Islam and the Governing of Muslims in France

Islam of the Global West

Series editors: Kambiz GhaneaBassiri and Frank Peter

Islam of the Global West is a pioneering series that examines Islamic beliefs, practices, discourses, communities, and institutions that have emerged from 'the Global West'. The geographical and intellectual framing of the Global West reflects both the role played by the interactions between people from diverse religions and cultures in the development of Western ideals and institutions in the modern era, and the globalization of these very ideals and institutions.

In creating an intellectual space where works of scholarship on European and North American Muslims enter into conversation with one another, the series promotes the publication of theoretically informed and empirically grounded research in these areas. By bringing the rapidly growing research on Muslims in European and North American societies, ranging from the United States and France to Portugal and Albania, into conversation with the conceptual framing of the Global West, this ambitious series aims to reimagine the modern world and develop new analytical categories and historical narratives that highlight the complex relationships and rivalries that have shaped the multicultural, poly-religious character of Europe and North America, as evidenced, by way of example, in such economically and culturally dynamic urban centres as Los Angeles, New York, Paris, Madrid, Toronto, Sarajevo, London, Berlin, and Amsterdam where there is a significant Muslim presence.

American and Muslim Worlds Before 1900
Edited by John Ghazvinian & Arthur Mitchell Fraas

Amplifying Islam in the European Soundscape: Religious Pluralism and Secularism in the Netherlands
Pooyan Tamimi Arab

Islam and Nationhood in Bosnia-Herzegovina: Surviving Empires
Xavier Bougarel

Islam as Critique: Sayyid Ahmad Khan and the Challenge of Modernity
Khurram Hussain

Sacred Spaces and Transnational Networks in American Sufism
Merin Shobhana Xavier

Islam and the Governing of Muslims in France

Secularism without Religion

Frank Peter

BLOOMSBURY ACADEMIC
LONDON • NEW YORK • OXFORD • NEW DELHI • SYDNEY

BLOOMSBURY ACADEMIC
Bloomsbury Publishing Plc
50 Bedford Square, London, WC1B 3DP, UK
1385 Broadway, New York, NY 10018, USA
29 Earlsfort Terrace, Dublin 2, Ireland

BLOOMSBURY, BLOOMSBURY ACADEMIC and the Diana logo are trademarks of Bloomsbury Publishing Plc

First published in Great Britain 2021
Paperback edition published 2022

Copyright © Frank Peter, 2021

Frank Peter has asserted his right under the Copyright, Designs and Patents Act, 1988, to be identified as Author of this work.

For legal purposes the Acknowledgments on p.vi constitute an extension of this copyright page.

Series design by Dani Leigh

Cover image © Brian Stablyk / gettyimages.co.uk

All rights reserved. No part of this publication may be reproduced or transmitted in any form or by any means, electronic or mechanical, including photocopying, recording, or any information storage or retrieval system, without prior permission in writing from the publishers.

Bloomsbury Publishing Plc does not have any control over, or responsibility for, any third-party websites referred to or in this book. All internet addresses given in this book were correct at the time of going to press. The author and publisher regret any inconvenience caused if addresses have changed or sites have ceased to exist, but can accept no responsibility for any such changes.

A catalogue record for this book is available from the British Library.

Library of Congress Control Number: 2020949134

ISBN: HB: 978-1-3500-6790-5
PB: 978-1-3502-1453-8
ePDF: 978-1-3500-6791-2
eBook: 978-1-3500-6792-9

Series: Islam of the Global West

Typeset by RefineCatch Limited, Bungay, Suffolk

To find out more about our authors and books visit www.bloomsbury.com and sign up for our newsletters

Contents

Acknowledgments		vi
Introduction		1
1	Beyond an Orderly Vision of Politics	15
2	The Social Republic	47
3	Rationalizing Integration	67
4	Islam and Society: Entwinement and Differentiation	91
5	Teaching Freedom	119
6	"The History of Some is not the History of Others"	137
7	Islam and Fiction beyond Freedom of Speech	165
8	Islamophobia and the Critique of Integration	191
Conclusion		203
Notes		209
Works Cited		251
Index		295

Acknowledgments

An earlier version of this book was submitted as a habilitation thesis to the Institute of Islamic Studies and Modern Oriental Philology at the University of Bern. My thanks go to the members of the committee, and in particular to Reinhard Schulze for many good discussions, advice, and comments. I revised the manuscript while working at the College of Islamic Studies, Hamad Bin Khalifa University and would like to thank everyone who made this a pleasant and stimulating experience.

This book builds upon research conducted at the Department of Comparative Cultural and Social Anthropology at European University Viadrina in Frankfurt/Oder as part of the research group "Muslims in Europe" funded by the Federal Ministry of Education and Research. My gratitude goes to Werner Schiffauer and the colleagues in Frankfurt/Oder for fruitful collaboration and exchanges. Many thanks also to Dietrich Reetz, who led the research group, and to its members.

I am grateful to all those who gave of their time to think about this research. At all stages of the project, discussions in classrooms and offices both enriched and challenged me; as did the conversations and interviews I had with various interlocutors in France. Parts of this research were presented in various academic settings and I owe thanks to the organizers and to participants and audiences for their feedback. I would like to mention specifically the International Institute for the Study of Islam in the Modern World (ISIM) in Leiden, where work on this project began, the Canadian Centre for German and European Studies at the University of Montreal, the network "Configurations of Muslim Traditions in European Secular Public Spheres" funded by the Netherlands Organisation for Scientific Research, and the European Commission-funded project "The Semantics of (Anti-)Racism and Tolerance in Europe" coordinated by Silvia Rodriguez Maeso. Finally, thanks to Lalle Pursglove from Bloomsbury Press for helping make this book become a reality, Kambiz GhaneaBassiri for thoughtful comments and exchanges, and to the anonymous reviewers for their valuable feedback.

Responsibility for any errors in this work remains my own.

Introduction

This book examines how Muslims and other French debate the implications of secularism for the social life of Islam in the French Republic. This is not a book, however, about how Islam fits into the secular republic. Nor is it about the question of whether or not secularism—*laïcité*—constitutes a workable framework for the practice of Islam. Without any doubt, these are important questions, if only because they are so frequently asked. Nonetheless, they are partly misguided as they tend to underestimate the difficulties involved in conceptualizing secularism. This is amply demonstrated by a large body of literature that has emerged more recently and unraveled some of the certainties which have shaped debates about the compatibility of Islam with secular orders. One part of this literature has drawn attention to the contingency and internal complexity of secular politics (see, e.g., Baubérot 2015; Bertossi 2016; Koussens 2016; Portier 2016), incidentally raising the bar for any typology of secularisms. Other studies have critically interrogated basic assumptions in studies of secularism and redefined their objects and modalities. They have variously problematized, one might say in shorthand, the secular-religious binary which is constitutive both of secular discourse and secularism studies.

This binary is more obviously fragilized by the now commonsensical critique of the concept of religion which redirects attention to "the politics of defining religion" (Beckford 1999). The same holds even more true for the reconceptualization of the secular, formerly conceived as mere absence (of religion), now a constructed object with a history. As José Casanova writes, "theories of secularization, as well as secularist social science, have avoided the task of analyzing, studying, and explaining the secular, or the varieties of secular experience, as if it is only the religious, but not the secular, that is in need of interpretation and analytical explanation" (Casanova 2011: 56).[1] This approach to the secular implies transcending to some degree dualist perspectives on religion and the secular. This is clearly expressed in the statement, by Talal Asad, that the secular is "neither continuous with the religious that supposedly preceded it (that is, it is not the latest phase of a sacred origin) nor a simple break from it (that is, it is not the opposite, an essence that excludes the sacred)." Asad takes it to be "a concept that brings together certain behaviors, knowledges, and sensibilities in modern life" (Asad 2003: 25). Importantly, the secular here is not simply external to religion. Rather, the concept of the secular "articulates a constellation of institutions, ideas, and affective orientations that constitute an important dimension of what we call modernity and its defining forms of knowledge and practice—both religious and non-religious" (Hirschkind 2011). From this perspective, the study of secular-religious entanglements comes into view as a central field for the study of religion (von Stuckrad 2013).

These reflections have been taken up and elaborated in a number of different ways in studies focusing on France (Adrian 2016; Amir-Moazami 2006; Caeiro 2011; Donnet 2013; Fernando 2014; Jansen 2013; Jouili 2015; Mas 2006a, 2006b). I want to suggest here that one upshot of the above is that an orderly vision of secular politics appears to be built upon shaky ground. In an orderly vision of politics, secularism is described as a political doctrine about the need and benefit of differentiating state and religion; this doctrine finds expression in a legal corpus specifying the place of religion in society, defining and delimiting religious liberties and thus the conditions under which individuals can practice their religion. To put it simply, secularism is conceptualized as a unified and stable order and the compatibility of Islam with a given secular order can be assessed on the basis of its legal and political framework. When questions are raised about the adaptability of Islam to *laïcité* and vice versa, they are asked from the perspective of an orderly vision of politics. This study argues that such orderly visions of secularism, to different degrees, misrepresent what Muslim intellectuals and activists engage with in France. They misconstrue the intellectual task which an engagement with the secular French context implies and the conditions under which it takes place. How can secularism be defined so as to examine secular politics in its complexity and to take into account the instability of this regime?

In this study, I focus on two factors. They have to do, first, with the fact that secularism does not simply grant the right of religious freedom; it also involves a perpetual attempt to govern the usage of freedom by people of varying religious persuasions. It is because of this concern for governing how freedom is practiced that arguments made in the course of debates about secular politics intermingle references to political principles and the law with very context-specific claims about Muslims' identities, lived experiences, and social power. To put it differently, secular politics is not contained within the private–public distinction so prominent in theories on secularism or secularization. Second, secular politics is complex because religion as its object of regulation is not simply given. "Secularism without religion" sums up a situation where conventional notions of religion and worship cover only one part of the social meanings attached to the terms Islam and Muslim and where the notions "Islam" and "Muslims" are continuously configured and contested. This is a context where secular politics is as much about defining and delimiting the province of religious liberty as it is about identifying aspects of religion, debating how to make sense of it, and deciding "what is really the issue" (Amiraux 2007).

Let me elaborate this. First, as critical studies of secularism emphasize, while secularism promises equal freedom (and largely legitimizes itself through this promise), secular politics also implies more or less explicit and clear ideas about the kind of people—and the kind of religions—that should be allowed to benefit from it. Thus, secularism is centrally associated with civil rights—but it cannot be dissociated from multiple attempts to regulate practices of freedom. These attempts rely upon complex mechanisms of government, i.e., efforts at "directing, ruling, controlling, mastering, guiding, leading, influencing, regulating the affairs, actions, policies or functions of others in a manner that claims or is accorded authority" (Rose 1998: 119). As democratic governments function within shifting and reversible power relations with their citizens and involve multiple actors beyond the state as well as diverse knowledges and ways of reasoning, there are profound limits to widespread accounts of secularism that emphasize systematicity.[2] This thesis will be substantiated throughout the ensuing pages.

The second factor accounting for the complexity of secular politics has to do with the fact that the object of secular politics is not simply Islam as "religion." Of course, Islam is routinely discussed as religion and worship and, more particularly, referenced as the "second religion" of France in terms of numbers. This is, however, not the only way in which Islam is apprehended. Moreover, to classify something as "religion" does not necessarily exclude it from other descriptions. In the social space of France, multiple descriptions of Islam coexist and often function simultaneously in various kinds of interrelations. Thus, this study also examines how Islam (or specific dimensions of it) is configured as a social object and becomes associated with various identities, institutions, and practices in relatively specific social spaces, how it emerges as the marker of a collective memory whose relation to France's memory needs to be amended, how it becomes an object which is fictionalized in multiple ways, and how it is defined as culture.

The complexity of the reference to "Islamic" matters and "Muslims" highlighted here can be fruitfully incorporated into the study of controversies about the visibility of Islam (Göle 2002, 2010; Jonker & Amiraux 2006; Salzbrunn 2019). This "visibility" should not blind us to the fact that debates about secularism very often make reference to entities which one cannot observe as such in the sensory world. By this I not only mean that secular politics is essentially dependent upon prognostics of the future (Foucault 2009),[3] but also that a good deal of debate about Islam implies concepts of order—"constituent models," as Foucault put it (2005)—for which there are no primary sensory data. Consider concepts such as "identity" (and its Other "alterity"), "memory", or the set of notions related to "society" and the "social" to which crucially important references are constantly made in French debates. Drawing on Foucault and related literature, this book attempts to convey this complexity by approaching debates about secular politics as the interplay of political rationalities. Rationalities are defined here as the "changing discursive fields within which the exercise of power is conceptualised" (Rose & Miller 1992: 175). Political rationalities are, in other words, resources available in society which enable the reflexive practice of power; they allow people to reason and justify, in public or private, a specific exercise of power, its means and ends. For the purpose of this study, social, historical, and aesthetic rationalities are directly relevant. To sum up, the space of secular politics is multidimensional in the sense that the "same" object is discursivized differently and made to appear in different manners. It is multidimensional in the sense that different knowledges interact in it. Based on how these knowledges are used and combined with each other, assessments of the state of social power may differ, and the double question "What ought to be done?" and "What can be done?" with regard to Muslims in France may give rise to different answers.

Levels of Analysis

How does adopting a complex, rather than orderly, view of secularism, as outlined above, affect analytical approaches to the study of the discourses of Muslim organizations and intellectuals in France, more particularly of discourses emanating from the network of public Islam? I will argue here that this perspective opens up three overlapping levels of analysis. These analytical levels relate respectively to the entwinement of Islamic discourses with other knowledges, integration defined as a changeable, reversible, and unstable relation of power, and ethics.

First, this approach directs attention to hitherto often neglected levels and modalities of differentiation and entwinement between "France" and "Islam."

Analyses of Islamic practices and discourses routinely make references to the French political order and, more particularly, the republican regime. This emphasis is notably justified given the revival of republicanism and its increasing impact on political debates since the 1980s (Furet et al. 1988; Chabal 2015). Important studies on French and European Islam have examined interrelations between Islamic traditions and European societies and politics; they have examined, notably, how the *fiqh* or Islamic legal tradition has been actualized in European legal systems.[4] In this study, I seek to broaden the various descriptions of France to other sources of knowledge about the context in which the Islamic tradition is reproduced. This move brings into focus new modes of differentiation and entwinement between France and Islam. Islam and Muslim are rationalized in multiple ways (as is France) and these rationalizations are not simply external to Muslim discourses and activism but are in many ways productive of Muslim discourses and subjectivities. Let me add that the simple opposition internal/external is not able to capture the broad range of modalities through which these rationalizations become productive in Muslim discourses; as shall become apparent, "internal" covers a large gamut of strategical usages of and engagements with secular rationalities. Olivier Roy's work has demonstrated the importance of examining the reconfiguration of Islam in Western contexts in particular. According to Roy, an essential condition of this process is the delinking of religion and culture triggered by processes of globalization (2004). In many ways, this study seeks to contribute to such an analysis. Bringing in new sources, primarily from historical and social studies as well as fictional writings, I examine new domains in relation to which the designation of Islam as religion becomes meaningful.

On a second level of analysis, this study examines how Muslims participate in the (re)configuration of the politics of integration in France. I have stated above that secularism cannot be dissociated from multiple attempts to regulate practices of freedom. In this study, integration designates the broader political configuration within which changing forms of regulation occur. At its moment of emergence, this configuration is strongly marked by assimilationist aims (Lorcerie 1994; Geisser 2005). The process of integration is envisioned as modifying cultural attributes of immigrants and thus conjoining what is separate, i.e., the national and the immigrant communities. Beyond the often-noted ambiguity of the term, references to integration, at the most basic level, assert that even if they have settled and, in many cases, acquired French citizenship, immigrants have not yet arrived in France. However, it would be wrong to associate references to integration in a stable manner with assimilationist projects. What I want to emphasize here is that integration politics has to be conceptualized as a "relation of power"[5]—that is, a relationship which is "changeable, reversible and unstable" and which necessarily presupposes that its subjects are free in the sense that they dispose at least of "a certain form of liberty" (Foucault 1988: 12).[6] The study of integration politics as a reversible power relation starts from the fact that the reiterated assertion of the problem of integration implies the possibility to assess—and revise—claims about the state of integration. At the same time, references to integration raise the questions "What kind of policies are suitable?" and "Which knowledges should inform them?" This is a process where the otherness of Islam is constantly redescribed in relation to changing and contested notions of normative Frenchness; it is a process where the answer to the question "Which factors constitute obstacles to inclusion of Muslims?" is formulated in very different ways in the decades spanning the early 1990s and the late 2010s.

Broadly speaking, the third level of analysis concerns ethics, i.e., the "ethical problem of the definition of practices of freedom" (Foucault 1988: 3) as this plays out in the French secular order. Put another way, the focus here will be on deliberations about the practice of freedom by Muslims and how those who are deliberating draw upon various rationalities when trying to make sense of their specific space of action and reflecting upon modes and aims of government of oneself and others. In this perspective, Muslims are placed at the intersection of three dimensions of governance: to govern others; to let oneself be governed by others (or to refuse this); to govern oneself. It is at this intersection that Muslim discourses of this study's protagonists intervene in different ways, and this is how they will be studied. In other words, I conceptualize these discourses in their entwinement with the politics of integration. I examine how deliberations on the practice of freedom by Muslims interrelate with diverse rationalizations of integration, what it requires, and its reform, critique, and so forth.[7] This perspective grants ethical questions considerable space without denying, of course, that law is a powerful determining force of both social life and the changing configuration of the objects and spaces of ethical reflection.

Public Islam

My entry into the debates on secularism and Islam in France is via the study of discourses issuing from a network centered around the figure of the Swiss academic Tariq Ramadan and the federation *Union des organisations islamiques de France* (Union of Islamic Organizations of France, or UOIF), renamed

Musulmans de France (Muslims of France) in 2017, which was created in 1983 (see notably Kepel 1991; Marongiu 2002; Maréchal 2008; Fournier 2008; Dazey 2019).[8] I designate this network public Islam. It is a network which displays a broad range of internal differences, as shall become apparent. However, the actors here also share one commonality, namely their commitment to the public relevance of religion. This network occupies a particular place in French Islam and is singularly well suited as a case study of Islam and French secularism, as it is intellectually the most vibrant Muslim network in France and has the greatest outreach capacity into the broader public.[9] While Tariq Ramadan, who has been touring France since the early 1990s, has become the most widely known Muslim intellectual in France (and probably in Europe), the federation *Musulmans de France* also has an exceptional status, primarily as the sole federation which has since the early 1990s made significant (and, broadly speaking, successful) investments in institutions for education and research on the one hand and youth work on the other.[10] The institutions built so far may appear less than impressive in absolute terms. A different picture emerges, however, if they are placed in the French context, where Islamic organizations have a predominantly local structure and a relatively low level of professionalization.[11]

Musulmans de France is, at its core, a federation of Muslim associations whose central aim is to provide spaces for prayer. It is one of the big Muslim federations which have been, since the 1990s, in regular dialogue with successive French governments leading up, in 2003, to the creation of a largely dysfunctional representative organ, the *Conseil français du culte musulman* (French Council of Muslim Worship, or CFCM).[12] Contrary to the other major federations, which cooperate closely with the governments of Morocco, Algeria, and Turkey, *Musulmans de France* presents itself as an independent organization related to and inspired by the Muslim Brotherhood. Having said this, *Musulmans de France* is, in a nutshell, both more and less than a federation of mosque associations. Three factors underlie its particular status: its investment in education and youth work; its efforts to elaborate and promote a discourse on French Muslim citizenship; its public visibility and numerous interventions in French debates.

Musulmans de France has itself opened two education facilities, both named the *Institut Européen des Sciences Humaines* (European Institute for Human Sciences). They provide courses in Arabic and Islamic sciences. The first was set up in 1991 in Château-Chinon in Burgundy and, the second in 1998 in Saint-Denis. *Musulmans de France*, set up by students from North Africa who still constitute its leadership, soon realized the importance of developing educational content in French and reaching out, through public conferences, various media, and other events, to younger generations. This is one of the reasons why it has been an important player in the Islamic revival among young French with Muslim backgrounds since the 1980s.[13] Another significant vector in the educational work by *Musulmans de France* are its student wing *Étudiants Musulmans de France* (Muslim Students of France), founded in 1989, and its youth organization *Jeunes Musulmans de France* (Young Muslims of France), founded in 1993.[14] A second factor underlying its special position relates to the organization's early interest in reflecting upon issues raised by the settlement and citizenship of Muslims in France. Since the early 1980s, the group has addressed the question whether and under what conditions Muslims can be residents and citizens of France. Through its institutions and members, it has exercised a decisive influence on the emergence of Muslim discourses which argue that Islam and French citizenship can exist together harmoniously. As this book will show, *Musulmans de France* constitutes a lively space for debate where the telos and conditions of French Muslim life in a secular state are reiteratively thematized in relation to changing political configurations. *Musulmans de France* is also a central player in the European Council for Fatwa and Research, created in 1997. This institution, as well as the federation's own *fatwa* board, has made widely noted contributions to the "contextualization" of Islam[15] in Europe. Third and finally, *Musulmans de France* and Tariq Ramadan have been important actors in the French public sphere. The rise to prominence of *Musulmans de France* starts with the first headscarf controversy in 1989, when its president wrote a public letter to the prime minister to defend the legitimacy of this practice in the framework of French law (Kepel 1994: 252–8). Since then, *Musulmans de France* has been pivotal to making certain segments of the Muslim population audible and visible in the public sphere. Its annual Easter meeting at Le Bourget in the Paris conurbation attracts large crowds; talks and debates between intellectuals, politicians, members of the organization, and Tariq Ramadan are an important feature of this event. As will become apparent in the course of this study, both Ramadan and *Musulmans de France* are widely known and often referred to by a broad range of actors in public debates.

My interest in these actors is as contributors to public debates. This is not a study of public Islam, its organizations, activists, or intellectuals[16] and nor is it a study of French secularism and Islam in all its interrelations. Rather, critically interrogating orderly visions of secularism, I use the case of public Islam to study modes and conditions of Muslim engagements with the secular order and possibilities for contributing to its transformation. Neither is this a case study of political Islam in France and its transformation. Such studies have been proposed notably by Maréchal (2008), Amghar (2006 & 2008), Ternisien (2005), and Vidino (2010). I consider the heuristic value of this approach limiting. One important reason for this has been explicated categorically by Jonathan Lawrence with regard to "Political-Islam federations" in Europe more generally: "These groups behave not as branches of a new 'Comintern,' but as domestic European organizations with domestic-oriented leadership and exclusively domestic political demands. Political-Islam leaders may retain allegiances to and symbolic membership in international networks, but their daily activities—and their constituencies' interests—are undeniably domestic and routine in nature" (2012: 94).[17] To approach these groups as representatives of public Islam is to take account of the fact that controversies about Islam in France cannot in any way be reduced to any issues raised by political and/or transnational Islam. Rather, controversies about Islam have to do with governing a newly arrived "religion" whose identity and power—a notion which is variously understood—are the object of divergent assessments in society.[18]

* * *

Chapter one outlines my hypothesis that secularism cannot be dissociated from varying attempts to regulate practices of freedom. I discuss how we can explain— and study—the controversies about the identification of Islam and Muslims which repeatedly occur in the course of these regulatory practices. I explain why this identification of Islam is necessarily contested and complex: because there is no neatly bounded, nondiscursive object Islam as "religion" and because a diverse set of rationalities are available and used in this process of identifying what is to be regulated and to what end. This is also why a set of three questions—"Who are Muslims?", "What is normative Frenchness?", and "How should Muslims be governed?"—is a constitutive part of secularism as it becomes effective in the case of French Islam since the late 1980s.

Now, the very idea that secular policymaking intrinsically depends upon knowledge of particular religions may seem to contradict widespread claims that in France the state simply abstains from identifying its citizens in ethnic, religious, or racial terms. Rather, the principle of abstract equality supposedly characterizes relations between the state and its citizens. In the game of national representations of political traditions (Kastoryano 2002), this element is crucial for constructing a certain notion of France as a republic. Thus, the foundational claim that secularism is based on a strong nexus between power, knowledge, and subjectivity stands in tension with, or implies a critique of, a certain idea of the French Republic.

Chapter two outlines this critique in some detail and substantiates it. Drawing on Jacques Donzelot's work *L'invention du social* (The Invention of the Social) (1994), it outlines how the emergence and institutionalization of social sciences since the late nineteenth century has reconfigured republican notions of abstract citizenship and created new ways of classifying and differentiating between citizens in order to govern them. Moving on to the pioneering study of contemporary French Islam, Gilles Kepel's *Les banlieues de l'Islam* (The Banlieues of Islam) (1987), it then studies how Muslims and Islam become inscribed into France—i.e., into its spaces of governance—through social rationalization. Kepel's book offers a brief illustration of what such rationalizations allow their practitioners basically to do, namely to simultaneously normalize Islam—by describing it with universal categories—and particularize Islam by situating it socially (roughly speaking, in the urban periphery areas designated *banlieues* which have come to be equated with degraded housing estates). The ambivalence reflected in this description points to the politically diverse usages which can be made of this rationality and which will be discussed throughout the book.

Chapter three takes the case of the *Haut Conseil à l'Intégration* (High Council on Integration, or HCI), created in 1990, to examine how social and other rationalities cofunction in political practice when defining answers to the questions "Who are Muslims?", "What is normative Frenchness?", and "How should Muslims be governed?" This is a study of how integration is defined between an imaginary of national sovereignty (central to much integration discourse) and the multiple, changing limitations entailed by the liberal framework which, since 2003, is undergoing a process of partial redefinition in relation to religious freedom. In this context, social rationality, up until 2002, played a major role in the reasoning of the HCI. Above all, this rationality allowed the HCI to configure Islam as identity and, departing from this discursive construction of Islam, to formulate means to change and reconcile Islam with the French context. While this rationality has a liberal potential, it is employed here to fuel and to direct the changing of Islam. Put differently, its usage is aimed at enabling the state to cross the private–public boundary.

Chapter four examines how Muslim authors reflect, in changing ways, upon the situation of Muslims in society. The basic aim here is to show that a social rationalization of France, even if often rudimentary, is an essential and important element in Muslim thought. Focusing on the debate about integration, this chapter examines the interrelation between social rationalizations of France and definitions of integration, i.e., its problems and requirements. My starting point here is that, beyond important differences in the milieu of public Islam, there is a tendency to reconfigure basic elements of integration policies within a broader ethical framework as a contribution to society and a self-willed process of change which depend upon certain social and political conditions. I then study how this assessment of social and political conditions has changed since the turn of the millennium. This has led to a rethinking of integration policies, displacing the focus to nonimmigrants and state authorities. At the same time, the understanding of how Islam interrelates with society changes. While the fundamental notion that Islam must be lived (also) in society is not abandoned, the distinctiveness of societal processes and the need for specific social policies is highlighted. In essence, the socially transformative power of Islam as religion is—indirectly—downgraded.

Chapter five narrows down the focus and shifts it to didactic discourses addressed to Muslims as ethical subjects in the *banlieue*. It examines specific imaginings of the ethical subject by authors in the milieu of public Islam. More particularly, I examine how ethical discourse interrelates with social rationalizations, and how these enable it to be inscribed in the space of France and thus configure a particular way for the Muslim subject to relate to citizenship. This ethical discourse relies on social rationalization in several ways, notably in the way it approaches and describes the shared conditions of subjectivation, the problems and risks likely to be encountered by individuals in the *banlieue*. Its key link with the rationality of the social is a negative one. Indeed, the primary aim of this ethical discourse is to define the work on the self which a Muslim subject must undertake in order to transcend the forces of social determination. The basic aim is to eliminate these forces, which these authors decipher by means of this rationality.

Chapter six examines the renarration of histories of France and Islam since the late 1990s. The context for this is the increasing dissemination of postcolonial thought and a memory regime which postulates both the centrality of collective memory to the core of the individual self and the possibility to shape memory through structural processes. In this context, diverse and often radically opposed counter-histories of France proliferate and regularly trigger broad public debates. Counter-history refers here, drawing on Foucault, to historical accounts based on "a principle of heterogeneity: The history of some is not the history of others" (Foucault 2003: 69). Counter-histories undo the unity of the nation as it is constructed in historical narrations, they interrogate how the exercise of power relates to principles of legality and legitimacy and, more generally, they problematize positivist assumptions about historical truth and bring to the fore questions of interpretation and representation. The chapter concentrates on counter-histories that seek to establish entwinements between Islam and France while at the same reshaping these entities variously. More precisely, the focus is on two usages of counter-histories, one aiming to provincialize histories of France (or certain dimensions), while the other seeks to write Islam into France. Through these histories, Muslims are identified as a relatively distinct memory collective inside the French population. That is, a new kind of entwinement of France and Islam is enacted whose precise contours and conditions are the object of debates among Muslim actors.

Chapter seven continues the critical reassessment of the orderly vision of secular politics by concentrating on the role of fiction, i.e., cartoons published by *Charlie Hebdo*, the novel *Soumission* (Submission) by Michel Houellebecq, and videos produced for the Muslim film festival *Mokhtar Awards*. The distinction between fiction and reality is central to the "orderly vision of politics" where the focus is squarely set on normative issues and debates, in particular the question how to reconcile freedom of expression with various limitations on free speech classified as forms of hate speech, abuse, or defamation on the grounds of religion, race, or ethnicity. This chapter seeks to reframe part of this approach to fiction in two ways. On the one hand, examining the controversies about *Charlie Hebdo* (from 2006 until 2015), I will show that they do not conform to conventional ideas of secular politics; that is, they cannot be reduced to a normative conflict about where to draw the line between the religious and the secular. This is partly so because the divergences which provoked controversy run deeper than divergent values or different interpretations of the cartoons and comprise multiple questions about Islam and France. On the other hand, via two case studies, fiction itself will be studied as a means to rationalize aesthetically the objects, aims, and conditions of government. In the context of these case studies, I leave aside the question of the ontological status of fiction and focus on the function it fulfills as "a means of telling us something about reality" (Iser 1975: 7).

Chapter eight examines the effects produced by introducing—in the early 2000s—the term Islamophobia into public debate. While activism against Islamophobia in the sense of discrimination concerns only a limited number of religious practices, my purpose here is to examine the application of the term Islamophobia, by now judged irreversible, as part of a broader critique of integration politics. This critique, prepared in many ways by activists from the milieu of public Islam, shifts the focus from Islam to other obstacles to inclusion faced by French Muslims, namely certain attitudes and views of Islam by non-Muslims. Taking the case of the *Collectif contre l'islamophobie en France* (Collective against Islamophobia in France, or CCIF), the most prominent association in the field, this chapter examines arguments developed in the course of mobilizing against Islamophobia and assesses their critical leverage in the debate on integration. It contemplates how Islamophobia is becoming the framework for a new governmental configuration aimed at certain groups of the French non-Muslim population and discusses whether the mobilization against Islamophobia gives rise to new arguments which have the potential to restructure the debate on integration and alter its disorderly nature.

1

Beyond an Orderly Vision of Politics

In October 2018, two prominent investigative journalists, Gérard Davet and Fabrice Lhomme, published a book titled *Inch'Allah: l'islamisation à visage découvert* (Inshallah: Islamization Uncovered). The book promised to provide new insights into the "Islamization" of Seine-Saint-Denis, a department bordering Paris. In terms of population, it is one of France's largest departments, home to more than 1.5 million inhabitants. In the following weeks, the authors, sometimes accompanied by the five aspiring journalists who had done the actual research,[1] toured radio and television shows in order to present the book and discuss the results of this investigation. The discussions, while certainly in some ways particular to this book, nevertheless are in one central sense typical for the debate about Islam in France: this debate is complex and does not fit into a single framework. In a first step, three dimensions of complexity can be named. The debate is complex because central features of the French normative order—e.g., notions like *laïcité*, or freedom of religion—are defined in divergent ways by participants; they are contested and changing. It is also complex because participants in this debate base their arguments not just on general principles, such as equal freedom. Such principles are certainly important, but at the same time these arguments rely upon and cannot be separated from factual claims about the particular case of Islam and Muslims. As claims about French norms regularly prove controversial, they trigger a second kind of debate. Secularism is a discursive context where general and particular reasons, normative and factual arguments, and diverse knowledges are constantly entwined. Finally, it is complex because of controversies relating to the identification of Islam and Muslims and the definition of Frenchness. Before addressing how this complexity can be explained and how it affects Muslim actors, let me illustrate this constellation with the case of *Inch'Allah*.

Inch'Allah is a book which sets out to describe and problematize the "Islamization" of Seine-Saint-Denis. However, the grounds upon which this can be done are, to different degrees, contested or unclear among participants in the public debate. The authors Davet and Lhomme distinguish "Islamization" from the "broader phenomenon" "Islamism"—a "fundamentalist political ideology"— and define it with a citation taken straight from the dictionary as "'to convert to Islam' and/or 'to apply Islamic law to various sectors of public and social life'" (2018: 11).[2] Why would the application of "Islamic law" (by whom and how?) constitute a public problem? The question is worth asking as "Islamization" seems to have a lot to do with practices covered by civil rights. As the two official authors put it at one point, "Islamization" is basically about the very broadly defined "return of religious feeling" (*sentiment religieux*) (2018: 14). The stories told in *Inch'Allah* are about people who, individually or in groups, practice and refer to Islam and do so increasingly: in schools, universities, canteens, workplaces, doctors' practices, trade unions, and local politics. Would this be illegal in a country where the right to manifest one's religion "as long as … (it) does not interfere with the established Law and Order" was enshrined in the Declaration of the Rights of Man and of the Citizen more than two centuries ago (France 1789)? A country where religious freedom[3] includes the right to proselytism even if this latter right, as the freedom to manifest one's religion, can and has been limited (Fortier 2008)?[4]

One well-known answer to this question would be that the place of religion in France is not only decided with reference to freedom of religion, but also to the famously polyvalent and contested notion of *laïcité*, enshrined in the constitution since 1958.[5] The notion *laïcité* is often defined as implying some kind of privatization of religion. The background for this notion of *laïcité* is the idea that the exercise of citizenship presupposes freedom of thought which in turn requires emancipation, through reason, from any kind of doctrine which limits the individual's autonomy; it also requires that citizens—as citizens— transcend their particular identities (Baubérot 2001; cf. Laborde 2008a). This understanding of *laïcité* has directly shaped more recent debates around legal restrictions de facto aiming at Muslim practices, namely the hijab and the so-called "burqa."[6] In the debate about *Inch'Allah*, reference to a normative notion of privatized religion is made, for example, by journalist Léa Salamé in a radio show with the journalists Davet and Lhomme. Salamé distinguishes between the "right to practice one's religion" on the one hand and the "construction of a full-blown way of life" by Muslims on the other. According to her, it is the latter, more expansive notion of religion, as it were, which is problematic and this is the object of the book.[7]

As I said, this kind of claim to the necessary privatization of religion is often considered to be an essential element of *laïcité*. Importantly, such a claim cannot be easily substantiated on the basis of how the judiciary defines *laïcité*;[8] one dimension of the complexity of debates about Islam has to do with this fact. The *Conseil d'État* (Council of State) identifies three basic elements in *laïcité*, namely "state neutrality, freedom of religion and respect of pluralism." Here, *laïcité* is not identified with privatization of religion ("religion is not a purely private matter"), but described as a condition for "religious diversity" in France. This includes the presence of religions in the "public square" "provided that no problems of public order emerge" (2004: 272, 276).[9] The greatly diverging views on the public status of religion go hand in glove with strikingly different assessments of "Islamization" and its problematization. A quarter-hour into the radio debate cohosted by Léa Salamé, the first question from the audience was read and it directly contradicted most of what had been said before. Camille called in to ask the two authors "in which sense is it a problem that people turn to Islam?" This question was highly critical of the book project, as was signaled by the fact that Camille found the two authors' positions strikingly similar to those of Éric Zemmour ("I feel like I'm listening to Zemmour").[10] A controversial bestselling journalist who has been convicted several times for incitement to hatred, Zemmour has become perhaps the most prominent face of anti-Islam discourse in France.[11]

This association with an extreme-right discourse was of course rejected by the journalists from *Le Monde* who, it must be added, were not surprised by it. In the preface to *Inch'Allah*, Davet and Lhomme situate themselves in the broader debate by claiming the middle ground and describing their task as merely reporting facts:

> How does one make a reasonable and nuanced voice heard between the "*ultra-laïcards*" and other Islamophobes for whom wearing a veil, having a long beard, or not eating pork is more or less equivalent to playing the game of the fanatical killers of Daesh, and, at the opposite end, those, often labeled as "islamo-leftists" (*islamo-gauchistes*), who paradoxically "essentialize" Muslims and present them as the new "wretched of the earth" (2018: 12).

In contrast to both those groups, who are summarily accused of ignoring "the field" (*le terrain*), the central objective of their book is precisely to provide more knowledge about what is happening in Seine-Saint-Denis. This claim to neutrality may seem naive and it can easily be contested in light of some statements made by the authors.[12] Nevertheless, the statement points to a crucial feature of this debate. It is not just a debate about how to apply the principles, rules, and procedures identified with *laïcité* to the case of Islam. Nor is it simply a debate about whether Islam—as a particular set of beliefs and practices—can find its place in the Republic. While both these issues are surely important, they are being debated (and debated in this manner) because of the perceived transformative power of some Muslims—and assessing this transformative power and how it affects Seine-Saint-Denis now and in the near future is what the book *Inch'Allah* is ultimately about. In other words, *Inch'Allah* is not simply a prosecutorial inventory of "a dissenting Islam" (*islam revendicatif*) which, for all the authors' claims to neutrality, is depicted in strikingly negative terms (2018: 14, 9). Rather, it also sets out to inquire into a changing societal power context. This interest in the changing context constitutes common ground in the debate about French Islam for a range of actors with sometimes very different outlooks. *Inch'Allah* does not limit itself to documenting normative transgressions, however defined, but investigates why the development called "Islamization" is occurring, how it changes people, both Muslims and other French, their identity, norms, social practices, and the context in which they live; it aims to identify realistic options open to public authorities when engaging with this development, and it examines whether this process is likely to continue. Against the background of great concern across the political spectrum about weaker "social cohesion," these questions have widely been considered essential since the early 2000s (Portier 2016: 274). The two authors Davet and Lhomme frame this set of questions with reference to a need to fight *communautarisme*, the term for processes of "disintegration" resulting from a subaltern community-building project, and, to a lesser extent, with reference to *laïcité*.[13] Notably, they also refer to national identity. Depending upon how these notions are defined (they are not in *Inch'Allah*), there may obviously be a huge overlap between them. All three can (and do) contribute to situating Muslims as yet-to-be-integrated into the national community of citizens. The reference to national identity is significant here as it marks an awareness—again typical for the broader debate—that the normative grounds for defending a particular notion of national identity (here, basically one that excludes visible Islam) are quite limited. As the two authors write, one can argue that national identity is constantly evolving and adapting to change, which leads Davet and Lhomme to ask rhetorically: "[A]re the increasing claims of those French of Muslim confession not legitimate?" (2018: 15).

So far, the examples have illustrated two kinds of complexity in the debate about Islam. They have to do, on the one hand, with the usage of different normative registers, notably religious freedom and *laïcité*, which are not consensually defined. In a poll from 2015, a majority of more than 80 percent agreed that *laïcité* is important both in public schools and for the identity of

France. However, they fundamentally disagreed on its meaning. 32 percent associated it with the separation between politics and religion, 27 percent with freedom of conscience, 17 percent with the equality of all religions, and 17 percent with the reducing of influence of religions in society (IFOP 2015).[14] On the other, this complexity results from the entwinement of general normative questions about the public status of religions with questions about the particular case of Islam and Muslims and the transformative social power ascribed to Muslims. Now, an additional dimension of complexity results from disagreement about what "Islamization" has to do with which Muslims and with Islam as a causal factor of behavior. These questions were raised, in different ways, in a popular TV show which assembled a panel of guests to discuss the book with its official authors. The program was called "Islamization—fact or fake news?".[15] One of the panelists, former politician Karim Zéribi, emphatically asserted the need for "combating" Islamization so that *laïcité* could prevail, but he considered the evidence for "Islamization" presented in *Inch'Allah* insufficient and merely "anecdotal." Ultimately, he found the term "Islamization" inappropriate, having asked the fundamental question "How many people in Seine-Saint-Denis are actually Muslim?" and challenging the claim in *Inch'Allah* that it was now about half the population. Like many others in the debate about Islam, he claimed (incorrectly)[16] that the collection of statistical data on religion is totally prohibited in France but referred at the same time to 6 million French Muslims (a serious study estimates them at 3.98–4.3 million).[17] In this case as in many others, the complexity of secular politics is simply ignored or denied. Zéribi argued that not only were the vast majority of Muslims not concerned by the behaviors described in *Inch'Allah*, but that the authors had created "confusion" by treating phenomena like the growing consumption of halal food as "Islamization."[18] For Zéribi, the increasing importance of halal food was about "business" and he disconnected it from issues relating to values, i.e., *laïcité* and the Republic. Other panelists likewise voiced concern about the superficial treatment of "Islamization." Journalist Agathe Aupoux deplored the way that the naked facts reported as relating to Islam were not in any sense "placed in perspective" and that no "sociological data" had been provided. Another panelist, musician Doc Gynéco, lamented the lack of discussion about "why people turn towards the spiritual," the reason, in his view, being the deficits of "the system" in France. The two authors Davet and Lhomme basically acquiesced. Indeed, they had themselves mentioned that "Islamization" has to be seen in many ways as a response to failures of the state and an attempt to "fill a gap and offset unacceptable shortcomings" (2018: 14).

Secularism Beyond a Sovereign Model of Power

These are merely snapshots from the debate about *Inch'Allah*. Nevertheless, they suffice to make apparent what I suggest is one major characteristic of the broader debate about Islam, namely its complexity. To put it simply, discussions about the status of religion and the limits of religious freedom refer to diverse and variously interpreted normative frameworks which are, in addition, to some degree changing. In turn, the question of how to delimit religious freedom is entwined in discussions about *Inch'Allah* with the questions "Who are Muslims?" and "What is Islam?". By asking these questions (even in a haphazard manner, as is often the case), the focus of discussion partially shifts from Islam to society; at the same time, the category "Muslim" is temporalized. This complexity is noteworthy, I want to suggest here, as there is a tendency to conceive of secularism in an overly orderly vision of politics as a well-ordered regime. An orderly vision of politics refers here to an understanding of secular politics where identifying the object of politics (here "Muslims" and "Islam") is seen as basically unproblematic, so that the focus tends to be on analyzing the normative frameworks—e.g., republican or liberal—used in politics. Consequently, the discursive encounter between Islam and France, as expressed for example in the writings of Muslim authors, is primarily construed as the engagement with political and legal theories. My starting point here is that this approach to secularism misconstrues (and to various degrees neglects) the constitutive link between secularism and epistemology, i.e., between secular politics and diverse constructions of Islam and Muslims. I contend that the construal of secularism as a well-ordered regime prevents us from identifying *what* Muslims engage with in the ongoing debates about secularism and Islam.

The orderly vision of politics can be described in a more systematic manner by drawing on Foucault's conceptualization of juridical conceptions of power.[19] Juridical refers to a particular function of the law and a particular kind of power exercise, namely that of specifying rules of permission and prohibition (and related sanctions). These four features can be summed up schematically as follows. Power is represented as something which is possessed by someone; from this perspective the distinction between those who exercise power and those who are its subjects is unproblematic. Power is exercised primarily by defining limits to what subjects are allowed to do, i.e., power relates to freedom and the exercise of power can be identified and described without any ambiguity. Power is unified in the state, and finally it is exercised over subjects preceding it. It is because power is imagined as unified and clearly localizable (through its reference to the state, representing the democratic sovereign, and through the fundamental relation established between power and law) that the question of its legitimacy—central to debates about secular politics on Islam—can be asked. A central element of Foucault's work is his criticism of this perspective on power as sovereign power, as commodifiable and repressive (Brown 2006). In a well-known statement, Foucault pointed to the discrepancy between the functioning of politics, on the one hand, and the way we reflect upon it (i.e., as centralized, reified, bounded, and legal), in political philosophy or elsewhere, on the other, by saying that "we need to cut off the king's head: in political theory that still has to be done" (2000: 122). Doing this opens up a perspective in which power "travels along threads of discourse by which we are interpellated and which we also speak, thereby confounding distinctions between subjects and objects of power, or between agents, vehicles, and targets of power (Brown 2006: 69). Analytic attention will be extended to "the range of subjectifying and often unavowed powers that coexist with legitimate forms of sovereignty" (Brown 2006: 68).

Governing Religious Freedom

Talal Asad has elaborated a framework for a study of secularism incorporating the above criticism. Central to his work and other studies building on and elaborating his approach is the differentiation between the political doctrine of secularism and the secular as an epistemic category (Asad 2003). The politics of secularism becomes intimately tied to the (re)making of regimes of knowledge, subjectivities and religions in ways that enable the establishment of regimes of differentiation. The secular and secularism, in this perspective, being "interdependent" (Asad 2003: 24), the functioning of secular regimes of differentiation is thus analyzed in relation to their dependence upon factors which far surpass the field of law and politics as conventionally defined.

Asad's perspective on secularism can be designated as critical in the sense that the constitutive association between secularism and the protection of religious freedom—so central to the orderly vision of secularism—is problematized. In this perspective, our attention is directed to examining the "normative models of practice, behavior and religiosity" (Mahmood 2010: 293) which determine secular politics. These models are authorized by both state and civil society actors, and hence secularism cannot be reduced to a state affair—with the state always operating as a point of origin or reference—and nor is it merely a matter of drawing boundaries between the state and religions. This approach moves us away from orderly visions of politics and shifts our attention to the field of government of French Muslims. At a general level, government as "the conduct of conduct" is defined as the "management of possibilities" (Foucault 2000: 341), all those "practices that constitute, define, organize, and instrumentalize the strategies that individuals in their freedom can use in dealing with each other" (Foucault 1997: 300). The central activity for the government of Muslims is that which "makes individuals subjects" (Foucault 2000: 331). In simple terms, individuals are made subjects through a double process. This process implies the objectification of individuals, in various regimes of veridiction (e.g., law, history, sociology, fiction) as particular kinds of subject. At the same time, it implies that individuals recognize themselves as these kinds of subject and become tied to their "own identity by a conscience or self-knowledge" (Foucault 2000: 331).

At this point, it is incumbent to clarify how this approach relates to the principle of religious freedom. More precisely, the question needs to be asked: If I approach secular politics by postulating a link to government, i.e., attempts to structure the usage of freedom by individuals, how does this affect my understanding of the principle of religious freedom? Is the proclamation really an empty promise or a mere mask of power? Pointedly said, nothing could be more misleading. The controversies about secularism in France are unintelligible if we disregard how freedom, as established in law, is real in the sense that formal liberty and equality are a fact. This is where the analysis of government starts—but it does not stop there. Government presupposes that the state has retreated from directly intervening in the vast spaces where citizens lead their private lives and agents of civil society assemble and organize.[20] It is this retreat which makes government—all those activities by state and other actors aiming to structure the possible field of action of others—possible in the first place. More precisely—this precision is crucially important—this retreat makes attempts at government possible. How successful these attempts are is another matter entirely and will be dealt with in the course of this study. In other words, to postulate that French secular politics cannot be dissociated from the government of Muslims does not mean that religious freedom is in fact always governed, i.e., the object of successful systematic attempts to shape the usage of freedom of others. It means that the widespread acceptance of the principle of religious freedom is closely tied to the expectation by the state and broad segments of the population that religious subjects conform to specific norms. More generally, it is dependent upon the expectation that religious subjects can be (re)formed. Both expectations, as I shall show, are, from the point of view of many French, continuously frustrated; this is an essential part of the story to be told here.

Islam as Exceptional Object in Knowledge Production

This schematic outline of government which I just gave may be misleading in that it suggests a degree of coherence which in fact cannot be found in French secular politics. Saba Mahmood points out, when referring to the prescriptive models of religiosity implicit in secular government, that they are "often unstable and mutually contradictory" (2010: 293). This remark holds true for France. Indeed, when thinking about how to operationalize the study of secular government in the case of France, we immediately run up against the problematic fact already mentioned that the terms "Muslim", "French", etc., are contested and defined in diverse ways in public, whether in relation to specific matters or more generally.

How to deal with this analytically? One response to this problematic emphasizes the exceptional status of Islam and Muslims as objects of knowledge production. In this perspective, the confusion around the terms "Islam" and "Muslims" is, analytically speaking, a minor problem and does not relate intrinsically to secularism nor does it have a strong connection to knowledge production. It is considered a problem, rather, of the dissemination of representations which are beyond the pale of legitimate knowledge. The increasing usage of the term "Islamophobia" crystallizes this tendency to emphasize that the public debate about Islam and Muslims, insofar as it problematizes Islam, often lacks a solid scientific basis. While there is vehement disagreement on how to define the term "Islamophobia" (and whether to use it in the first place), it deserves underlining that there is wide if implicit agreement on the core meaning of the term (and it is this agreement, importantly, which enables or incites controversy).[21] Thus, the kernel of the concept Islamophobia—designating its causally significant dimension—refers to mistaken perceptions of Islam and/or Muslims or attitudes toward them.[22] These negative perceptions and attitudes are mistaken since they are indiscriminate, the reason why they tend to be considered illegitimate, even if they are not necessarily justiciable, and potentially dangerous.[23] This understanding of the term will also be used here even if the analytical work done by this concept in this study is very limited.

It needs to be emphasized that this definition of Islamophobia, as Jörg Stolz puts it pointedly, "has the effect of 'pathologizing' Islamophobia: an islamophobic person or institution is said to act on 'false' assumptions" (2005: 549).[24] This basic structure—an opposition, more or less pronounced, between knowledge and various forms of ignorance—is clearly discernible in French studies on Islamophobia. Thus Hajjat and Muhammad conclude their study with the statement that "the magnitude of the 'Muslim problem' is above all a matter of perception: the more the perception of the Other is hostile and restrictive, the bigger the 'Muslim problem' will appear" (2013: 263). The authors call for a "'secular' (*profane*) approach" to studying why "social actors use the Muslim reference" and consider that the "essentialization of 'the Muslim'" is "one of the foundations of Islamophobia" (2013: 263). Geisser, in his pioneering work *La nouvelle islamophobie* (The New Islamophobia), does not dwell so much on essentialism, but rather emphasizes that the "ideologues" who talk about fear of Islam do not have any knowledge of "lived Islam" (*islam vécu*) in France. While he recognizes that they may read the same authors and use the same words, "beyond appearances, we do not talk about the same issue." Unlike him, he comments, what prompts these "ideologues" to write is an Islam which is purely "*imagined*" and "*fantasized*" (Geisser 2003: 115; emphasis in the original).

Depending upon how one evaluates the scope of Islamophobia in public debates, assessments of their rationality will differ. The limits of the rationality of these debates are emphasized in proportion to the importance given to Islamophobic discourse. The positionality of the researcher and the conditions of possibility for public criticism deserve attention. If the object of study is more or less fantastical representations of Islam as an alterity figure and various mythologies of France (see, e.g., Scott 2007: 7–10), the scholarly engagement with the public debate is to a large degree concerned with uncovering the untruth of the debate. To put it another way, to conceptualize the study of public debates with a focus on Islamophobia tends to bolster an orderly vision of secular politics. It distracts scholarship from exploring mainstream regimes of science and knowledge. This is so because the term "Islamophobia" is based upon the division between reasonable (differentiated) and unreasonable (undifferentiated) thought which in turn is associated with the distinction between legitimate diversity of opinion on the one hand and illegitimate speech about Islam founded on erroneous representations on the other.

Secular Rationalities

Pursuing my aim to restore the secular discursive context in which Muslim actors function, I suggest a partial shift of focus, from political ideology on the one hand and from confusion, misperceptions, and misrepresentation on the other, to the multiplicity of rationalities involved in public debates. These rationalities are not simply the object of consensus, nor are they fixed, but they are widely shared and they are, literally, essential to the public debate on secular politics in France. As such, they deserve closer scrutiny. In one sense this study argues that the scholarly concern with Islamophobia broadly speaking—racializing, essentializing, monolithic representations of Islam and Muslims—underestimates to different degrees how reasonable (and closely connected with scientific discourse) the French public debate in fact is. Needless to say, the word "reasonable" does not imply any normative judgment, and does not refer to one reason, but to multiple rationalities which are not always easily compatible with each other if looked at logically. Nor does it imply that all members of the public necessarily validate the ways in which participants reason. However, it does mean that the modes of reasoning can be understood in their particularity.

There is, thus, a problematic of knowledge about French Islam which transcends questions of Islamophobia. At the most general level, this problematic needs to be understood as a result of the existence, in French society, of a variety of institutionalized knowledge resources which make it possible to describe and make sense of Islam and Muslims, and to define in what ways they are relevant to government, i.e., in what ways they further its interest or are detrimental to it. I want to argue here, then, that government, for the purpose of a study of secular politics on Islam, needs to be conceptualized in such a way that we can grasp and name the distance between "things in themselves" and how they appear in governmental reason. The task is to operationalize Foucault's claim that:

> Government is only interested in interests. The new government, the new governmental reason, does not deal with what I would call the things in themselves of governmentality, such as individuals, things, wealth, and land. It no longer deals with these things in themselves. It deals with the phenomena of politics, that is to say, interests, which precisely constitute politics and its stakes (2008: 45).

Let me add that a similar conceptual claim can be made independently of this theoretical perspective. Tariq Modood, in a study of European secular politics, has proposed a typology of "five types of policy reasons"—religion as truth, religion as danger, religion as utility, religion as identity, and worthiness of respect—which may lead the state to be interested in religion (2010: 7). The basic assumption in both approaches is that a plurality of possible interests can be perceived to be associated with Islam and Muslims. Drawing on studies of governmentality, I conceptualize this diversity of knowledge resources as political rationalities.[25] As they are not authorized by any religious tradition, they can be considered secular rationalities. Apart from the juridical rationality discussed above, there are three rationalities which crucially enable the government of Islam and Muslims in France in the period from 1989 till the present. Here they are named social, historical, and aesthetic, based on their respective epistemological perspective. At the most basic level, rationalities are defined here as the "changing discursive fields within which the exercise of power is conceptualised" (Rose & Miller 1992: 175). We could say that political rationalities are resources available in society which enable the reflexive practice of power; they allow people to reason and justify, in public or private, a specific exercise of power, its means and ends. Of course, these discourses are not limited to scientific discourses. A rationality functions in relation to a specific notion of truth but is not necessarily scientific. In France, aesthetic rationalizations of Islam—e.g., in novels or movies—are of great importance. Fiction will be examined here both as an object of legal and political deliberations, notably with regard to freedom of expression, and as a mode of public reasoning. Note also that the concept of rationality does not imply that power is always fully rationalized, but that it *can* be rationalized. More generally, a "political rationality" needs to be distinguished from a "system." Wendy Brown stresses that "it is precisely the difference between a 'rationality' and a 'system' that is significant in Foucault's reformulation of the political." A political rationality is not "coherently bounded, internally consistent (or internally contradictory)" and cannot be reduced to "abstract principles." Furthermore, rationalities should not be confused with "systems of rule"; rather, they constitute partly contingent "orders of practice and orders of discourse" (Brown 2001: 115f.).[26] In this study, these rationalities are defined and differentiated with reference to three features. (Needless to say, these definitions are strictly tailored to suit the cases examined here.) First, in relation to their epistemology, i.e., the epistemological structure of reality they postulate; second, in relation to the kind of aims and tasks of government which they render thinkable, debatable, and realizable; and finally, in relation to the forms of subjectivity they presuppose and reproduce.

Only a broad summary outline of these rationalities can be given here. In terms of epistemology, social rationality assumes the existence of social forces— generated by various kinds of interaction between the actors in a given space— which constitute conditions for who they are, what they do, the relationships they form, and the institutions which emerge in this space. The central assumption of historical rationality is "France," understood as maintaining on certain level(s) an identity in the course of historical change. As pointed out before, the definition of France's identity is controversial. This holds true in particular for its historical rootedness, i.e., for the specific ways in which past, present, and future interrelate in France. So the shared assumption is limited to the notion that history matters to the content of contemporary French identity. Aesthetic rationality, meanwhile, assumes the existence of forms of representation which are not mimetic, i.e., which manifest their fictive status yet are meaningful in relation to the real world as conventionally understood and contribute to understanding the latter. In terms of subjectivity, social rationality—to simplify—conceives of the social as being basically prior to the individual. The subject is made to appear in its social specificity (in contrast to the abstract legal and political subject) and probability. Historical rationality presupposes a remembering subject, i.e., a subject who constitutes its relation to self and others, its bonds, commitments and obligations, partly through an understanding of the history of things and humans, in particular of France. In aesthetic rationality, the subject is conceived as universal in the sense that it has the fundamental capacity to consume—and be moved by—works of fiction and thus participate in the shared world of fiction. As to the aims and tasks of government which are rationalized and debated in these manners, social rationality allows social forces to be taken into account, in diverse and sometimes conflicting ways, as causal factors in the exercise of power. Social rationalizations of Islam routinely ask or demonstrate how social conditions or state policies have contributed to the emergence of Muslim religiosity in general or specific dimensions of it, how they have shaped them and determined their significance—and how changes in these conditions or other policies would affect Muslim religiosity. This rationality allows Muslims (and their practices) to be particularized by locating them in social space; at the same time, it can be used to dissolve the particularity of Islam by reducing it—to varying degrees—to the social forces underlying it.[27] The most central task rendered thinkable by historical rationality is to shape, through the writing of French history, how French remembering subjects—Muslim and others—identify (or not) with France. The writing of history is invested with great hopes as to its potential for furthering the inclusion into the national community of hitherto marginalized groups. At the same time, the writing of history can disunite the sovereign power of the state by making apparent the disjuncture between what is rightful and how power is exercised. As to works of fiction, they are produced with the claim to enable specific understanding, or experience, of aspects of reality: be it what is conventionally held to be reality; a reality which is obscured; the reality as it is lived by other humans; the interior reality of humans; or a possible future reality, etc. They regularly function in mutual relations of competition or complementarity with other rationalizations of Islam. As I shall show, the introduction of these rationalities not only allows us to map modes of reasoning beyond references to law and political theory, but also to grasp in a systematic manner the broad range of matters—relating notably to social policies and historical memory—which have become related to Islam and Muslims in the framework of integration policies. While these matters—and the moment and way in which they have become relevant—are partly contingent, these connections between religion and other matters are by no means simply coincidental, specific to Islam, or due to some kind of misfunctioning of the secularist order. Rather, they are enabled by routine procedures of government rationalizations.

Regulating Worship and Governing Muslims

Now, circling back to the question of how to deal analytically with the fact that basic terms in the public debate on Islam are contested in their definition, I will use the concept of political rationalities here to show in which sense the difficulty of determining unambiguously what is Islam and Muslim is an essential part of secularism in France.[28] The "things" of government can be seen differently and this has important consequences for debates about secular politics. It would be wrong to deny that French secularism implies normative models of subjectivity; that is, it would be impossible to deny that debates about rights are often routinely tied to an understanding of what kind of subject can be the bearer of this right and who cannot. Debates on secular politics do establish systematic connections between the management of worship practices on the one hand and the examination of Muslim subjects and their attempted government on the other. However, it would also be wrong to consider that these normative notions of religion and subjectivity are always readily identifiable. In response to this I want to underline that relative indeterminacy is an important feature of French secularism. This relative indeterminacy can be represented in the following three questions, which summarize schematically recurrent topics in debates about the governance of Muslims, topics which are often but not necessarily related to each other. First, what kind of subjects are French Muslims? How can they be described, i.e., what are necessary features of the category Muslim and how many individuals are to be included in it? How can this group be internally differentiated? Second, what kinds of subjectivity are appropriate for Muslims in France as French subjects? To put it another way, what is distinctive about non-Muslim French subjects and how should normative Muslim subjectivity in France be defined? That is, what kind of subjectivity is in France's interest? Finally, how can Muslims be governed in general and how should the subjectivation of Muslims be governed in such a way that the national interest is achieved? More generally, what is the structure of power in French society and how is it evolving? So briefly, the questions are "Who are Muslims?", "What is normative Frenchness?", and "How can Muslims be governed?". The importance of this last question can hardly be overstated as it opens up normative-theoretical reflections on difference to the observation of transformations in French society and to the question "Who triggers and/or controls these processes of change?". As we shall see all through the book, this set of—highly political—questions is practically omnipresent in French public discourses on Islam.

These three groups of questions have become central to debates about Islam since the early 1990s. They recur in discussions about the legal status and correct policy response to specific religious practices: headcover, halal meat provisions, workplace prayers, mosque constructions. The importance of these questions is widely recognized and, more often than not, no longer needs to be acknowledged, i.e., there is no real need to argue the public importance of knowing and learning more, in whatever way, about Muslim lives in France in all their dimensions, not least in areas commonly regarded as private. Note also that these three questions describe a formal structure of debate. Different forms of reasoning can be used to answer them. For example, Muslims can be characterized in terms of different criteria (social, cultural, religious, etc.) and knowledges. Likewise, the term "interest" leaves open on what basis the interest of France is determined. It only postulates that any public discourse about Muslim subjects in France needs to prove that Muslim subjectivities are not detrimental to France's weal. Last but not least, the very definition of the French normative subject is not fixed.

Integrating Muslims

I have introduced the concept of political rationality to facilitate analysis of the diverse and entwined logics at play when identifying Muslims, normative Frenchness, and modes of government. Having emphasized the complexity and the potential for discursive fragmentation, I will now take a closer look at the framework for debate which these three questions outline. Although this framework has been critiqued, it has not yet been superseded, and it centers on integration into the French nation.[29] Nation refers here to a formal political structure, "something more cohesive than a mere aggregate of persons who happen legally to belong to the state" (Brubakers 1992: 21), supposing an inside/outside division and postulating that citizenship and identity need to be in equation; as to the relevant features of identity and what counts as being in equation, they can be diverse. Adapting Foucault, one might say that the consideration of France as a nation-state functions in debates about Islam as the—always already contested—"principle of intelligibility of what is, but equally of what must be" (Foucault 2009: 376). In these debates, it is regularly presupposed that the (re)production of the population as a nation, as a bounded group definable with reference to certain traits (primarily but not exclusively, the usage of French language), is a task of the state.[30] Since the debates in the 1980s about reforming the nationality code, it is highly politicized (Feldblum 1994). Pointing to the nation-state as a principle of intelligibility is not meant to deny that this principle is contested from various sides; this is indeed a major topic in this study. However, the power of the nation-state framework—relying, ultimately, on forms of "banal nationalism" (Billig 1995)—to shape debates about Islam is a condition for these contestations.

In this study, I follow Sayad's argument that immigration, broadly speaking, is political because it implies a challenge to the national order—founded on the distinction between inside and outside—and exposes its contingency (1984, 1999).[31] Emigration and immigration "are a cross-check or a borderline situation which force us to reflect on the notion of the nation, obliging the latter to reveal its truth" (1984: 189). In other words, they raise questions about how to define what the nation is and by which criteria membership is determined. In this perspective, the most important condition for conflicts about Islam in France is the fundamentally contingent nature of the nation and Islam's status as a newly arrived religion. Once questions are asked about the definition of normative Frenchness and what constitutes the nation in all its particularity, the answers vary not only in content, but also in their mode of reasoning. Again and again, questions emerge about incoherencies and contingencies on which the notion of a bounded French nation is predicated. It is this ongoing debate of which the issue of secularism and Islam is a central part.

Immigration constitutes a "national problem," according to Sayad. The problematic nature of immigration is reflected in the fact that it is constantly presented as provisional, in the face of all the available knowledge that contradicts this "illusion of the provisional" (Sayad 1984). As for the situation in France, maintaining the "illusion of the provisional" became strictly impossible in the course of the 1980s.[32] However, the term integration serves fundamentally to indicate—or, rather, repeatedly assert—the unaccomplished nature of immigration irrespective of whether immigrants have acquired citizenship or not. It serves to identify one kind of immigration as a national problem, in Sayad's terminology, and to assert the state's power to address it. At the moment of its institutionalization, e.g., in the *Haut Conseil à l'intégration* (High Council on Integration, or HCI) created in 1989, the discourse on integration was motivated by a desire to assert the sovereign, i.e., unconditioned, power of the state to effectively assume the task of guarding the nation against undesirable immigrants. This assertion of sovereignty— which manifests itself in the simple claim that immigration is unaccomplished whatever the real status of immigrants is according to the law—is, at its most basic level, what dominant discourse on integration seeks to accomplish.[33]

Analytically, the discursive link between integration and secularism is crucial for this study. By positing this crucial link, Muslims are not naturalized as immigrants nor is integration ascribed a self-evident status. Rather, the power struggle about integration, the definition of normative Frenchness, the (self-) identification of Muslims, and the modalities and possibilities for government come into focus without presupposing a fixed concept of religion, Islam, or France. It needs to be emphasized that this struggle is not only about specific policy measures, but about the conditions—notably, the kind of reasonings— under which the future of France and French Muslims is debated. Foucault's statement is applicable here: "Discourse is not simply that which translates struggles or systems of domination, but is the thing for which and by which there is struggle, discourse is the power which is to be seized" (1981: 52f.).

Recognizing Islam: "Religion" and "Worship" in State Discourse

If *laïcité* politics is complex, then partly it is because it involves multiple acts of identifying Muslims and relating these identities to notions of normative Frenchness. A more comprehensive analysis of this complexity needs to incorporate four modes of identifying the Islamic in the present context, which I will now briefly present. I will start by examining the conceptual grid shaping how state institutions deal with Islam. Essentially, there is recognition of Islam as one religion among others. Next, I shall address usages of "Islam" as a proper name—meaning that the word "Islam" is not used as descriptive of any object. This usage is central to Islamophobic speech. I then turn to human and social sciences on the one hand and fiction on the other. Both fields display structures which enable very diverse representations of Islam and thus contribute to the complexity of secular politics. If, as I said, the dyadic relation between the secular and the religious is of limited value as an analytical framework for French secular politics, the last three modes are part of the reason.

Let me first observe how state institutions recognize Islam.[34] A crucial question to be discussed here relates to the very category religion or, more precisely, the two closely related and partly overlapping notions worship (*culte*) and religion as they are used in official judicial and legislative documents in France. Briefly, these two notions, both more or less ill-defined, do not seem to pose a major obstacle to recognizing as religious practices those practices which the majority of Muslims identify in this manner.[35] (Needless to say, this does not imply that they are necessarily considered permissible in France.) However, as mentioned above, state policies around Islam and Muslims are complex, in the sense that they are based on heterogeneous rationalities, and this also applies to conceptions of religion. Apart from the juridical concepts of worship and religion, other to varying degrees coherent notions of religion and/or worship come into play and serve to further qualify and distinguish between variously acceptable and unacceptable religions or practices; these distinctions may affect the legal status of a religious group or religious practice and/or how public authorities deal with it. As Winnifred F. Sullivan, Elizabeth Shakman Hurd, Saba Mahmood, and Peter G. Danchin showed with regard to the "legal and political enforcement of rights to religious freedom and other related regimes of management, including toleration and accommodation of religious diversity," they "necessarily involve a dividing of legal religion from illegal religion—good religion from bad religion." Separations of this kind are established on the basis of "an ongoing set of unresolved and competing dichotomies dividing religion as individual or communal, private or public, spiritual or material, belief or practice, chosen or given, Protestant or Catholic, Western or Eastern, peaceful or violent, utopian or locative, universal or particular" (Sullivan et al. 2015: 7).

State institutions have not provided a full-fledged definition of religion.[36] This at first sight astonishing fact is characteristic of the legal framework. It is worth quoting Francis Messner, who writes that "the French regime of separation is characterized by the existence of legislation for worship groups (*cultes*), but above all the nonexistence of a status for worship, i.e., a precise legal regime. Having been abolished by the law of 1905, it was replaced by an ensemble of isolated mechanisms which are susceptible to be applied to the religion which demands it" (Messner 2001: 45). While the term "worship" has not been defined in law,[37] "exercise of worship" was defined by the *Conseil d'État* in 1997 as "the celebration of ceremonies organized in order to accomplish certain rituals or practices by persons assembled by shared religious belief." A previous decision—which refused to recognize a group of atheists as a worship association—indicates that worship is connected to faith in a deity.[38] This definition—implying a deity, rituals, belief, and a group of people—is to a significant degree typical, not only because judges simply refrain from defining the term religion, but also because of its conventionality. The "largely descriptive and traditional" character of juridical definitions of religion has been emphasized (Woehrling 2003: 29) and the "very traditional and full of common-sense definition" of worship has been highlighted by jurists (Rolland 2005: 59).[39] Although this framework does not seem to produce negative effects for the recognition of Islam and Muslim practices, other groups fare less well.[40] There is much, often implicit, agreement between Muslim actors on the one hand and state institutions on the other about which practices count as Islamic. One (partial) exception to this is the "burqa" (whose status among Muslims is contested). While the *Conseil d'État* branded it a "radical practice" of Islam,[41] French legislators attempted in 2010, albeit without success, to label it non-Islamic in the law prohibiting the wearing of face veils in public.[42]

In simple terms, the legal framework does not simply place Islamic practices beyond the pale. However, this obviously does not mean that these practices are automatically considered permissible in France; if some are not and/or are contested in their legality, this has partly to do with additional qualifications of specific practices and/or Islam in general. To illustrate this, the hijab was recognized as Islamic practice by the *Conseil d'État* during the first headscarf controversy (1989).[43] Ever since, various actors in France have attempted to restrict its usage and/or attempted to persuade Muslim organizations and authorities to declare it nonobligatory.[44] In the course of these attempts to circumscribe the place of the headscarf, multiple arguments were put forward about the headscarf as a religious practice, the *banlieues* and *laïcité*.[45] To different degrees, these arguments imply a conceptual framing of the headscarf which necessarily problematizes it and renders its legality precarious. Importantly, the French government redefined the headscarf as a "religious sign," a term which is used in the law banning the headscarf. Talal Asad underlines the discrepancy between the government's conception of the headscarf and that of a woman who wears "the veil as an obligation of her faith": "*if her conscience impels her to wear it as an act of piety*, the veil becomes for that reason an integral part of her self. For her it is not a *sign* intended to communicate something but *part of an orientation, of a way of being*." In contrast, the government's approach turns the hijab into a "*displaceable* sign" (Asad 2006: 501; emphasis in the original). This framing of the headscarf is closely related to the general notion that religion is basically belief and external practices are not an essential part of it. During one of the hearings conducted by the parliamentary Debré Commission, set up to investigate the "question of wearing religious signs at school," chairman Jean-Louis Debré declared: "Religion is an inner process (*démarche*); one is a believer (*croyant*), one has the faith. We carry it within us." This notion of religion led him to ask Fouad Alaoui, then secretary-general of the UOIF, whether wearing a "sign" such as the hijab was not "an act of proselytism" and thus prohibited. Alaoui failed in his repeated attempts to make the members of the Commission grasp the distinction between two alternative perspectives on the hijab, i.e., as implementation of a "religious prescription" versus usage as a "religious sign" which, in his view, had no religious basis (Commission Debré 2003: II, 427).[46] The notion of religion championed by Debré and many others cannot simply undo the classification of hijab as a religious practice; they cannot ignore the problematic of religious freedom. However, this understanding of what is and what is not essential to religion is one factor among several which render the status of hijab highly precarious.[47]

The basic point here is that state practices for identifying religions are complex; they are not limited to the categories of worship and religion, nor does this process necessarily involve an either/or choice (which the above remarks may lead one to think). For example, French state institutions are regularly called upon to examine whether a given space, practice, or institution is related to worship (*culte*) or culture (*culture*) or whether both categories apply. The significance of this issue has partly to do with a national architectural heritage constituted by tens of thousands of churches, which are owned by the state and used, almost exclusively, by the Catholic Church. While case law based on the law of 1905 declares the usage of these buildings for worship to preclude other uses, today they are often simultaneously designated for worship and for cultural functions in the broad sense (Fornerod 2006). In the case of Islam, this fuzzy relationship between cult and culture arises with mosque associations, most of which are not registered as worship associations (*association cultuelle loi 1905*) but adopt the more flexible format of a nonprofit or cultural association (*association loi 1901*). In short, when it comes to associations, the boundary between religion and culture is often blurred.[48] While French governments sometimes appeal for clearer distinctions to be drawn between religion and culture,[49] the opposite trend can also be observed, with calls to revise the association format for worship so as to broaden the potential range of activities of these associations (see, e.g., Commission Machelon 2006).[50] Note that the question whether or not an association qualifies as a worship association is not automatically answered by state agencies when dealing with associations. This is partly because an association becomes a worship association by declaration and not by authorization from the *préfecture*. Only if a worship association applies to benefit from any of its privileges will its status be reviewed.[51] This is merely one example for a much broader phenomenon where other categories, in addition to "religion" or "worship," are used in processes of identification.[52]

Islam as a Proper Name

If the meaning of the terms "Islam" and "Muslims" is controversial in France, this is partly because both can be—and are—used as empty signifiers or as "proper names," as Saul A. Kripke puts it. This usage is central to what I have termed Islamophobia above. When a term is used in this way, it is not descriptive of an object. From this angle, the—never fully achieved—boundedness of terms such as "Islam" and "Muslim" does not depend upon any features shared by those who are thus designated (and only by them). Rather, it is this name which—partly—fixes and gives unity to an otherwise polysemic field of elements. As proper names, "Islam", "Muslims", etc., individuate the carrier of the name without characterizing it in a manner only fitting this carrier (cf. Kripke 1972).

Perhaps the most widespread usage of Islam and Muslim as empty signifiers—noted in much of the literature—configures Muslim as racialized ethnicity or descent group (Meer & Modood 2009, 2019). Here, "Muslims" refers to a descent group whose origins are located in immigration movements from "Islamic" countries. One example may serve here to illustrate this kind of usage of "Muslim" which does not describe any group with features only fitting this group, but which is, importantly, nevertheless likely to be understood by a vast majority in French society. This example is from 2012, when President Sarkozy was commenting on the killing of two French soldiers by Mohamed Merah.[53] Sarkozy rejected the "amalgamations" made in extreme-right statements blaming the killings on "radical Islamism" and immigration. Sarkozy stated: "I remind you that two of our soldiers were—how to put it? Muslim, in any case in appearance, as one was Catholic, but (Muslim) in appearance." In this example, the speaker Nicolas Sarkozy stumbles when he realizes that he is using the term "Muslim" in two different and conflicting ways, namely racialized and religious, and attempts to disambiguate the meanings of the term. Heavily criticized and ridiculed, the statement was nevertheless understood; that is, everybody understood whom Sarkozy was trying to name, to wit "immigrants" or "descendants of immigrants" from North Africa, in particular from Algeria.[54] This statement is adduced here merely to illustrate a broader and diverse spectrum of racializing, essentialist, or monolithic usages of the terms "Muslim" and "Islam." Whether and to which degree these terms have an explanatory function depends upon how precisely they are employed.[55] These usages are widespread and they constitute one important reason for controversies about this cluster of terms.

The Secular Order of Things

To understand the complexity of secular debates and acts of identifying what is Islam(ic) and Muslim, it is indispensable to consider some general conditions shaping knowledge claims about Islam made today. In this respect, I shall draw on Foucault's study of modern sciences, and more particularly of what he terms human sciences, in *Les mots et les choses* (The Order of Things) (1966). The equivocal term "human sciences"—used in multiple ways in France in the 1950s and 1960s—refers, in Foucault's context, roughly speaking, to psychology, sociology, anthropology, text analysis, history, and anthropology (Descombes 2016: 68f.). The utility of Foucault's observations as applied here, marginal to his broader concerns in *Les mots et les choses*, resides in the fact that they highlight how the notions of visibility and reality—in relation to objects of study—have been immensely complicated with the rise of modern human and social sciences. Structurally speaking, these sciences imply reasons why rationalizations of Islam are essentially incomplete, ongoing, and contested. Moving up to the most general level, we can say that Foucault's observations allow us to throw some light on the insecure and contestable nature of the secular order of things.

Order—in Foucault's perspective—enables us to answer the question why "we say that a cat and a dog resemble each other less than two greyhounds do, even if both are tame or embalmed (...)" (2005: xxi). If we want to answer this question, i.e., if we want to establish "even the simplest form of order," we need "(a) 'system of elements' – a definition of the segments by which the resemblances and differences can be shown, the types of variation by which those segments can be affected, and, lastly, the threshold above which there is a difference and below which there is a similitude" (Foucault 2005: xxi). Now, the emergence of modern sciences considerably complicates the basis upon which order can be constituted. It opens up more choices for constituting order and making sense of things.

The general reason has to do with the fact that the emergence of modern sciences not only relates to a "transcendental reflection" (2005: 265) on the subject, but "opposite" to this, to a second reflection concerned with the "being itself that is represented." In this second case, the "foundation of ... unity" of representations is found in a different kind of transcendence. Foucault refers to concepts such as labor, life, and language which "in their being ... are outside knowledge, but by that very fact ... conditions of knowledge" (2005: 265). The ambivalent status of these "objects"—in relation to in/visibility—is emphasized by Foucault, who describes them as "those never objectifiable objects, those never entirely representable representations, those simultaneously evident and invisible visibilities, those realities that are removed from reality to the degree to which they are the foundation of what is given to us and reaches us" (2005: 265).

The first point to make here is that a much more complex understanding of the relation between visibility and reality establishes itself at the threshold of the modern world: "(T)hings, in their fundamental truth, have now escaped from the space of the table" where order was constituted on the basis of their differential characteristics (2005: 259). Another way to put this is to say that these "objects" or "forms"—language, labor, life—"prowl around the outer boundaries of our experience" (2005: 265).[56] They are "'transcendentals'" (2005: 265) or, "the 'quasi-transcendentals' of Life, Labour, and Language" (2005: 271). Now, while these observations are useful for problematizing notions of reality, and representation they are indirectly connected only to human sciences in Foucault's account.

First of all, let me outline the central characteristic of these sciences. Human sciences—in Foucault's reading—have the essential characteristic that their object and condition of possibility are representations made by humans. Human sciences are not concerned with "an analysis of what man is by nature" (2005: 392), namely a living, speaking, and laboring being. Rather, human sciences are concerned with "that living being who, from within the life to which he entirely belongs and by which he is traversed in his whole being, constitutes representations by means of which he lives, and on the basis of which he possesses that strange capacity of being able to represent to himself precisely that life" (Foucault 2005: 384). Thus, "biology, economics, and philology must not be regarded as the first human sciences, or the most fundamental" (2005: 383), although the last two sciences imply activities specific to humans. Rather, a rough "division" of the field of human sciences would refer to three "interlocking" regions, namely psychology, sociology, and analysis of literature broadly speaking (2005: 387f.), which stand in a position of "duplication" to the aforementioned sciences, i.e. biology, economics, and philology (2005: 387f.). In other words, they do not have a positive object of study (Sabot 2014: 155) but are rather derivative of more or less complex representational entities created by humans, entities which may ultimately take shape as science.

The "originality of human sciences"—and this is a feature which greatly contributes to complicating the task of representation—is the fact that "they seek the basis of man's active role as a subject (i.e., his power of representing objects) in this very unthought" of humans (Gutting 1990: 212). Foucault emphasizes this aspect: "On the horizon of any human science, there is the project of bringing man's consciousness back to its real conditions, of restoring it to the contents and forms that brought it into being, and elude us within it" (2005: 397). He adds "a 'human science' exists, not wherever man is in question, but wherever there is analysis – within the dimension proper to the unconscious – of norms, rules, and signifying totalities which unveil to consciousness the conditions of its forms and contents. To speak of 'sciences of man' in any other case is simply an abuse of language" (2005: 398).

This analysis of non-thought dimensions is enabled, generally speaking, by a number of concepts taken from the empirical sciences, namely signification and system, function and norm, conflict and rule. Foucault argues that "meanings (signs), functions, and conflicts can all be represented without appearing to consciousness." Thus, this set of concepts—or "constituent models", as Foucault calls them—makes it possible to speak about, explain or interpret phenomena in a manner which is unconnected (but not necessarily in conflict) to how the humans studied consciously represent this matter to themselves: "(T)he human sciences have been able, for example, to speak intelligibly of the function of social practice, of a conflict within an individual psyche, or of the meaning of a myth, even though the society, individual, or culture in question has no awareness of it" (Gutting 1990: 212). To what extent the general emphasis placed upon the unthought in the last stage of the development of human sciences is valid in this form is of no concern to me here. For the purpose of this study, it is enough to say that this is clearly a significant aspect of scientific knowledge as it broadens the range of possible representations—and of possible conflicts about representations—and contributes to complexity in debates about Islam.

The basis of this complexity lies in the fact that the emergence of human sciences implies the emergence of new entities, namely the "constituent models" mentioned above. Such models or concepts literally constitute what these sciences study (in contrast to models of formalization or metaphorical models). They "make it possible to create groups of phenomena as so many 'objects' for a possible branch of knowledge ... They play the role of 'categories' in the area of knowledge particular to the human sciences; they ensure their connection in the empirical sphere, but they offer them to experience already linked together" (Foucault 2005: 389). In this study, this can be applied to the notions "the social" (or "society") and "memory" in the relevant sciences, i.e., the social and historical. The social refers here to the basic notion, developed in the nineteenth century, that "society ... was an entity that could have causal effects on individuals' actions. What a human being thought and did was determined by her or his position in a society, in a social structure" (Wagner 1999: 144). Memory refers here to the socio-psychological complex shaping how individuals and groups define their identity through acts of recollecting and forgetting. As in the case of society, the knowledges that enable rationalizations of these matters emerged in the late nineteenth and twentieth centuries (Perthes 2008). In brief, the cluster of concepts and methods relating to the social and memory offer multiple means to reconfigure the visible features of what is studied.

The "Transcendental Mobility" of Human Sciences and the Postcolonial Critique of Sciences

The emergence of human sciences signals a reconfiguration of representative mechanisms. In this new context, "man appears in his ambiguous position as an object of knowledge and as a subject that knows," as an "observed spectator" (Foucault 2005: 340). There is a second, closely related dimension to the functioning of human sciences which needs to be mentioned here as it also complicates the rationalization of Islam and Muslims. It has to do with an inherent tendency for a specific kind of self-examination in the human sciences. Representations being both an object of study and a condition of possibility for the human sciences, Foucault claims that "[t]hey are always animated, therefore, by a sort of transcendental mobility. They never cease to exercise a critical examination of themselves" (2005: 397). In the day-to-day functioning of human sciences this "transcendental mobility" manifests itself through multiple acts of auto-demystification or unveiling: "... unlike other sciences, they seek not so much to generalize themselves or make themselves more precise as to be constantly demystifying themselves: to make the transition from an immediate and non-controlled evidence to less transparent but more fundamental forms.... It is always by an unveiling that they are able, as a consequence, to become sufficiently generalized or refined to conceive of individual phenomena" (2005: 397).

If we move up one level from mechanisms internal to science to the constitution of scientific fields or sciences, we can add that the "peculiar configuration" of human sciences (2005: 387), that is, their being in a position of "duplication," "can serve *a fortiori* for" human sciences themselves. Not only is it possible "to treat in the style of the human sciences (of psychology, sociology, and the history of culture, ideas, or science) the fact that for certain individuals or certain societies there is something like a speculative knowledge of life, production, and language a speculative knowledge of life, production, and language – at most, a biology, an economics, and a philology." Foucault concludes that "this is probably no more than the indication of a possibility which is rarely realized and is perhaps not capable, at the level of the empiricities, of yielding much of value" (2005: 386f.).[57]

In contemporary France, since the 1980s, this inherent mechanism of (auto-)demystification and transcendental mobility has become actualized and produced effects that have significantly reconfigured the conditions under which Islamic matters are debated. Put simply, multiple and diverse acts of demystification are accomplished in this context by exploring the connections between knowledge production on the one hand and identity construction (and its historical conditions) on the other. To put it differently, knowledge production is looked at from the perspective of the constitutive relation between self and Other. The basic relevance of this connection—conceptualized in greatly diverging levels of complexity—is widely recognized and has a status akin to a commonplace which manifests itself, notably, in widespread references to other(ization) or alterity and Islam as the Other of France, Europe, or the West.[58] This development is due to the broader and multiply mediated impact of postcolonial thought and not least the work of Edward Said disseminating the notion that a logic of otherness is crucial for the formation of certain identities.[59] Twisting Foucault a bit, we might say that in this context claims about Islam are regularly met with the question "who did the interpretation": "interpretation finds itself with the obligation to interpret itself to infinity, always to resume" (1994: 277). This reshaping of the discursive context obviously cannot be understood as solely emanating from practitioners of human sciences, but is, as Foucault shows, enabled and reproduced by their structures and it is in this respect that I include it here in the reconstruction of the discursive context of secularism.

Considering the period covered here, the critical study of France conceived as a postcolonial space—"post" designating here simply the impossibility of a clear break with colonial history—and implying the scrutiny of modern French cultural production, including notably academic scholarship in relation to Islamic and Oriental matters, is of substantial importance. As Vincent Geisser put it with regard to scholarship on Islam, French scholars work in an academic environment which has been reconfigured by the "'mental decolonization' of the social sciences and the fall from grace of the Orientalist tradition" (2012: 355).

Since the 2000s, it can be said that French public life has been partially reshaped by postcolonial awareness. Particularly in the aftermath of the 2005 riots, postcolonial thinking arrived in the broader public sphere and contributed to a new kind of ongoing society-wide reflection on the presence of the colonial past.[60]

As I said, this development is partly due to Edward Said's study on Orientalism translated into French in 1980,[61] but cannot, of course, be reduced to his work which, in any case, is not free of ambivalences (Marzouki 2004). As this study also deals with scientific work on Islam, it needs to be mentioned, as Thomas Brisson has notably shown,[62] that there has been a history of fundamental transformation in this field of Islamic studies since the 1950s, acquiring more pace and scope in the 1960s in a context of major institutional changes in universities. Writing before the publication of Said's work, Maxime Rodinson had already noted the end of philological dominance and "the inescapable need" for "contact with other disciplines," notably social sciences, as essential results of this process (1974). Finally, Edward Said himself repeatedly quotes the article "Orientalism in Crisis" by Anouar Abdel-Malek, who, writing in 1963, had already drawn attention to the crumbling authority of Orientalists.[63]

This complex set of developments led to important reorientations in major French publications on Islamic matters after the Iranian Revolution of 1979. Achcar, in his article "Orientalism in Reverse," has argued that a certain continuity of orientalist thought in France since the 1970s can be observed, albeit with some central axioms of orientalism now being reversed. To put it simply, while the new brand of orientalists still see "the religion of Islam" as essential to the region and peoples of the Orient, they do not consider that this constitutes an obstacle to modernity and modernization; rather, they conceive of Islamism in particular as an agent of modernization (Achcar 2008: 24f.).

In the field of studies on French Islam, the publication of *Orientalism* brought changes of a different order.[64] Here, I would argue, the concrete agenda of auto-demystification—an agenda shaped directly in response to Said's critique—was and remains to "de-exceptionalize" Islam and Muslims. This may seem hardly worth mentioning in the sense that this development aims to correct a manifest error. It simply integrates the study of Islam belatedly into the human and social sciences. However, that would not be entirely correct, as this development contributes to configure the production of knowledge on Islam in particular ways. In fact, it creates a kind of blind spot in academic scholarship and public knowledge on Islam, due to an emphasis on disproving what is seen as a centuries-old tradition of homogenizing and essentializing. Great efforts are being undertaken to indicate the existence of individualizing processes in French Islam and to render the plurality of Islam apparent: "There is not one Islam..."[65] More generally, this development translates into multiple efforts to demonstrate how Islam is malleable and socially transformed and in essential respects such as its relation to modernity, secularism, or individualization, similar to other religions, notably Christianity.[66] One example for this line of argument is Olivier Roy's statement in the introduction to his study on "globalized Islam" that "Islam cannot escape the New Age of religions or choose the form of its own modernity" (2004: 6). Basically, great interest remains in criticizing Orientalist perceptions of Islam and Muslims, but few attempts are made to go beyond this critique and develop a sociology of French Islam which does not reduce Islam to a mere epiphenomenon of social processes or the result of individual appropriations of discourses and practices. Likewise, there is little interest in examining the question of how to think about unity in diversity, i.e., whether observable differences between Muslim practices and discourses can be integrated into or presuppose a broader framework, namely Islam.

Furthermore, the striving to "de-exceptionalize" this field of study needs to be considered in its institutional contexts. This aim implies notably a critique of approaches, identified with Orientalism, which are exclusively relying on textual sources. Importantly, this critique is made in a context where the status of academic Orientalism inside the academy is undergoing, since approximately the 1990s, a rapid and remarkable decline (Mission de réflexion sur la formation des imams et des cadres religieux musulmans 2017: 28–31). As a consequence, the knowledge necessary for engaging in whatever way with the textual tradition of Islam, and with its scripture in the first place, have been dwindling, severely restricting available options to study the contemporary Islamic intellectual production in France.

In brief, I want to underline here that the integration of Islam and Muslims starts in a context where representations of Islam are critically revisited through the lens of the self–other dynamic[67] and philosophical anti-essentialism has become a powerful influence in social sciences (Modood 1998). As a consequence, this is a context where references to Islam as a causal factor (as opposed to social factors) easily smack of essentializing Orientalism and where scientists specializing in the study of Islam often regard references to the particularity of Islam—central in debates about integration—as a primary object of their critique. It seems, then, that auto-demystification led to a significant but by no means complete discrepancy between public and expert discourses on Islam. As we shall see, this fact is of some importance for the content and development of Muslim discourses on Islam in French society.

The Truth of Fiction

To argue that in politics, the necessary reliance upon systems of representation, is a source of ambiguity and confusion is not a surprising claim to make. It could be said that the emergence of modern political science in the West is coterminous with this recognition. In *Leviathan*, Hobbes insists on the various negative consequences which follow from the often ambivalent meanings of words and images. While Hobbes believes that words are the "light of human minds," they need to be provided with "exact definitions" and "purged from ambiguity" (1994: 26). The disturbing ambivalence of words is, from his point of view, only one element of his broader concern with the instability of signs. Generally speaking, "(f)rom the perspective of the new political science, the illness of politics resides in the words and signs, images and scripts which signify but to which no uncontested meaning could be ascribed" (Balke 2007: 64; see also Pettit 2008). Here, I have raised a much more specific argument, drawing on *Les mots et les choses*, about the historical emergence of human sciences and how this affects possibilities to order and interpret what is visible in today's France. Human sciences, to the degree that they contribute to secular knowledges, considerably complicate the task of representing "religion." The visible manifestations of what is classified as Islamic worship can be reordered and interpreted in strikingly different ways without necessarily negating the classification as religion. Both the sciences of the social and the science of history and memory offer a large number of concepts to reconfigure Islam, to order and interpret what is (in) visible, as well as new means to govern and justify the importance of government.

I now want to discuss the last constituent factor in the relative indeterminacy of secular politics in France and, at the same time another central element of modern epistemological orders: fiction. Very briefly, the main argument here is that fiction—i.e., works which explicitly indicate their difference from a representation of reality claiming to be mimetic—cannot be considered as merely imaginary or the opposite of reality. Fiction cannot be simply excluded from the political rationalities which are employed in debates about Islam and which I propose to study here. If fiction is defined in simple opposition to reality, it will not be possible for analysis to capture the public significance and interest which aesthetic rationalizations of various aspects of social life including Islam elicit. The relationship needs to be conceptualized differently. Here, I will follow Henrich and Iser, who suggest that fiction, made for certain usages, refers through its usage to reality while at the same time "exceeding" it (1983). Numerous works of fiction are not situated, either by their creators or by the public, simply in an autonomous sphere with its own kind of particular reasoning—i.e., with a limited sphere of validity—which functions alongside that of other fields without being able to connect with them.[68] On the contrary, the acknowledgment and affirmation of a difference to mimetic representation is often combined with the claim that they enable a specific understanding, or experience, of aspects of reality: be it what is conventionally held to be reality; a reality which is obscured; a reality as it is lived by other humans; the interior reality of the human mind; or a possible future reality, etc. From a different angle, we might add that a flat denial of any "problem of appearance and reality" in social life (Trilling 2008: 209), and of fiction as one forum where it can be engaged, misses out on an essential dimension of public deliberation in secular France.[69]

Complex relations of rivalry and mutual determination have shaped the position of literature vis-à-vis the social sciences since the nineteenth century. Novelists have claimed to do the work of sociologists, while sociologists have drawn on works of fiction (Lepenies 2002), aspiring to conduct "a more dispassionate and scientific scrutiny of life than had ever been attempted before" (Watts 1957: 11). More generally, Robert Nisbet has proposed that the arts and sociology should be considered mutually determinant, building on significant similarities in their respective practices.[70] Focusing his reflections on nineteenth-century sociology, Nisbet conceptualized one link between them as "theme." A theme as defined by Nisbet is constituted by a question and "an ordering of experience and observation in a special focus": "'Reality' is indistinguishable from what is perceived under the influence of, in interaction with, theme" (Nisbet 1976: 31, 36). Themes identified by Nisbet as specific to the arts (i.e., writers and visual artists) and sociologists of the nineteenth century are "*community, authority, status,* the *sacred,* and *alienation*" (Nisbet 1976: 41; emphasis in the original).

Drawing upon Nisbet, I want to suggest a much more specific theme for the present context of France and this study: the reconfiguration of identities and structures of power in the multicultural society of France. This theme integrates, of course, the three questions outlined above: Who are Muslims? What kind of subjectivity is appropriate to them? How should they be governed—and how can they? In this formulation, the focus shifts from Islam, Muslims, and integration to a general question about changing identities and power structures in the multicultural context. Nisbet places a strong emphasis on the shared assumptions implicit in a theme.[71] Needless to say, his emphasis contradicts the approach chosen here. Beyond the basic existence of what my analysis terms "identity," "change," "power," and "multiculturalism," there is considerable disagreement not only on the results but on how to answer the associated questions. The above definition implies a logical tension in the way fiction relates to reality. My aim here is not to resolve this tension. Rather, I want to insist on the simple fact that in French debates the distinctions operated by participants between reality and fiction are "complex" ones and partly obscure, but that the possibility of making such distinctions is nevertheless widely accepted. This is part of the secular discursive context.

Conclusion

Approaching the study of French secularism requires due attention to its complexity. A conceptualization of secularism as a well-ordered regime, as a regime set up to determine the legitimate place of religion in public, runs into problems for two reasons. One has to do with the fact that the object of secular politics is not simply Islam as religion as it is defined conventionally. Broadly speaking conventional notions of religion and worship, often implicit, are important for French state institutions in their relation to Islam. "Secularism without religion" sums up a situation where these conventional notions cover only one part of the social meanings attached to the terms "Islam" and "Muslim." This is a situation where the notions Islam and Muslims are continuously reconfigured in different ways, with sometimes great and sometimes limited consequences, by various actors including Muslims.

Secularism is not one-dimensional as the objects of secular politics are multiple and not one. Other categories beyond religion or worship, whose importance may vary, come into play in secular politics; hence the need to broaden the range of rationalities of secular politics. The other has to do with the fact that secularism cannot be reduced to a formula where a separation is enacted and a space of absolute nonintervention for the state is created. Rather, the state, and other actors, seek to govern how people make use of their freedom. In the case of Islam in France, this desire is strong and persistent. It has taken shape in the governmental politics of integration into the nation. This is not to say that political ideologies and notions of a legal order do not matter. More particularly, republicanism, and the often noted principles of abstract equality, and notions of separation, are without doubt important for politics. But these ideological references have to be placed in a political constellation which is much more heterogeneous. Here, the public/private boundary is routinely crossed and Muslim lives and subjects are investigated (as the private matters); Islam is constantly examined in its specificity as one religion and social group. The kind of arguments which result from combinations of these diverse rationalities is the object of the following chapters.

2

The Social Republic

Introduction

In 2005, two prominent intellectuals, Alain Renaut and Alain Touraine, published a book of conversational debates about *laïcité*. The exchange between the two authors turns around the challenges French society faces and the options available for dealing with cultural diversity. Not surprisingly, references to the law prohibiting the wearing of headscarves in public schools, which had just been adopted by parliament (March 15, 2004), are omnipresent in the book. What may surprise, however, is that Renaut and Touraine disagree about the reasons which led to the adoption of this law. Renaut argued it was a specific interpretation—or rather, from his point of view, misinterpretation—of the republican idea. This misinterpretation led the state to adopt a law which excludes schoolgirls wearing a headscarf, while paradoxically justifying this exclusion with reference to a political order supposed to be universalist.

In his response to Renaut, Touraine argued that the causes leading to the adoption of the law were "on the whole sociological." Having himself been a member of the Stasi Commission (2003), which had recommended to the French president the adoption of the anti-headscarf law, Touraine pointed out that inside the commission there was no agreement "on how to define the principle of *laïcité*," nor did the commission's members agree on "the place which is due to cultural rights in France." The Stasi Commission's near unanimous support for the law[1] and the public's approval of it do not amount to a "philosophical" argument nor do they indicate, according to Touraine, "a principled rejection of cultural differences." Rather, the commission had "discovered" that the "social bond" was threatened, by (unnamed) groups and Muslim practices of self-segregation, and this triggered a response in form of a law. Put differently, in Touraine's view, it was the rise of Muslim "communalism" (*communautarisme*) which led to the law (Renaut & Touraine 2005: 28–32).[2]

The disagreement between the two intellectuals—about the identification of the "problem" at hand, i.e., the object of state policies—is another illustration for the disorderly character of secular politics which I have discussed in the previous chapter. If I mention this case here, this is in order to illustrate that disagreement about secular politics is regularly "thick"; not only is there disagreement about the ends (or means) of policies, but the very problem to be tackled is not determined in an identical manner. As this case shows, this pluralism of political rationalities can generate significant effects. It matters, for example, whether the prohibition of the headscarf should be understood as a sign of the "principled rejection of cultural differences" by the French government or rather, as Touraine argues, as a decision highly contingent upon a particular and changing social context in the *banlieues*. In other words, whether or not a religious practice— here, the headscarf—is rationalized in its social embeddedness can make a difference not only to how the decision is justified, but also to what the decision is intended to achieve or in plain terms what it is about.

This chapter will examine in more detail the diverse effects as well as the conditions of rationalizing Islam and Muslims in their social embeddedness. The more general aim of this chapter is to complicate accounts of the significance of political thought, more particularly republican discourse broadly speaking, on debates about Islam. Republican implies here not only a reference to *laïcité*,[3] but more generally to the singularly important role played by public authorities in the organization of collective life in France. As is widely known, this role cannot be disconnected from the "permanence of an illiberal temptation linked to the absolutization of popular sovereignty and the pretensions of a state creating society (*l'État l'instituteur de la société*)" (Rosanvallon 2004: 11). In studies about Islam in France, the republican regime of France and republican political discourse are rightly emphasized. This emphasis is notably justified given the revival of republicanism and its increasing impact on political debates since the 1980s (Chabal 2015; Furet et al. 1988). Put simply, the existence of an "illiberal political culture in France" cannot be denied. Having said this, it is important to take into account that it was never uncontested (Rosanvallon 2004: 12).[4] Diverse institutions and modes of reasoning coexist inside the space of the Republic; focusing on social rationality, this chapter sets out to show how this matters to debates about Islam.[5]

As a first step, I will briefly outline here changes in political thought induced in the course of the nineteenth century through what Jacques Donzelot has dubbed "the invention of the social" (1994). Fundamentally, these changes are triggered by the recognition of the distinctive and irreducible nature of the social, i.e., by the fact that society is a distinct form of association: "The question what turns a grouping of individuals into a society is not the same as Rousseau's famous question 'what is it that makes a people a people.'" Society is made "of actions rather than will," and "these actions, taken in their materiality, make it a heterogeneous and shifting reality whose unity is never assured." As to the study of society, "the kinds of cohesion, connection or conflict" inherent in it cannot be reduced to anything else and they "cannot be analyzed, and certainly not evaluated, according to a preestablished juridical norm" (Karsenti 2006: 3).

The emergence of the social as a distinct entity will transform political thought in important ways. In the context of this study, it is important to mention, in crude terms, that the dissemination and banalization of social rationality both creates new obligations and possibilities for governmental action in society and complicates significantly the usage of a juridical vocabulary in political discourse. For example, the status of political equality, such an important notion in republican thought, changes in relation to the emergence of social thought; henceforth, it cannot be simply dissociated from social equality. Figuring out how the two interrelate empirically and how they should relate to each other has become a central political question, a question which also impacts debates on French Islam and the forms of religiosity specific to it.

In a second step, after these general observations on the interrelations between republican and social thought in France, this chapter examines social rationality in practice, i.e., it studies how questions about Muslim identity and about desirable and possible forms of government are reflected upon.[6] I will briefly discuss the history of knowledge production on French Muslims before the 1980s and then examine the pioneering study on French Islam, *Les banlieues de l'islam*, by one of France's most prominent Islamic studies experts, Gilles Kepel (1987). While written just before an explicit government policy of integrating Islam into France was elaborated and before the revival of Islam among young French became a public concern, this multidimensional study prefigures basic elements of social rationalizations of Islam that continue to be important—i.e., practiced, debated, critiqued—until today.

Among other things, it examines the social meaning of Islam in the context of postmigration and thus answers the question, "Who are Muslims?". It also initiates reflection on why there is a need for government and what are the possible modalities of government. At the same time, Kepel's study aims to inscribe Islam in a differential manner into the national space as a particular religion, raising the question of how this newly established religion in France affects the transformation of French national identity.

A Republic Unlike Any Other?

Why is it that the term "Republic" signifies much more in France than "what is fundamentally, after all, one possible answer to that ancient, universal question about what constitutes the best political regime" (Renaut 2005: 65)? More specifically, is the focus on republican political theory —or, put differently, the identification of France with the republican regime—in studies on Islam in France and French secular politics analytically warranted?

The study *The Politics of the Veil* by Joan Scott (2007) will serve here to briefly illustrate why current conceptualizations of French secular politics often connect it closely with the republican regime. More specifically, I am interested in her analysis of the conditions which have enabled this conflict of 2003 to take on the virulence it has. Scott refers to the civilizational discourse which has, particularly after 2001, been so central to commentary on Islam. However, she is adamant that what is at stake in this conflict is not culture however defined. Rather, in her view, this conflict and the omnipresent references to culture broadly speaking are "the *effect* of a very particular, historically specific political discourse" (Scott 2007: 7; emphasis in the original). While Scott addresses racism and "post-colonial guilt" (2007: 10), her focus is on French republican political theory and its understanding of equality as sameness:

> That equality is achieved, in French political theory, by making one's social, religious, ethnic, and other origins irrelevant in the public sphere; it is as an abstract individual that one becomes a French citizen. Universalism – the oneness, the sameness of all individuals – is taken to be the antithesis of communalism. And yet, paradoxically, it is a universalism that is particularly French.... France insists on assimilation to a singular culture, the embrace of a shared language, history, and political ideology. The ideology is French republicanism.
>
> Scott 2007: 11f.

According to Scott, this kind of political theory has provided the fundamental arguments enabling the legislative to adopt the law prohibiting headscarves as a sign through which the individual's religious affiliation is manifested. The headscarf conflict is from this perspective a process through which the notion of equality as sameness is further extended, via the law of March 15, 2004, in the field of gender relations. Broadly speaking, Scott's study, like others (see, e.g., Sternhell 1986; Noiriel 1988; Silverman 1992; Amselle 2001; Silverstein 2004; Lochak 2010), approaches France as a Republic by concentrating on a number of contradictions which are internal and constitutive of her. We are far removed from the kind of analysis that considers the actually existing republican political regime as merely a not-perfect manifestation of the idea of the Republic.

Having said this, the conceptual identification of France as Republic needs to be further elaborated and to some degree, complicated. Republicanism is important. However, the analysis of secularism should not be reduced to a critical engagement with certain kinds of claim to universalism and equality made in the name of the secular Republic. The opposition between universalist and differentialist thought does not constitute something like a general frame for how people reason in debates about Islam nor how they legitimate or critique state policies. These notions combine in various ways with other modes of reasoning, as I will discuss now, and ultimately form a much more heterogeneous discursive context with a broad range of criteria for defining (il)legitimate forms of diversity in French society.

The Invention of the Social

Here, I will scrutinize in what sense France can be described as a Republic, exploring how the category of the social has durably transformed juridico-political discourses on the Republic since the late nineteenth century. Donzelot writes the story of how the social and social policies emerged. His point of departure are the developments which followed the rapid failure of the Second Republic—in fact the first republican regime to realize the principle of "universal" suffrage for male citizens—after violent confrontations between revolutionaries and the national assembly in June 1848 put an end to the alliance between the bourgeoisie and workers. In the wake of this revolution, it became manifest that the language of rights (*language du droit*) was not able to create consensus. In the contractualist framework, so prominent among defenders of the Republic since the time of the Revolution, the law had been regarded as an element that united people while safeguarding their liberties. The establishment of law and the abolition of privilege were seen as the crucial step toward restoring the natural functioning of society, a society reconciled with itself. After 1848, however, conflicts around the "right to work" revealed the insufficiencies of contractualism and brought to the fore the problem of the state, hitherto ignored: how was its legitimate role of intervention in societal structures to be delineated? How interventionist should the state be? In the following decades, an opposition emerged between two groups, broadly speaking. On the one hand, those who championed a society free from state intervention; here the language of rights was used to "defend individual freedom and the autonomy of society against state encroachment, or some kind of despotism of the masses." On the other hand, those who wanted the state to reorganize society in order to establish their understanding of equality, thereby favoring a society which was subordinate to the state. The seriousness of this conflict lies in the fact that it "invalidates the republican response to the problems inherent in social life, by discrediting the Rousseauan model of a society founded upon a social contract which can be deduced from the general will and which respects the freedom of everyone" (Donzelot 1994: 49f.). Put differently, the Second Republic of 1848 was "caught ... between its new *political responsibility*, based on a requirement of justice, and its *civil responsibility*, based on respect for freedom"; it "found itself already paralysed" (Donzelot 1993: 107; emphasis in the original).

Donzelot argues that this conflict between liberals and social revolutionaries set the stage for a new interest in developing social rationalizations. Two aspects of the ensuing developments are of interest to this particular discussion. First, broadly speaking, invention of the social indexes a process driven by multiple factors which fundamentally implies a recognition of the social as a distinct part of reality with its own specific laws of functioning and specific means of government; in Donzelot's study, the introduction of insurance for workers—collectivizing the risk of accidents—and the establishment of multiple "social rights" are the most important of these. Second, the emergence of the social is closely entwined with a reconfiguration of political thought. One indicator for this is the term (collective) solidarity which, at the turn of the twentieth century, is both a recognition of and response to the relative autonomy of the social and the challenges it poses to order. Solidarity refers to the idea that the social can be regulated by the state. The principle of solidarity both justifies and contains the role of the state in the social sphere; it lends legitimacy to state policies which seek neither the wholesale transformation of society nor the simple preservation of inherited structures: Solidarity "aims to mitigate society, not reorganise it" (Donzelot 1993: 108). In this sense, Donzelot argues, the discourse of solidarity constituted a means for the Third Republic "to resolve the antinomies inherent in its *political foundation* on the equal sovereignty of all" (1994: 121; emphasis in the original).

The rise of social policies thus indicates an important and durable modification in the matrix of republican politics. The preeminence of political equality as a cornerstone of the Republic is fragmented; the social becomes a central field where the Republic and its telos need to be realized and themselves become the objects of various attempts to realize them. The legitimacy of the Republic, in the eyes of the citizen, is measured against the general progress of society to which the state has pledged itself, and which it realizes by institutionalizing various "social rights" for French citizens and thereby putting into practice the principle of solidarity.

Like others, Donzelot sees the Republic as a project which is characterized not least by its constitutive antinomies. In fact, he shows how the invention of the social makes it possible to address the problems generated by the relative indeterminacy of the principle of sovereignty. Importantly, this problematic of contradiction leads him beyond the field of political thought narrowly defined to focus upon other—social—modes of rationalizing politics. The upshot of this is that republican political thought cannot simply be considered the master discourse whose structure and key concepts—such as, for example, abstract universalism—are that of French public debate in general. At the same time, this raises the question how strong and central the connection between secular policies and republicanism is. Is secular France secular-republican or is this connection to some degree contingent? The above discussion points to the latter option. The process of the "invention of the social," which has durably reshaped parameters of political reasoning in France, is inseparable from a critical engagement with key aspects of republican thought, notably contractualism.[7] The discursive space in which republican political thought functions today—in various kinds of combination with other modes of reasoning—is highly heterogeneous and this fact needs to be considered when analyzing debates about Islam. The first element of the present context to be discussed in relation to these debates is what I call here social rationality.

Politics after the Invention of the Social

In paving the way for my analysis of debates about Islam in France below, there is a need to define social rationality as it relates to the governance of Muslims.[8] As I said before,[9] social rationality is defined in terms of its content, i.e., the epistemological structure of the reality it implies, its function, i.e., the kind of tasks and aims of government it renders debatable, and the form of subjectivity it presupposes. The following systematizing description is not a blueprint for how to rationalize. Rather, it indicates how one can rationalize and reasonably expect to be understood. Moreover, as these definitional elements all circle around government, it is incumbent to say that the field of usages is not exhausted by government. Rationalizing Islam in a social perspective is not necessarily about what should and could be done, but regularly about explaining facts with reference to what has not been done. More generally, it may of course be used for making sense of situations from a social perspective—as described below—in argumentative contexts where the primary concern is simply to win the argument or win over the counterpart.

On the epistemological level, as we have seen, this rationality constitutes a new object in relation to which governance is exercised: the social. The social designates here the space of direct or indirect interaction between humans that conditions individual actions and subjectivities. The social makes certain actions and subjectivities more likely than others. This general definition needs to be extended by two concepts. The first is that of social function, which describes an important mode of reasoning particular to this rationality. The truth claims generated by this rationality regularly imply a view of society as a functional ensemble. That is, the phenomena—institutions, practices, processes, groups, and subjectivities—to be rationalized are not conceived of in a substantivist manner, but are constructed in ever-changing ways according to specific relations of interdependence between them, which become intelligible as part of a functional ensemble. As a result, this rationality enables distinct truth claims to be made about religion as one functional element in the analysis of society. In other words, religion becomes reconfigured as a social entity whose constitution and effects can be analyzed to some degree independently of what Muslims say Islam and being Muslim mean. Importantly, these claims also have a bearing, whether intended or not, on the way in which the various political or other imperatives associated with its government at any moment in time, are debated.

Second, the rationality of the social is closely bound up with defining notions of normality, i.e., average forms and values of social practices and subjectivity in a specific milieu. In Durkheim's formulation, normal refers to what is "related to [*tient aux*] the general conditions of collective life in the social type under consideration" (1982: 97). The notion of social normality offers a basis for defining the ever-changing degree of acceptable deviancy, along with the probability that specific events in this milieu will happen (Foucault 2009; Hacking 1990). It is in relation to these notions of normality and the anticipatory calculation of probability that decisions are made about when and against whom "society needs to be defended" (Foucault 2003). Durkheim's notion of normality has attracted heavy criticism. However, in response to Giddens's claim that "No aspect of Durkheim's writings has been more universally rejected than his notion of normality and pathology," Hacking points out that, for all this criticism, "for much of the century before Durkheim, and ever since, we have regularly used 'normal' to close the gap between 'is' and 'ought'" (1990: 163). Considering this statement from the French perspective, one needs to add that claims about normality are very much contested. Nevertheless, these arguments are made and clearly are significant for debates.

As to the political tasks which are rendered thinkable through the rationality of the social, the most important potential this rationality offers lies in calculating and predicting the individual practice of freedom. In a nutshell, it promises to make freedom appear as determination through social factors. Bauman's description of the relation between the rise of sociology and modern government is helpful in identifying the interest in the rationality of the social. According to Bauman, sociology emerged in a context where it was hoped that by "cracking the mystery of the deployment of free will in the production of necessity, regularity, norms and recurrent patterns of thought and action" (2005: 366), foundations could be established for a new kind of government. This government would be based on the assumption that it is neither necessary nor desirable for the state to intervene in all spheres of society, but that it should resort to different kinds of regulatory power, i.e., a kind of power which is not imposed externally, but which determines the conditions of freely willed action, the criteria of rationality, and the forms of subjectivity. In other words, the object addressed by the rationality of the social consists of entities which are in principle apt to be governed by regulatory power applied to domains with partly distinct laws of functioning into which one cannot and does not wish to intervene directly.

These observations indicate the underlying ambivalence of the social. The social is first and foremost simply a space which cannot be collapsed into political society and which has its own entities and laws of functioning (Foucault 2009: 449).[10] However, to say that it is distinct in no way implies that it is unrelated to politics. The social is not simply one element of a tripartite division into political society, society, and private sphere. Rather, its status in relation to politics is fundamentally ambivalent. Donzelot makes this point by writing that the social is "this hybrid species which has been constructed at the intersection of the civil and the political" (1994: 10). From Donzelot's perspective, the social is hybrid in the sense that the emergence of this space implied a new kind of politics aimed at appeasing political conflicts between liberal and socialist groups, notably by collectivizing risks and responsibilities through the institution of social rights. In a sense, it is a politics whose primary aim is depoliticization.[11] If we abandon the historical perspective, the social appears to have an ambivalent status with regard to politics, in the sense that the state needs to regulate it, since it is a condition for politics, but can only do so to a limited degree. The social is relatively autonomous or, rather, prior to political society, since the individuals who constitute the latter are shaped by it in ways the state cannot fully control.

As pointed out above, the boundaries and relations between the social and political are to some degree always open and being redefined; the kind of autonomy which is ascribed to the social and the degree to which it is efficiently regulated vary. Nevertheless—and here my discussion is already addressing the third dimension of this rationality, its subject form—this rationality implies the basic notion that the acts of individuals, their identity and relations to others are not simply the result of the individual's freely willed decisions, but derive to some degree from broader social processes which are prior and external to the individual. Here we have a reformulation of the old question about how to generate human dispositions which enduringly enable citizens to live together and submit to the law. By introducing the concept of the social, political allegiance to the state and the law, as formulated in the idea of a civil contract, is considered to be partly enabled by—or dependent on—social ties. The issue of political order is thus also—or some would say only—a question of social cohesion. Henceforth, the human can be conceived as either a political animal or a social one (Koselleck 1991). There is now a new set of criteria—namely those derived from expertise on the social—for judging what makes policies realistic, efficient, legitimate, and good. Suffice it to say at this point that the relation between the social and the political is heavily contested and these conflicts inform controversies surrounding Islam in France.

To sum up, the rationality of the social presupposes a specific form of subjectivity and defines the aims and modalities of government in relation to it. As pointed out already, the process through which individuals become specific kinds of subject is rationalized as socially conditioned. The notion that society is in a sense prior to the individual implies a specific restriction which is placed upon the free will of individuals. While this restriction can be considered as merely one more restriction placed upon free will, it is important here to underline that this restriction cannot be separated from the emergence of the entity society, which permits new ways to govern citizens and creates new forms of rights and responsibilities incumbent on the state and its citizens. The rationality of the social enables a variety of actors to intervene in multiple ways, directly or not, in society in order to shape processes of subjectivation and determine what counts as a legitimate subject.

La Politique Musulmane

The argument so far has been that French political thought has been reconfigured by the invention of the social. Reconstructing the secular discursive context of contemporary France has led us back to the second half of the nineteenth century. This raises the question how the social rationalization of Islam as it has been practiced since the late 1980s relates to earlier debates on Islam and Muslims in France. Muslims have been present in metropolitan France in numerically significant numbers since the early twentieth century, their numbers rising dramatically during World War I. Ever since, their number has been counted in the hundreds of thousands.[12]

This long history notwithstanding, the 1980s do mark a new beginning. This was not simply because the number of Muslims residing in France increased rapidly in the 1980s nor because of the accelerated speed with which Muslim institutions have been created since the 1980s to make Islam more visible in the public square.[13] Rather, it has to do with the overall limited interest expressed by French academics in French Muslims. It is often remarked that a number of Orientalists, including some of the most prominent French scholars, directed their scholarly interest, even if only to a small degree, to Muslims living in France. This applies to both Louis Massignon (1883–1962) and Robert Montagne (1893–1954).[14] The work of these and other scholars is closely entwined with the institutionalized emergence in France, since the late nineteenth century, of a policy—*la politique musulmane de la France*—that seeks explicitly "to take into account Muslim realities in the internal and external action of France" (Laurens 2004: 57) and, in a more narrow sense, to manage Algerian immigrants since the 1920s (Rosenberg 2006; Sellam 2006).[15] Henry Laurens writes that "Muslim politics (*la politique musulmane*) is first of all the accumulation of knowledges necessary for taking action" (2004: 57). The creation of special university chairs, research centers, and advisory bodies constitute crucial elements of the institutional framework of the knowledge production enabling policymaking. This setup, however, disintegrates with the end of the Fourth Republic (Laurens 2005: 279f.).[16]

Considering the intimate connection established between Islam and immigration, it is noteworthy that the study of immigration into France in general was largely neglected until the 1980s. This disinterest finds a clear-cut confirmation in the number of university theses on immigration. Gérard Noiriel reports that from the 1950s until the mid-1960s, only a dozen theses on this topic were defended, in the 1970s about eighty, whereas in the 1980s more than three hundred theses have been defended (Noiriel 1988: 16). According to Noiriel, in the field of history, this long-time neglect is related to an understanding of France's identity which is mostly conceptualized as self-sufficient in the sense that it is disconnected from immigration and understood as fully formed at the eve of the Revolution. However, the remarkable absence of immigration as a factor shaping France and French identity in the field of history contrasts with the situation in other disciplines.

The first major studies on foreigners in France, in the 1920s and 1930s, were produced by scholars in the fields of demography and geography. In the course of the 1930s, the theme of "assimilation" became an important problematic in immigration studies and remained so until the 1950s (Noiriel 1988: 36f.). Roughly speaking, the late 1950s again mark another break. While the very first study on "Algerians in France" produced by the *Institut National d'Études Démographiques* (National Institute of Demographic Studies, or INED) in 1955 was announced as the first of its kind, the INED abandoned the topic of immigration soon afterwards (Escafré-Dubet & Kesztenbaum 2011).[17] In sociology, unlike demography, a certain disinterest in acknowledging immigration into France, let alone studying it, was visible in the interwar period; Maurice Halbwachs and Marcel Mauss, for example, persisted in viewing France, in contrast to the United States of America, as a country of emigration, whereas it was by then an important site for immigration (Noiriel 1988: 30f.). Since the 1950s, however, Noiriel notes that changes had been taking place in sociology, partly related to the massive buildup of research institutes in France at that time: "the institutional phase of social sciences which started in the late nineteenth century comes to an end" (1988: 44). A new generation of sociologists turned toward studying immigration. Their focus was set on economic aspects; their general outlook had altered in comparison to previous scholarship. Noiriel identifies "an inversion of the dominant discourses in the previous period," where nation-state interests directly guided research. However, the object of study—immigrants—remained fully externalized to French history and society and the presence of immigrant workers was seen as a strictly temporary phenomenon (Noiriel 1988: 47f.).[18]

The *Banlieues* of Islam

Social rationalizations of Islam start to become widespread in the course of the 1980s. One early example of such a rationalization, to be discussed here, is provided by one of the pioneer studies on French Islam, *Les banlieues de l'islam* (1987), by Gilles Kepel.[19] The case of Kepel illustrates how social rationalization functions, what it allows practitioners to do, and more particularly how it contributes to answering the three questions: "Who are Muslims?", "What is normative Frenchness?", and "How should Muslims be governed?". Gilles Kepel is one of the most prominent and prolific scholars working on French Islam and, more generally, on political Islam in the Middle East. His work continues to attract a lot of criticism.[20]

In Kepel's study, the social rationalization of Islam answers three questions, facilitating a definition of the need, the aims, and possibilities for the governance of Muslims. First, the social rationalization of Islam places it within the French space of government. It does so by identifying the conditions which determine the genesis of Muslim religiosities and the different forms it takes; at the same time identifying factors which allow for change. In brief, the rationalization permits a functional analysis of Islam, in the process of which its status as religion is reconfigured. Second, by identifying the social conditions enabling forms of Muslim religiosity and the social functions fulfilled by the practice of Islam, this rationality allows statements to be made about the—relative—normalcy of practices of Islam, normalcy being defined here as the relation between the probability of certain phenomena and the average conditions prevailing in a given social milieu. Importantly, the demonstration that certain practices are normal in the above sense can be used, as we shall see, to partially alter the public perception of Islam. Note that both these questions contribute to answering the question "Who are Muslims?". Put differently, they allow assessments to be made of the difference or similarity of Islam and Muslims in relation to other religious groups and/or immigrated communities. Third and last, social rationalization offers a springboard for assessing needs and realistic possibilities for government in light of prognostics about the future development of Muslim religiosity and, more generally, the future and challenges facing postmigration society. In this respect, as we shall see, social rationalization can offer precious advice to political reflections as it makes statements about the power configuration in which things and subjects emerged and can be transformed (or not). The importance of this kind of reflection on the relative power of social groups, in debates about Islam, cannot be emphasized enough.

Kepel's starting point is the recognition that France faces a new and specific situation. Whereas in the early 1970s, the *hexagone* (mainland France) counted not even a dozen mosques and prayer rooms, there were more than a thousand in 1987 and about 600 registered Islamic associations. As the title of the book *Les banlieues de l'islam* suggests, they are strongly concentrated in the suburbs of French cities, the milieu which is central to this and almost all subsequent studies on Islam. Kepel's central hypothesis is a functional explanation of this process. He argues that this rise of religiosity and the "social affirmation of Islam" (1991: 16) is in no way a natural process but should be seen primarily as "a mode of settlement" for some Muslims (1991: 14). While the study pays great attention to a number of transnational elements and how they shape the "birth of Islam in France," primacy is given to national factors—quite simply in the sense that the "demand for Islam," as Kepel puts it, emerges in the postmigratory context. From this functional perspective, the turn to Islam and the creation of a network of Islamic associations are directly comparable to other forms of "settlement" (*sédentarisation*) and "integration" in earlier times. Kepel refers to the experience of the communist party and the workers' movement in France as providing a mechanism for integration (cf. Courtois & Kepel 1988). In this mobilization of immigrants alongside workers, a process of integration was initiated which ultimately led to the dissolution of socialist and communist identities. As Kepel points out, the settlement process of immigrants that began in the 1970s displays features similar to this "classical scheme," but also other features which "seem to set it apart" (1991: 12). The perspective adopted here by Kepel (and in many later studies on French Islam) is a functional one, in the simple sense that it pertains to an analysis of how a given social function can be fulfilled by different institutions, religion being among them. It is by examining how Islam as religion functions in the process of integration and comparing it to how previous processes of integration were achieved—partly in different ways—that Kepel can develop his central argument about how Muslims settle in France.

Kepel ascribes a second form of function to Islam in the light of a major debate since the 1980s about the growing number of "second generationers" who turn to Islam. Kepel mentions this trend in his study, remarking that it has been noted by several observers but only since 1986, and that he had not recorded it in the early stages of his own research (1991: 386).[21] He nevertheless provides one functional explanation which is supposed to account for the fact that the Jama'at al-Tabligh seemingly played a pivotal role in this process. Quoting a member of the organization, he argues that "the strict Islamic framework for the life offered by this pietist movement offers an attractive response" to an existence "without order or finality," such as that of the "unemployed youth of the *banlieues*" (1991: 376). This line of reasoning was destined for an important future.[22]

The rationalizations of Islam sketched out here define a normalizing perspective on Islam as religion. Outlining a social milieu within which the practice of Islam fulfils a given function signals the normalcy of this practice in relation to a particular set of social features. Kepel himself is aware of this normalizing potential and pleads the case for a positivistic analysis of "the social fact of the birth of Islam" (1991: 10). In his introduction to the book, Kepel criticizes the absence of studies on immigration from Muslim-majority countries, which he explains by certain restrictions on the topic. He thus writes: "According to some, it is illegitimate or inappropriate to study Islam in France. Such a project is in fact suspicious. It would only end up displacing the *tête de turc* from fairs of earlier times to the intellectual field, it would offer a specious description of immigrant populations and the cultural pretext for discriminating against them." But, as Kepel points out with reference to the rise of the extreme-right movement in France, "the circumspection of some becomes aphasia and opens up the space for the noisy phantasms of the others." In his view, "only a thorough analysis of social phenomena without any concessions can break this vicious circle" (1991: 10). At the end of his study, Kepel relates his findings to the issue of terrorism in France, which was, at the time of publication of this study, not yet the major concern it later became, notably after the Paris bombings in 1995. His reflections do not sound unfamiliar today. Criticizing the media for incriminating certain groups or individuals while judicial investigations are still underway, he argues that a certain type of reporting about so-called Islamic terrorism exerts a negative impact on the national situation: "By assigning only one descriptor – Islamic – to the terrorist networks who stand accused, the weekly [*L'Express*] is creating a problem which will burden the future of Islam in France with a heavy legacy" (1991: 379).[23]

However, the main challenge lies elsewhere, he believes, namely in how Muslims become part of the French nation, that is, as what kind of subjects, and how this process of settlement affects French national identity. Indeed, while Kepel repeatedly refrains from forecasting trends in the number of Muslims, notably French Muslims, his analysis presupposes that Islam will be an enduring part of France, a fact with important consequences for French national identity. The book ends with an assertion that "the birth of Islam and its development in the *banlieues* of the Hexagon are already obliging French society to revisit the definition of nationality and to invent a new and dynamic affirmation of itself" (1991: 384). Here, Kepel is using the results of his study for an analysis and prognosis of the evolution of French society and identity. Having identified the "social affirmation" of Islam as one mechanism of "settlement," Kepel reflects on the modalities of this process. Here, he refers directly to the distinction, central to republican discourse, between a citizenship identity which is strictly individual and one which is bound to one's community. In this perspective, he asks whether the settling of immigrants will lead to a process of integration, defined here as individual absorption into French society and implying the "dissolution" or "at least weakening of bonds of communal allegiance," "the feeling of national belonging superseding it," or to a process of "insertion," leaving strong communal structures intact. In the first case, Muslims "can practice their religion in the framework defined by the secular state, they can abandon or change it if they so wish." A "consistorial institution" would in this case "mainly take care of issues of worship (*culte*) and ritual" and not be able to "determine decisively" the politics of community members, even if it might interact with public authorities. As to the second option, "insertion," its subject would be a community—"ethnic, religious or other"—whose "leaders or spokespersons" would try to achieve the "monopoly of representation to public authorities" (1991: 381f.).

While Kepel's reflections are founded on political options essentially open to the state, which allow it, in principle, to condition the future development of Muslim identities whose genesis he has rationalized, he notes that the political option that would seek to transform these identities has been ruled out. As evidence, he hints at the "careful" avoidance of the term "assimilation" by sociologists and social workers. The future, he feels, is probably one where existing social identities among Muslim immigrants are perpetuated because there is a lack of political will to change them. While describing earlier settlement processes as a mere phase of insertion before the "machinery of assimilation" took effect, Kepel sees the broader societal context to be quite different today, as the French no longer assume assimilation to be the objective: "Some find that this term ... reeks of colonialism, Western domination and cultural violence. They prefer insertion, assuming that it is not traumatic" (1991: 384).

I have introduced Kepel's study (1987) as one of the pioneering analyses of French Islam. In one sense, it would be more accurate to say that it is *the* pioneering study.[24] A look at studies published in the mid-1990s indicates a major difference—the great emphasis now placed upon French-born Muslims or the so-called second generation, which only appears at the margins of Kepel's account. Another rapidly emerging theme is the reinterpretation of the Islamic tradition in the French context (e.g., Babès 1997; Césari 1998). In spite of this shift, the basic questions about the needs, aims, and possibilities for government continue to be discussed. No proper survey of this broad field of research can be given here. However, it is possible to indicate four major divisions in order to situate Kepel's early work in the wider scholarly context of the then emerging field of studies on French Islam and briefly outline other ways of using social rationalizations of Islam.

Four analytic decisions have a major impact on how social rationality is put to use. The first one relates to the spatial framework in which Islam is situated. Kepel's study, as I said, locates the factors triggering the demand for Islam in the French context and more particularly the movement of settlement of migrants. At the same time, Kepel examines, often with considerable detail, transnational factors—e.g., the Iranian Revolution—and movements, such as the Jama'at al-Tabligh and the Muslim Brotherhood and how they attempt to satisfy this offer and, more generally, shape developments on the ground.[25] In Kepel's study, the emergent French Islam is basically grasped in doctrinal or ideological categories which, importantly, transcend national space. Other approaches are possible. This is shown, for example, by Farhad Khosrokhavar's study *L'islam des jeunes* (Youth Islam) (1997), which partly deals with the same movements. Unlike in *Les banlieues de l'islam*, the connection between ideology and analytical categories is far less direct; for example, the network of *Musulmans de France* is grouped together with *Jama'at al-Tabligh* under the category "neo-communitarian Islam." Another alternative is offered by François Burgat (2003), who has outlined a distinct approach to the study of political Islam. The point of departure of his analysis is the critique of the excessive ideologization—in the eyes of Western analysts—of opposition movements using an Islamic political vocabulary.[26]

A second decision concerns the notion of identity which is used when studying integration. Jocelyne Césari introduces her study *Être musulman en France: associations, militants et mosquées* (Being Muslim in France: Associations, Activists, Mosques, 1994) by drawing attention to the polysemy of the term identity and emphasizes that her study does not understand the term in a way which would allow, as it were, individuals to be slotted into collectivities defined as having fixed attributes. Note that this is basically what Kepel does in the first part of this study, where fifty-eight Muslim interviewees are classified in four categories (ranging from communitarian "insertion" to individual "integration"). Rather, identity is understood as composite—Islam, migration, postcolonial memory as its main sources—and never fixed. If identity is approached in this processual manner, the schematic opposition between "insertion" and "integration" gives way to a complex scenario with a broad range of relevant factors, outcomes, and policy choices.

A third decision is about locating sites of interpretive authority in French Islam. Introducing the series of interviews conducted in France, Kepel raises the familiar question, "Who speaks for Muslims?" (1991: 26). In France, one influential response to this question is, to put it simply, nobody. In this perspective, processes of individualization are presented as characteristic for the current context of France. Islam is, as sociologist of religion Danièle Hervieu-Léger writes, "just as any other of the great religions in the societies who 'exited religion' (*sorties de la religion*) a tool-box, a stock of symbolic references from which individuals – in the absence of any semantic code which imposes itself upon them and society as a whole – can draw elements" and use them to make dimensions of their life meaningful (1989: 86). The hypothesis of individualization tends to render the entire politico-theological problematic of the integration of Islam into a secular country obsolete (see, e.g., Roy 2002).

Finally, the social rationalization of Islam can be used to invalidate the current debate about Islam and shift attention to ask: What does this debate tell us about French society, culture, and politics? This is the question Bruno Étienne proposes in the beginning of his book *La France et l'islam* (France and Islam, 1989). Referring to Kepel's study and the research undertaken by his own team, Étienne considers that it is now possible to "think the question of Islam in France in terms which are not strictly speaking sociological." Rather, the "problematic" around which he develops his study departs from the notion that the "debate about Islam" "says more about French society than about Islam itself" (1989: 10).

Conclusion

This chapter started with a reflection on the analytical place of the republican order in studies on French Islam. While the important role of republicanism needs to be acknowledged (and historicized), drawing on Jacques Donzelot, I showed how republican thought was reconfigured in the second half of the nineteenth century through the invention of the social. To put it very simply, social rationalization—in an endless number of variations—allows for the particularizing of citizens and it reconfigures the meaning and effects of legal and political equality. From this it follows that the normative and epistemological frameworks of conflicts about Islam—in which participants constantly invoke the Republic and its values—are perhaps more complex than is sometimes assumed. I then sketched out a rough definition of social rationality as it relates to the governance of Muslims and illustrated the usage of this rationality, dwelling on the case of Gilles Kepel's study *Les banlieues de l'islam* (1987).

The above summary of Kepel's study illustrates how Muslims and Islam come to be inscribed into France and the spaces of government. Islam becomes, simultaneously, normalized and particularized, i.e., represented as a specific kind of religion fulfilling certain functions. In the process, the need and possibilities for government are elucidated. The summary of Kepel's argument—as well as of some major counterperspectives—demonstrates that the political effects of social rationalization of Islam are complex. One is reminded of what

Johan Heilbron wrote about the early days of social theory and the difficulty of identifying it with a "specific political outlook" (1995: 271; cf. Habermas 1980). The next chapter, dedicated to a study of reports published by the High Council on Integration (1990–2012), will allow us to analyze in more detail the functioning and effects of social rationality in the framework of integration policies.

3

Rationalizing Integration

Introduction

In October 1999, Jean-Pierre Chevènement, the French Interior Minister, sent an invitation to the leaders of five Muslim federations including the UOIF's president, Lhaj Thami Brèze, six mosques with a particularly broad outreach, and six prominent individuals.¹ He wanted them to take part in a "consultation." Also known as "*al-Istichara*," this process was to garner huge media attention in subsequent years with an agenda devoted to "the situation and problems of Islam" in France, and above all how associations running Muslim prayer spaces could create a unified national structure to act as an official partner for the public authorities in matters relating to Muslim worship.² Chevenement's initiative seemed to mark a significant change in French policies away from outsourcing the management of state relations with mosque associations to foreign governments toward the incorporation of Islam (Laurence 2012). In 2001 a framework was adopted for the future institution—the *Conseil français du culte musulman*—and in 2003 elections were held for the first time.³

Before the consultation got underway, the minister asked the participants to sign a document entitled "Principles and legal foundations governing the relations between the public authorities and the Muslim religion in France." By signing this text, "Muslim groups and associations" declared that they "solemnly confirm their commitment to the fundamental principles of the French Republic and in particular to Articles 10 and 11 relating to the freedom of thought and freedom of religion in the Declaration of the Rights of Man and of the Citizen, as well as to Article 1 of the Constitution establishing the secular nature of the Republic and its respect for all faiths and, finally, to the provisions of the Law of 9 December 1905 on the Separation of the Churches and State."⁴

The document briefly summarizes some basic rules about religious associations, mosques and prayer spaces, officiating ministers (*ministres du culte*) and other religious officials (*cadres religieux*), chaplaincies in hospitals, prisons, and the armed forces, private schools, Muslim dietary and sartorial practices in public institutions, the management of cemeteries, and dispensations on Muslim holidays. The declaration concludes that "full adherence to these principles" expresses the "will to join and integrate into the legal framework which organizes and guarantees the free exercise of religions and the secular nature of institutions in France."

This initiative strikingly illustrates a basic premise of integration policies, namely an assumption that the relationship of Muslim subjects to French constitution and law is not only unclear, but potentially problematic and in need of clarification. Notably, the lack of clarity and problematic potential is, to some degree, disconnected from what Muslims actually do. This is not to say, of course, that the Ministry of the Interior does not care whether Muslims respect the legal norms or not. The main purpose served by this document, as it points out, is to give Muslims the "opportunity" to bind themselves openly to the French order by highlighting their wish to be part of this legal framework and of the community of citizens whose affairs it regulates. In other words, what matters to the authors are intentions—the text was initially called "Declaration of intent regarding the rights and obligations of the Muslim faithful in France"—rather than mere acts.

The text, and the ministry's approach more generally, drew fire from various angles.[5] Critics found it paradoxical to ask the representatives of French Muslims, many of them born as citizens of the Republic,[6] to commit themselves to a legal order which was already theirs anyway. Chevènement denied suspecting all Muslim associations of disloyalty to the Republic as the *Ligue des droits de l'homme* (Human Rights League) and other actors had alleged: "However, it needed to be affirmed in public that there is no conflict in principle between the tradition of Muslim worship and the legal organization of religions in France" (Zeghal 2008).[7] The ministry's attitude was labelled neocolonial by Soheib Bencheikh, who had participated in the consultation for a while as a delegate of the Algerian Grand Mosque of Paris.[8]

In the years that followed, state policies on Islam and Muslims were frequently called (neo)colonial by activists, intellectuals, and the broader public.[9] Some authors note a remarkable similarity, and sometimes continuity, between French Algeria and contemporary France with regard to state attempts to control Islamic institutions and, more generally, Muslims by intervening in religious affairs (Geisser & Zemmouri 2007).[10] If we understand "colonial" as referring to a context of domination, this label does not at first seem far-fetched. Indeed, by insisting that Muslims sign the declaration before the consultation process could begin, the ministry was, one might argue, illustrating the state's ability to define, in seeming violation of citizenship laws, what kind of relationship to France certain groups, here Muslims, can legitimately claim for themselves. This ability underlies the entire enterprise of the integration policies to be discussed in this chapter. Upon second glance, however, some doubts emerge, for the whole procedure surrounding the signature also reveals certain limits to this power. For one thing, the government's dependence on Muslim actors was already evident when the initial title was changed. Moreover, the document had originally mentioned the right to change one's religion, but this was abandoned at the request of the UOIF.[11] Finally, the official document referred essentially to associations as if they were worship associations, which have a specific legal form in France, ignoring the fact that most Muslim associations were actually constituted as nonprofit associations,[12] and sought to confine their activities strictly to worship. The UOIF, however, added a passage on the possibility for Muslims to set up associations for cultural, educational, or other purposes (Ternisien 2000; Zeghal 2008).[13]

While this episode might in itself be seen as a minor conflict between government and Muslim actors, I will argue here that it forms part of a more general feature of state policies on Islam. Indeed, they are characterized by a disparity. On the one hand, many state policies regarding Islamic matters and Muslims are fundamentally inspired by and refer to an imaginary of national sovereignty, an imaginary founded on the notion that the state wields ultimately unconditional power to safeguard France and Frenchness. On the other, the means available to implement these policies are restricted in multiple ways.[14] Patrick Simon points out that "there is a striking mismatch between discourses and policies on immigration and what migration statistics tell us" and adds that "the ability of the state to define and enforce its objectives is even more questionable in the case of integration policy" (2014: 196).[15] This disparity crucially determines the space of possibilities for state policies on Islam[16]—as well as for the work of Muslim associations—and the debates about integrating Islam grapple with it repeatedly.

I will examine this configuration by looking more closely at the HCI. The HCI is not seen here as typical of any specific position or outlook—if only, as I will show below, because the positions it adopted changed significantly over the years, and so did the broader societal and political context in which and upon which it reflected. Rather, it offers a concrete case for studying the debate around three questions: Who are Muslims?, What is an appropriate Muslim subjectivity?, and How can Muslims be governed? Examining how these questions are answered and how the ends and means of integration are defined provides a first opportunity to flesh out and specify the claim that integration politics should be conceived as a changeable, reversible power relation. On a more general level, I will argue here that integration policy has rendered the French legal order "ambivalent" with regard to the citizenship of immigrants and the regulation of Islam as worship. On the one hand, integration policy is indissociably tied to the fact that immigrants have become citizens or are potential future citizens, and that the rights conferred by citizenship (or residence) are not merely theoretical. In other words, the basic mismatch between the sovereign imaginary of integration and the instrumentalities of power available, which are fragmented and in multiple ways limited for both external and internal reasons, remains even if its form changes. On the other hand, integration policy is a sustained effort to change or qualify the rights of immigrated French or future citizens. The term "ambivalence" seeks to capture the instable status of legal rights which results from these efforts. Ambivalence refers to the fact that the law is always indispensable, but insufficient for describing the actual position of the objects of integration policy in the French community of citizens.[17]

The *Haut Conseil à L'intégration*

The HCI was created in 1990 and ceased operation, as its mandate was not renewed, in 2012 when the Socialist Party came back into power. The *Observatoire de la laïcité* (Secularism Observatory), a monitoring body initially set up in 2007, began its work in 2013 and has taken over any issues relating to secularism from the HCI.[18] The broader context for creating the HCI was provided by the debates about immigration and the Nationality Code which set in after 1983. Until that time, immigration had mostly been excluded from politicization by a consensus between parties on the left and right (Feldblum 1999: 38f.; see also Favell 2001; Weil 2004). This consensus broke down during the elections of 1985, largely because the National Front mobilized against immigrants, in particular from North Africa. In 1987, Prime Minister Chirac convened a commission of experts, whose televised deliberations attracted great interest; he charged the commission to reflect upon a reform of the Nationality Code, which ultimately failed.[19] The conflicts which erupted around the headscarf in 1989 provided a new forum for the debate on citizenship and nationality. By then, parties on the left and the right had already partially realigned their positions on immigration and citizenship. Most notably, this reorientation was reflected in the centrality accorded by both sides to voluntarist notions of citizenship and an increasing emphasis on the boundedness and homogeneity of the nation.[20]

The HCI (from 1994 onward) comprised twenty members from a variety of backgrounds, including civil servants, politicians, academics, and representatives of civil society.[21] The HCI was directly accountable to the French prime minister, who would usually call upon the HCI to examine a specific matter. The HCI and its members "which benefit from a real echo in the media" (Beaugé & Hajjat 2014: 31)[22] often dealt with questions relating to Islam. The recommendations made by the HCI in the 1990s and 2000s contributed directly to a number of major policy fields, including policies to combat discrimination from the late 1990s,[23] the gradual introduction from 2003 of integration contracts including a civic education, component[24] and ongoing attempts to extend the ban on wearing headscarves beyond public schools.

Integration

Before I start analyzing the reports issued by the HCI, let me briefly outline how I use the term "integration." Many studies have challenged the very feasibility of defining the term "integration." Gérard Noiriel asserts, for example: "The absence of a rigorous definition of this term has given everybody the chance to use it as he or she sees fit" (2005: 9). It is true that understandings of integration differ (and the work of the HCI will provide further evidence for this, too). Nevertheless, it can be said that—since the 1980s—the term has certainly been understood as referring to the integration of immigrants. As Françoise Gaspard put it, "when a book with the title *La France de l'intégration* (The France of Integration) is published, everybody understands what it is about" (1992: 15), namely immigrants.[25] Second, the main object of integration policy is immigrants from Muslim countries, i.e., a cultural group broadly defined. Finally, the term is understood as basically normative and as describing the present situation as one where immigrants have failed to arrive in French society. It is understood as postulating a need to conjoin something that is illegitimately separate. Logically, this task presupposes the definition of groups and their differences and, importantly, the identification of problematic differences. As I argued earlier, the question of what needs to be done by whom—in the context of integration policy—is an open one, as I shall show in this chapter and throughout this study.[26] The focus on the difference of immigrants can be contested and abandoned, it can be reoriented toward an analysis of societal structures and discrimination, and toward identifying necessary changes in society and politics, as I shall elaborate. At its outset, however, integration policy was strongly associated with assimilationist aims.

The definition outlined above matches the HCI's definition of integration.[27] In its first report, the HCI emphasizes the specificity of the "French model of integration" (HCI 1991). This specificity is defined in a standard way as a polity model founded on a "*logic of equality and not a logic of minorities.*" Consequently, the "institutional recognition of minorities" (as in the United Kingdom) is excluded as a policy option in matters of integration and elsewhere (HCI 1991: 19; emphasis in the original). However, rejecting a definition which conceptualizes integration as the middle way between assimilation and insertion, the report presents integration as a process aiming to "incite the active participation in national society of varied and different elements, while accepting the subsistence of cultural, social and moral specificities and considering true that the whole is enriched by that variety and that complexity" (HCI 1991: 18). Placed in context, the reference to cultural enrichment through diversity sounds more ambivalent. In this same report, the HCI problematizes the cultural identity of immigrants. Noting that "legal integration is accomplished rather easier than elsewhere," it adds that "the levels of unemployment, certain forms of marginalization, identitarian clashes, urban and suburban violence seem to indicate a relative failure in the system of formal identity" (HCI 1991: 53). This first report also clearly propounds the notion that immigrants can be understood as cultural groups and classified according to their cultural distance from or proximity to France. More recent immigration movements are seen to differ from previous ones in that they come more often from regions further away from "Europe" and thus require a "more sustained integration effort" (HCI 1991: 51). The next report placed a starker emphasis on the centrality of culture. Here, the HCI acknowledges that employment, housing, and social protection are key to achieving integration, but then concludes by stating that "it is without doubt ultimately a matter of culture" (HCI 1992: 33). This idea of culture leads us to the nation-state. By settling in France, immigrants have made the choice, "consciously or not," for a "national community defined by a history, traditions, and a system of values." The report continues to define the challenge of integration for society as "welcoming this diversity while preserving its cohesion" (HCI 1992: 33).

From the perspective sketched out above, integration is very much about modifying the culture of immigrants by taking French culture as a yardstick. It would be difficult to make a strong distinction between integration and assimilation.[28] This assumption is applied directly to Muslims. The HCI states clearly that "transplanted Islam cannot be lived the same way (here) as in the countries of origin of those who adhere to it" (HCI 1992: 34).

Culturalism

Is it justified, then, to conclude that the HCI's discourse is culturalist? If culturalism implies constituting a group as a cultural community, ascribing stability to it and turning essentialized culture into "a universal explanation" (Fassin 2011: 785), the application of this term to the HCI is, in important ways, misleading.[29] As we just saw, the HCI reports do refer to immigrants from specific nations or regions as homogeneous groups defined through their culture, i.e., as "bearers of *a* culture, located within a boundaried world, which defines them and differentiates them from others" (Grillo 2003: 158; emphasis in the original) and significantly through their cultural distance to France. The issue of integration is ultimately considered to be a matter of culture and in this sense the discourse of the HCI is culturalist (cf. Bouamama 2010: 47f.).

However, this is not the end of it. The political reflection which is engaged here on integration—and here the HCI's work is far from unique—is not based on self-sufficient culturally stable groups. Very much to the contrary, a major aim of the HCI is to understand and, in a second step, shape processes of change in identity. Such an approach is already formulated, albeit in a rough and a priori manner, in the first report, where an affirmation of cultural identities threatening national cohesion is explained as socially conditioned: "It is natural that those who are hit head-on by precarization and xenophobia seek in the warmth of community or in religious identification a refuge against exclusion" (HCI 1991: 19). Indeed, the HCI's implicit claim is that the government of immigration, and more particularly Muslim immigration, is possible because Muslims can be changed in a favorable political and administrative context.[30] Thus, if culturalism denotes "imprison(ing) concrete historical societies in a substantialist definition of their identity by denying them the right to borrow, to be derivative, that is, to change" (Bayart 2005: 245), then the term is not applicable here.[31]

The desire to understand and shape processes of change in identity is closely connected to the officialization of the category "immigrant." The career of this term illustrates how policies of integration seek to reconfigure basic political categories, and notably the legal understanding of citizenship, in order to enable the state to identify new objects of government. In the context of new concerns about immigration since the 1980s, this term has become indispensable to public discourse, and it is in this context that it has acquired new scientific status in official discourse. The work of the HCI, and more particularly its cooperation with the INED via the HCI's member Michèle Tribalat, was of great importance in this respect (Spiré 1995; HCI 1991; Tribalat 1989).[32] Until 1989, French government discourse only distinguished, on the basis of legal categories, between "foreigner" and "French." In 1989/90, as a veritable integration policy came into play, the statistical and political categories became complicated and the term "immigrant" was officially defined and introduced by demographic experts (Tribalat 1989). "Immigrant" was henceforth to refer to persons born as foreigners outside France and residing indefinitely in France, *with or without* French citizenship (Spiré 1999: 55). The major shift in the categories used for identifying citizens of France, which the official definition of immigrant accomplished, is spelled out explicitly by Tribalat: "While the concept of foreigner refers to a legal status open to modification, that of immigrant is based on an invariable characteristic, namely that of being born abroad" (1989).[33] This "invariable characteristic" was then extended to the descendants of immigrants, designated here as "persons of foreign origin" and defined as "born in France with one parent (or grand-parent) having immigrated to France" (HCI 1991: 16). The introduction of these two categories in the work of state-funded research institutions of course begs the question whether it infringes on the principle of the unity of French citizens, a pillar of republican thought. This problematic—which, as I said, is constitutive of a social rationalization—is fully recognized, as the following statement demonstrates, for the HCI hastens to add:

> [T]he notion "person of foreign origin" has no legal value whatsoever. In fact, nationality is indivisible. Otherwise we would risk falling into the logic adopted by the Vichy regime, for which the number of a person's French ancestors could be a key, whether to the right to work as a civil servant, or to retaining the benefits of naturalization, or to the status of Jews....
>
> HCI 1991: 16[34]

What, then, is the function of the cluster of terms around "immigrant" in the HCI's deliberations? First, by introducing this terminology it became possible to measure the "demographic contribution" to France made both directly by immigrants and indirectly by their offspring (Tribalat 1989), and to try to appease the vigorous criticism of previous census data, which had been berated for not indicating the real number of "foreigners" (Tribalat 1989; Spiré 1999: 51). The strategy for tackling this challenge is set out in the HCI's first annual report (1991), where reference is made to its remit, defined by the prime minister, "to banish the phantoms surrounding the presence of foreigners in France, by replacing the fragmentary, dispersed, and sometimes incoherent, or simply incomplete information we have today with the most accurate knowledge possible about data on immigration flows and the evolving presence and legal status of foreigners on French territory" (HCI 1991: 7).[35] Second, and this is the central point for this study, this cluster of terms realigns social and scientific classifications to the new needs of government; it allows the identification of diverse groups among "immigrants," subsequently scrutinized—in different ways—by the HCI, by demographers, or by other actors. I want to emphasize here that this category "immigrant" can serve different ends. A brief look at two major demographic studies on immigration to France may illustrate this. In 1995, Michèle Tribalat presented the results of a study on "immigrants and their children" led by the INED. The central aim of this study was to measure "assimilation," defined as the "reduction of specificities through the mixing of populations and the convergence of behaviors." Put simply, the researchers concluded that "assimilation is happening" (Tribalat 1995: 216). In 2015, INED presented the results of another major study, *Trajectoires et origines* (Trajectories and Origins). This research project explicitly distances itself from a "normative approach to integration according to which practices and behaviors of immigrants and their children should converge on a reference embodied by the majority population." Aiming to reformulate "problematics in relation to the question of discrimination," the researchers examine differential abilities to access social resources (language, work, education, …) and the effects of discrimination on the construction of identities (Beauchemin et al. 2015a: 22). The need for integration policy as well as its aims are thereby redefined. One important result of this second research project is that "it is always the same groups who are disadvantaged," namely descendants from immigrants from the Maghreb, Turkey, and sub-Saharan Africa (Beauchemin et al. 2015b: 607).

Who are Muslims?

How does the HCI then identify Muslims? In line with what I outlined above, the HCI applies a set of terms and distinctions to describe and analyze Islam and Muslims. There is a worry that Islamic normativity collides with gender equality (see, for example, HCI 1995: 32). However, the problems associated with Islamic normativity are limited to a small number of questions and the HCI emphasizes that Muslims have accepted the "social and political order of France" (HCI 1992:

43). The HCI also identifies some manifestations of Islam as *intégriste* ("fundamentalist") and voices concern over "certain advances" of fundamentalism in France (HCI 1995: 45; see also HCI 1997: 23, 33). It points out at the same time that "the most radical form" of Islam remains "nevertheless marginal" (HCI 1995: 45). Only in very few cases is a clearly identified group labelled with one of the categories with tendential illegitimacy (*intégriste*, Islamist), the only numerically significant group being *Jama'at al-Tabligh*. The UOIF is described as defending a "conservative vision" of Islam (HCI 2000: 33). However, the HCI's description of *intégriste* associations is easily applicable to the UOIF. In fact, the HCI considers that the "often educational" activities of these groups are part of a broader strategy to "implant" themselves in the *banlieue* and "to make new recruits among the marginalized, who may drift off into terrorism" (HCI 1995: 45).[36] Furthermore, the HCI discusses the national and/or ethnic heterogeneity of Muslims, which it concludes is limited in the sense that "the by and large dominant group of persons originating from the Maghreb follow a common Islamic tradition" (HCI 1992: 41). Finally, the HCI proposes a number of distinctions between Islam as culture and Islam as religion or faith (a question which, given the absence of any official data on the number of Muslims, is closely entwined with repeated attempts to determine adequate criteria for estimating the size of the Muslim population).[37]

These distinctions between culture and religion are not unimportant; for example, the fact that "youth," i.e., the immigrants' descendants, practice a superficial Islam (*islam peu profond*) can be combined with the claim that they have "massively adopted French cultural values" (HCI 1995: 34).[38] However, the effects of the distinction between culture and religion are more complex than the language quoted above might suggest. A "superficial" practice of Islam might nevertheless require state regulation. Significantly, the report adds that this cultural practice of Islam "has implications for the public life of the persons concerned (arrangement of spaces and times of work, food in collective institutions such as schools, prisons, army)" (HCI 1995: 34), and this is clearly one of the central concerns of the HCI. The "reality of Islam in France" which interests the HCI relates to "the concrete conditions in which Muslims live their faith, practice their worship, or manifest their identity" (HCI 2000: 35). Extending its focus to public behavior, the HCI finds it difficult to distinguish between what is specific to Muslims and what to those who "belong to a socio-cultural milieu." Examples of the behaviors in question include gender-typed patterns of differential treatment of teachers by parents or students, and social pressures on students not observing Ramadan. The HCI considers that these "nevertheless" can be related "more or less directly to an adherence to the Muslim religion" (HCI 2000: 52).

Briefly, the HCI identifies what is of interest to its work with reference to the external practice of Muslims. However, this external practice is not conceived simply as worship, whose exercise the law of 1905 guarantees and regulates, but rather as the practice of a cultural Muslim identity which, in the case of the immigrants' children, regularly gives rise to claiming of civil rights. The HCI's take on the immigration of Muslims relies fundamentally upon the notion that religion, or more particularly Islam, is a central element in the identity of immigrants and their offspring. It is this conceptualization of Islam as one determinant in the subjectivation of immigrants which legitimates, in part, the HCI's—and more generally the state's—interest in Islam:

> It seems crucial that neither the public authorities nor French society as a whole should confine themselves to conceiving Islam only in its spiritual dimension. It is not for the Republic to integrate religion. However, the politics of integration apply to Muslims as to the other members of the population whose religious practices, meaning as much their culture of origin as the dogma itself, contribute to forging identity.
>
> HCI 2000: 22

What is an Appropriate Muslim Subjectivity?

The HCI's thoughts on the appropriate way of being Muslim in France are characterized by a divergence of aims. This divergence of aims reflects the ambivalent structure of integration policy. While fundamentally relying upon an imaginary of sovereignty, integration policy is shaped by multiple constraining factors which to some degree deflect the government's attention from the original aims. On the one hand, the HCI makes clear that it favors and considers necessary a reform of Islam in France (even if the individual reports vary in assigning its contours). On the other hand, the HCI lays great emphasis on harmonious relations between Islam and the Republic. Which is to say that it aims to prevent Muslims from making contentious claims—for example, about freedom of religion—and from politicizing this issue. Consequently, as the HCI realizes that this politicization is influenced to some degree by real problems of unequal treatment, many of the concrete measures proposed by the HCI are not about a reform of Islam, but quite simply about enabling existing Muslim institutions to put their religion into practice.

As to the first aim, the reform of Islam, the HCI expresses an unambiguous general unhappiness with the dominant understanding and practice of Islam in France. While the HCI considers it "unrealistic, dangerous, and unacceptable" to count on the "progressive erasure or even disappearance of Islam in France" in the context of integration policies, there can be no doubt that it feels the kind of Islam practiced in France should change as part of the integration process (HCI 1992: 47f.; for a similar statement see also HCI 1995: 44). A major task identified in 1992 was to "trigger [the creation of] a high-level cultural institution" (HCI 1992: 50). This institution "would exercise the critical theological function necessary to develop a representation of faith which takes into account the needs of persons confronted with cultural displacements" (HCI 1992: 50). Note also that the HCI vigorously supports the project of "a 'critique of Islamist reason'" (HCI 1995: 46) and deplores the fact that "those who defend a secularized and reform-oriented Islam are deprived of a space to speak" (45). The HCI also addresses more specific wishes for changes in Islamic practice. This is most explicit with regard to conflicts about the headscarf. In the report "Islam in the Republic" (HCI 2000), the HCI clearly states its wish to assimilate Muslim women. It recommends that pupils should be alerted to the fact that "the sexual inequality which the wearing of headscarves implicitly denotes is at odds with the social norm in our country" (HCI 2000: 77). This indicates that the HCI's opposition to forms of Islam which postulate "a clash between the Western world and the Arabo-Islamic world" and its quest to prevent "cultural marginality" (HCI 1995: 46) cannot be simply dissociated from assimilationist objectives.

Finally, the HCI not only aims at reforming Islam, but also seeks to shift the categorical boundaries of Islam from religion to culture. In fact, the HCI notices and is worried by the fact that Islam is such a central element in the identity of French Muslims. This is most clearly spelled out in its conclusion of the report "Islam in the Republic," where the HCI argues the importance of "knowledge of the culture of origin," because "not knowing it quite often turns Islam into the only reference for identity" (HCI 2000: 79). A proper teaching of "Muslim culture" is thus deemed necessary: "Such efforts allow everybody to discover or appropriate for themselves Muslim culture in its historical and cultural dimensions and not only a solely religious one" (HCI 2000: 79).

As to the second overarching objective, the government of Muslim subjectivation patently aims for a subject whose interaction with state authorities and the public is free from disruptive factors. Claims-making by Muslims who do not shy away from conflict and provoke reactions by state authorities is a recurrent theme in all the reports. The notion that claims made by Muslims distinguish the present period from the previous one is central to the HCI's reasoning. Surveying the function and development of associations, the HCI observes that earlier associations stand out for their "very great discretion and modest claims about enhancing the conditions of worship" (HCI 2000: 24). It is worth noting that the HCI ascribes a political dimension to Muslim claims with a direct bearing on the freedom of religion. Thus the HCI describes the conflicts around school students wearing headscarves as a "trial of strength" between institution and pupils (HCI 2000: 51).

How Can Muslims be Governed?

As to specific measures, given that no project for an Islamic theological institute in France acquired concrete form (HCI 2000: 71)—a situation which broadly speaking continues today in spite of repeated debates about the training of imams (Zwilling 2014; Mission de réflexion sur la formation des imams et des cadres religieux musulmans 2017)—the HCI does not formulate many proposals for reforming Islam. By contrast, the measures it puts forward for dealing with Muslim practices and social behaviors are much more elaborate and provide insights into how the HCI envisions the governance of Muslims and how it legitimates its positions with regard to French law, the notion of *laïcité*, and the institution of the Republic.

In its reports during the period 1991–2002, the HCI persistently approached Islam and Muslims from a social perspective. More precisely, the HCI conceptualized Islam as part of a relatively specific social milieu, characterized as a disadvantaged postmigration context subject to forms of xenophobia or discrimination. This is visible from the first report (HCI 1991: 19) up until the report "Islam in the Republic," which frames the issue of Islam in a much more systematic manner as one where the issues of religion, society, and citizenship are entwined and cannot be dealt with in isolation (HCI 2000: 8, 56, 78). Constantly blurring the distinction between private and public, the HCI's ultimate aim is to help French Muslims identifying with the Republic and to engage in a process of rethinking certain aspects of their religious practice. The HCI identifies two general fields of action for state agencies. The most far-reaching policy field concerns the social exclusion of immigrants and their descendants, which tends to have a detrimental effect on their identification with France. One of its recommendations was to set up the equality body called the *Haute Autorité de lutte contre les discriminations et pour l'égalité* (Equal Opportunities and Anti-

Discrimination Commission) (2004). Second, the HCI takes a big interest in the material conditions in which Muslim worship is exercised. Like social conditions, these are deemed to have an important influence on shaping Muslim subjectivity, and in many ways these conditions are deficient. HCI recommendations address the construction of mosques, i.e., how planning permission is awarded (or not) by public authorities and how these can indirectly contribute to the financing, and responses to a variety of Muslim practices in public spaces, notably school, around diet and nutrition, death and burial, the festivities and ritual slaughter associated with Eid, and wearing the headscarf.

Let me briefly outline the HCI's reasoning in this field by taking as an example the construction and financing of mosques (HCI 2000).[39] The HCI describes the contemporary situation as characterized by too few mosques, many in poor condition, and argues that this situation presents "several problems" with regard to "the good integration of Islam" and "religious freedom" (HCI 2000: 36). The HCI argues its position not only on the basis of equality, i.e., "the principled problem which is that access to worship varies depending on the religion" (HCI 2000: 37). It also highlights the consequences of the current situation for Muslims and their relationship to the Republic: "... this situation creates, notably among the youth, a **feeling of injustice** which turns against public authorities.... This feeling of frustration leads sometimes to symbolic claims which go beyond the purely material question" (HCI 2000: 37; emphasis in the original). Five years earlier, the HCI had already argued that local authorities need to take an interest in the construction of places for Muslim worship: "[I]t is better to organize places of worship by taking into account the imperative of social cohesion and public peace than to let spontaneous places of worship be set up in an improvised manner that disrupts the neighborhood" (HCI 1995: 27).

Ever since its first report, as pointed out above, the HCI had been emphasizing the specificity of the "French model of integration" (HCI 1991). While the HCI referred repeatedly to a particular French polity model, the distinctiveness and clarity of this model had been partly lost, and this well before the HCI's deliberations reached the stage of practical problems and concrete recommendations. In fact, once the HCI set out to think through the central guiding principles of state policies in relation to each other, the policy matrix turned out highly complex. The understanding of *laïcité* described here certainly addressed the liberties of citizens and the resulting spaces where the state should not intervene. However, this principle was explicitly not seen as merely delimiting a space of nonintervention for public authorities. On the contrary, the recognition of freedom of conscience and state neutrality was coupled with the principles of equality and public order, and both of these were held to legitimate direct state intervention in religious matters, since the state had an obligation to counter inequality and a duty to maintain public order (HCI 2000: 42–7, 51, 58f.).[40] Also, the HCI made it clear that the state had a general obligation to examine even matters pertaining to the private lives of citizens: "If, as has already been pointed out, the public authorities are incompetent to deal with religious affairs when they refer to freedom of conscience and free exercise of worship, they cannot be uninterested in the consequences, in public space, of belonging to Islam" (HCI 2000: 56; cf. HCI 1995: 42). The term "identity," of course, designates one such connection between private and public life. Evidently, this interpretation of the principle of laïcité does not result in a regime of separation between the state and religions and between public and private spheres, even if this claim is also at times put forward by the HCI (e.g., HCI 1992: 36; HCI 2000: 53).

As I will show in the next section, the privileging of a social rationalization by the HCI during this period was directly contested, and it was abandoned after 2002 when almost all the members of the HCI were replaced. The relative contingency of its policies resulted partly from the simple fact that the legal rules applied in any given case were subject to diverging interpretations. Once the HCI set out to survey the laws applicable to the construction and financing of worship spaces, it was confronted with a complex framework giving rise to very different practices. Local authorities regularly refused building permits. The authorities were seen as "unwilling" partly because of "electoral considerations" (HCI 2000: 61f.). The state institutions, particularly prefects, were urged to facilitate grants of planning permission for mosques by local authorities. The HCI also noted that local authorities were increasingly keen to promote integration and "seek the means to financially aid construction or the transformation of buildings into prayer rooms" (HCI 2000: 38), e.g., through agreements to lease and develop a municipal property, or by issuing local authority guarantees for loans to a mosque association.[41] The HCI also noted, in the light of efforts to aid associations financially, that there had been a "rise of illegal practices" on the part of local authorities, which were "neither isolated nor exceptional" (HCI 2000: 39, fn. 30).

The HCI (2002–8)

Let me recapitulate: the social rationalization of Islam promises to make apparent and to some degree governable the social conditions framing the acts of individuals and the formation of subjects. The possibility of government presupposes, of course, the existence of spaces of freedom; it is these spaces, where individuals lead their contingent lives, which are made apparent through this rationalization as spaces of relative determination. From this perspective, the benefit of this rationalization emerges clearly. The potential drawback is the following: As government is performed indirectly, it always implies, from the point of view of coordination, some kind of recognition, acceptance, and indeed involvement with the subjects and behaviors at which government is aimed. Hence the aim of changing the kind of Islam which is preached and practiced implies at least some kind of support for the establishment of educational institutions and the construction of mosques. The aim of having Muslim identities that are compatible with a solid identification with France demands that the infrastructure for Muslim worship be considerably expanded. And so on.

Now, there are two potential objections to such acts of recognition and involvement by the state in the process of social government. With regard to Islam, this form of government can be seen—and indeed is seen—as contravening the law and, more particularly, the principle of secularism. But more importantly, and this is the problem to which I allude here, such acts of government necessarily imply a claim that state power is limited and that cooperation, in some way, with other actors (who of course cannot be fully controlled) is necessary. An example for this problematic is provided by Muslim associations. The public status of "immigrant associations" is significant since the early 1980s; in the 1990s–2000s, a new kind of associative actor, centered on the "moral, social and local," largely replaces the more civic-oriented actors from the previous decade (Leveau & Wihtol de Wenden 2001: 12f.).[42] In this context, the HCI contemplates at length what kind of role Muslim or cultural associations (might) play in the process of integration. The HCI rejects cooperation with "Islamists" and warns public authorities to "not be satisfied with the illusory tranquility which a strong Islamist control over difficult neighborhoods provides" (HCI 1995: 45). Having said this, a number of factors suggest that associations could play a positive role, even if the question of funding by public authorities for religious and cultural associations is problematic. According to one report, "(t)he role of associations in the process of integration seems nevertheless interesting to the HCI" (HCI 1995: 41). This interest the HCI takes in the work of associations results precisely from its reflection on the perceived limits of state power vis-à-vis the "structures of French society" (HCI 1995: 42).

A similar argument is proposed with regard to the confrontation around Muslim headscarves in public schools. The HCI, against the background of a legal context that rules out a general exclusion of the hijab (in 2000), defends dialogue with students and parents and opposes the exclusionary approach because it incurs a risk of a breakdown in communication: "But above all, the testimonies of several actors in the field indicate that an expulsion pure and simple from the school community of young girls who persist in wearing the headscarf would serve to confine them even more within their particularism, whatever the motives – eminently diverse among teenagers – for donning it may be" (HCI 2000: 6f.). This line of thinking almost sacrifices any autonomous capacity for action and has often been criticized, as the report itself points out.[43]

The counterposition was prominently defined in 2003 by the abovementioned report of the Stasi Commission,[44] which conducted an inquiry that year into the "application of the principle of laïcité" and, above all, the issue of the Muslim headscarf in state schools (Commission Stasi 2003). The Commission's members recommended the adoption of a law prohibiting ostensible religious signs in state schools.[45] In its report, this recommendation was based on a simple argument:

> The Commission, after listening to positions on all sides, considers that the question today is no longer about freedom of conscience, but about public order. The context has changed within a couple of years. The tensions and conflicts in schools around religious questions have become too frequent. The normal course of teaching can no longer be guaranteed. Pressure is exerted upon young girls of minority age, forcing them to wear a religious sign. The family and social milieu sometimes impose choices on them which are not their own. The Republic cannot remain deaf to the cry of distress from these young girls.

The Commission claims here that the phenomenon at issue simply does not qualify for government, as the relative liberty of the individuals to be governed is simply not given. The Commission asserts that the conditions necessary for a relatively unconstrained development of young Muslim women no longer prevail.[46] The conditions which might normally be expected in the private sphere, where individuals are free to choose their way of living in a context of limited social determination, have been disrupted by the emergence of a power context imposing direct constraints—i.e., the girls' families and the broader milieu—and this is why the state should step in.[47] The recommended law, adopted on March 15, 2004, unambiguously delimits the space of freedom through a sovereign decision and allows an assertion to be made, in the case of headscarves, about what laïcité stands for.[48] Let me note in passing that, at the same time, the opposite argument was made in order to justify the creation of the CFCM and the inclusion of the UOIF in it.[49] Defending the CFCM against widespread criticism, Interior Minister Sarkozy drew attention to the need to accept things that have become normal in order to transform these phenomena as much as possible by initiating—indirectly—mid-term or long-term processes of change: "Demonization only produces radicalization. One more time: France must accept itself as it is: diverse. One should not fear this diversity, but seek to create opportunity from it" (2004: 91).[50]

Put briefly, social government works with and through the social conditions for acts and subjectivities; it seeks to transform the latter via the former. In this sense, it is the exact antithesis to sovereign, i.e., undivided and unconditioned, power. It will always tend to disappoint those who wish for a centralized policy asserting fixed standards of right and wrong. It will always disappoint those who think of politics as a constituent power, i.e., as the power which constitutes the social, and not vice versa. Such a view has been expressed by Dominique Schnapper, an observer of "integration" for several decades, who has warned that social policies and the mere integration of individuals into systems of objective interdependence do not suffice to guarantee the cohesion of society (2003: 25).

This view of politics becomes one of the central themes guiding the reorientation of the HCI's work after 2002 under the chair of Blandine Kriegel (2002–8). How does the HCI argue its departure from the previous policies? The HCI criticizes the emphasis placed on the social dimension of integration policy: "The result of this was that it only talked about fighting racism and, on a more banal level, about fighting discrimination" (HCI 2006: 17). Rejecting this "purely moralizing" and "depoliticizing" approach, the HCI seeks to reintroduce the "strictly political dimension of the debate (who is to integrate, into what and how)" (HCI 2006: 17). Writing at the time of the uprising in the *banlieues* (October–November 2005), which triggered broad debate about the failure of integration policies, the HCI claims that this "depoliticization" of integration policy has been a demonstrable failure, as attested in particular by "all forms of withdrawal and identitarian tensions" (HCI 2006: 17).[51] The new policy is committed in central aspects to classical notions of republicanism and emphasizes the notion of contract and individual. Integration policy is defined as "the definition and realization of a shared civic project common to all inhabitants of a country" and its citizens, and it is this project which has as its starting point the conclusion of an integration contract between the Republic and the immigrant (HCI 2004: 83).

Now, as already intimated, the HCI does not perform a full-blown reorientation in its reasoning. The HCI seeks at this point to distinguish its approach from previous policies by emphasizing that the new policies will go beyond a purely negative approach aimed at controlling and limiting immigration on the one hand and fighting discrimination on the other. Nevertheless, the HCI demonstrates an awareness that certain social conditions need to be met in order to ensure that young French people of immigrant origin can identify as French. In presenting a series of equal opportunity initiatives, exemplifying the "positive" approach to integration, it typically notes that one of the consequences of unemployment is that "the young, often with degrees, feel excluded from our collective project" (HCI 2006: 42). The same reliance on a basic notion of subjectivation processes guided the HCI in its support, beginning in 2003, for a better representation of diversity on "pale TV screens" (HCI 2006: 78).[52]

The HCI (2008–12)

In its final period of activity, the HCI focused far more on issues around *laïcité*, adopting an unambiguously restrictive position on public expressions of religion (Hennette-Vauchez & Valentin 2014).[53] In this sense, it directly contributed to the "regime of *new Laïcité* that has been consolidating in France since the mid-2000s" and that "may well be read as a threat to human rights" (Hennette-Vauchez 2017a: 312). This is a regime which extends the obligation of neutrality for the state and civil servants to citizens; *laïcité* can thus become the antonym of religious freedom. For example, the HCI suggested extending the ban on "conspicuous religious signs" to universities—the suggestion failed to garner sufficient support—and advocated the prohibition of religious signs, i.e., the headscarf, for mothers accompanying schoolchildren on excursions. In 2012, this contested practice by some schools was formally recommended by the Education Ministry but then rejected by the *Conseil d'État* (December 23, 2013) clarifying that parents accompanying schoolchildren cannot be subjected to the principle of neutrality.[54] The HCI adopted a similar—illiberal—position in the ongoing controversies about limiting religious freedom at the workplace (HCI 2011). While the precise effects of legal changes on religious freedom in this field are difficult to assess, the developments which have taken place are very significant. In 2013, a court ruled that the duty of neutrality—imposed on all civil servants—can be applied to any enterprise and its personnel if charged with a public task.[55] Furthermore, it is now possible, under certain conditions, for private companies to impose a duty of neutrality on their employees.[56] The HCI also favored restrictions on the manifestation of religions by users of public services; in this regard, however, the changes enacted have been very limited (HCI 2007).[57]

From the standpoint of various observers, including to some degree the HCI, this development toward restriction or prohibition—in other words, the reshaping of *laïcité*—is likely to threaten basic conditions for the success of integration policies. This awareness can be detected in reports by the HCI. When, in 2010, the HCI decided to entrust a working group, formed by some of its own members and staff from the Education Ministry with the task of defining a pedagogy for *laïcité*, the need for this working group was argued with reference to the fact that in "numerous situations in school" the principle of *laïcité* had been rejected as "contradictory to the freedom of expression, notably religious" (HCI 2012: 163). The aim was to enable teachers to develop a discourse which not only reminds pupils of the principle of *laïcité* and respect for it,[58] but which can justify the principle and respond to those who criticize its application on grounds of "cultural oppression and the negation of religious freedom" (HCI 2012: 163f.).

The conflict identified here by the HCI, between exclusionist policies toward Islam and Muslims on the one hand and the basic aim to encourage French Muslims to accept and identify with central principles of the Republican order on the other, is increasingly recognized. In response to this, the think tank *Institut Montaigne*, an important contributor to the debate about integration, criticized plans for extending the requirement of neutrality from public servants to users of these services, stating: "These developments do not seem likely to ensure the serenity of debates about *laïcité*" (Institut Montaigne 2013: 5). Drawing upon a report it had commissioned in 2010,[59] *Institut Montaigne* quoted Gilles Kepel, who had argued at the end of the study that it was "without doubt the weak appeal of the secular promise (*la promesse laïque*)," particularly among the Muslim interviewees, which "most" invites reflection (Kepel 2012: 24; Institut Montaigne 2013: 4). In line with this, *Institut Montaigne* draws attention to "the crisis of legitimacy of *laïcité*" and the alienation which state policies produce among French Muslims in particular: "The malaise seems to be strongest in neighborhoods under the wing of urban policies, where Islam has a strong presence. There, *laïcité* is perceived as an indirect criticism of the poor assimilation of populations with immigrant origins" (Institut Montaigne 2013: 1, 4). Rejecting the claim that new laws are needed, it emphasizes the need for pragmatism, local initiatives, and consultation with all stakeholders.

The reflections captured by *Institut Montaigne* about strongly divergent views—among French—of the secular order are part of a broader debate, also taking place in the political field, about the aims and means of integration policy. After the accession to power of the Socialist Party in 2012, this question was examined in two reports—the second one consisting of five distinct studies—commissioned by the government in an attempt to reinvigorate and rethink integration.[60] While these reports, for lack of political support,[61] triggered public debate but no significant policy change,[62] they reveal how controversial the definition of "integration" has become. They show, as I said previously, that the focus on the difference of immigrants can be contested and abandoned, that it can shift toward an analysis of societal structures and the identification of necessary changes in society and politics. Moreover, these debates indicate that, largely in contrast to the early stages of integration policy, when researchers of a "Republican nationalist" bent played an important role in legitimating state policies (Lorcerie 1994), the contributions made by academic experts in this debate today cover a wide range of diverse positions.

Both reports, to different degrees, propose to reframe integration policy. Thierry Tuot, State Councilor and author of the first report, defines integration in a first step as the "social phenomenon through which the major role of real or supposed origin as a factor in the social difficulties encountered by a person" is "dispelled" (Tuot 2013: 11). However, Tuot primarily problematizes the term "integration," one reason being the difficulty of defining the entity into which subjects should be integrated. "How to measure" integration into a society which is "dispersed, tribalized, internationalized, individualist, fragmented" and where "multiple belongings ... unconcerned about coherence" have replaced centuries-old communities and agents of socialization (Tuot 2013: 13)? Instead of integration, he prefers "inclusion" and proposes empowerment (*mise en capacité*) and, broadly speaking, social measures as the central aim and tool of policy. Put simply, Thierry Tuot reorients the focus of integration policy—or rather, inclusion—away from immigrants as distinct group(s) toward social structures.

This shift of perspective in integration policy is in a sense limited by Tuot's approach to cultural identities and the accompanying issues. Questions of cultural difference are discussed, but at a general level they are minimized by a strict refusal to recognize cultural groups: the state has "no right nor obligation" to identify cultural groups (Tuot 2013: 66). In some cases, cultural change is downplayed in its significance: "the 'Muslim question' [is] a pure invention of those who ask it," claims Tuot, elsewhere referring explicitly to debates about the burqa (Tuot 2013: 62, 64). Tuot recognizes that cultural change poses challenges to many French but is resolutely optimistic: "an evolution of [the nation's] mental landscape" (Tuot 2013: 65) is in his view possible.[63] In contrast to this, the results of the five working groups which were established in the follow-up to Tuot's report pay much more attention to questions of cultural recognition and to recognition in a broader sense. These working groups, each presided over by two experts, drew their members mostly from practitioners in the concerned societal fields.[64] Not only are the proposals more numerous and specific, they also address more directly the kind of general changes which will be needed in societal structures and identities if the aim is to create an inclusive society. One suggestion is to rethink the history of France—and related memory acts—to take account of the crucial role played in it by immigration.[65] "Mutual learning" is necessary in order to "reconcile national and multiple identities," but this process is possible and enriching (Lamarre & Maffessoli 2013: 9ff.).[66] Given the scope of the desired transformation, changes must be made to training for various professions, e.g., mediation or teaching. "History of immigration, slavery and slave trade, history of colonialization," "interculturality," and "religion and *laïcité*" are the three threads which need to be introduced (Lamarre & Maffessoli 2013: 51f.). The proposal, in order to create "a sufficiently shared feeling of belonging", is to "tackle the logics, processes, and practices which hinder this positive identification with a political community." In this respect, the report calls attention to how "social boundaries" are created by, for example, ethnicization, alterization, or racialization. Discussing how to address these issues, the requirement for change is described here as moving from the current policy approach, which reads "public problems" like racialization as problems specific to certain sections of the population (e.g., immigrants), into an approach which develops truly "public policies" (Dhume & Hamdani 2013: 7, 10f.). Through these and other recommendations, these reports taken together completely overturn the hitherto dominant perspective on how to tackle a successful integration policy.

Conclusion

I have argued that integration discourse—as expressed by the HCI—emerges out of the relation between the imaginary of a sovereign nation and the de facto limited capacity of the state to act in a unified and unconditioned manner with regard to immigration. It emerged originally as an attempt to reconfigure this context by creating and continuously (re)defining a new policy field where entry to the nation is to be controlled and managed by the state.

This examination has shown how Islam and Muslims have been socially embedded, particularized, and located in the complex hierarchies of social power. Doing this involved—in a complex process full of abiding conceptual unclarities and ambiguities—reframing Islam primarily as an identity which functions in a postmigratory milieu. Subsequent chapters will provide evidence of how influential this social positioning of Islam has become and how it plays out. This analysis has also highlighted in various ways the relative instability and the (changing) limits of state power. As I said, integration repeatedly invokes or refers back to the sovereign power of the nation to decide over its future. This imaginary contrasts significantly with how the debate on integration politics is conducted in these reports. The notion of integration is refracted by the heterogeneity of rationalities of power, which regularly leads to controversial debates about the aims, means, and objects of integration. Important limitations characterize the space of possibilities inside which integration is rationalized. These limitations are either inherent to governmental rationalities, as is the case with social rationality, where transformative action presupposes recognition of and working with what exists, e.g., Muslim associations or federations; or else these limitations emerge when, partly in critical response to the social approach, the state attempts to redefine and diminish the spaces of freedom, as the French Republic did with regard to Islamic practices after 2003. The perceived disidentification of Muslims with the core principle of *laïcité*—understood as a response to this process—acts as a different kind of relative constraint on state action.

What about *laïcité*? References to *laïcité* are crucially important in the proposals made by the HCI. Of course, as has often been noted, these references are based on different understandings of how to define and differentiate the secular and religious. Looking at these differences from the perspective adopted here, the distinction frequently drawn between a more and a less "liberal" approach—a juridico-political distinction—is not sufficient. Indeed, when taking into account how social modes of reasoning are used for government, it becomes apparent that invocations of freedom and nonintervention can be entwined with an interest in, and attempt to, structure spaces of freedom. This is part of the ambivalence of the legal order. The following chapter will examine how authors in the milieu of public Islam construe it.

4

Islam and Society: Entwinement and Differentiation

In April 2000, Lille-Sud, home of the Al-Imane mosque, was the site of violent clashes between the youth and the police. The clashes erupted in reaction to the death of young Ryad Hamlaoui, who had been shot in the back by a police officer. In the days of unrest that followed the killing of Ryad Hamlaoui, various attempts were made by different parties to calm the situation, and they were successful. Amar Lasfar, *recteur* (rector) of the Al-Imane mosque, intervened repeatedly to address the hundreds of people who gathered in the afternoons to honor the deceased. Speaking in the name of Ryad Hamlaoui's family and appealing both to Islam and to common sense, Lasfar helped to defuse the situation and discourage disorder (*Le Monde* April 17, 2000; April 20, 2000; cf. November 20, 2001 and *Al-Urubbiya* 18: 11f.). The incident in Lille attracted nationwide attention and the interior minister had to make a statement to parliament. Referring to the "pacifying role" played by some members of the Muslim community, he mentioned Amar Lasfar explicitly (*Assemblée Nationale*, April 26, 2000).

Later, Lasfar, who became president of the UOIF in 2013, commented upon these events in more detail (Bouzar 2001: 37–45).[1] He not only highlighted his contribution to resolving the crisis (two days after the killing, he believed, the situation was "close to Intifada");[2] he also spoke about his broader vision of the role mosques play in society and more particularly in the *banlieues*. For Lasfar, the events after the death of Ryad Hamlaoui—the fact that the mosque and Lasfar himself as its *recteur* could mediate successfully, even if not without friction, between the youths, parents, and the municipality—showed that the mosque association is "an unavoided and unavoidable representative of a community in its broadest dimension."[3]

The community the *recteur* refers to is not easy to define. When explaining reactions among young people after the killing, Lasfar's analysis summarizes the importance of "being Muslim, to have Muslim benchmarks, to have a Muslim identity" (Bouzar 2001: 40). However, this community is not simply constituted by individuals identifying as Muslims or associating in one way or another with a prayer space. Rather, emigration (Lasfar invoked his commonalities and "symbolic link" with all "young emigrants" in Lille), family ties, culture (a shared "Arab" identity in France that was starting to supplant ethnic or national identities of primo-migrants), and class (social misery in Lille-Sud is a unifying thread in his account) all come together to define a group for which a mosque can be more than a space for prayer. All this, claims Amar Lasfar, has made him "Brother Amar," distinguishing him from most other adults in the neighborhood: "My position allows me not to lose this connection" contrary to those "who are paid by political agencies which are, incidentally, responsible for the misery of the young."[4] While Lasfar's narrativization of April 2000 tends to focus on events, he also mentions that his mosque basically functions as a community center. Readily acknowledging that the mosque attracted only a small percentage of the younger generation, Lasfar asserted that its services were nevertheless used by more children than all four older community centers in the neighborhood put together. Quoting the interior minister, he argued that many problems faced by the police would never arise if other associations worked in the same way as his.[5]

Lasfar's account of these incidents in 2000 inscribes Islam and Muslims into society. More precisely, he simultaneously outlines how mosques are situated in and can shape the *banlieue* and its inhabitants. His vision of the mosque's role has political implications: Lasfar's narrative presents the mosque and its leaders as partners, to some degree indispensable, to the public authorities. This bid for partnership crucially rests upon Lasfar's claim to have influence over young people in his neighborhood. At the same time, by highlighting communal identity and structures, social problems, and problems of governance in his description of the *banlieue*, Lasfar's account partly converges with basic assumptions of integration policy. Among these convergences are the idea that the *banlieue* is a semiautonomous region which necessitates particular policies and measures, and a developing notion of Muslimness which is to some degree disconnected from how those who call themselves Muslims would describe themselves.

Basically, Lasfar's views on the role of the mosque and Muslim associations are far from exceptional in the milieu of public Islam (even if he is perhaps more optimistic and outspoken than others). Certainly, his statements are potentially controversial, partly because his understanding of the role of a mosque conflicts with a central republican notion—dating back to the Revolution—that relations between citizens and the state should be direct and unencumbered by intermediate bodies of any kind.⁶ However, his views on the role of Muslim associations are seen as a serious option by various politicians, as the deliberations by the HCI in the last chapter indicate (and see below).

In the milieu of public Islam, many actors have persistently argued, with varying degrees of complexity, that Islam is a factor conducive to social stability which strengthens the belonging of Muslims as citizens in the Republic. References to the harmonious conjunction of Islam and citizenship are frequent in statements published by the UOIF. The general program of the Union (2001–5) bears the motto of an "authentic and civil Islam" (*un Islam authentique et citoyen*). The leaders of the UOIF stress the possibility for Muslims, much as members of other religious groups or humanists, to contribute to the welfare of French society in its entirety; Muslims are called upon to do so "as citizens and on the basis of their Islamic values and their ethics" (e.g., Jaballah 2000). The contribution Muslims can make to broader society as Muslim citizens is a prominent theme in the writings of Tariq Ramadan. Ramadan's vision of mosques is similar to that of Lasfar: "The mosques which are multiplying in Europe and the United States, rather than seeing them as signs of invasion, should translate as *promises of social stability* because they nourish a positive local engagement" (Ramadan 1994: 124f.; emphasis in the original). Ramadan conceives of Islam as a transformative force, as this statement makes clear: "In England, France, Belgium and the USA, identification with Islam or its discovery succeeds where repression or expensive social programmes have failed" (2001a: 222). Tareq Oubrou claims: "We helped many young people to get out! Contrary to what is often believed, there are many imams who do their work well in the neighborhoods. They help the young to refind their dignity without inciting them to break with their environment. It is thanks to the integrative discourse of imams that many young people became French in the 1980s" (2012: 18; see also 128).

The confidence reflected in these statements is an essential part of how actors in this milieu debate the conditions of life in France. Having said this, their perspectives on societal conditions are more complex than the above statements suggest when considered in isolation. Muslim actors in this milieu routinely ascribe transformative power to Islam. They understand Islam as a tool for individual reform and social change, asserting in various ways Islam's capacity to further the integration of Muslims into society. Two countervailing factors complicate this view. First, various dimensions of life in France are considered problematic in light of the requirements for a Muslim life. The question of what kind of change Muslims can effect in society is thus entwined with the question whether or not Muslims need to adapt to French society (for reasons external to them)—and if it is permissible for them, according to Islamic normativity, to adapt. Or, to put it differently: Does France really constitute a hospitable environment for Islam? Moreover, and more generally, the question of what kind of change Muslims can effect in society is entwined with the question of whether or not Muslims are also changed by the society in which they live.

There is a second factor complicating the social mission of Muslims. It is largely contingent upon the extraordinary series of events which considerably broadened and exacerbated the various problems associated with Islam. As I mentioned already, the headscarf debates in 2003/4 reinforced the hijab's association with sexual inequality and violence against Muslim women (and between defending secularism and liberating these women),[7] but also with a number of other "broad social dangers" (Bowen 2007). Since the early 2000s, there has been increasing public concern over the rise of anti-Semitic acts. One question regularly raised in this connection is whether there is a specific causal link with Muslims.[8] With the outbreak of riots in the suburbs of practically all major cities in October 2005, a phenomenon whose impact on public opinion was highly significant,[9] new links were established between Muslim identity and urban violence. While public reactions to these disturbances often displayed an inability to make sense of the events, their aims and their causes, a number of prominent voices, including politicians, implicated Islam in various ways.[10] Finally, since the early 2000s, the societal context has been reshaped by a growing fear of radicalization and measures taken to detect or prevent it. Concern with what, since the early 2000s, has been called radicalization (Guibet-Lafaye & Rapin 2017)[11] does not constitute a full-blown rupture in perceptions of Islam. As we saw in the study by the HCI, Muslims have been subjected since the mid-1990s to "an anticipatory – or prospective – analysis which aims to discern future risks of social or political conflicts arising from this part of the population which it conceives as part of an Islamic milieu." Within this analysis, the conduct, practices, and identities of various kinds of Muslims, as well the activities of their associations, have been routinely problematized by public authorities (Peter 2008a). Having said this, the political concern with radicalization following the attacks of 2012 and 2015 has placed things on a new level (Halpérin et al. 2017; Mechaï & Zine 2018; Sèze 2019).[12]

I analyze the debates about this power constellation in three steps. First, I outline conceptual convergences and affinities between integration discourses and the matrix within which varying visions of Islam in France are propounded in this milieu. Fundamentally, these convergences are set against the background of reconfiguring integration in a broader ethical framework as a self-willed process of change and societal contributions by Muslims which depends upon certain social and political conditions. As suggested already above, the conditions for making such contributions were deemed favorable by many actors in the late 1990s; the potential for entwining Islam and society in mutually beneficial ways was considered high. This changed significantly in the course of the 2000s, when the criticism that social questions had been unduly "Islamized" became widespread. In this criticism, which features prominently in the thought of Tariq Ramadan, greater emphasis was placed on the distinction between society on the one hand and Islam on the other. Without abandoning the fundamental notion that Islam is lived necessarily in society, more attention was given to the distinctiveness of societal processes and the need for specific social policies. In a third and last part, I will briefly discuss how this critique of the "Islamization" of social issues is, directly and in other ways, contested in the context of concern with "radicalization."

France as a Problem-Space

Actors in the milieu of public Islam differ considerably on a number of points. There are, however, certain commonalities. At one level of analysis, these commonalities result from dealing with the problem-space of France. As I said, these actors engage with a number of general questions about the permissibility, aims, and possibilities for Muslim life in France. At another level of analysis, these commonalities emerge from how they go about answering these questions and what kind of preconception of France guides these answers.

I want to suggest here that this conception combines three broadly defined, related elements. First, the context is referred to as a secular, liberal democracy. From such a perspective, this context raises the question of whether the terms of citizenship in a liberal democracy are acceptable to Muslims from the point of view of Islamic jurisprudence.[13] Of course, the question of how, on Islamic grounds, to justify belonging to secular countries is, indeed, pivotal in a debate to which actors in the milieu of public Islam have made major contributions.[14] Second, the reference to a liberal and secular order implies reference to certain lines of separation which structure this context (and, it is argued, are crucial for enabling the diversity of ways of being French), the most important— and, nominally, the least controversial —being that between citizenship and religion. As already pointed out, these separations relate to a number of conceptual distinctions, such as the distinction between religion and culture or the distinction between the religious and the social. The apparent stability and orderliness of the above is complicated by the third element feeding into conceptions of this context. It is characterized as a "society," a space of unequal power relations where "some can act on the actions of others" (Foucault 2000: 343). Answering questions about the possibility, aims, and permissibility of Muslim lives in France implies situating Muslims in society and reflecting upon the power relations within which they operate. It implies considering the effects of (changing) unequal power relations on the Muslim community, and whether and how they can be changed; at the same time, it involves reflecting upon the responsibilities which follow from this configuration for Muslim organizations and their leadership.

Visions of Integration: The *Union des Organisations Iislamiques de France*

References to integration—in the sense of joining what is, but should not be, separate—are frequently made by the Union. The very name of the *Union des organisations islamiques de France* is an acknowledgment of this notion of integration. Three years after its foundation in 1983, the group changed its name by one word, from "in France" to "of France." This substitution was intended to indicate its stronger national embeddedness. According to the Union's president Lhaj Thami Brèze (1992–2009), this change is part of a larger process of "gradually weav(ing) a reading of Islam which takes the French context into account and does not enter in confrontation with society" (UOIF 2006: 20). Commenting on the recent name change to *Musulmans de France*, the current president, Amar Lasfar, called it "self-evident" in the light of the earlier change, implying further progress on the road to integration (La Croix 2017).[15]

The concrete measures taken to further this process are concentrated in the fields of jurisprudence and education. The Union's overriding intellectual concern remains how Muslims can act and live their Muslim lives, defined in accordance with Islamic sources, within the framework of the French Republic. To find answers to such questions, a scholarly body was set up in 1997 with the explicit aim of elaborating an Islamic jurisprudence for Muslims in Europe.[16] The existence of this fatwa council, some of whose members count among the Union's leadership, notably Ahmed Jaballah (president of the Union, 1984–92, 2011–12), is cited by the Union as proof of its commitment to contextualizing Islam and its "desire for integration" (Jaballah 2003: 138). The same motive is given for creating its *Institut européen de sciences humaines*, designed to train religious experts in tune with the French context.[17] Note that contextualizing is conceived as a form of adaptation inherent to the Islamic tradition. Scholars like Ahmed Jaballah have clearly stated that "adaptation" to changing contexts is an essential part of this tradition, whether in Europe or in "Muslim societies," and is by no means "the sell-out of religion" (Jaballah 2000).

In addition to tradition, the framework for contextualizing Islam is constituted by the conceptual distinction between citizenship on the one hand and religion on the other. In the Charter for European Muslims, adopted in 2008 by the Federation of Islamic Organizations in Europe (FIOE, the federation, now named Council of European Muslims, to which the Union is affilliated), this idea is expressed programmatically:

> Muslims of Europe are urged to integrate positively in their respective societies, on the basis of a harmonious balance between preservation of Muslim identity and the duties of citizenship. Any form of integration that fails to recognize the right of Muslims to preserve their Islamic personality and the right to perform their religious obligations does not serve the interests of Muslims nor the European societies to which they belong.
>
> FIOE 2008

This statement proclaiming the essential aim of "preserving" Muslim identity, which presupposes a categorical distinction between secular citizenship on the one hand and Muslim identity on the other, comes close in tenor to discourses within the Union. It is an essential link in the argument that citizenship of Muslims in the West is permissible. Building on this distinction, the Union has consistently advocated "positive integration," and the idea notably that Muslims should be "active, productive and useful citizens" (FIOE 2008).

By placing the emphasis on secular citizenship and its logic of separations, integration is thus divested of any assimilationist implication in the Union's discourse. This is, however, not all that is said when reflecting upon modalities and possibilities for Muslim lives in Europe. There is an awareness that questions of social power need to be brought in. This is manifest, for example, in the statement that Islamic norms (i.e., those which are not fixed) may change "depending on the strength or weakness of the umma," as one French member of the European Council for Fatwa and Research (ECFR) puts it (Bishri 2005: 240).[18] It is this consideration of social power which can lead to certain convergences with a notion of integration that implies transformation of Muslim identities. Basically, the argument is that French Muslims have not yet fully arrived in society for both social and cultural reasons, and that other French have not yet properly arrived in multicultural France. For this reason, life in France for any French Muslim, at least for now, poses difficulties.

This argument is systematically made by Ahmed Jaballah (2008). Examining the relationship between citizenship and the preservation of Muslim identity, Jaballah essentially maintains that the requirements of citizenship can be reconciled with those of preserving Muslim identity. He examines the question on two levels. First, there is the legal framework, where Islamic obligations are discussed in light of positive law. Jaballah considers why French Muslims can and must accept the democratic form of the state and positive law. His reasoning here is conducted on quite a general level, and he does not, for instance, discuss any specific country. Jaballah then turns to what he calls "the reality" of European Muslims. How is this reality described? The author tries to emphasize the positive aspects. He notes that there have been "without doubt" changes allowing "more interaction with society and positive integration," but he adds immediately that many obstacles remain in the exercise of citizenship rights (2008: 269). Jaballah refers to two kinds of factors, one relating to Muslims, the other to society at large. With regard to the latter, he mentions the negative image of Islam propagated by the media, the political strategies that contribute to racism and Islamophobia, and discriminatory practices on the job market. At the same time, he identifies factors inside the Muslim community. One cause is Muslims' lack of openness toward society and a tendency to prefer isolation, especially among the "first generation" who were immigrants to France and those with limited linguistic skills; another derives from the ethnic links—supported by some who do not want to see Muslims become active citizens—that continue to divide Muslims and stand in the way of integration into broader French society. A last factor has to do with Islamic currents preaching the self-segregation of Muslims, a call which, the author notes, has been received favorably by some "fervently religious" youths among the "new generations."

A cross-cutting theme in Jaballah's reflections—and here, he converges with integrationism—is the idea that certain social and cultural conditions are necessary for Muslims to exercise their citizenship fully. These include "knowledge of society, its language, its culture and customs" (Jaballah 2008: 271). These conditions, as the author repeatedly points out, are fulfilled by the French-born generation of Muslims. In this sense, the entire argument is based on a clear separation between the law on the one hand and lived reality on the other. The distance between these two orders is caused, to a significant degree, by social and cultural factors specific to Muslims and by the hostility of French toward Islam. Although Jaballah is also critical of French politics and society, he reflects on how this gap can be closed by changes in Muslim identity and attitudes, which he perceives as ongoing.

Both his distinction between law and reality and his gesture toward a fuller future to be achieved through changes in the Muslim community indicate some convergence with the assumptions underlying integration discourse. Importantly, integration is not a right of the state which can be demanded from Muslims, but something Muslims should want and strive for themselves. This convergence is not simply the result of an uncritical attitude toward the Republic, even if there is, ultimately, acceptance of the fact that membership in the polity is differentiated by factors beyond the law. Rather, it is the result of a double reflection: on the sources of social power and how access to them is differentiated according to cultural identity, and on how Muslim identity is shaped through social factors, although this aspect is less developed in his writing. This perspective leads Jaballah to conceptualize the current situation of Muslims in terms of a disjuncture between citizenship status and social power, and to contemplate a future when this disjuncture will be overcome, to some degree naturally, by the passing of time and generational change.

Visions of Integration: Tariq Ramadan

Tariq Ramadan's writings and activities seem, at first sight, removed from any overlap with assimilationist notions of integration. This is not only because he rejects the idea that the existing system in France cannot be modified in the process of integrating Muslims. Noting that, due to the stronger Muslim presence, "the social landscape has changed a bit," he wonders, in a general manner, if it "isn't necessary to reconsider things ... without questioning the basic principles of *laïcité*" (1994: 94) in order to enable policies which are more accommodating of Muslim demands.[19] The weightier reason is that Ramadan's primordial aim, from the outset, is to mobilize Muslims, to orient and enable their "efficient *social participation*" (1994: 123; emphasis in the original).[20] Broadly speaking, this participation, whether through specific interventions or more generally, bearing testimony to Islam in a materialist society which has forgotten God, is to have a transformative impact on society (1994: 126, 131). From Ramadan's point of view, his interest in Muslims' social participation sets him somewhat apart from the leadership of the Union. Introducing the French translation of the first fatwa collection issued by the ECFR (2002), Ramadan spells this difference out by asking whether Muslims should not abandon "the 'logic of fastidious adaptation' [to the European context] in order to 'protect themselves,'" which he identifies with the work of the Council, in order to "open up for [Muslims] new horizons of contribution and renewal" (2002: 15). Instead of "wondering *whether and how they would be accepted*," Muslims need to accomplish the "most important mission" they are entrusted with, "an infinite self-sacrifice for social justice, the welfare of mankind, the environment, and all forms of solidarity" (1999: 150; emphasis in the original).

Leaving aside the question whether Ramadan's description of the Council's thinking is correct,[21] I want to underline here that he ties the aim of "contribution"—i.e., of a critical contribution by Muslims to European societies— to relatively specific conditions to be fulfilled by Muslims, both individually and as collectives. Importantly, these conditions are perceived by him from the beginning—albeit to different degrees and for different reasons—as problematic. For this reason, the mobilization of Muslims with a view to their social participation becomes contingent upon their (changing) sociocultural profile which in turn shapes their understanding of Islam. To put it simply, it is this perspective on the conditions of Muslim mobilization which establishes a link between debates about integration on the one hand and Ramadan's broader intellectual project on the other.

It is from this perspective that Ramadan, in the introduction to his first book *Les musulmans dans la laïcité* (Muslims in the Secular Order), chooses a problematization of European Muslim identity as a framework for his study. Referring to the emergence of "*the famous second generation*" of Muslims, he asks whether "we will be able to find a way to live Islam while being respectful of both our religious obligations and the law of the host societies?" (1994: 20; emphasis in the original). Here, Ramadan's politico-theological framing of his study converges, to some extent, with a variety of voices in the integration debate questioning the compatibility of Islam and the republican order;[22] one example— Interior Minister Chevènement's letter to certain Muslim leaders—was discussed in the previous chapter. Note that Ramadan also accepts as a fact—even if it may contradict the law, as he points out twice—that Muslim citizens are often seen as foreigners. This makes it incumbent upon them to "seek to understand the references, the history, and the symbols of the universe and the humans welcoming them"; at the same time, they need to communicate, not in a "reactive manner," who they are (1994: 88).

But how does Ramadan define identity? Ramadan equates identity with the expression of the most fundamental elements of being Muslim. Four dimensions of identity are indicated, i.e., worship including faith and spirituality; a "principle of rationality and responsibility" which permits Islamic sources and context to relate to each other; the transmission of Muslim identity through education; and finally, "action and participation" in projects geared toward social justice (1998 [1994]: 33). Expressing Muslim identity is possible in Europe. One "can clearly state that the legal framework guarantees and protects the expression of this identity" (1998 [1994]: 34). Discussing how Muslim identity relates to national identity, Ramadan pursues the standard line of argumentation in the Union, which consists in establishing distinctions:

> To be a Muslim signifies to uphold a trust (*amâna*) which gives a meaning to one's life: it is to be inhabited and imbibed by an overall conception of life, death and destiny, directed by the belief in a Creator. Philosophically speaking, 'Muslim identity' answers the question of being and as such it is basic and fundamental, since it justifies life itself. The concept of nationality, as it is understood in industrialised countries, is of a completely different nature: as an element of identity, it structures – within both a given constitution and a given space – the way one is to deal with his fellow citizens or fellow human beings. Muslim identity is an answer to the question 'Why?', whereas national identity answers the question 'How', and it would be absurd and stupid to expect geographical attachment to come first or to solve the question of being (1999: 163).

With regard to how Ramadan assesses the French context as a power configuration, it is worth noting that this discussion of "nationality" implies a remarkable dismissal of the appeal and power of the national as a point of reference for solidarity, culture, and thinking. This downgrading of the nation is part of a broader approach to the historicity of France and the West. Whereas "Arab peoples"—"as all peoples from the South"—"cannot nor do not want to flout their cultural and religious traditions which define and shape them" (2011: 37), history in the West is primarily characterized by discontinuity. It *is* change, one may say, or more particularly, it is the history of doing away with religious and cultural obstacles to liberty and creating a space for diversity. This partial downgrading of culture is reinforced by the fact that Ramadan considers the cultural identity of European nations to be in crisis. Thus Ramadan writes in 1994[23] that Islam has a valuable contribution to make in that its "culture and faith challenge France and the West: 'French, English, or German ... citizens of Europe, what is your culture?' To us this question seems worth asking today."[24]

In these writings, Ramadan establishes Muslim identity as unambiguously distinct from citizenship and shields it from state intervention, but this is not all he has to say about identity. Rather, Ramadan is convinced of the need for a process of social and cultural change by Muslims which he believes has already started and whose progress he regularly monitors. Ramadan outlines his vision on integration in a book of conversations with the Swiss intellectual and politician Jacques Neirynck entitled *Peut-on vivre avec l'islam?* (Is Cohabitation with Islam Possible?, 1999). Ramadan argues that the analysis of integration should take place on three levels which, in effect, implies a temporal order: that is, the analysis builds on a distinction between the act of entering the new home country and what comes afterwards. Here as elsewhere, he emphasizes the need to consider both social and economic factors on the one hand, and religious and cultural factors on the other. The first phase is the "process of immigration in the strict sense." The second level is about how Muslims perceive their environment and how this changes over time. Ramadan considers that "a profound analysis will show that their perception and their evaluation have changed in the course of generations. The first migrants considered themselves to be passing through, some generations later their children feel European, at home, members of the only society which they know. The memory of exile has ceased to inhabit them and their gaze changes, very naturally" (Neirynck & Ramadan 1999: 193). The third level is "the direct result of the second." At this stage, argues Ramadan, "it becomes necessary to revisit the scriptural sources in order to think through the stages of juridical adaptation. A triple form of integration needs to be coordinated: identitarian – in order to remain loyal to one's conscience in a new context; legal – in order to determine the kind of relation one needs to establish with the legislation in a given country; social – in order to determine what is possible in terms of civic engagement" (Neirynck & Ramadan 1999: 193).

Ramadan describes a long-term, and open-ended, process of acculturation which is notably enabled by changes in education and economic status—the first migrants who came "were destitute, poor, and little educated"—and which leads the "children of immigrants" to feel "at home" in Europe and to want to revisit the sources of their religion and ponder the forms and aims of their civic activism (Neirynck & Ramadan 1999: 195). Culture is an essential category in this process. As Ramadan has elaborated (1998 [1994]: 36ff.), Muslims need to distinguish clearly between religion on the one hand and culture (and civilization) on the other. As he identifies Islam with "values and precepts," nothing stands in the way of "thinking a sartorial conduct, an artistic and creative expression – a culture – which mobilizes French energies and takes into account national context and customs while at the same time respecting Islamic values and precepts" (1998 [1994]: 37).[25]

The above analysis makes apparent some significant overlaps with discourses on integration. From both Ramadan's perspective and that of integration discourse, Muslims do not simply arrive in European societies when the "process of immigration in the strict sense" (see above) is over. It makes sense to speak about integration after immigration,[26] and this is the most basic assumption of debates about Islam. Importantly, since the mid-2000s Ramadan has reevaluated the achievements, obstacles, and conditions associated with the process of integration in a more systematic manner. In an essay titled "Integration – a conceptual trap?", published originally in 2005, Ramadan seems to fundamentally question the concept of integration: "What can it signify in the mind of political actors *to integrate* women and men who are already French, Belgian, Swiss, or other citizens?" (2008b: 75; emphasis in the original). Introducing the notion "post-integration," Ramadan voices multiple criticisms of integration policies: they are less necessary than often thought, misguided in their orientation toward religion and culture, and counterproductive. In brief, state policies need to be reoriented (2010a: 67–73). In "Citizenship, Identity and the Sense of Belonging," originally published in 2008 as a report on education for the City of Rotterdam and subsequently published in French, Ramadan explains that the notion of postintegration is about the "diagnosis of problems which our societies face": "Certainly, there are individuals (and sometimes new migrants) who still have problems with cultural and/or religious integration, but what the new generations of citizens and (long-standing) residents encounter has nothing to do with these difficulties". Rather, their problems are socioeconomic and call for "adapted social policies" (2008b: 87). Religious integration has been achieved, he claims: "Millions of Muslims are, in fact, already proving every day that 'religious integration' is an accomplished fact, that they are indeed at home in the Western countries whose tastes, culture and psychology they have made their own" (2010a: 125).

Ramadan has not abandoned the notion of a sense of belonging, a feeling which is enabled and shaped by social processes. Rather, he has become aware that integration policies as currently practiced are obstructive: "The all but obsessive discourse about the 'integration' of new citizens is an objective impediment to the positive development of a feeling of belonging." (2010a: 67F.). As this statement indicates, the basic validity of the category "sense of belonging" is not questioned.[27] Rather, he argues that "the different modes of 'integration' (linguistic, intellectual, social, legal, cultural, and religious) have become or are becoming obsolete: what remains is the ultimate stage, which is psychologicl as well as intellectual and which nurtures, and is nurtured by, the sense of belonging." (2010a: 67). It is here that the "construction of a new We" comes into play:

It is a matter of greatest urgency to set in motion national movements of local initiatives, in which women and men of different religions, cultures, and sensitivities can open new horizons of mutual understanding and shared commitment: horizons of trust. These shared projects must henceforth bring us together, and give birth to a new 'We' anchored in citizenship. Of course, 'intercultural' and 'interfaith' dialogues are both vital and necessary, but they cannot have the impact of the shared commitment of citizens in the priority fields: education, social divides, insecurity, racisms, discriminations, and more (2010a: 130).

Visions of Integration: Tareq Oubrou

Tareq Oubrou's work, in line with the above approaches, emerges out of the perception of the presence of Muslims in France as new and exceptional. Oubrou, who officially left *Musulmans de France* in 2018,[28] has been prominently contributing to debates on the contextualization of Islam in France since 1998, when he presented his project for a *sharî'a de minorité*, minority here referring to "spatio-temporal exceptionality (political, social and cultural)" and not to demographics.[29] Like Ramadan, he believes that Islam as religion can be expressed and connected with multiple cultural forms which can be clearly distinguished from religion; a cultural process of change inside the Muslim population is necessary and desirable. Whereas Ramadan uses the distinction religion/culture to support the creation of French-Islamic cultural practices, Oubrou sets his sights rather on what he calls "acculturation."[30] At times, Oubrou strongly emphasizes a common culture: "The culture of French Muslims is in principle the same as of all other French" (Colombani & Oubrou 2017: 80). He has criticized the ECFR as "far too Arab."[31] Unlike Ramadan,[32] and much more in line with the Union's leadership and the Council, Oubrou remains aloof from any kind of activism.

Oubrou accepts integration—in principle or as a basis for negotiations—as an ethical obligation for Muslim citizens and a political task for the state. He believes that the presence of Muslims in France is not a problem in terms of law and the "values of the Republic." However, the situation looks different on the cultural level: "particularly with regard to mentalities, culture, and the *tectonics* of their evolution."[33] Put positively, Oubrou deduces an ethical obligation for Muslims to change certain dimensions of their practice of Islam from his understanding of French society in its historicity. This is the starting point for his evolving project and constitutes a fundamental convergence with integration policy discourse.

Oubrou regularly describes French culture, notably shaped by Catholicism and secularism,[34] as not easily changeable, and he keeps encouraging Muslims to engage in a process of cultural integration—while at the same time insisting that religious freedom rights cover Muslim practices (2004: 218).[35] Fatwas are the essential tool to facilitate integration. Oubrou's fatwas seek "to avoid sociocultural fracture with the majority by taking into account the dominant cultural environment," thus accepting "a certain social constraint for the visibility of Muslim practice" as part of the context.[36] In order to safeguard "the secular equilibrium of French society," he recommends not issuing Islamic norms which may obstruct a Muslim in his life and "prevent him from realizing a social, material, and even spiritual advance."[37] A Muslim who has chosen to practice Islam "needs to be offered norms which do not handicap him in their social, affective, spiritual, economic ... life."[38]

Oubrou's project has sometimes met with hefty criticism. This has partly to do with the fact that an isolated reading of certain statements by Oubrou could suggest that he is preaching assimilation: "The responsibility of Muslims, for me, comes first because it is for the newcomers to adapt themselves to the Republic and France, and not the other way around" (2019: 22). In some of his publications, Oubrou seemingly applies this adaptive approach to the hijab, performing a radical change of his position which, not surprisingly given the topic, was widely noticed. In line with the Union, which has long supported the right to wear the hijab, Oubrou was initially a strong advocate of the duty to wear the headscarf (Babès & Oubrou 2002). Later, he declared that covering the hair was "a simple implicit recommendation and not an obligation" (2009: 84).[39] While Oubrou criticized the headscarf bans in France as curtailing individual liberties, he believed it was a "mistake" to support practices like the "veil, which is erroneously called 'Islamic'" and is, in his view, dispensable, particularly given its negative perception in France (2009: 70; see also 80f.).[40]

This line of argumentation prompted criticism that Oubrou relies excessively on contextualization and, wrongly, perceives the assimilation of Muslims in France as unavoidable (Bahri 2009). Given the significant dislike of the hijab in France, Oubrou's rereading of the sources[41]—leading him to "preach the invisibility of Muslims of France" (*oumma.com* 2013)—might be seen as a matter of political expediency which paid off, as Oubrou was awarded the Legion of Honor in 2013 by the mayor of his hometown Bordeaux, Alain Juppé.[42] Similar arguments are made regarding some of Oubrou's statements concerning Palestine.[43] While it is not possible—simply because Oubrou's work remains unfinished—to fully appraise the degree to which the implementation of the methodological notions and principles sketched out above can be considered assimilationist, his writings flag up two major limits to self-assimilation which help to properly situate his thinking and clarify some misperceptions.

First, Oubrou in no way simply bows to public concerns about Islam uncritically or sees them as legitimate injunctions to adapt. Rather, he calls his opponents out by repeatedly stating that debates about Islam are in truth not really about Islam, but about various dysfunctional aspects of society. In a discussion about the burkini, he points out that "Islam has become a pretext for not confronting a profound crisis" (2017: 109) in the way French society defines itself. Similarly, when asked about two controversies (related to the burqa and virginity as a condition of marriage), rather than responding directly, he declares that "Islam allows evolving debate about topics which remain, all things considered, quintessentially Western or French (*occidentalo-occidentaux ou franco-français*)" such as "the condition of women, democracy, human rights, freedom of expression" (2009: 53; cf. 2012: 97f.). While Oubrou, as I said, problematizes certain forms of visibility of Muslims, notably the hijab,[44] the causes of this problem are unrelated to Islam and lead back to a critique of French society: "One has to have the courage to recognize that the problem of 'aggressive visibility' of Islam in France hides in fact, in a surreptitious and subliminal manner, [the problem of] the relation to the Arab." (Colombani & Oubrou 2017: 93f.).[45] Another reason for the negative perception of the hijab is a simple misreading of this practice. Adopting "the prism of its Judeo-Christian tradition," the headscarf was wrongly associated by French with the "submission of woman. However, for Muslims, it is in reality about the submission to God." (2016: 167). Oubrou seems little interested in debating issues such as "polygamy, the legitimacy of slavery, the illegitimacy of adoption, or cutting off the hand of thieves," arguing that "99% of majority Muslim countries do not apply these prescriptions" anyway (2017: 98f.). A certain difference is discernible here compared with Tariq Ramadan who, in 2005, started a global campaign for a moratorium on corporal punishment, stoning, and the death penalty (a campaign, incidentally, which was criticized as unnecessary by Ahmad al-Rawi, the chairman of the FIOE).[46]

Second, it deserves underlining that Oubrou's highly conflictual recommendation to embrace discretion in the case of the hijab is not typical of other concrete outcomes of his "theology of acculturation." To take another controversial case, halal slaughtering, Oubrou proposes as a compromise solution—as part of what he calls "minimalist orthopraxy" (*orthopraxie minimaliste*)—that the stunning of animals before their killing should be accepted as long as it is not "lethal" or "brutal" (2016: 187f.).[47] Leaving aside the issue of whether this basis for compromise is at all realistic, this view is less "minimalist" than another option he identifies, namely a "generalized dispensation allowing [Muslims] to eat any kind of meat apart from pork" (2012: 86).[48] Once again, Oubrou's study of slaughter methods combines contextualization with a critique of the context, i.e., a highly critical analysis of the place of animals in European traditions of thought. Furthermore, the widespread demand that slaughter without stunning be prohibited is problematized and deconstructed here, for example, as the ideological discourse of "Western civilizational progress" (2016: 172-5, 183-7).

Governing the *Banlieue*

In the early 2000s, the conditions for defining the relation between Islam and society changed, even if not in every respect enduringly. The discursive parameters were reconfigured both by the creation of institutional relations between Muslim associations and the government, and by the riots in the autumn of 2005. The imminent creation of a representative body, the CFCM inaugurated in 2003, seemed to open up new prospects for Islamic actors with regard to their public legitimacy and visibility. Moreover, it became apparent while the CFCM was being set up that some Muslim federations would benefit particularly from these new prospects, as the functioning and electoral mechanism of the CFCM privileged those federations controlling a sizeable number of mosques.[49]

The creation of the CFCM was widely experienced as a potential turning point in relations between Islam and the Republic, a moment when the Republic's institutions were realigned to a changing society. For the Union, the creation of the CFCM and its own integration within it consecrated the fulfillment of a long-cherished aim to be recognized, in spite of its relationship to the Muslim Brotherhood, as a legitimate element of the French Islamic landscape and an official interlocutor for the public authorities. As already indicated,[50] the Union's inclusion was not self-evident, as the justification by Interior Minister Sarkozy amply demonstrated. Sarkozy did emphasize that this policy was, at its most basic level, designed to realize equality of religious freedom while fully respecting the limits imposed on this freedom by the principles of *laïcité*. In this respect, Sarkozy stressed the legality of the Union's practice of Islam: "I take note of the fact that the UOIF responds to the aspirations of those among our compatriots who wish to live their religion with a degree of rigor. It [the Union] must do so in conformity with republican principles, and it can do so. This is why this 'fundamentalism' has been taken into account in the CFCM" (2004: 86; see also 64).[51] Sarkozy also presented the Union's inclusion as one piece of a necessary response to a changed societal context in a now more diverse France: "France has become multicultural, multiethnic, multireligious ... and she was not told about it"; "France has to accept herself as she is – diverse (*multiple*)" (2004: 22, 91).[52] Repeatedly, he emphasized the need to wake up to reality[53] and to tackle extremism in its various forms by recognizing Islam as part of the Republic: "First of all, I emphasize that the emergence of Muslim fundamentalism in our society results primarily from clandestinity, from non-recognition of Islam as a religion of France, from the absence of debate and the refusal to create an institution representing Islam in its entirety. Who contributed to the rise of fundamentalists, *intégristes*, or Islamists? What led to this situation? Resistance to change (*immobilisme*)!"[54] Note that Sarkozy did not fail to point out the particular benefits accruing from cooperation with the Union: "The reality is that the UOIF is doing, at the grass-roots level, useful work against the more dangerous enemies of the Republic, namely the Salafis" (2004: 84).

The Union's integration into governmental schemes for shaping and controlling Muslims, suggested here in Sarkozy's remarks, echoes self-descriptions from inside the Union. For example, the assertion by Abdallah Ben Mansour, the Union's secretary-general, that "Muslim associations are doing a better job than the DST [intelligence agency of the Ministry of the Interior] ... at preventing Islamist infiltration in France."[55] After the creation of the CFCM, concrete help was provided by the UOIF for the fight against Salafism.[56] The evolving, seemingly close relationship between the interior minister and the UOIF gave rise to many comments and critique of various kinds. This relationship was critically discussed in circles sympathetic to the Union. In 2005 Yamin Makri, cofounder of the *Union des Jeunes Musulmans* (Union of Young Muslims) and the *Collectif des Musulmans de France* (Collective of French Muslims),[57] reflected in an article entitled "Les 'nouveaux notables' de la République" ("The 'new notables' of the Republic") on the fruits of the Union's strategy during the past decade of making institutional recognition the "absolute priority." According to Makri, the outcome of this was that the "border" between "cooperation, adaptations, necessary concessions, compromise, and trade-offs ... becomes less and less clear and more and more debatable." Makri illustrated this worrisome development, from his point of view, with reference to recent events. In the run-up to the CFCM elections in 2005, the Union welcomed the leadership of the Grand Mosque of Paris—historically the trusted partner of the French government and its main tool for preventing a more autonomous organization of Muslims—to its annual meeting in Le Bourget.

Listening to the speeches, the historical dividing line between, on the one hand, "consular" Islam, controlled by foreign governments in cooperation with Paris, and on the other, independent Muslim federations such as the Union no longer seemed relevant to Makri.

While Makri's critique emerges out of a broader reflection on the transformation of "reformist" movements in the Muslim world toward a form of conservative pietism proper to the *petit bourgeois*, his concern about the "notabilization" of the Union's leaders responds to a very particular political context. This was a context in which the possibilities for religious actors, not least Muslim actors, to cooperate with the government were exceptionally great and where the concessions and compromises mentioned above could be defended, albeit not without difficulty. This context was shaped notably by Interior Minister Nicolas Sarkozy (2002–4, 2005–7), who, as minister and later as president (2007–12), strongly asserted his belief in the public relevance and singular role of religion as a source of morality and meaning for humans.[58] In his first stint as interior minister—in contrast to his second stint—Sarkozy included Islam in this view of religion. In a context where anxieties about the *banlieue* were growing, Sarkozy highlighted the role of religion by contrasting it to social factors: "I consider that, these past years, we have overestimated the importance of sociological questions, whereas the religious fact, the spiritual question, have been largely underestimated" (2004: 13). Much like the Union, Sarkozy emphasized the religious option as particularly relevant to the *banlieue*[59] and used the term "Muslim" to cover both a religious and a cultural identity, thus raising the stakes attached to the recognition of Islam.[60]

The particularity of this conjuncture needs to be underlined, primarily because the context was to change rapidly and sometimes dramatically in subsequent years. The CFCM, almost from its beginning, struggled with internal conflicts; as a consequence, it was unable to tackle practical issues and did not succeed in establishing itself as the institutional Islamic actor that had been so sorely lacking in the public sphere.[61] The erstwhile close relationship between the Union and Sarkozy soon became seriously strained[62] as Sarkozy turned to more repressive discourse and policies in the *banlieue* and chose national identity—increasingly framed as Catholic identity—as a major theme in his successful presidential campaign (2006/7), engaging a rhetoric that included a number of widely noted anti-Islamic elements.[63] In brief, the policies of Nicolas Sarkozy in relation to the creation of the CFCM and the Union strikingly illustrate the flexible and contingent nature of secular politics in France.

The Critique of "Islamization"

Some months after the publication of "The 'new notables' of the Republic," riots broke out in Clichy-sous-Bois after the violent death of two youths, and soon spread to many other cities. The riots started on October 27 and prompted the government to take the extraordinary step of declaring a state of emergency on November 8. In this context, the Union published a fatwa on November 6 entitled "Fatwa on the disturbances affecting France."[64] The Union claimed to have received numerous telephone calls on its fatwa lines from individuals and associations after the riots started, and the fatwa was then issued "in response to demands probably emanating from those families most affected by the destruction of (their) cars (and from local imams powerless in face of the situation)" (Caeiro 2006b). In the fatwa, the Union stated clearly:

> Every Muslim living in France, whether citizen or guest, has the right to demand the scrupulous respect of his being, dignity and belief, as well as to act for greater equality and social justice. But this action (...) must never take place against the teachings recalled above and the law which regulates common life.

While the Ministry of the Interior as well as various interfaith groups welcomed the fatwa, strong criticism was expressed by some Muslim actors. The popular web forum *oumma.com* published an op-ed headed "La 'fatwa' hallucinante de l'UOIF" ("The amazing UOIF 'fatwa'"), in which it took issue with the approach:

> But this "fatwa" ... attaches social problems to particular communities and religions, giving credence to the idea that the motives of the 'vandals' are rooted in their alleged *islamité*: they are delinquents because they are above all Muslims, or rather, the way the UOIF argues, "bad Muslims", because the "vandals" are not upholding the verses of the Quran."

Criticizing the Union's willingness to work for the Ministry of the Interior and its desire to act as "the community police of the consciences of Muslims of France," the article asserts that the Union is in fact "Islamizing" what are simply and exclusively grave acts by criminals.[65]

Adopting a broadly-speaking similar perspective, Tariq Ramadan joined the debate shortly after *oumma.com* had published its opinion piece. Ramadan's reflections partly tread familiar ground. As in previous interventions, Ramadan argues that the recurrent debates about "integration" and "identity" disable people from seeing the real problems, which are social; they have to do with xenophobia and institutional racism. Identifying a broader context of exclusion and inequality in various forms, Ramadan concludes that "(t)heir violence, drawing on illegitimate means, is a reaction which is unfortunately understandable..." (2005a).

For Ramadan, however, the *banlieue* crisis also plays out within a broader context in which the relationship between society and Islam are being reassessed and redescribed. This reassessment implies conceptual work. He highlights the need for clear categorical boundaries—notably between the religious and the social—and urges Muslims to remind politicians and the general public not to "Islamize" or "culturalize" problems in society (2008: 105).[66] Ramadan's strategy is clear: it aims to save "real" Islam from some of its supposed manifestations, and it is this reference to the social—whose power and autonomy are at times greatly emphasized in his reflections—which allows him to do so.[67] Implicit in this reference is a reassertion, direct or otherwise, of an image of the Muslim population as particularly affected by social problems and vulnerable to exclusion.

Addressing the appeal of "radical" forms of Islam, Ramadan offers a social explanation: "To those who assert themselves as French or British, it is made understood that they are first of all Arab, Asians, or Muslims. How could certain individuals, socially and/or psychologically marginalized, not be attracted by literalist or radical discourses which tell them that they are rejected for who they are and that there is no other way than to confront identities and civilizations." (2005a).

In 2006, in his programmatic position paper "Manifesto for a New We" (2008c: 110–19), Ramadan elaborates more systematically on how to conceive the relation between Islam and society. The central idea here is that the differences between orders and categories—such as religion, culture, society—should be carefully respected without, however, ignoring possible connections between them (2010: 126). This, Ramadan argues, is the best way to deal with what he repeatedly terms legitimate fears and anxieties about Islam and Muslims among the broader public:

> One of the most effective ways of responding to legitimate fears is to separate problems into their component parts, but without disconnecting these closely related elements. 'Deconstructing without disconnecting' means that we accept, first and foremost, the obligation to distinguish what is strictly religious in nature from educational, social, or immigration-related issues, and then analyse how cause-and-effect relationships are established at the sociopolitical grass roots (2010: 126).

He proceeds to give a simple illustration of such cause-and-effect relationships: "Seen in this light, unemployment, school failure and delinquency have, as we already mentioned, no connection with Islam. Yet it is vitally important to grasp the reasons that Muslim citizens and residents bear the brunt of failure in these very areas" (2010: 126).

The leaders of the Union totally rejected claims that they had contributed to "Islamizing" societal problems. The Union's president, Lhaj Thami Brèze, pointed out that the Union, concerned about "social cohesion," had made use of the "means" available to religious actors, notably by issuing "directives." Furthermore, continued the president, the fatwa did not simply equate all rioters with Muslims, but sought "to interpellate" "those who considered or declared themselves Muslims" (Brèze 2006).[68]

The Critique of "Islamization" and its Critique

In the 2010s, the critique of "Islamization" lost nothing of its relevance. On the contrary. The attacks of 2012 and those in 2015 stimulated vehement debate where the causal role of Islamic factors was central. The questions to ask here, then, are: Was this critique of "Islamization" as propounded by Ramadan, Oubrou, and others, heard at all, and did it garner any support?

In short, this critique was heard, and more to the point, it converged with other voices warning of the dangers entailed by "Islamizing" various phenomena, not least those designated as jihadism.[69] At the same time, it had to confront two important countervailing tendencies. One relates to the fact that Ramadan's critique, similar to most other critiques of "Islamization," identifies societal dysfunctions as one major cause of the social ills to be explained. This inversion triggered accusations of apologism and a broader debate about the usages of sociology. Second, a critique of "Islamization" that focused on identifying the causes of phenomena had limited bearing on the debate about jihadism that was being conducted in the tense political context after the attacks of 2015 and the declaration in November that year of a state of emergency, not to mention its subsequent perpetuation.[70] Here, the immediate and primary interest was not in ultimate causation, but in identifying potential future jihadists. From this angle, and independently of any assumptions about the causes of jihadism, Islamic practices were seen as important indicators of "radicalization" and used to identify suspects, setting in motion a powerful tendency to render all Muslim appearing individuals suspect.

The fact that Ramadan's critique of "Islamization" found support in this context is not surprising. His critique centrally implies not only a distinction between Islam and the social but a downgrading of Islam as a causal factor in society; in this sense, his approach converged markedly with basic outcomes of social rationalizations of Islam, a discourse which carried some public weight. Recall the brief presentation of contemporary French scholarship on Islam. One important feature of this scholarship is the emphasis placed on how Islam— practices, discourses, institutions and the functions they fulfill—is shaped by and dependent upon social forces. From this perspective, which has become in many ways commonsensical, Islam as it can be observed in France is actually made in France—a notion concisely and pointedly expressed in the following statement by François Burgat about the responsibility borne by society: "We will have the Muslims which we give ourselves" (2016: 277).

The stress on societal responsibilities is not alien to studies on jihadism.[71] In a general study on radicalization, Farhad Khosrokhavar writes that the "new forms of extremism of which jihadism has been the dominant form for more than a decade" are the "indicator" of "profound malaise" in society. While Khosrokhavar acknowledges that one could consider this extremism a matter of "individual responsibility or religious radicalism," he chooses to conclude within a much broader perspective. Radicalization, in his view, is "one of the spaces where the malaise of a number of citizens in a world deprived of real citizenship is being played out" (2014: 184).[72] With an eye to France, Khosrokhavar warns: "When exclusion is paired with stigmatization, the mixture can become explosive." One tendency among "groups doubly deprived of means of political expression" is "to express their revolt through violence, radical Islamism being one of these modes of expression" (2014: 19). On a similar note, Fabien Truong writes that the combined action of the police and the courts on "a population which has no problem recognizing itself – French by birth, immigrant by descent, and Muslim by faith – can take on the shape of organized persecution."[73] Considering their "imaginaries" and the "'biographical resources'" produced by "*our* society," the author asks how anyone can be surprised if this leads, "in the long term and in some cases" to "wanting to bestow death in a spectacular manner" (Truong 2017: 200; emphasis in the original). Note that the claim that Islam (in whatever form) is not the ultimate cause of jihadism does not need to be based upon the argument that social malaise is the real cause. Olivier Roy, the most prominent theorist striving to 'de-Islamize' jihadism, rejects the claim that the "radicalized" have a "typical social and economic profile" (2017: 62). More generally, Roy refuses to situate jihadism analytically in the space of both the *banlieues* and the "community of Muslims" which, as he wrote pointedly in an opinion piece in the aftermath of the attacks in January 2015, simply does not exist (Roy 2015). In Roy's view, "the radicalized" are young, uprooted individuals (i.e. they belong to a second generation or are converts); they "invent the Islam which they oppose to the West"; "they are not integrated into the local religious communities (neighborhood mosque)"; "they do not work for the Islamization of society, but to realize their fantasy of sick heroism" (2015).

Presented in such concise form, Roy's argument may seem to constitute a remarkably clear-cut case of 'de-Islamizing' jihadism. This is, indeed, how Roy's work is often, albeit incorrectly, debated—for example, by Gilles Kepel and François Burgat in a series of widely noted exchanges in the French media.[74] Both authors, although coming from opposite directions, attribute a hypothesis to Roy which is far more straightforward than his actual writings allow. Kepel, in a text coauthored with Bernard Rougier, criticizes Roy because by framing his research in terms of "radicalization"—a term branded a "smoke screen" by the authors—he has "diluted" the phenomenon and ruled out thinking its (Islamic) "specificity," "even in a comparative manner" (Kepel & Rougier 2016). François Burgat, more sympathetic to Roy, considers that the latter refuses to "focus in any way on the Salafist variable" in the explanation of jihadism and supports this view (2016: 279).[75] In fact, Roy's argument in its fully developed form does not, as he emphasizes repeatedly, "exonerate" Islam or Salafism (2016: 15, 61, 99, 110). Roy does insist that there is no relation of "causality" between Islam or Salafism on the one hand and radicalization on the other (2016: 110). Nevertheless, Salafism—and here Roy casts doubt on his former distinction between quietist and *takfiri* Salafism—does raise legitimate concerns for policies of security and prevention (2016: 99, 102). As to Daesh, the Islamic State of Iraq and the Levant, Roy—noting the incomplete nature of his analysis and that more research on "the religion of Daesh" is needed—sees "important differences" between the "Islam of Daesh" and Salafism, but also maintains that they share a "common matrix" (2016: 102, 107, 110).[76] Ultimately, there does not seem to be much of a gap between Roy's "Islamization of radicality" thesis (2016: 15) and the claim that "Islam" is a necessary but insufficient condition of the process leading these individuals to take action.[77] The latter claim is, of course, widely made today in diverse forms. The complexity of Roy's argument—i.e., the difficulty of distinguishing unambiguously and conclusively between "religion" and "violence"—is worth mentioning here, as it is part of a broader trend in debates about Islam and "Islamization" since the public emergence of Salafism (see below).[78]

The critique of Islamization, then, is itself subject to critique and confronted with two sets of countervailing forces. One line of argument, which harks back to debates about urban delinquency and violence,[79] targets how social rationalizations are used in debates on jihadism. Following the attacks of November 2015, Prime Minister Manuel Valls made a number of widely reported statements attacking those who sought to "explain" what had happened by adducing social, sociological, or cultural factors. His critique culminated in the claim "explaining is already a little bit excusing." Expressed in such a polemical form, Valls's critique seems absurd. Not surprisingly, some responses merely aim to clarify an apparent underlying misunderstanding, namely, as sociologist Bernard Lahire put it, the confusion between "understanding in the most rational manner possible what exists," which is the task of the social sciences, and "judging or suggesting means for transforming it."[80]

However, the controversy is not simply the result of confusion. As the examples reported above show, sociological work, while not itself enouncing moral judgments, can of course change the conditions for making moral judgments by casting light on structural forces of determinism—and this is what can often be observed in this case. Abandoning the idea of fully autonomous choices and exclusively individual responsibility does not mean that notions of choice or responsibility are totally abandoned. However, judgments become conditional and absolute condemnation impossible. Moreover, as regards our concrete case, the above examples show that any debate around jihadism becomes entwined with mostly devastating portrayals of the state of French society.[81] All this is not to say, of course, that the causes of this controversy, where questions of method are frequently raised,[82] are exclusively rooted in sociological techniques. More simply, as Dominique Schnapper suggests in her intervention, the issue has a lot to do with the specific kind of politics pursued by many sociologists today and the related failure to practice the disengaged critique they preach: they "pretend not to give in to the spirit of times," but "the dominant spirit of their milieu" shapes what they critique and what they do not critique, according to Schnapper. For example, the critique of racism in Western countries is "easy," as "it is the norm" today; to study "racist practices" such as the enslavement of black Africans in other contexts, however, is much less so.[83]

This line of critique is shared by a diverse group of authors whose focus, however, is not specifically on sociology, but more generally on conceptualizations of Islam. This interest in new conceptualizations is largely nourished by a dissatisfaction with approaches that reduce Islam simply to a social epiphenomenon and marginalize it in the course of analyzing jihadism or French

Islam (see, for example, Birnbaum 2016; Taguieff 2017; Manent 2015). This (emerging) debate also revisits the now commonsensical distinction between Islam and Islamism. Rejecting such neat separations between legitimate religion (Islam) and an illegitimate ideologized avatar (Islamism) as insufficient for identifying responses to the challenges France faces, a more relational perspective which does not label Islamism as a priori areligious is proposed. Note that this reframing of Islamism implies raising questions about how violent interpretations of the Qur'an are enabled and facilitated—but not caused—by the text. Thus, Islamicist Adrien Candiard draws a comparison with how Nazis were able to make use of Wagner or Nietzsche, arguing that this usage would have been impossible, for example, in the case of Kant and Haydn (2016: 28). By adopting this level of analysis, Candiard reformulates standard questions about the relation between scripture and violence; the problem scrutinized is no longer (crudely) conceptualized in terms of "determination" but rather in terms of "code," as it were. The potential scope for problematizing Islam widens.

A second set of powerful factors shaping the reception of the critique of Islamization needs to be mentioned. After the attacks of 2015, government policies focused more explicitly on Islam in its relation to violence, often strongly differentiating between Islam and Salafism, the latter being more and more explicitly designated as incompatible with the republican order. Not until 2014 was an official strategy for prevention of radicalization and support of families launched (April 29, 2014). This entailed a state subsidy for a newly created *Centre de prévention contre les dérives sectaires liées à l'islam* (Center for the Prevention of Sectarian Deviances Linked to Islam, or CPDSI), directed by Dounia Bouzar and charged with "deradicalizing" youth.[84] As the name indicates, the problematic issue of justifying this direct intervention by the state in religious matters is partly resolved by designating these matters as "sectarian deviances" and attaching the CPDSI to the *Mission interministérielle de vigilance et de lutte contre les dérives sectaires* (Interministerial Mission for Vigilance and Combat of Sectarian Deviances, or MIVILUDES) dealing with such phenomena.[85] The original directive on the prevention of radicalization dating from 2014 addresses the issue of religion in extremely concise terms ("These actions cannot ignore the religious dimension of radicalization, which needs to be discussed with trusted religious officials who will be able to evaluate how to tackle this with youth..."). This question has been more explicitly thematized since 2015 as part of a campaign alerting the public to the phenomenon of "radicalization" and providing tools for detecting it.[86] As the authors themselves state, the indicators of "radicalization" highlighted by the campaign, such as adopting new dietary or sartorial habits or dropping out of sport where it is a mixed-gender activity, seem to establish close links between the "practice of an *Islam rigoriste*" and "radicalization." Admittedly, this connection is explicitly disavowed, and the campaign material emphasizes that no generalizations can be made about precise trajectories of "rupture."[87] Nevertheless, this campaign and others like it, in addition to statements from government members about "weak indicators of radicalization" (such as no longer drinking alcohol), will not fail to produce stigmatizing effects for (those perceived as) Muslims (and other French). In a nutshell, since the attacks of 2015 Salafism as a specific trend in Islam has been more and more explicitly designated as a problem. There has been a perceptible tendency to give in to the "temptation to combat certain religious attitudes" which are legally speaking unproblematic (Sèze 2019: 167).[88] This development has far-reaching consequences and is not limited to government policies focused upon potentially threatening phenomena linked to Salafi trends to the exclusion of other components of the Islamic landscape.

Conclusion

This chapter has examined how Muslim actors engage with integration policies. Integration policies are often associated with injunctions to integrate. Such injunctions are rejected en bloc by some from inside the milieu of public Islam.[89] This, however, does not mean that integration is simply not a concern for actors in this milieu. In this chapter, I have approached integration as a power relation which is "changeable, reversible and unstable" (Foucault 1988: 12). As an element in a reversible power relation, the reiterated assertion of the problem of integration implies the possibility to assess—and revise—claims about the state of integration and society, definitions of Islam, and normative Frenchness. References to integration raise questions about what kind of policies are suitable in a given context and which knowledges should inform them. These questions are answered by the actors examined here in a series of analytical descriptions of the changing situation of France—as a nation, a cultural space, a society—and how she interrelates with Islam and Muslims.

The foundation for their reflections on integration is a liberal vision of the French polity where a system of separations guarantees liberties for everyone. From this perspective, society figures as a distinct space which requires certain adaptations from Muslims who in turn will be better equipped to actively contribute to the (re)shaping of social life. In other words, these multilayered visions of Islam in society are characterized by ambivalence. Thus Tareq Oubrou's project of *sharî'a de minorité* reflects on modes of "acclimatizing" the practice of Islam to this space while at the same time envisioning the advent of fundamental changes: "Can we already postulate that, in the 21st century, Western civilization will be, in its religious base, Judeo-Christian-Muslim?" (1998: 27). On a different level, this ambivalence is manifest in the double image of French Muslims: "at risk," on the one hand, of exposure to significant social problems, while called upon, on the other, to contribute actively to shaping society.[90]

Note that these challenges occur in a context where Islamic associational resources are limited and their buildup continues to be slow. The CFCM being dysfunctional almost from inception, there is no national Muslim actor with significant institutional resources and/or weight in public debate.[91] Reiterative debates about Islam have extended the scope of ills associated with it beyond what was imaginable.[92] The need to differentiate and distinguish between Islam and various issues not intrinsically related to it becomes more important, while the emphasis placed upon the transformative power of Islam diminishes. As I have shown, the critique of the "Islamization of social problems," enacted in more or less complex forms by these actors, can rely upon a much broader discursive context structured by social rationalizations of Islam. At the same time, this critique of "Islamization" is itself the object of critique. More than ever, the correct approach to make sense of things potentially related to Islam is contested.

5

Teaching Freedom

In this chapter, the focus will shift to pedagogical discourses addressed to Muslims as ethical subjects in the *banlieue*. At the most general level, the question I will address here relates to another dimension of the entwinement of Muslim discourses with the secular context, namely how the ethical subject is imagined in the milieu of public Islam. Broadening the horizon beyond juridically centered debates in this group, this chapter inquires into how ethical discourse drawing on social rationalizations inscribes Islam in the space of France and thus configures citizenship for Muslims.

I understand ethics here, drawing on Foucault, as one part of "morality" (Foucault 1990: 25–8). Different meanings of morality need to be distinguished. Morality can refer, first, to the "moral code," i.e., "a set of values and rules of action that are recommended to individuals through the intermediary of various prescriptive agencies." It also refers to the "real behavior of individuals in relation to the rules and values that are recommended to them." Finally, it can refer to what is called ethics, my focus here, "the manner in which one ought to 'conduct oneself' – that is, the manner in which one ought to form oneself as an ethical subject acting in reference to the prescriptive elements that make up the code." Ethics, then, presupposes a distinction between the agent and the ethical subject of an action.

In this last respect, Foucault emphasizes, four dimensions of how individuals constitute themselves as ethical subjects can be distinguished: the ethical substance, i.e., "this or that part of himself" which the individual problematizes and constitutes "as the prime material of his moral conduct"; the mode of subjection, i.e., "the way in which the individual establishes his relation to the rule and recognizes himself as obliged to put it into practice"; the ethical work— or the techniques of the self—undertaken by the subject "not only in order to bring one's conduct into compliance with a given rule, but to attempt to transform oneself into the ethical subject of one's behavior"; and finally the telos, a certain "mode of being of the ethical subject." Here, the emphasis is not on the morality of the action itself, but on the moral dimension accruing to an act through "its circumstantial integration and by virtue of the place it occupies in a pattern of conduct" that "commits an individual, not only to other actions always in conformity with values and rules, but to a certain mode of being" (1990: 26ff.).

With regard to these four dimensions of self-cultivation, ethical discourses may diverge or converge. Here, my focus is on ethical discourses whose commonality is situated on the level of telos, a telos defined on the basis of social rationalizations. Briefly, my argument is that this kind of ethical discourse relies on social rationalization notably in the way it approaches and describes the problems and risks likely to be encountered by individuals in the *banlieue*. Its key link with the rationality of the social is a negative one in that the primary aim of this ethical discourse is to define the work on the self which a Muslim subject must undertake in order to transcend the forces of social determination. The aim is to render dysfunctional their effects which are deciphered by these authors by means of this rationality. On a general level then, this ethical discourse is concerned with the freedom of the individual, and this freedom is discursively delimited and debated by socially rationalizing the subjects' milieu as a power context.

The following three cases illustrate different examples of this ethical discourse. Their authors are members of a new generation of public intellectuals in the milieu of public Islam. Taken together, these cases illustrate a level of discourse on life in France, broadly speaking, which incorporates juridical reasoning, but to different degrees decenters it. This ethical discourse problematizes Muslim subjectivity in relation to adverse forces, and this implies, directly or not, that the power of Islam to overcome these forces is also more patently manifest. This problematization refers to different dimensions of subjecthood, and as the following analyses will make apparent, the authors discussed here differ on numerous points. What they share, first, is the aim of describing a kind of subject who is able to achieve positive freedom, i.e., able to overcome determining factors, be they internal or external. Their second, closely related, aim is to turn Muslims into citizens actively participating on an equal footing in the life of society. They diverge with regard not only to their elaboration of ethical work on the self, but also their different evaluations of the place of ethics in relation to Islamic normativity and in relation to active citizenship.

Spirituality and the Reform of One's Self

The first case I will discuss is that of Sofiane Meziani, a prolific writer and teacher from Lille. Meziani pursues a great number of activities within this milieu.

A founding member of the Lille branch of the student organization *Étudiants musulmans de France*, he teaches ethics there at the school created by the affiliate of the UOIF and also works at the institute associated with Al-Imane Mosque. He is a regular speaker at public events in the Lille region and elsewhere in France. Meziani has published many books, mostly short, which cover a broad range of topics and genres. They include a biography of the Prophet Muhammad for young readers,[1] two novels about young French who find their way to Islam and reorder their lives,[2] a work on the modern crisis of meaning,[3] and an essay on dysfunctional French democracy.[4] While Meziani's publications are in various genres and cover different topics, a transversal theme emerges, namely interrogations about the diverse effects of modernity's fundamental crisis and how to satisfy humanity's essential quest for meaning—and this is where ethics comes in. His first book, published in 2008, is an essay entitled *"L'islam entre cœur & intélligence"* ("Islam between Heart and Intellect") with the subtitle *"Un pas vers la réforme par un retour à l'essentiel"* ("A Step Toward Reform by Returning to Essentials").[5] Whereas this book offers a general introduction to Islam, Meziani's second book *"Réforme ta vie"* ("Reform Your Life") outlines a specific ethical practice.[6] In his first book, Meziani had already defined his distinctive position by contesting the usefulness of legal debates about Muslim citizenship in France. Rather, the question to ask is how to cultivate and maintain one's spirituality: "The crucial question today is not so much whether the laws of Islam are compatible with those of Western society. This question is outdated. Rather, the question to ask is how to preserve and intensify one's spirituality in the middle of modernity? How to live remembering God in a society which is cut off from Him?" (Meziane (*sic*) 2008: 41).

This shift away from normativity to spirituality is characteristic of Meziani's thought. This is not to say that he ignores or disregards Islamic normativity; in fact, he spent a year in Cairo studying, among other things, legal theory (*uṣūl al-fiqh*). Nor, as already indicated, does he shy away from politics. He is very much engrossed in French and international issues, publishes commentaries on political events in French Muslim websites *oumma.com* and *saphirnews.com*, and seeks to mobilize support for Palestine in Lille.[7] Ethics occupies a central place in his work and a central notion here is reform. This notion designates first of all the movement of an individual Muslim or a collective to achieve control of the self by working on it systematically. In his early work, a prominent keyword for the telos of this work on the self is "success." In a nutshell, it designates the ability *not* to be determined by the social milieu in which one lives, i.e., the ability to pursue one's way regardless of the surrounding social forces. On his website, Meziani has described himself as someone who, growing up in one of the "most infamous neighborhoods," has acquired and exercised this ability in his life:

> Like most of the youngsters living in these sensitive and marginalized zones, he could not avoid getting involved with crime during his youth. Although he grew up in a family where Islamic values were upheld and the respect of principles was sacred, Sofiane succumbed nevertheless to the temptations of the wild life. However, he soon caught himself from his terrible fall, the experience of which led him to help save and preserve the youth from this ruin which almost caused his perdition ...
>
> Since that time, his aim is clear: to nurture hope and provoke a positive rebirth among the young French of Muslim confession (2009c).

Just like in this account, the probabilistic forces of determination unleashed in this milieu are present in his writings, even if schematic. Delinquency, failure at school, and drugs are the most prominent effects of this social determinism:

> With regard to ethics, we cannot claim to be good models. Delinquency, drugs, robbery and all these scourges are mostly found among the youth of our community. We have to acknowledge this knowing that the source of these evils is in no way a religious one, since they are in absolute contradiction with Islamic principles (2009a: 69).

Meziani's approach to ethics has partly developed as a reflective intervention in the conditions of subject formation which characterize this milieu. On a fundamental level, the motives shaping this intervention are identical to those at work in the cases below. In all of them, a central concern is the relative weakness of Muslims, individual Muslims, and/or the collective of Muslims. In a social rationalization, this weakness of Muslims is defined negatively as being molded in one's conduct by social conditions specific to the milieu of the *banlieue*. The main motive is to acquire strength, more precisely the strength necessary to overcome relative determination by one's environment.

Meziani's reflections are similar to those of other voices in the milieu of public Islam with regard to his understanding of the politics of citizenship. Fundamentally, the public benefit or even the imperative of entwining citizenship with Muslim ethics is undisputed. While Meziani at times merely expresses his desire for the Republic to gain from Islam—"As devoted citizens, let us make our country benefit from our values and our ethics. Let us put our faith in the service of our citizenship"[8]—he is also very clear about the need for Muslim ethics to discipline youth in the *banlieue*:

The French State retreated in cowardly fashion from part of its territory, namely the so-called 'difficult neighborhoods'. Just as in the old days, France is divided in two: but rather than 'those at the top' and 'those at the bottom', we talk about the France of the *banlieues*. This France is regularly summoned to court by the judges, whereas the France of the affluent clings to its legal experts. We have come to believe that we can no longer expect politics to resolve these social problems. Rather, we need to draw on the principles and values of faith in order to reform behaviors and to take on this challenge that is so ignored and despised. In other words, we will ask religion to succeed where politics has failed! (2009a: 70).

In a later article, responding to the aforementioned study on Clichy-sous-Bois and Montfermeil directed by Gilles Kepel (2012),[9] Meziani again stressed the need for an Islamic educational investment in the "popular neighborhoods."[10] While not denying outright the "pertinence" of Kepel's study, he nevertheless disagrees with some of its conclusions. Notably, he objects to the claim that a turn to Islam is the "cause or symptom of social and geographic decline in certain neighborhoods." Things are more complex insofar as this turn relates to a much more fundamental existential malaise, generated by capitalist society, which pervades all of French society. Nevertheless, the case of Islam remains, to some degree, specific, given that one reason for educational investment is a desire to "avoid ... that youth in the course of their quest for meaning become easy prey for certain *rigoristes*."[11]

Overcoming social forces of determination is a common objective, but Meziani's reflections lend it broader and particular meaning, for he stresses the importance of choosing a way of living and an aim in life which match one's individuality. Whereas his second book provides practical advice about how to transcend the milieu, his novels (published later) narrate the stories of young Muslims, Safwan and Luciano, who live unhappy and morally reprehensible lives precisely because they are unable to present their authentic selves. In his first novel "*L'ambition du vainqueur. Un intinéraire au service de la réforme*" ("The Champion's Ambition: A Journey in the Service of Reform"),[12] the narrator characterizes the protagonist by saying that "[t]he path which he had embarked upon did not correspond to his personality."[13] Meziani also sets himself apart from other voices in the milieu of public Islam in that he has developed a precise vision of how believers can gain control over the self and acquire the strength for self-determination. In "*Réforme ta vie*," Meziani had outlined a seven-step program for Muslims seeking self-transformation. This program overlaps in some respects with more widely held positions in the milieu of public Islam, notably with regard to the role of knowledge. As Meziani writes: "Knowledge is our means of reform without which no change is possible. Knowledge allows you to clear the fog which prevents your spirit from discerning."[14] Evaluating the links between knowledge and obligatory Muslim practices, Meziani writes that "Everything started with science and not with prayer or fasting, because practice too needs a degree of understanding which is acquired through the search for knowledge."[15] More importantly, a second indispensable element of any reform and a main source of strength lies in the individual himself. A recurring feature of Meziani's thought is the idea that individual Muslims can decide, to some degree, who they want to be. For example, one dimension of reform is will, and the desirable aim is to be optimistic. This is seen by Meziani as a choice for a specific outlook on life and on one's own experiences: "Optimism consists in never giving up, however many and however bad the failures one experiences on the way. Such a person will be able to read and conceive of any ordeal in a positive manner."[16]

A keyword in this conception of human character is the term "ambition." The plot of "L'ambition du vainqueur" is crucially structured by the emergence, in the mind of the protagonist, of an ambition, i.e., the orientation of his will towards achieving a specific aim. Drawing on *The Alchemist* by Paulo Coelho, ambition is described as being driven by the will and indeed the necessity "to realize a personal legend": "He had fixed an aim in his head, and his will to win suppressed all psychological barriers which posed obstacles. Success is more a question of will than of effort. Success is reserved for those who want it, who have the will."[17] The frequent reference to psychological and self-help literature in this novel is emblematic for how self-formation is imagined as a process of reflection and introspection that allows the individual to reshape themselves. Thus, in the case of Safwan, ambition replaces the psychological "pattern" of failure, defined as an "auto-destructive mechanism deforming reality."[18] Having said this, in the programmatic essay "*Réforme ta vie*," the most central element on the individual path toward a new self is what he calls spirituality, and more particularly prayer. As Meziani puts it, this path is possible "only if it is animated by the consciousness that you have of the divine presence."[19] Meziani emphasizes strongly that worship is a source of "energy and light" for Muslims.[20] In particular, praying is a means to overcoming difficulties: "The believer communicates his frailties and weakness to God, who will give him hope, confidence and internal peace. Prayer keeps us away from bad actions, '*keep up the prayer: prayer restrains outrageous and unacceptable behavior*' (29/45)" (Meziane 2008: 48f.; emphasis in the original).

Praying is also the main source of power which allows some individuals to perform extraordinary actions: "Praying in the middle of the night was the secret of all the great men who marked the history of Islam, first among them Muhammad, God's messenger. (...) It [praying at night] is also a means to find power and energy. In fact, all great reformers, like Hasân al-Bannâ, drew their strength, their energy and above all their ever-lasting love from praying at night."[21] With regard to prayer, Meziani takes care to emphasize that the contemplation of the heart takes precedence over the correct execution of the gestural sequences which constitute and structure prayer. Likewise, he affirms the predominance of a "deep comprehension" of the Qur'an before its memorization.[22]

Muslims Contributing to Human Civilization

While Meziani's work is inscribed into a perspective where the key to change is spirituality, Mohamed Ramousi, our second case, manifests a very different approach to how Muslim citizenship can be fully realized or, in his words, how Muslims can contribute to the universal project of advancing the civilization of humans. In brief, unlike Meziani, who declared this topic outdated, Ramousi grants considerable attention to legal questions associated with Muslim citizenship.[23] Ramousi is fundamentally ambivalent about this debate in the sense that he simultaneously engages certain aspects of it while denying these questions the very right to be debated. This is because the *fiqh* debate about citizenship continues to be bound up with the question of whether or not Muslims can be citizens. As I shall show, this ambivalence about the legal debate on Muslim citizenship is part of a general feature of Ramousi's thinking. On the one hand, adopting a totalistic perspective, he conceives that citizenship for Muslims is already given and indisputable; on the other, he is obliged to acknowledge, repeatedly, that the right to citizenship of Muslims is to different degrees doubted and contested on multiple sides, including by Muslims. This is where social rationalizations of Muslim practices—their identity and tendency to "imitation" (*taqlīd*)—come into play. As in the previous case, the general aim is self-mastery, i.e., to cease being an object of social determination. More specific aims are full identification with civic identity and, ultimately, an active citizenship whose contribution is defined in terms of civilizing humans.

Ramousi, who is from Wallonia, graduated from the IESH in Château-Chinon, works as a teacher of Islamic sciences in Belgium, and is the author of a number of works dealing with comparative *fiqh* of acts of worship and Qur'anic exegesis. In 2012, Ramousi published his first book, *La citoyenneté: clef d'une contribution civilisationnelle des musulmans d'Europe* (Citizenship: Key to a Civilizational

Contribution by European Muslims). It is here that Ramousi, with a geographic focus on France and Belgium, elaborates in systematic detail his perspective on Muslim citizenship. As I said, much of the book is devoted to addressing a number of controversial questions associated with Islam in Europe that have been central to *fiqh* debates for a long time. Thus, Ramousi examines whether democracy can be reconciled with the notion of God's sovereignty, he considers the "delicate matter" of political participation in a "non-Islamic government," and he attempts to clarify the notion of *al-walā' wa-l-barā'*— translatable as loyalty to God and other Muslims and disavowal of anything un-Islamic[24]—which is central to all those who regard Muslim political participation as illegitimate. Here, as elsewhere, Ramousi engages key notions of Salafi thought; he does not, however, name the proponents of the positions he criticizes. While he exerts a considerable effort to engage with legal debates, Ramousi is not arguing that the debate about the (il)legality of Muslim citizenship should be continued. On the contrary. This is apparent from the very first page, when he announces that his basic approach assumes Muslim citizenship "as a given."[25] Not surprisingly, Ramousi is critical of the term "integration." Examining usages of the word, he argues that it designates "moving from one place to another, ... implying adaptation." Referring to contemporary young people, he points out that they did not and do not move; they are "sociologically different from those who have just arrived from Morocco or Senegal." Instead of integration, he finds the term "inclusion" more appropriate when it comes to those born here.[26]

Very soon, however, he is obliged to acknowledge the contested status of citizenship and, even if implicitly, the diverse sources of power which render citizenship efficient. These contestations, coming from different sides, are simultaneously acknowledged and derided. When referring to (unidentified) Muslim critiques of citizenship, they are scornfully dismissed. Ramousi notes that he is obliged to take account of the "Kafkaesque position" of those "categorically rejecting any citizen discourse" and declaring illicit the residence of Muslims in Europe—without leaving the continent, however.[27] In Ramousi's view, addressing such questions is part of a much broader and ongoing project, namely the necessary elaboration of a "referenced theological discourse"[28] in Europe. This approach is shared by a large section of the Union, where there is a widespread idea that the dissemination of more "radical" practices of Islam derives from mere ignorance.[29] Ramousi accordingly argues that among those who reject Muslim discourses of citizenship "there are rarely any with a recognized theological education."[30] The net result of this intra-Muslim criticism is difficult to evaluate. On the one hand, Ramousi and others not only criticize divergent positions, but devalue them as ignorant. On the other, the fact that at least some of these positions are constantly rehearsed and debated at length and in considerable detail not only gives them public space but de facto recognizes them as an element of scholarly debate.

While Ramousi discusses legal issues about citizenship, he is keen to transcend debates about citizenship in order to think about the "role" of Muslims in society. He sees this role as a "civilizational" one, the term "civilized" being understood by Ramousi as designating a superior state of evolution. Its opposite is the absence of self-mastery, i.e., being the object of one's "primitive instincts," which renders any evolution impossible.[31] This civilizing role acquires concrete shape in Muslim activism based on spirituality and ethics oriented toward justice, honesty, respect for the other, and protection of the environment.[32] Ramousi argues that he offers Muslims a new starting point for reflecting upon their societal role: "Working for justice means accepting a qualitatively new philosophical point of departure which allows Muslim thought to recharge, to move on from debates like the one about establishing the caliphate (...)."[33]

Now, as I said, Ramousi's aim to start a debate about the constructive role of Muslims in society is threatened by various forces who undermine the apparent evidence of Muslim incorporation into the nation. Ramousi describes the condition which he seeks to transcend as that of the "eternal allochthonous,"[34] i.e., an individual defined by the ineffaceable relation between Muslimness and foreignness. He analyzes this condition as the effect of various mechanisms: Certain Muslim and racist discourses play their part, as does the "sociological reality" to which he draws attention, i.e., the "real and/or psychological ghettoization which occurred in history" to the first generation of immigrants and "has marginalized the following generations until today."[35]

It is important to underline that Ramousi does not easily accept the idea that "sociological reality," by which I mean here the relatively particular position of Muslims, determines Muslim identities in this manner. More generally, he does not easily accept the fact that social differences matter. At times, his argumentation is thus very much indebted to a liberal imaginary in which the category "religion" is understood to be fixed, bounded, and fully separate from other social fields. From this perspective, "religion" is subtracted from any kind of power struggle and can be combined—in an identical manner and notwithstanding the particularity of a given religious tradition—with citizenship in any country. Belgian Muslims simply constitute a religious group like any other in Belgium: "There is also a worldwide Christian community without their adherents being considered less French or less Belgian."[36] Ramousi is therefore astonished to note that some exclude Muslims as Muslims from the national community, unlike other social groups with a more recent history of migration.[37] Ramousi's underlying assumptions here are, first, a system of separations, and second, the endless flexibility and utter emptiness of national cultures and identities. On this basis, Ramousi asserts that identity is not determined once and for all: "Identity is not the object of any determinism! It changes."[38] Thus, "diversity is possible, compatible, natural, inevitable, without compromising citizenship."[39]

Ramousi clearly remains attached to an imaginary—which he continuously seeks to reassert as self-evidently normative—in which social groups are divided into neatly bounded categories and the law ensures their equality. Nevertheless, his study incorporates a variety of sometimes elaborate reflections on mechanisms which disrupt the equality of Muslims and ghettoize them. These reflections are not limited to the rejection of Muslims by hegemonic opinion or the phenomenon of Islamophobia. A long chapter is devoted to a critical examination of the influence of foreign countries on European Islam. Ramousi writes, "Maghrebi paternalism and Saudi influence are an obstacle to the emancipation of European Muslim thought, and simultaneously they to some extent prevent the definition of European Muslim identity."[40] Secondly, Ramousi sets out to examine how European Muslims are themselves contributing to their exclusion from full citizenship. Ramousi's fundamental conviction is that "Muslims are full citizens and need to define themselves,"[41] but he is obliged to recognize that this perspective is far from shared by other Muslims, who are trapped in different modes of "imitation." On the one hand, there are those who claim that Muslims should follow the examples set by Muslim countries; on the other, there are those who prefer to follow models of European countries.[42]

Ramousi's take on this issue is both "theological," i.e., on the level of *fiqh*, and also argued with reference to the "social perspective."[43] After concluding that imitation (*taqlīd*) itself can be criticized within the Islamic tradition, Ramousi turns to the social dimension and examines mechanisms of imitation. The social context in which imitation is conducted is modelled, generally, as a relation between dominant and dominated, the latter naturally tending to imitate the former.[44] This position is rejected by Ramousi who, drawing on Ibn Khaldun, argues that the position of the dominated is explained *not* so much by the qualities of the dominant, but rather by the weak performance of the dominated themselves. As this performance is capable of improvement, the solution is not imitation, but rather "work upon oneself to change and evolve."[45] This work upon one's self should be directed by Islamic spirituality, and more precisely oriented toward imitating the Prophet. Ramousi is fully aware that there are further obstacles inhibiting this kind of work, above all an "inferiority complex" which is inherited and reactuated in relation to the white "ex-civilizer."[46] He offers various illustrations of the impact this inferiority complex continues to have on Muslims today: admiration for converts (*"he is purged of any genetic impotency because not born Muslim"*—159; emphasis in the original), glorification of "marriage to a converted woman," the constant jokes perpetuating ethnic prejudices or, by inversion, total rejection of the dominant model, as practiced by, for example, the Nation of Islam or those Muslims who seek to fashion themselves according to a model "which is as opposite as possible to those whom they seek to 'confront'." [47] Ramousi's point of departure is the notion that human characters are not given, but emerge and consolidate in a specific situation. Since individuals are personally responsible for maintaining (or altering) this situation, they are indirectly "the principal architect" of their own character, and this, in Ramousi's view, creates a "positive perspective" for tackling the inferiority complex.[48] The key to resolving this problem lies unambiguously on the level of "thought" and "self-perception"; the aim is to attribute fresh value to identities which have been devalued, often through colonialism.[49] Ramousi stresses the potential for tackling this inferiority complex. Citing the psychologist Alfred Adler, he recalls that the work of compensation triggered by an inferiority complex can trigger the emergence of genius, "and in this respect we find the model very interesting."[50]

Ramousi's concern with and his conceptualization of "imitation" practiced by Muslims is to some degree unique. However, the fundamental question around which his reflections circle is not specific to his approach. It is a question about the link between the positive freedom achieved by individual Muslims and the rejection of Muslims by the society in which they live. What links might there be between the fact that Muslims do not obtain full self-mastery, i.e., remain unduly objects of social determination, and the state of those societies where Muslims are exposed to rejection? Briefly, this question induces a politically charged redefinition and extension of the "responsibilities" of Muslims. It is not a question that Ramousi formalizes. Other authors in this milieu have approached this topic in a more explicit manner, as the last case, Farid Abdelkrim, will illustrate.

"Damn France?!" Shifting Perceptions of Social Determination

Farid Abdelkrim is from Nantes. He presents himself as an "author, comedian, producer [and] ex-president of Young Muslims of France."[51] Abdelkrim has a long career working in Muslim associations. Until 2006 he was an active member of the Union. He was a founding member of its youth organization and served on the Union's executive board. During this time, he was one of the most prominent voices of the so-called second-generation Muslims and one whose numerous activities provided him with multiple audiences. Abdelkrim has authored several books. The first, partly autobiographical, is an essay called *Na'al bou la France?!* ("Damn France?!"), which appeared in 2002.[52] In the same year, he published a self-help book for young people about "hidden realities" of Islam and sex.[53] This was followed in 2005 by a series of vignettes on the state of Islam in France called *La France des islams. Ils sont fous ces musulmans?!* ("The France of Islams: These Muslims are crazy?!").[54] In addition to this, he has edited and translated a selection of invocations compiled by Hasan al-Banna, has written comic scenarios for children, and has been performing as a comedian in one-man shows and producing video clips. In 2015, Abdelkrim published a book titled *Pourquoi j'ai cessé d'être islamiste* (Why I Stopped Being an Islamist), in which he described at length his experience in the UOIF.[55] The book is noteworthy largely because of the public criticism Abdelkrim levelled at the Union. While some of the criticism voiced here and in later publications was perhaps only of limited interest to the general public, Abdelkrim did associate his erstwhile companions with processes of "radicalization" and pointed to "troubling similarities" between the Muslim Brothers and the Islamic State with regard to the notion of the caliphate.[56] The book also articulates a more general revision of his earlier views on life in France as a French citizen. When it comes to rationalizing the French context and defining the ethics of citizenship, Abdelkrim has thus provided two visions which in many ways are strikingly different.

Na'al bou la France?! is written in a conversational tone, typical for all of Abdelkrim's writings, and addressed to young Muslims. A short book, it is composed of a long sequence of short chapters recording the author's fast-moving snapshots from the Muslim community, social debates, and personal life. These reflections begin with a biographical sketch centering on how Abdelkrim became a Muslim and how this turn to Islam in fact changed his life. This story is essential to the book, in that the ethical advice which Abdelkrim offers his readers is closely related to and validated by his experience. Note that Abdelkrim seeks to reject the role of a spokesperson for a specific social group; the blurb on the cover reads: "I do not pretend to be representative of whomsoever, or to be an example," only to add, four lines later, that the book is written "with the conviction that some will recognize themselves in certain passages of this book,"⁵⁷ and these readers are the targets of Abdelkrim's frequent exhortations that they should change their way of life.⁵⁸

The question of how individuality relates to broad processes and discursive structures is central to the entire book. In brief, the message Abdelkrim seeks to convey concerns the way in which young Muslims perceive and represent to themselves the conditions of their life in France and the options available to them. In this respect, Abdelkrim oscillates between two modes of rationalizing Muslim lives. On the one hand, the entire book strongly relies upon social rationalizations and narrates how individuals are determined in relatively predictable ways by their milieu, characterized by multiple forms of discrimination, and thus become certain kinds of subjects—subjects who, as the title of the book indicates, may turn away from France. Likewise, the depiction of delinquency as relative normality is founded on the notion that what is normal is bound up with the general conditions of life of a milieu, here the *banlieue*. This reliance upon the rationality of the social is crucial for making sense of Abdelkrim's narrative and not least for the author's hope, indicated above, that others will recognize themselves in his writings. It is, in part, his social rationalization of Islam which allows him to formulate an intelligible narrative. On the other, Abdelkrim again and again emphasizes the potential for transforming this context. In brief, he insists on the difference that Islam and being Muslim can and, indeed, must make. This difference that Islam can make is played out primarily on the level of the individual. Abdelkrim quotes the Quranic verse "God does not change the condition of a people [for the worse] unless they change what is in themselves" (Qur'an 13:11) to conclude a long exhortation, reiterated many times throughout the book, reminding young Muslims that each and every one of them can be an agent of change.⁵⁹ Abdelkrim's narrative relies upon the social rationalization of the subjectivities of young French suburbanites while simultaneously arguing that every single individual can drop out of this context and choose to fashion himself in a different way: "Islam will help you to open your eyes. Yeah! And even if you do not become a tiger, at least you will avoid becoming a jackal."⁶⁰

The kind of Muslim subject envisioned by Abdelkrim is identified in condensed form as a *citoyen à part entière*, i.e., a citizen who exercises their rights and obligations fully, and most importantly, who is not shy to state their demands for justice, which are summarized in a list at the end of the book. In brief, this is a citizen who can no longer be ignored and who is able to mount a real Muslim lobby.⁶¹ That Muslims can and must act and become active citizens is argued repeatedly throughout the book in different ways. Abdelkrim's call to his readers to become active is presented as feasible with reference to the somewhat abrupt claim, made in the middle of the book, that social reality is complex and shifting. After devoting dozens of pages to manifestations of hostility toward Muslims, Abdelkrim states that "we see glimmers on the horizon of the mutual acceptance which will impose itself."[62] Rejecting "unilateral visions" of the causes shaping the condition of French Muslims, Abdelkrim urges his readers to assume their responsibilities.[63] As in the case of Meziani and Ramousi, the emphasis here is on will, determination, and faith. Abdelkrim also quotes from Hasan al-Banna, who begins his "Epistle to Youth" by declaring that an idea becomes reality if the belief in it is strong enough.[64] More than feasibility, it is the obligation to act which is emphasized. It derives from a whole web of other obligations identified by Abdelkrim. He refers to the obligation toward God, "expecting from you that you strive towards perfection,"[65] toward "the old": "Yes, you have to succeed because you have a debt towards the old. They consented to make so many efforts for you. The amount on the bill is the sum of their suffering and sacrifice."[66] Finally, he invokes the general obligation toward the community: "Do you think that it is enough to get out on your own to find peace. No! Because as a young Muslim, it is your responsibility not to be stingy with the favors that have been showered upon you. You belong to a community, do not forget to whom you are joined."[67] The pivotal justification for this exhortation to act, however, is that a way of acting implies a way of being. It is here that the normative obligation and the criterion of feasibility are reconciled and coherence can be achieved by the individual. Acting in the way he describes both presupposes and induces a specific mode of being, one that is immanently positive and, indeed, the only one which preserves or even restores the individual's dignity. Hence, after asking rhetorically how much a person can actually shape their own life and society in general, he asks his readers: "At this price – a total inability to shape the course of your life – don't you ever wonder if life is really worth living?"[68] This "illusory comfort" comes at the price of dignity.[69] The way out of this situation is prefigured, according to Abdelkrim, by those who have chosen "with conviction and pride the old proverb which says 'It is better to live one day as a tiger than 100 days like a jackal.'"[70]

It is apparent from the above analysis that Abdelkrim's advocacy for Muslim citizenship is not simply an Islamic plea for the legitimacy of the French legal order. Rather, it is a text describing how one can become a Muslim citizen of France in a particular context, which in its broad outlines is deciphered through the rationality of the social. Abdelkrim's text designates the mode of being which is particular to the subject position of a Muslim citizen. This subject position is circumscribed by its constituent reference to the French legal order and at the same time by the fact of its precarious efficiency with regard to Muslims. Abdelkrim outlines what kind of character traits "young Muslims" should cultivate in order to be able to relate to this legal order in all its uncertainty: sense of responsibility, conviction, determination, pride, and a sense of belonging to the community of Muslims are essential attributes. By doing this, Abdelkrim describes a mode of self-government which politicizes Muslim identity and simultaneously subtracts fundamental structures of French society from this process. While the scope of injustices to which Muslims are submitted is set out at length—the precarious status of legal equality and equal freedom being a central condition of his ethical reflection—and while Muslims are called upon to commit themselves to changing this context, criticism is, in fact, levelled primarily at Muslims themselves for their inactivity.[71]

In his later writings, however, this concern with the ethics of citizenship gives way to a critique of Islamism and, more generally, to an inquiry into factors internal to Muslim communities which constitute obstacles to the emergence of "Islam of France."[72] The reference to the well-worn notion "Islam of France" is not coincidental. At the most basic level, Abdelkrim's later texts propose a new perspective on the necessary and desirable conditions for rooting Islam in France while at the same time rigorously questioning, as a former insider, the Union's claim to be working toward this aim. As he explains in *Pourquoi j'ai cessé d'être islamiste*, he now believes that "the Islamist approach of religion constitutes undoubtedly a real obstacle" to the social and cultural adaptation of Islam to the French context.[73]

This is not to say that the book is framed as a full-blown critique of political Islam. While Abdelkrim is disconcerted about the effects of the Union's binary worldview and their exclusivist claim to truth, he also acknowledges the accomplishments of "the organization of the *Brothers*," i.e., building mosques, and seeking to organize the representation of Islam and to provide association-based structures for young Muslims. Moreover, part of his criticism of the Union is aimed simply at general organizational features, i.e., the absence of critical internal debates, or the dearth of qualified human resources combined with a certain lack of self-reflection among the Union's leaders. The latter, in Abdelkrim's view, fail to fully realize that they are overwhelmed by the tasks which are theirs and unable—with the exception of Tareq Oubrou—to produce anything but superficial discourse.[74] "God is practically not invoked anymore. He is ignored. Obscured. Replaced by the religion everybody talks about."[75] The blatant disrespect for the separation of politics and religion, to which state institutions and politicians greatly contribute, is identified as a major obstacle to incorporating Islam into France.⁷⁶ Equally important to the confusion between politics and religion as an object of critique is the confusion between culture and religion, i.e., Arab and Muslim identity. The hegemonic status of Arabic in the Union and in many French Muslim communities is a favorite target for Abdelkrim, who contrasts this with other Muslim associations and authorities where interaction with the French context is more comprehensive.

In the course of this critique, Abdelkrim repeatedly considers how to describe, in general terms, the social context of France as experienced by Muslims. In particular, he addresses the question which slowly made its way onto the public agenda in the course of the 2010s: Is France "a resolutely anti-Islam country," as he pointedly puts it.⁷⁷ Abdelkrim attacks variations on this claim from a number of angles. In this respect, the entire book is marked by constant attempts to disrupt (negative) stereotypical readings of the French context: "Complexity characterizes any society and all those who constitute it."⁷⁸ Whereas Abdelkrim used to produce anecdotes and dialogues to flag a general state of affairs, now he chides those who use "snapshots" to describe the social context for obscuring the broader picture and focusing attention on negative "clichés."⁷⁹ Abdelkrim does not deny the existence of "injustices." However, he does seek to conciliate ("the situation seems to me far from being that somber and tragic") and to spread optimism, in contrast to the "prophets of the apocalypse" who declare "all of France" to be racist, or—and Abdelkrim puts this word in quotation marks—Islamophobic.⁸⁰ Importantly, Abdelkrim insists that these "prophets" have no authority to speak for Muslims, whose "silent and discreet majority" do not support such activism and "most often ignore it." ⁸¹

To match this criticism, Abdelkrim sets out to narrate his biography a second time. Whereas his narrative from the previous decade was solidly situated in France, and the Algeria of his parents was mentioned only in relation to historical and political issues, it now appears as the place of an early "brief conversion" which prepares his later turn to Islam;⁸² the description of his family's biannual sojourns on the southern shore leads him to reject the well-known cliché of being "neither from here nor there": "As far as I am concerned, and as far as my memory allows me to say, I felt I was both from here and from there."⁸³ Whereas the first narrative simply assumed a distinction between "us"—immigrants—and "them," Abdelkrim now dwells on the years before he "started to consider himself an 'Arab.'"⁸⁴ He explains the phase after his father's death, when he reconfigured his social milieu on an ethnic basis and drifted into delinquency, as the result of an "unfortunate conjunction of events" which fundamentally had to do with "a lot of ignorance" on the part of all concerned.[85] These and other revisions obviously do not allow Abdelkrim to brush aside all those elements he once used to construct visions of a divided—racist or Islamophobic—France. However, by resolutely focusing on the individual level, Abdelkrim can shift attention to the relative contingency inherent in his trajectory and the diversity of ways in which other French interacted with him. This, he claims, opens up a new take on "immigration and the so-called problems of integration": "This is good to know. To understand. And to explain. Secure from crude perspectives hastily cobbled together."[86]

Conclusion

This chapter has examined a specific kind of ethical discourse addressed to Muslims in the milieu of public Islam. This discourse, I have argued, is primarily an attempt to define the conditions of subjectivity which enable Muslims to achieve positive freedom, i.e., self-mastery. To a significant degree, these conditions are defined by relying, albeit in a negative way, upon the rationality of the social. Social rationalization offers one means to relate subject formation on the one hand and (self-)government on the other. It permits a definition of the conditions of subject formation and more particularly the power effects of social determination and, *ex negativo*, of the kind of subject able to overcome them. The analysis has thus identified a distinct level of discourse where an effort is undertaken to adapt Muslim discourse to the so-called context of France. This process of adaptation thus takes place not only on the level of normativity, but also on that of the practices comprised by work on the self and its telos. The analysis of ethics is important, since it is part and parcel of the discourse on the citizenship of Muslims. In this respect, the analysis has, first, opened up a new perspective on the fragmentation of discourse in this milieu, which concerns notably the place of law in debates about citizenship. Second and more fundamentally, it has highlighted a shared feature. The perspective on citizenship is broadened beyond normative assessments of the context to include the question of how (the experience of) this context can be changed, i.e., how to become the kind of person who is able as a Muslim to assume civic rights and obligations.

6

"The History of Some is not the History of Others"

Introduction

December 2, 2005 marked the 200th anniversary of the battle of Austerlitz (in today's Czech Republic), where the French army under the leadership of Napoleon I won a decisive victory over Russia and Austria. On the French side, the commemoration turned out to be a complex matter. In fact, it was no secret that the government hesitated and ultimately did not participate prominently in celebrating what is sometimes considered the most glorious battle fought by the emperor.[1] The reason for the cautious—or, as some felt, foolish—attitude had to do with a controversy about Napoleon Bonaparte which erupted shortly before the anniversary. In a publication titled *Le crime de Napoléon* (Napoleon's Crimes), Claude Ribbe, a writer and filmmaker, had publicized the widely ignored fact that Napoleon Bonaparte had reestablished slavery in the colonies in 1802, after its abolition throughout the empire by the National Convention in 1794.[2] It was finally abolished in 1848 under the Second Republic. Moreover, in his attempt to recover direct political control over Saint-Domingue—soon to be independent Haiti—the French expeditionary corps sent on Bonaparte's orders had, according to Ribbe, perpetrated "genocidal" massacres; the methods used, Ribbe claimed, prefigured the "politics of extermination" of Jews and *Tsiganes* during the Second World War. Ribbe's verdict was unambiguous: "Napoleon, unfortunately, is indeed a criminal; and of the worst kind" (2005: 12).[3]

Ribbe's book triggered multiple reactions. While the tonality of the book was often criticized, the facts he reported could not easily be dismissed and gave additional weight to questions which had become central to French public debates in the early 2000s. One of these questions stems from the impossibility of reconciling the reintroduction of slavery by the First Consul of the Republic with the latter's fundamental principles of liberty and equality.[4] Napoleon's act disjoined state power from the underlying principles of its law. Importantly, this disjuncture between the law and the exercise of power is recognizable in other parts of French colonial history, too.[5] What does this discrepancy indicate about the Republic and its aspiration to embody universal principles? Does this discrepancy affect its claims to legitimacy and how? One answer to this double question was given in early 2005 by a newly created small, but influential postcolonial movement, *Indigènes de la République* (Natives of the Republic).[6] In its foundational text, the "Republic of equality" is declared to be a "myth" and the "colonial past-present" of France is brought to the fore. Referring to fields such as employment, housing, health, education, or judiciary, the authors claim that the French republic in its dealings with postcolonial French continues colonial policies, even if state actions cannot be reduced to these policies.[7]

A second question relates to how acts of commemoration define the parameters of belonging to the nation, how they unite or divide the national community, and recognize or negate the existence of particular social groups in its fold. As the media reported demonstrations by associations of French citizens from overseas territories against the "glorification" of Napoleon and the foundation of a *Conseil représentatif des associations noires* (Representative Council of Black Associations, or CRAN), Austerlitz raised a question about how a leader whose policy was to divide the French should figure in national memory. Given the historical division of the nation, what about the legitimate place of particular identities in the official memory of present France, where the recognition of any identity other than national identity is often rejected as pernicious fragmentation of the country (*communautarisme*)?[8]

These questions were vociferously debated. An indicator of their intensity is an op-ed penned by Pierre Nora, internationally renowned historian, publisher at Éditions Gallimard, and member of the Académie Française, in response to the government's handling of this matter (Nora 2005a).[9] In this polemical text, whose title "In defense of the natives (*indigènes*) of Austerlitz" alluded to the postcolonial *Indigènes de la République*, Nora tried to come to terms with the altered power context of the politics of commemoration.[10] Indeed, Nora's work had contributed greatly in the 1980s to shaping public interest in memory in France. Through the publication of the multivolume *Les Lieux de mémoire* (Sites of Memory), which in more than a hundred entries, incidentally, does not offer anything on Napoleon or his battles, Nora provided the "vocabulary and grammar" for booming commemorative practices (Valensi 1995: 1272).[11] Now, a "nobody" like Ribbe, author of a "confused" pamphlet, had seemingly managed to evict Austerlitz from official French memory. As Nora made clear, Austerlitz has an essential place in French history.[12] In his critique of the state-engineered occultation of Austerlitz's memory, Nora tried to portray the entire controversy as ridiculous (a "farce"), the outcome of a mixture of ignorance and political opportunism. However, Nora's intervention in the controversy also unwittingly showed how difficult it is to disrupt and disable the logic of a moral critique of history which had led the government to avoid celebrating Austerlitz. In fact, his critique can hardly be distinguished in some places from Claude Ribbe's position. In the conclusion, Nora becomes almost a contributor to the revision of French history when he suggests removing Napoleon's tomb and replacing it with a monument dedicated to the Unknown Slave. What Nora intended as an ironic suggestion to expose the absurdity of morally judging the past and interpreting it with contemporary frames was welcomed some days later by Claude Ribbe, who found the idea of a monument honoring slaves excellent.

The controversy about Napoleon is but one moment of a broader process, closely linked with debates about French colonial history that gradually took off in the 1990s. These debates altered the conditions for self-representation of the Republic through history (Bancel et al. 2003; Blanchard et al. 2005; Bancel et al. 2010).[13] In this context, Ribbe's account of Napoleon's crimes functions as one of many counter-histories of France. Counter-histories, as Foucault used the term, reject "[t]he postulate that the history of great men contains, a fortiori, the history of lesser men, or that the history of the strong is also the history of the weak." Counter-histories introduce instead "a principle of heterogeneity: The history of some is not the history of others" (2003: 69). Counter-histories undo the unity of the nation as it is constructed in historical narrations, they interrogate how the exercise of power relates to principles of legality and legitimacy, and, more generally, they problematize positivist assumptions about historical truth and bring to the fore questions of interpretation and representation. In all these ways, they provide potential points of challenge to the state's claim to neutrality.

Counter-histories make manifest the political potency of historical knowledge and both the importance and difficulty for the state to control it.[14] Historical narratives can support or subvert the state's account of itself (Citron 1987), and they also can play a crucial role in (re)describing the identity of the population and structures of power. The introduction of the term "*indigène*" as a name for postcolonial immigrants and descendants, mentioned above, is but one example for how a new perspective and vocabulary to discuss politics and the logics of social power in France can be forged; other examples from extreme-right milieus can be added (see below).

This chapter examines how history's potential to act as a principle of heterogeneity has unfolded in France, helping to reconfigure the Republic and redefine conditions for debating citizenship of Muslims and the place of Islam in the public sphere. More particularly, it will show how Muslims are identified as a relatively distinct memory collective inside the French population. This enacted a new kind of entwinement of France and Islam whose contours and conditions are debated among Muslim actors. The writing of French history is becoming a new condition for Muslim subjectivity; this subjectivity is now interlacing with another political rationality and with the power struggles about legitimate and desirable modalities of Frenchness which it enables. As in the previous chapter, the analysis will emphasize how the emergence of constituent models—here, "memory"—changes the basic terms of debate and government; it creates both the possibility and the contentious need for governmental action.

Beyond the Unitary Regime of Memory

The starting point for Claude Ribbe's critical account of Napoleon is a plural vision of France. His critique is grounded in his concern for French overseas territories whose inhabitants constitute, according to him, a distinct group of citizens of subaltern status for whom the history of Napoleon matters in particular ways (Ribbe 2005). While cultural pluralism has a problematic status in most understandings of the Republican order, a number of more recent changes have facilitated the official recognition of particular identities and thus decentered unitary conceptions of France.[15] In the context of this discussion, two issues— related to diversity and memory—need to be mentioned.

Since the 1990s, references to the term diversity have become frequent in French politics, notably in relation to efforts at countering discrimination (Doytcheva 2010; Lantheaume 2011). The redescription of France as diverse is, however, contested, as indicated, for example, by the failure to approve President Sarkozy's proposed amendment to the preamble to the Constitution with a reference to "respect for diversity." Moreover, the notoriously polyvalent term "diversity" is used in different ways. This also applies to the state education system, where the elements constituting what is named diversity vary, just as in other spheres of society. Having said this, the introduction of the term certainly reconfigures various practices by state institutions based on the idea of the abstract universal citizen. Thus, the notion of diversity, as used by the state education system, reshapes expectations of teachers, who are now called upon to take various forms of diversity into account. An incitement has been created to perceive students in relation to their "cultural origin." The construction of a shared culture is now premised upon the "cultural and religious diversity of France" (Lantheaume 2011).

In the teaching of history more particularly, successive revisions of national history programs reflect, in different ways, an increasing recognition that multiculturalism matters: "The struggles against discriminations and for diversity have become constitutive elements of educational policies in all member states of the European Union" (De Cock 2015: 249). Since the late 1980s, the important role of history classes in meeting the purposes of integration policies has been recognized (Lorcerie 1991), with controversial debate about who is to integrate into what. In the course of the 1980s, "new memorial injunctions" started to determine the writing of history programs, and since the 2000s the range of actors involved in the process has widened; the education ministry increasingly receives applications from various groups seeking to integrate their histories into the program (Legris 2010: 499). School curricula have been revamped within a more plural vision of the history of France; however, this process is slow, contested, and, as de Cock argues, not linear (2015: 278). As for the teaching of colonial history, De Cock dates the emergence of "significant changes" "which allow the study of the colonial situation and memory controversies (*enjeux de memoire*)" to 2008 (*collège*) and 2010–12 (*lycée*) (2018: 283; see also Nef 2017). Islam as a civilization and religion had integrated as compulsory material in history programs since 1957. However, in the late 1980s it still occupied "a limited place, all in all hardly less limited than the other important religious phenomena" and confined to non-European contexts (Lorcerie 1991). This situation has partly changed. Since the 2000s, against the background of long-standing, widespread concerns about the religious ignorance of young French, religious phenomena have been granted increasing space in teachers' training and in teaching in schools across all subject matters (Carpentier 2004).

As far as official acts of commemoration are concerned, the starting point for the pluralization of national memory, amid a proliferation of local memories and processes of patrimonialization, can be roughly dated to the 1980s.[16] This process of change is closely associated with the notion of a *devoir de mémoire* (duty to remember), a moral injunction widely promoted in France in the 1990s that helped to legitimate a critical and problematic revision of national history (Lalieu 2001; Ledoux 2013a).[17] Johann Michel has analyzed this fragmentation of national memory in terms of the partial and contested transcendence of the "memorial regime of national unity" which since the 1980s has coexisted, often uneasily, with the "Shoa memorial regime of victimhood" (*régime victimo-mémoriel de la Shoah*) (Michel 2011). This memorial regime is defined by the integration of the Holocaust into national memory and, more generally, the revision of perceptions about the Vichy regime (1940-4) and French resistance to the German occupation.[18] Importantly, it pluralizes French memory by recognizing distinct memory groups among the French. At the same time, commemoration shifts from honoring those who died *for* France to those who are, more or less explicitly, presented as victims *of* the state (either the French state or a foreign state). Importantly, Michel argues that the "Shoa memorial regime of victimhood" serves also as a "matrix" for various groups defending other memory causes (Michel 2010: 69, 117), in the majority of cases without success, which are related to the wrongdoings of France. True enough, this memorial regime exerted a broader impact on the regulation of memory.

In 1990, the first of the so-called memory laws—the *loi Gayssot*—was adopted; it made Holocaust denial a punishable offence. In 1995, President Chirac acknowledged the responsibility of the Republic for the deportation of Jewish citizens during the occupation; his predecessor François Mitterrand had controversially refused to acknowledge this fact in 1992. Throughout the 1990s, debates raged about the Algerian war—the designation "war" was not adopted by parliament until 1999 (Stora 1999: 128-35)—and the role of the French army. The debate about the Holocaust, Vichy, and Algeria became closely entwined in 1997 when Maurice Papon went on trial for deporting French Jews to Germany, because in 1961 Papon had been the police prefect of Paris and responsible for repressing the Algerian demonstrations in support of independence, when hundreds were killed by police on October 17 (House 2001). In the following years, a number of laws began to regulate specific memories and memory practices. In 2000, a national day of commemoration was declared for the "victims of racist and anti-Semitic crimes by the French state" and to honor "the Righteous of France" (Law 2000-644, July 10, 2000).[19] One year later the above-mentioned *loi Taubira* branded the slave trade and slavery a "crime against humanity" (Law 2001-434, May 21, 2001).[20] The adoption of the law marked a process, initiated by associations, of nationalizing a memory which had previously been largely confined to overseas territories. Since the 1990s, the term "descendant of slaves" (*descendant d'esclaves*) had spread in France as a social category.[21] Moving beyond the national space, the "Armenian genocide of 1915" was recognized as such in January of the same year (Law 2001-70, January 29, 2001).[22] Similar acts of recognition by France have been taking place in relation to overseas territories. The New Caledonia Agreement (1998), for example, contains an ambivalent reference to "the dark sides of the colonial period, even if it was not devoid of light" (cf. Stora & Lecère 2007: 23).

The divisive potential of memory politics became more fully visible in 2005, when several events intersected to create a nationwide debate on France's colonial history and its memorialization. The springboard was a legislative bill adopted by parliament on February 23, 2005, the culminating point of the "pro-colonialist" memory defended by the right-wing government elected in 2002 (Michel 2010: 135).[23] In its most controversial section, the law expressed a positive assessment of colonialism and made it obligatory teaching in schools. Section 4 provided that "school manuals will recognize in particular the positive role of the French presence overseas, particularly in North Africa, and will give the history and sacrifices of the French soldiers from these territories the prominent place they deserve" (Law 2005-158, February 23, 2005). The broad debates about the "positive role" of colonialism intersected with the nationwide riots which obliged the government to declare a state of emergency on November 8 (using a law enacted during the Algerian war). In this particular context, the hypothesis of the "colonial continuum" acquired unprecedented relevance for a segment of the French media, who alluded to the postcolonial dimension of the riots (Bertrand 2006a: 112f.).

The controversial section of the law was abrogated per presidential decree in February 2006. Moreover, in 2008, a parliamentary commission set up to examine "memory-related questions" (*questions mémorielles*)[24] recommended that parliament limit its engagement with history to "resolutions" instead of adopting laws (Assemblée Nationale 2008).[25] The commission stressed the importance of avoiding further conflicts about memory, although it refrained from abrogating existing memory laws. Nevertheless, this did not put an end to the parliamentary regulation of memory. This was partly due to a 2008 framework decision by the European Union (2008/913/JHA) requiring member states to punish conduct which is "publicly condoning, denying or grossly trivialising crimes of genocide, crimes against humanity and war crimes." The law adopted in 2011 to transpose this decision into national law (*loi Boyer*) was declared unconstitutional in 2012. Furthermore, the memory controversies led to an equally controversial debate about national identity. During the presidential election campaign of 2007, candidate Nicolas Sarkozy had made "national identity" a theme of his campaign and in this context the polemical critique of the rewriting of French history—denigrated as "repentance"—figured prominently in his speeches (Lefranc 2008). After his election, Sarkozy effectively created a "ministry of immigration, integration, national identity and solidarity development," dissolved in 2010, but only after initiating a major and inconclusive public debate (2009/10) about the question "What does it mean to be French?".[26] In 2003, it had been decided to create a national museum of the history of immigration in an attempt to integrate immigration into the national heritage (Wahnich 2017). The contested legitimacy of this project became apparent when its opening in 2007 was deprived of an official ceremony (Gruson 2011; Thomas 2013).

Memory and the Remembering Subject

The widespread public concern with memory-related issues illustrated in the above outline is contingent upon a relatively specific notion of memory. Indeed, the great public and academic interest in memory (the "memory boom") dates to the 1980s (Winter 2007). Until then, the notion "memory" was hardly used in social scientific and humanistic studies. Kerwin Lee Klein points out that Raymond Williams's *Keywords* published in 1976 has no entry for the term, while the *Dictionary of Social Sciences* of 1964 claimed that "the word verged on extinction" (2000: 131).

While the polyvalence of the term memory has been often noted (Berliner 2005; Winter 2007), the semantics of memory—how its emergence "rework[ed] history's boundaries"—and its constitutive effects can benefit from clarification (Klein 2000: 128, *passim*). For this study of rationalizations of French history, a double feature of memory needs to be highlighted. This double feature unfolds as a pair of opposites which simultaneously characterize memory. On the one hand, memory connotes interiority. Quoting Michael Roth, Kerwin Lee Klein writes that, in the modern era, memory constitutes not only "the key to personal and collective identity," but "the core of the psychological self" (2000: 134). Since the late nineteenth century, newly emerging sciences of memory and forgetting have provided a "surrogate for the soul," as Hacking puts it (1994: 50). Psychological concepts in discourses about memory (notably trauma) abound. Klein states that while references to Halbwachs's notion of collective memory are numerous and "although the new memory studies frequently invoke the ways in which memory is socially constructed, Freudian vocabularies are far more common than Halbwachsian or even Lacanian ones" (2000: 135; cf. Ledoux 2013b). Klein considers that this recourse to "Freudian vocabulary" is contestable considering the problems raised by moving from the individual to the collective level:

> ...in his important work on Holocaust memorials, *The Texture of Memory* (1993), James Young explained his reluctance to "apply individual psychoneurotic jargon to the memory of national groups" by pointing out that "individuals

cannot share another's memory any more than they can share another's cortex." Who could disagree with this reasonable proposition? And yet most historical studies of memory highlight the social or cultural aspects of memory or memorial practice to the point of projecting "psychoneurotic jargon" onto the memory of various national or (more often) ethnoracial groups (2000: 135).

We would, however, miss out on the central feature of contemporary references to memory if the implied association with interiority were not linked to the fact that memory is also physical and structural. Describing modern usages, Klein states that memory "is not a property of individual minds, but a diverse and shifting collection of material artifacts and social practices" (2000: 130). In other words, it is wrong—as Klein insists—to reduce the modern use of memory, "roughly," to the "rise of the modern self and the secularization and privatization of memory." Rather, there is a "convergence of archaic and contemporary meanings" of memory (2000: 132).

So how does the "memory boom" change the writing of national history?[27] For the purpose of this discussion of French memory politics since the 1990s, it is useful—drawing on Foucault[28]—to consider the notion memory as a "constituent model," that is as constituting an object for possible knowledges. As the above discussion makes apparent, the notion of memory establishes linkages between interiority on the one hand and institutions, social structures, and material artifacts on the other. This defines the boundaries of the new object memory for the purposes of both policymaking and knowledge production. The writing of national history thus becomes relevant in a new way and arguably more urgent: Individuals and collectives, now regularly conceived in psychological categories, are supposed to require public recognition of their particular historical identity by the state. Memory needs to be attended to, including the memory of the failures of the nation. The above notion of memory facilitates arguments for the great importance of and need to attend to memory politics.[29] One example for this is the following statement from an influential edited volume whose title *La fracture coloniale* (The Colonial Divide) gave a name to the French postcolonial predicament.[30] On the basis of "Freudian vocabulary," the postcolonial question is here ascribed the status of an inescapable task for the French public: "The appearance center stage of the 'colonial question' and its inevitable corollary, the postcolonial question ... is not an accident, a coincidence, but the symptom of a 'return of the repressed': the long occultation of this dimension of national history explains the disorderly and compulsive character of its unveiling" (Blanchard et al. 2005: 10).[31]

History and Sovereignty

The above developments are fundamentally driven by the circulation of counter-histories of France. It is these counter-histories—histories "of the deciphering ... and of the reappropriation of a knowledge that has been distorted or buried" (Foucault 2003: 72) —which seek to modify the "narratives of 'identity'" (Anderson 1983) generated or incited by state institutions. They are driven, to go back to Foucault's description of human sciences, by a kind of historiography which is properly speaking a human science in that it has increasingly assumed a metascientific perspective and is critically examining itself all the time: "Historiography begins when history sets itself the task of uncovering that in itself which is not history, of showing itself to be the victim of memory and seeking to free itself from memory's grip" (Nora 1996: 4).

A basic condition of possibility for these developments is a specific kind of disjunction, i.e., the state's dependence upon historical knowledge and the varying degree of independence under which historical knowledge is produced by a multitude of different actors. This can lead to various configurations combining conflict and cooperation between state institutions on the one hand and various actors wielding certain forms of historical knowledge on the other.[32] It is useful to recall this point not only as it indicates a limit to the state's sovereignty, but also because this relationship can be one of confrontation. Foucault discussed this relation by distinguishing between two opposed ways in which the writing of history can relate to the legitimacy and unity of state power (Foucault 2003).[33]

The first kind, designated Roman historiography, relates primarily to "rituals of power," i.e., its function is to "speak the right of power and to intensify the luster of power" (2003: 66). History, by recounting the deeds of sovereigns, establishes a juridical link between these individuals and power, and it uses "the almost unbearable intensity of power, its examples and its exploits, to fascinate men" (2003: 66). According to Foucault's account, a new kind of history-writing started to emerge from the late sixteenth century in England and France (2003: 118f.). This practice of history functions as a counter-history to the previous one. Its discourse threatens the power of the ruler, attacking its constitutive identification with law by supplying new historical narratives. A central distinctive feature of this second kind of historiography is that it proposes an analysis of the "State, its institutions and its power mechanisms" in "binary terms" (2003: 88). Instead of narrating stories about ancient and glorious founders of empires, this discourse shifts attention to "races," i.e., coexisting groups which "have not become mixed because of the differences, dissymmetries, and barriers created by privileges, customs and rights, the distribution of wealth, or the way in which power is exercised" (2003: 77). This binary-code-based narrative opposes organicist or functional conceptions of the social body (2003: 51) and is a direct challenge to the historico-juridical claim to legitimacy of the sovereign.[34]

In the 1990s, contesting the currently existing French state through radical counter-historical narratives using binary code was a significant phenomenon. The division constitutive of the analysis performed in counter-histories is, needless to say, defined in diverse ways. Perduring colonial domination is one way to define it, as we saw. In contrast to this, other—influential—authors from the extreme right draw the line of division, broadly speaking, between an internationalist elite and variously defined nonelite groups. From this perspective, the journalist Éric Zemmour refers to May 1968 ("The state was rescued, but not society") as the starting point of developments which brought a new, heterogeneous, elite to power which set out to radically change France. It is this elite-led "deconstruction" of France—in a liberal-individualist, antipatriarchal, and internationalist framework—which Zemmour in turn seeks to "deconstruct" in his bestselling book *Le suicide français* (The Suicide of France), revealing all its ruinous implications to the broader public (Zemmour 2014). "Islamization" is one of them and, for future generations of French, life as a "minority" in their "ancestral land" (Soullier 2019). Here, Zemmour's thought converges with another influential counter-history of France—today notably associated with Renaud Camus, author of *Le grand remplacement* (The Great Replacement), who also portrays the country as divided between an internationalist elite and the indigenous population. The latter is not only in the process of being replaced by immigration; at the same time, the cultural conditions for national resistance are being subverted through the "mediatico-political complex" (Camus 2012). In both cases, a binary code is used to describe society as the site of an ongoing war; what is at stake is the sovereignty of the French nation.

To put it briefly, the French context is characterized by the production of multiple counter-histories of France. Importantly, their critical charge and aims vary greatly. Counter-histories contest the universality of existing national histories, they make apparent divisions inside the population and modify memory regimes. However, their critique can go beyond this and radically delegitimize the existing political order. While the aims pursued by the authors examined here are often situated much more on the level of reforms, their discourses are in multiple ways conditioned by or contribute to the circulation of radical counter-histories of varying allegiance. The stakes attached to debates about history are not limited to defining what is an appropriate narration of the nation, but can extend to the legitimacy of the political order.

Narrating Europe's Difference

Different kinds of counter-histories of Europe and France have been generated in the milieu of public Islam since the 1990s and contribute to the multisited renarration of France. Counter-histories of Europe and/or France are important elements in some of the theoretical projects developed during this period. A number of authors outline in their writings a historical vision of Europe and/or France which contests, broadly speaking, the preeminence of these countries as sources of modern political orders. In other words, these authors criticize the universals derived from the particular histories of European countries (Chakrabarty 2000). This historical critique is, however, not directly connected to efforts to create conditions which would make it easier for Muslims to identify with France. Rather, the primary aim is to correct accounts of French history and certain institutions in order to enable a proper consideration of Islam in the present time. As I shall show subsequently, a different kind of counter-history, which equally starts to emerge in the 1990s, is more directly concerned with writing Islam and Muslims into the history of France and Europe and creating new spaces for Muslim identification.

An example for the first kind of account is provided by Moncef Zenati in "*La fraternité humaine en Islam*" ("Human Brotherhood in Islam," 2008). Zenati is a graduate of the IESH in Château-Chinon, translator of a number of Arabic reference works on Islam, and cofounder of the association *Havre de Savoir* (Haven of Knowledge), which is based in Le Havre. In this essay, Zenati examines the Islamic principles shaping relations between Muslims and non-Muslims, arguing that human brotherhood is one of them. This claim is a direct critique of two groups, those believers who practice a "literalist" reading of scripture and produce a socially disruptive vision of Islam by claiming that the legitimate only bonds are those between Muslims. Second, a group he ironically calls intellectuals, "obviously all of them specialists in Islam and the Muslim world," who portray Islam as inherently violent and negating basic rights to non-Muslims (2008: 9). More generally, Zenati aims to show that central values enabling the coexistence of different communities in France—tolerance is the key concept here —are an essential part of Islam. In the course of demonstrating this claim, Zenati also compares the record of early Islamic civilization in dealing with religious and ethnic difference to that of other political systems in history, including France. Taking examples from the history of Churches in the West and proceeding as far as the colonial negation of human rights in Algeria between 1830 and 1962 (2008: 71-83), Zenati highlights the multiple acts of violence which minorities had to endure. In brief, Zenati argues that Islam shares in the foundations of the French political order. Unlike France, he argues, Islamic civilization has implemented the principles essential to this order—tolerance and equality—all through history.

Zenati is here not interested in French history for the sake of history nor for the sake of memory; he does not wish to "reopen old wounds" (2008: 82). He merely alludes to the often ignored long history of Muslims in France dating back to the First World War, a history which, incidentally, includes his own family (2008: 5f.). His recourse to comparative historical outlines serves, quite simply, to properly appreciate the achievements of Islamic civilization (2008: 72, 82). A similar usage of history can be found in some of Tariq Ramadan's writings (which is not to say that this usage excludes other approaches to history). Ramadan analyzes European history primarily as a force of particularism which threatens universal equality and in particular the equal treatment of Muslims. Ramadan describes the history of Europe since medieval times as a "long history full of conflicts, excommunications and deaths" (1994: 25). He does assert in unequivocal terms that the end result of modern history, "secular society," constitutes "in a double sense a *liberation*"; human reason is liberated and the state is now a neutral arbiter in a society where different conceptions of the good can coexist (1994: 34; emphasis in the original). However, this history has not only led to the emergence of secular regimes, whose logic Ramadan associates with the principle of separation, but—and this is Ramadan's second perspective on European history—it has also shaped in a durable manner "modern Western thought" (1994: 26f. and *passim*). Basically, this experience has engraved in European thought the idea that the "religious factor is necessarily, essentially, anti-democratic" (1994: 31), that liberty needs to be defended against the domination, or claims to domination, of the Church, and that reason and dogma confront each other. According to Ramadan, the way in which Europeans today perceive religion is primarily shaped by the history of the Catholic Church: "What the Catholic Church did with its power has influenced all later considerations in the West about religion and the place which is due to it" (1994: 27f.).

While Ramadan recognizes the diversity of processes of secularization and the divergences between national secular regimes, he emphasizes that they hold in common a "kind of influence which the dominant religion had exerted on society until the 19th century. For all of them, it was about liberating the social field from an authority which, in the name of divine law, had muzzled social, political and scientific action." By adopting a comparative perspective on the history of Europe, centered on Roman Catholicism on the one hand and Islam on the other, Ramadan criticizes that the particular history of Europe has been given the status of a universal model. According to him, the conflict between "faith and reason" and the struggles about pluralism did not arise in Muslim societies because of the "very essence" of "Islamic civilization" (1994: 32f., 69).

In brief, one way to summarize Ramadan's analysis is to say that European history is in a double sense not the history of Muslims. It is a history which is by and large made not by Muslims. While Ramadan refers here and elsewhere to the important cultural influences from Arab-Islamic countries on medieval Europe (1994: 26, 77f.; Gresh & Ramadan 2000: 204), the "struggles which have led, in the course of history, to a new disposition of forces and institutions in Europe and the United States, have taken place without Muslims." Muslims live in Western society, "in this Western society which has been made without them and which has not taken into account their 'integration'" (1994: 35; see also 114). Secondly, it is a history which has created a dominant mindset which does injustice to the particularity and difference of Islam. It is because Europeans do not recognize the particularity of European history and the contingency of conflicts about religion that they tend to conceive of Muslims as a problem. Muslims, as Ramadan stresses, are "more than mere believers of a religion" because their identity "express[es] itself almost naturally in the social field" (1994: 36; see also 137f.). However, it is only through the lens of European history that this is necessarily problematic. It is this history which threatens to impede the equal application of law. History is here primarily conceived as the domain of particularity and because of that as a negative force hampering the realization of equality, which needs to be countered by mutual attempts to understand the other's history (1994: 17f., 36f.).

Remembering al-Andalus

A second usage of counter-histories aims to write Islam and Muslims into French history. The practitioners of this approach seek to demonstrate that France is, indeed, positively shaped by its multiple relations with Islamic and/or Arabic sovereignties in the past and by Muslims who have lived in France and its colonies, many of whom, most notably in the course of the twentieth century, fought for France as soldiers. Briefly, this approach seeks to write French history so that France can be commemorated in a manner which is inclusive of Islam and Muslims. While those approaching French history in this way may differ on a variety of points, they share in common a fundamentally productive approach to history, its rewriting and its remembering. The aim they pursue is to widen the possibilities to relate to France as a remembering subject, whether for Muslim subjects or others, and at the same time to entwine Islam and Muslims more closely with it.

One example for this approach to French history is provided by Charafeddine Mouslim from Bordeaux.[35] Mouslim, entrepreneur by profession, is also a historian, a former president of the regional representative council of Islam in Aquitaine, and a collaborator of Tareq Oubrou. Mouslim is a specialist in medieval Islam in France and has been working since the 1990s on a study which seeks to redefine the dominant perspective on Islam in medieval France (Mouslim 2014).[36] This perspective, says Mouslim, is centered around the battle of Poitiers— or Tours and Poitiers—which is conventionally dated to 732 and which set the army of Charles Martel, mayor of the Merovingian Palace, against that of 'Abd al-Rahman al-Ghafiqi, governor of al-Andalus. Importantly, al-Andalus had at the time encompassed the province of Septimania, in southwestern France, for several decades. 'Abd al-Rahman al-Ghafiqi's army was defeated and retreated, and he died in battle. After 801 forces from al-Andalus stopped crossing the Pyrenees, although naval incursions into Provence continued.

The place of Charles Martel in French imaginaries fluctuated considerably across the centuries and political usages of his figure do not exclusively refer to his role as vanquisher of the forces—described in various combinations as Arab, Berber, or Muslim—from the Iberian peninsula; his role as the founder of a dynasty has also been very important, particularly in moments of political transition in France (Blanc & Naudin 2015). Having said this, the battle of 732 features prominently in contemporary imaginaries,[37] the presumed site of the battle, near Châtellerault, became a heritage site in the 1990s (Basset 2013), the battle has acquired central significance for the far right as a major civilizational confrontation, and its importance is also indicated by the controversies it triggers. For example, in 2012, the battle of 732 caught national attention as a major memory site after debate following the occupation, by activists from the extreme-right *Bloc identitaire* (Identitarian Bloc, now *Les Identitaires*), of the site where the Union was constructing a mosque in Poitiers (Bloc identitaire 2012).

Mouslim objects to standard accounts of the battle on various grounds. The central place granted to the battle in the historiography of Islam in medieval France is problematic, as it sets up the relations between the local population and the invading forces from the south as one of violent conflict. Moreover, given that the battle of 732 is supposed to be where Charles Martel stopped the invasion by people from al-Andalus, it reduces their presence in today's France to barely two decades. In contrast, Mouslim's account radically downgrades the importance of the battle and its effects on later political and military developments. The battle is not the decisive victory that halted incursions from the south. Rather, the end of these incursions has to be explained with reference to factors internal to the history of North Africa and the Middle East. Just as importantly, Mouslim insists that the battle of Poitiers should not be equated with the early history of Muslims in France: "Can the Muslim presence on *terre gauloise* be reduced to a single event? Can a presence which has lasted centuries be reduced to a single battle to which later historians gave exaggerated importance?" (2014: 6). Mouslim reconstructs aspects of Muslim lives in the south of present-day France up until the fourteenth century[38] and asserts that the coexistence between different religious groups was "almost exemplary" (2014: 314). Finally, Mouslim reflects upon why the battle, in spite of its limited importance, became so central in various discourse from the twelfth century onward in France. He sees this as a broader process through which Saracens become the Other of Christians (2014).

Overall, conditions in academy are conducive to the production and circulation of such revisionist accounts; elsewhere the situation is much more somber. Mouslim's revision of historiography not only draws upon a long line of critical historians, going back to the late nineteenth century, who have questioned accounts of the battle of 732 (see, e.g., 2014: 115). It is also in full convergence with what Jacques Le Goff, prefacing a seminal work on the history of Islam and Muslims in France, calls a "strong tendency in current history," namely to analyze not only "political 'events', but also and above all the history of their construction as events" (2007: xiii). Needless to say this approach can ultimately obliterate some events, such as the battle of Poitiers, from history. This is its fate in the successful and widely noticed first global history of France, with contributions from more than a hundred authors (Boucheron 2017).[39] The entry on the eighth-century incursions into Frankish lands from Africa is centered around an arbitrarily chosen date (719) and only mentions the battle of Poitiers in passing, as the status of this "skirmish" supposedly depends upon its place in an "epic of the other" (Fauvelle 2017: 127).[40]

This reference to "the other" is typical for a broad range of studies on relations between Islam and Europe. More particularly, reference is made here to a particular form of alterity construction, namely that of "orientalization" (Baumann & Gingrich 2004), where the self is defined through negative mirror imaging. This concept is another powerful resource Mouslim can use in order to problematize claims about the existence of transhistorical civilizational conflicts between Islam and France or Europe. It is noteworthy that a simplified form of deconstructing identities in the framework of othering processes has acquired a commonsensical status in and beyond academia.[41] What is the added value of the concept of othering? Mouslim not only provides evidence which complicates or invalidates the binary perspective on Septimania, a region where local hostility toward the Frankish forces commanded by Charles Martel led to alliances between residents and the Andalusi forces; noteworthy instances of peaceful coexistence between religious communities are reported. Mouslim also proposes a metalevel argument, as it were, about the identity-constituting function of antagonistic discourse on Islam. Conflicts supposedly rooted in civilizational or religious differences are thus made to appear as mere effects of the process of defining the self through negative mirror imaging, here, as I mentioned before, a process initiated by the Catholic Church in relation to Islam. It is precisely identities antagonistic toward Islam which are subverted as their constitutive relation to the latter now comes into focus.

This reference to othering wields a significant argumentative force, but it does not simply do away with historical narrations of the battle in a civilizational framework. Rather, the clash between civilizational conflict accounts of Islam in medieval France and other narrations is, to a significant degree, simply polemical. Both sides tend to mutually reduce the opposing analysis to an ideologically driven historical discourse on identity. This is what the comedian turned bestselling historian Loràant Deutsch does in his historical guide to France, *Hexagone* (Hexagon), published in 2013, which includes an account of the battle of 732. A mocking summary of views of the battle as a nonevent is paired with the claim that these views are driven by "political correctness" (Naudin/Blanc/Chéryl 2013; On n'est pas couché 2013). In a handout published by *Les Identitaires* titled, "How to respond to the lies about the Battle of Poitiers?", the text likewise starts by asking why the claim, "The Battle of Poitiers did not take place," is made at all. The answer is simple: in a society committed to coexistence (*société du 'vivre-ensemble'*) where concerns about Islamization run high, the prestige of the battle of Poitiers—a battle which terminated "the Muslim conquest of Europe"—is awkward (Les Identitaires 2017).[42]

Mouslim's account crucially depends upon highlighting that al-Andalus is not limited to present-day Spain. Rather, in the early eighth century, the province of Septimania now in France was part of al-Andalus for roughly four decades. From a historical perspective, al-Andalus is thus also France; remembering al-

Andalus, then, can be a commemorative act of France. The attempt to integrate the history of medieval France with that of al-Andalus and thereby to create a transregional genealogy of Islam in France stretching back to the emergence of Islam also shapes Hassan Iquioussen's discourse. In one of his talks he describes the particular status of al-Andalus as a point of indistinction between Islamic and French history: "*Andalousie*, we understand each other, this is the south of France" (Iquioussen 2015b). Iquioussen hails from the region of Valenciennes in the utmost north of France and is one of the Union's most prominent conference speakers. Having studied Arabic and history at university, his knowledge of Islamic sciences is self-taught. Lecturing and touring France as a speaker since the 1980s, he is the founding president of JMF (1993). In 2012, he set up a successful YouTube channel; in his early career, he published numerous audiocassettes.[43] Iquioussen also works as tour guide and some of his published talks on history originate in this context.

Iquioussen approaches the history of Islam from different perspectives. First, Iquioussen seeks to demonstrate the significance of history by pointing out that the number of verses about history far surpass those about normative questions. Furthermore, he emphasizes that the study of history is important as it gives access to the "laws" which stably govern the life of human societies, like the law of alternation enunciated in the Qur'an: "We deal out such days among people in turn" (3:140). Other verses are read as an exposition of law and an injunction to unity: "and do not quarrel with one another, or you may lose heart and your spirit may desert you" (8:46) and "Hold fast to God's rope all together; do not split into factions." (3:103) (Iquioussen 2015a). Disunity among Muslims is, in Iquioussen's analysis, a major factor in the decline and loss of Muslim al-Andalus. Adopting a framework where history unproblematically continues to fulfill its function as a teacher of life (Koselleck 2004), Iquioussen underlines that "lessons" can be drawn from the past as history repeats itself (2015a).[44] At the same time, Iquioussen approaches history as a reservoir of narratives which permit the constitution of confident individual and collective identities. Equating history with memory, history-memory is held to fulfill an anthropological function as individuals need to know where they come from in order to flourish. Not only is this a distinctive human characteristic, but memory is an essential condition for the formation of "pride," Iquioussen maintains (2015a). This last aim, he warns his audience, is actively opposed today by certain groups who seek to make French Muslims detest France. This is why cemeteries for Muslim soldiers who died as "martyrs" serving France are regularly desecrated (Iquioussen 2014).[45]

The fact that many of these soldiers were recruited by force is not addressed (Dewitte 1991).

From this perspective, Iquioussen's talks on history, whether medieval or modern, pursue two related aims, namely to unmask the political strategies of certain historical narratives of Islam, in school textbooks or elsewhere, and to disseminate counter-histories enabling the construction of a proud French Muslim identity. In the counter-histories of medieval France, two themes are of overriding importance: first, the rejection of historical accounts, notably by "Orientalists," associating Muslim conquests with the imposition of Islam by force; second, the critique of all those histories which have obscured or eliminated Muslim contributions to Western civilization. While Iquioussen considers that Islam is a proselytizing religion and jihad served the aim of "making [Islam] accessible to people," jihad and the establishment of Muslim sovereignty in al-Andalus or elsewhere in no way entailed forced conversion. This is demonstrated, he argues, simply by the persistence of multireligious (and multiethnic) society (Iquioussen 2013).[46] Freedom of religion is an essential principle of Islam as it has been practiced since the earliest times; much in contrast to Europe, characterized by "the crime against humanity," the Inquisition (Iquioussen 2015d). This fact is crucial for the history of the Muslim presence, as it lends greater plausibility to the claim that the invading forces from North Africa were not viewed merely as hostile conquerors by the local population. Rather, a certain "complicity" characterizes their relations (Iquioussen 2015b, 2015d).[47] Renarrating the history of al-Andalus, Iquioussen aims not only to correct misperceptions about its history. As importantly, he seeks to relate al-Andalus to the broader history of Europe and to restore al-Andalus to its real place in history, as an essential link connecting the Renaissance period to the worlds of antiquity. Playing this multidimensional role was essential for Europe's transformation and it has been concealed in many respects;[48] this is but one of a series of features in current historiography and school textbooks which prevent Muslims from feeling proud as Muslims, and this is what he has set out to change (Iquioussen 2015a, 2015b, 2015c).

In Iquioussen's account, the history of France cannot be fully understood outside of cross-civilizational transfers. El Hadji Babou Bitèye, former EMF president and a history teacher, has reflected on the relational identity of France by drawing on the work of Lucien Febvre and François Crouzet, and more particularly their idea that pure, self-sufficient culture and civilization is impossible (Bitèye 2013: 63–70). Sketching out some well-known and lesser-known cases of interrelation and entwinement between the Middle East and the

West, Bitèye illustrates how to conceive of Frenchness, in line with Febvre and Crouzet, as benefiting (from cultural transfers), inheriting (from past generations of a diversity of men and women), and creating, or contributing to an ever-continuing "process of adjustment, adaptation and synthesis" (Febvre and Crouzet as quoted in Bitèye 2013: 70). When contributing to the continuation of the human undertaking (*œuvre humaine*), Bitèye concludes, one does so both as debtor and creditor (2013:70).

Divisive Memories

This general approach to French history, aimed at broadening the possibilities for relating to France as a remembering subject and for entwining France with Islam, is political, but it is not necessarily connected to debates about memory policies. In contrast to the above cases, Tariq Ramadan has intervened directly into these debates.

As discussed, Ramadan conceptualizes the historicity of France and Islam in a *longue-durée* perspective as civilizations; here, he posits a clear distinction between Islam and the West, which, however, does not exclude normative convergences between them, nor does this line of distinction translate spatially into a clear-cut boundary (Ramadan 1999). On a different level, Ramadan reflects upon colonial history and history of migration. In partial contrast to the civilizational perspective, history is here not a factor of difference necessitating a hermeneutical and conceptual effort by Muslims and other Europeans in order to enter into dialogue; rather, history tends to be perceived as part of what Muslims need to be included into. Discussing the case of Muslim immigration into Europe, Ramadan underlines the need to "revisit" the "histories of colonization and immigration" and to "reappraise" the contribution of immigrants to Europe. Note that this is coupled with the call to "promote" "above all," "the civilization of origin and the long memory of the descendants of immigration born in Europe" (Gresh & Ramadan 2000: 202f.).[49] The foundational idea is expressed in a book of conversations with philosopher and sociologist Edgar Morin, where Ramadan declared that "what bothers many French people from across the sea today is that they are told a History where their version, their perception, their experience of this History is not at all integrated" (Morin & Ramadan 2014: 34). Exclusion, for Ramadan, is hence "also an exclusion from common memory," and it is one field where the "integration of intimacies" has to be pursued (Morin & Ramadan 2014: 29).[50]

Ramadan's position on the rewriting of French history emphasizes three modalities. First, Ramadan wants French schools to "recognize and celebrate" what he calls "diversity and 'interfertilization,'" a term coined by Morin (Morin & Ramadan 2014: 34). Second, Ramadan is not interested in approaching colonial history from the angle of "repentance" (2014: 35). Writing in the first year of the Arab uprisings, he has been very explicit that "[the] time has come to stop blaming the West for the colonialism and imperialism of the past or for today's attempts at manipulation and control." (Ramadan 2012a: 13). Rather, he does believe that diverse memories have their place in the teaching of a "common history of memories" which would combine "the wealth of all our memories, explaining different points of view, and trying to understand collective consciousnesses and collective hopes as well as historical wounds and traumas" (Ramadan 2010b: 158). Third, he stresses the importance of reporting the historical past "as objectively as possible" (Morin & Ramadan 2014: 35). Next to objectivity, he advises a "critical spirit," which he believes is threatened by "passion" (Ramadan 2010b: 157).

Given that there is a profound mistrust about the divisive potential of the surging interest in collective memories, the overriding aim in Ramadan's thought is to maintain a unified framework in which the past can become an object of public deliberations. Aiming to entwine France with Islam, he never loses sight of this basic aim of unity; Ramadan's position is aligned with widespread concerns in France about the so-called competition of memories (see, e.g., Todorov 2004; Stora & Lecère 2007). Ramadan recognizes that "history, and the memories and traditions that fight over how events, values and references should be interpreted, have always been battlefields and the focus of power struggles" and in all likelihood will always remain so (2010b: 156). However, his aspiration is to construct an inclusive history and this aspiration is reiterated in many statements, as is his criticism of all those who pursue memory claims which considers to be divisive:

> Civilizations, cultures, nations, regions, 'ethnic French' (*citoyens de souche*), immigrants, former slaves or colonial subjects, the *indigènes*, all demand origins, a history and a memory that justify the way they specify their differences and, should the need arise, resist the way the other's memory instrumentalizes history. ... This economy of memories is very unhealthy, and the very opposite of what the rationalism that gave birth to modernity wanted: it is no longer a critical analysis, and it no longer integrates many different points of view into a historical study (2010b: 152).

Ramadan's reflections allow us to grasp another dimension of the complexity inherent in secular politics. Ramadan, as previously discussed, is fully committed to the aim of safeguarding and making publicly apparent the universality of the Islamic tradition in a context where Islam is primarily seen as a particular religion rooted in North Africa and the Middle East. The claim to universality partly depends on neat separations Ramadan establishes between religion and culture, religion and the social, or religion and nationality. The debate about memory is another context where these separations crumble, giving way to new entwinements, here between immigration, Islam as religion, and history.

This partial reconfiguration of Islam is noteworthy in relation to the scholarly debate about the thesis that Muslim religiosity is increasingly being disconnected from "culture" as part of a broader process in which Islam is losing its social authority (Roy 2004, 2007). The debates about memory constitute one—relatively significant—context in which a new kind of relational embedding of Islam occurs. This process also deserves mentioning for its direct political implications. In his statements, Ramadan identifies memory—with diverging emphases[51]—as a specific condition for the integration of subjects with ties to immigration and/or Islam. By doing this, he is able to make claims for the accommodation of Muslims, but at the price of delving more fully into the disorderliness of secular politics and further blurring the distinctions between religion, culture, and the social. Thus, Ramadan's discursive ability to set himself apart from the positions he wishes to criticize, such as the culturalization of social problems, is negatively affected by this. In a televised debate entitled "Colonization, *banlieues*: Is France guilty?", during the riots in autumn 2005, Ramadan did not draw a direct causal connection between the riots and memory politics, but he nevertheless emphasized the importance of "integrating" the histories of immigrants into "official discourse." When confronted with a criticism that his analysis of the riots was also based on cultural explanations, he referred to his argument, already discussed, that cultural and social factors need to be distinguished without "disconnecting them" (Culture et dépendances 2005).

Patriotism beyond Critique and Repentance

Ramadan demands the inclusion of Muslims into French history, a history which he critically reflects upon. This is manifest, for example, in his formulation that the history of France should paint a twofold picture: "the France of the light as well as the France of the shadows, of resistances as well as of collaborators"

(Morin & Ramadan 2014: 34). It is precisely this critical and ambivalent view of France which is rejected by *Fils de France*, an association and think tank aiming to promote Muslim patriotism. *Fils de France*, though a fringe association, has benefited from significant support and visibility since its creation in 2012.[52] Its former president and most prominent representative is Camel Bechikh, a member of the Union, former spokesperson for the *Comité de Bienfaisance et de Secours aux Palestiniens* (Committee for Charity and Support for the Palestinians), and one of the spokespersons of *La Manif Pour Tous,* the network which emerged in 2012 out of opposition to the introduction of same-sex marriage.[53] In 2016, the association *Fils de France* became the site of internal power struggles concerning its relation to the UOIF, causing it to interrupt its work. The starting point for these controversies was the posting of an interview by *Fils de France* with the former member of the Union, Farid Abdelkrim (see chapter five), in which he problematized the Union's relation to the Muslim Brotherhood (Fils de France 2016). The subsequent legal struggle for control of *Fils de France* was lost by Bechikh.

Bechikh is regularly associated with extreme-right milieus in France, and his talks are featured on the website of Alain Soral's extreme-right movement *Égalité et réconciliation* (Equality and Reconciliation).[54] Soral, an essayist and former member of the National Front who was convicted several times for anti-Semitism, benefits from considerable media attention (Chauveau 2014). Part of Soral's strategy for national reconciliation is to build bridges between the far right and French descendants from recent waves of immigrants, particularly from North Africa; Muslims constitute only one of the groups targeted.[55] When asked where the association *Fils de France* stands politically and why Bechikh speaks at meetings of groups close to or part of the National Front—whose president, Marine Le Pen, called for dissolving the Union in 2012—Bechikh responded that his contacts with these groups, which he describes as "Islamosceptic or even Islamophobe," arise out of the wish to pursue dialogue and to work for "appeasement," and not the desire "for a membership card." He is clear in identifying basic convergences between his views and those of the National Front about, for example, the importance of sovereignty, the critique of globalization, and the need to restrict immigration. Bechikh links the association to the "social capitalism" it identifies with de Gaulle, and has said that it is not far removed from the notion of "left on labor, right on values," the motto of Soral's *Égalité et réconciliation* (Fils de France 2014a; Bechikh 2012).

The positions taken by *Fils de France* are radically opposed to many taken by Ramadan. Ramadan's critical historiography in praise of carefully regulated diversity cannot be reconciled with the "both carnal and spiritual" love which *Fils de France* pledges in its charter to "our mother" France (Fils de France 2012a). Ramadan's analysis of fears about immigration as primarily an epiphenomenon of deep identity problems within society contrasts strongly with the demand by *Fils de France* for a halt to immigration. While these and other differences are real and important, they are partly enabled by a loosely defined shared matrix. First, there is the common distinction between Islam as a universal tradition on the one hand and the particular cultures of Muslim-majority countries on the other. While Ramadan makes this distinction in order to enable the emergence of a culture based on Islamic values and drawing on French cultural repertoires of expression, Bechikh aims at acculturation and not the creation of new culture. Here, Bechikh draws inspiration from Tareq Oubrou.[56] Second, there is the common aim to establish a distinction between the religious and the social, i.e., between the social identity of Muslims and their subjectivity as Muslims. As in the case of Ramadan, it is difficult for Bechikh to uphold this distinction fully. Referring to the "amalgam" between social issues and memory on the one hand and Islam on the other, Bechikh maintains the association's "ardent desire to distinguish all that." While Bechikh concedes that the confusion arises out of "legitimate" claims, the connection established here with Islam "enfolds" it "in an image" which he rejects (Fils de France 2014a).

Importantly, he claims, this disconnection between Islam as a "spiritual tradition" and the fields of history and culture is already established in a certain sense. It is established because, as Bechikh emphasizes in various formulations, Muslim identities are not tied anymore to North African histories and cultural spheres, but shaped by French culture. Patriotism, according to Bechikh in his address to the Annual Meeting of the Union in 2012, is "the fact of saying that we have in France a language, a history, a culture, an artistic production and that all this has played a part in constructing our individualities, our culture" (Fils de France 2012b). However, the limits of Muslims' patriotism and the particular constraints bearing upon it are recognized. He concedes that acknowledging this and articulating patriotism is difficult for many Muslims who, he claims, have "an undeclared love of France." History is a major reason why this is so: "our social psychology today is to have a selective reading of history by only picking out negative things from an ocean of positive things." The neglect of the history of alliances and relations between the Ottoman Empire and France, going back to François I and Suleiman the Magnificent, is one major example for this inclination (Fils de France 2012b).[57] Bechikh partly blames Muslim associations for this state of affairs because they have adopted a "discourse of victimhood." However, the responsibility also lies with various other groups, such as anti-racist groups like *SOS Racisme,* who have contributed since the 1980s to an "organized abhorrence of France" which *Fils de France* seeks to undo (Fils de France 2014c). With regard to Muslims as remembering subjects, the association believes that French Muslims must be offered a different, more positive perspective on the history of France. At the same time, the "blame game" needs to stop if Muslims are to find an "attachment point" for identifying with France (Fils de France 2014c).

Fils de France radically upgrades the notion of culture. The distinction often made between religion and culture thus takes on a new meaning; the scope of potential effects entailed by this distinction broadens considerably. This holds even more true for Abdelaali Baghezza aka Albert-Ali, a writer and conference speaker. Baghezza has been active in the Union's milieu since 1989, was a member of JMF, and has (co)authored two books, one on the headscarf controversy (Adjir & Baghezza 2004), a second one announced as "novel" and entitled *Marianne m'a tuer* (Marianne have killed me) (Baghezza 2007).

Baghezza is concerned with the construction of a "theology of rooting" (*enracinement*) (Baghezza 2014). Like Bechikh, Baghezza seeks to move beyond debates on citizenship, the contextualization of Islamic norms, and associational work. His normative reference is the Prophet, who declared his deep love for his native Mecca, and it is this "carnal relation with his native city" which inspires Baghezza in his thought. He sees himself as "following through to the end the reasoning initiated by the UOIF" by shifting the focus to how Muslims can "take root" culturally in France and shed off the "luggage" of cultural identities imported with migration (Baghezza 2010). Citing Qur'an 49:13: "and made you into races and tribes so that you should get to know one another"—a standard reference in the Union's milieu—and Qur'an 30:22: "Another of His signs is the creation of the heavens and earth, and the diversity of your languages and colors", Baghezza's point is that "the Divine will created people in distinct and homogeneous communities so that they should get to know each other and not so they should mix" (Baghezza 2012). Baghezza's description of mosque associations emphasizes how deeply this milieu is steeped in a specific culture, notably Maghrebi culture. While, like Bechikh, he upholds "the fundamentals [of Islam] without compromise" and considers Muslim life in France to be unproblematic, he wants to promote conditions for "striking cultural roots and ethno-cultural fusion, a fusion of races." At one point he defines the telos as the generation of "French Muslims who are like converts" (Baghezza 2013).

Of interest here is less the position Baghezza has come to adopt—including the option of remigration for culturally resistant groups—or his debate with others in the public Islam milieu about electoral options for Muslims and his proximity to the National Front (Baghezza 2012; Ennasri 2012; Makri 2012)[58], but rather his approach to French history. Both his books addressed at length the history—up to the present—of relations between France, Islam, and Muslims, whether in the metropole, North Africa, or elsewhere. This is also the central topic of Baghezza's second book, *Marianne m'a tuer*. The rationale for the book—which is "written in vitriol" as the "warning" on the book informs the reader—is outlined in a "letter from a son to his mother," here the personification of the Republic, Marianne. The son, Albert-Ali, tells her that the time has come for the public to know about her various wrongdoings: "It is important to reveal it in order to ask forgiveness and ultimately forget, in order to build a better future for our family and all my brothers and sisters." A second related aim is to make the readers doubt and question the knowledge about history they have received, notably in schools; the internally conflicted nature of the colonial Republic needs to be made apparent and "Republican myths" need to be shown for what they are (2007: 9f; 67). Baghezza then goes on to provide a survey of French views on Islam past and present and on the French state's dealings with Muslims. Describing the fate of those who "refuse[d] to grasp the profound sense of the tricolor civilization" (2007: 50), in Algeria or elsewhere, this historical survey produces a devastating record for the Republic; it does not exclude the occasional French who refused to give in to the "destructive instincts" that are part of human nature and opposed colonialism (2007: 96f.). The deconstruction of "Republican myths" is partly realized through portraits of major figures of history shown here as "defendants"; in contrast to this Baghezza presents a list of "forgotten master thinkers" among Muslims who prepared the emergence of modern Europe and who illustrate paradigmatically how "our destinies on both sides of the Mediterranean are linked" so that "it cannot be anymore said that we are the *Others*" (2007: 124f.; emphasis in the original).

In this book, Baghezza stressed the need to establish historical truth in order to forgive and start anew, but he later made it very clear that he had discarded this approach, an approach which he then identified with thinking that is alien to Islam and notably leftist. From Baghezza's point of view, reconciliation no longer depends on discovering historical truth, which has degenerated into a quest for "eternal vengeance": "Reconciliation for tomorrow takes priority over repeated condemnation of the past, eternal vengeance is a tradition for others than the children of Ismael" (Baghezza 2012). Here, Baghezza can be read as making questions of repentance, vengeance, and reconciliation his primary concern.[59] Adopting this reading, Yamin Makri (2012) considers that Baghezza misconstrues the stakes of the debate about colonial history and the Republic. The real question raised by this history is, in Makri's words, "more fundamental." This history makes one wonder what is the essence of the state in which colonial crimes could happen; how could they happen in spite of the values—such as human rights and *laïcité*—the Republic proclaimed to be its own. Makri's reflections thus turn on the repeatedly occurring discord between power and law and what appears as a fundamental division in society. He considers that this discord cannot be seen as accidental and attempts to show that the colonial enterprise is "intrinsic to the republican project." Moving beyond the case of the Republic, Makri suggests seeing France on a continuum with Athens, where democracy was instituted as a "system regulating and pacifying the conflicts of interests within the dominant group" while excluding the majority of the population.

Ultimately, however, the historical analysis of the colonial Republic, the democratic system, and the nation-state form is of limited value in Makri's framework. Given the supposed decline of the nation-state, this analysis serves primarily to identify what are nonoptions (namely participation in the democratic system). The elaboration of action strategies for the future departs rather from reflections on the global economic system and "productivism" (Makri 2012).

Conclusion

This chapter has examined how histories of France and Islam have been renarrated in the past three decades. A basic condition for this process is a notion of memory which postulates both the centrality of collective memory to the core of the individual self and the possibility to shape (collective-individual) memory through structural processes. Put differently, this concept of memory, as described by Kerwin Lee Klein (2000), potentially assigns memory great political importance and urgency and outlines a field of interventions for a variety of actors. From this perspective, I have examined how counter-histories contribute to establishing and shaping distinctions and entwinements between Islam and France. Counter-histories are stories which are told because the "history of some is not the history of others." This "principle of heterogeneity" (Foucault 2003: 69) entails usages of counter-histories which sometimes differ greatly. Two of these usages have been central in this account; one aims to provincialize histories of France or certain dimensions of them, while the other seeks to write Islam into France.

These counter-histories, to a significant degree, contribute to the nationalization of Islam. By conceiving Muslims as remembering subjects needing to identify with the history of France, the views of Islam and Muslims which are elaborated privilege, mostly in an implicit manner, connections to spatial, historical, and linguistic contexts that are important for French history. However, it needs to be added that the counter-histories examined here do not simply accept and reproduce national frames, but rather transform notions of France, even if they do so to different degrees. These counter-histories do not imagine France as already fully constituted, providing merely an Islamic supplement to her (cf. Thomas 2013). Rather, these counter-histories seek to codefine or alter conditions of speaking about France. They restrict the usage which can be made of French histories and vocabulary when studying the history of other spaces; they problematize whether and how, historically speaking, Islam and Muslims are external to France, that is, they reshape conditions for othering Islam and Muslims; they reconstruct genealogies of freedom of religion; they subvert accounts of Muslim invasions and civilizational conflict; they reflect on the relation between the writing of history and a moral critique of the past.

To be sure, some of these counter-histories considered separately are likely to have a limited impact. However, it is important to consider them in context and assess their likely reception and intelligibility. As I said, there is certainly a broad range of sometimes bestselling authors who, in very different ways, perpetuate a historiography of France-without-Islam, or in violent conflict with it. Importantly, a deep divide separates these authors from most practitioners of academic historiography (Offenstadt 2014; Noiriel 2019). In this latter field, the distinction between history and memory, which is an essential conceptual foundation of the critique of France-without-Islam expressed in counter-histories, is, in different ways, commonsensical. Likewise, a critical or, rather, skeptical examination of claims to pure and self-sufficient French identity, also central to counter-histories, is routinely undertaken.[60] Both facts seem to favor the renarration of histories about Islam in/and France; both raise awareness for the possibility that the history of France necessarily refers beyond herself, to "other" spaces and "other" histories.

7

Islam and Fiction beyond Freedom of Speech

Introduction

In the study of European Islam, fiction figures primarily as an object of secular politics. This is understandable as controversies about freedom of speech have become closely interconnected with controversies about Islam. The debate about freedom of speech, notably as it applies to works of fiction, has been a part of Islam controversies ever since the publication of Salman Rushdie's *The Satanic Verses* in 1988. In the 2000s, a nexus between Islam and freedom of speech solidified. The reasons were the publication, in various media in France and elsewhere, of various drawings[1] of the prophet of Islam, Muhammad, originally published in Denmark in 2005,[2] and then, in 2015, the killing of the staff of the satirical weekly *Charlie Hebdo*, who had reprinted them and later published multiple other offensive caricatures. Subsequent to these attacks, one of the biggest marches in modern French history, honoring the victims, took place in various French cities.

The dominant perception of the controversies surrounding the derogatory depictions of Muhammad conforms squarely to what I called the orderly vision of secular politics. These controversies were declared to be about freedom of speech. The cause of conflict was typically seen in the problematic connection between the right to freedom of expression on the one hand and the right to protection against hate speech,[3] "abuse" (*injure*), and "defamation" on the other. This latter set of rights is enshrined, via two major amendments to the 1881 law on the freedom of the press that date 1939 (*décret-loi Marchandeau*) and 1972 (*loi Pleven*) (Soula 2018). In Section 33 this law prohibits abuse of a person or a group on the grounds of an actual or assumed adherence or nonadherence to a specific religion, ethnic group, nation or race.[4] This legal norm was central to the court action initiated by all major Muslim organizations, including the UOIF, against *Charlie Hebdo* in 2006.[5] In this and similar cases, involving Muslim or Catholic associations, a central recurrent question is whether the injurious representation of a religion also implies abuse of its adherents or incites to "discrimination, hatred or violence" against them; only in the latter cases is it admissible to restrict freedom of speech.[6]

Continuing the critical reassessment of the orderly vision of secular politics, my aim here is not to discuss the legal and ethical question of how to evaluate the publication of cartoons depicting Muhammad or other related texts or images. Instead, in a first step, I wish to invert the perspective and examine what this controversy is about. In asking this question, I am contributing to the scholarship about the Muhammad cartoon controversy in 2005/6, which has highlighted that the cartoon controversy and "the disagreements and issues debated in this context, in fact comprised *several* controversies . . . if one describes and individuates controversies on the basis of what they are *about*, what their *occasion* is and *among whom* they take place" (Lægaard 2014: 123; emphasis in the original). In this, writes Sune Lægaard, the controversy is not at all exceptional. Rather, "an important element, and often the most important element, of any controversy is a meta-controversy over what the *terms* of the controversy are; public controversies are often centrally about what it is that is controversial and how it should be framed and debated" (Lægaard 2014: 135).

Here I want to draw on this idea in order to problematize certain understandings of secular politics. My discussion of the Danish cartoon controversy aims to show that this conflict does not conform to conventional ideas of secular politics; that is, it cannot be reduced to a normative conflict about where the line between the religious and the secular ought to be drawn. This is partly so because the act of publishing the cartoons and Muslim reactions to them are rationalized differently. The differences that provoked the controversy thus run deeper than mere differences in values or interpretations of the cartoons. While the normative question about how to balance freedom of speech and religious sensibilities is very important, it is not self-contained, and the differences in responses to it are inseparable from questions about Islam's relation to France. More specifically, how the normative question about the right to freedom of speech is answered relies greatly upon questions about Muslims and Islam: the aims and strategies of French Muslim critics of the cartoons; the national or national-global nature of their protests; the social power of Islam and Muslims in France. At the same time, it depends upon how the role and place of satirical critique and caricature are defined in present French society, and specifically the satire produced by *Charlie Hebdo*, which had been accused of racism since the very outset of the controversy.[7] Unpacking "the" controversy and examining the struggles about the identification of its objects is crucial because it helps to grasp the relatively complex and instable discursive conditions under which critics of the cartoons have operated.

I will begin by applying this perspective to legal and ethical debates about the cartoons in 2005/6. I will go on to a broader examination of how fiction is used to describe and rationalize Islam in France and various aspects of French society. Via two case studies, this chapter aims to shift our attention away from fiction as an object of secular government—notably an object in various adjudications about freedom of speech controversies—toward fiction as an aesthetic means to rationalize the objects, aims, and conditions of government, or to contribute to their rationalization. This approach presupposes, as I outlined in the first chapter, that fiction is not situated in opposition to reality. Leaving aside the question of the ontological status of fiction, the focus will be on the function it fulfills and the effects it produces in a particular context, i.e., how fiction is used, not always successfully, "as a means of telling us something about reality" (Iser 1975: 7). In this analytical perspective, the distinction between fiction and reality does not simply disappear, but neither does it constitute a boundary clearly separating two classes of speech about France and French Islam. The first case to be studied is an annual film festival and forum for a future Muslim cinema; the second is the novel *Soumission* (Submission) by Michel Houellebecq (2015).

Two Victims in Court

The controversy about the Muhammad cartoons is typical because the legal question so closely entwined with it is instable, in the sense that contextualized descriptions of the matter to be adjudicated differ significantly and conflict with each other. In another respect, however, this controversy stands out in debates about Islam. If we look at French controversies about Islam from a more general perspective, it is clear that the constitutive factor for most conflicts is the use of freedom rights by Muslims, or their demand to fully exercise them, in a framework of equality. To be sure, these conflicts are driven by assumptions of Muslim illiberalism. Conflicts about the hijab are importantly driven by critique of a duty to belong which is supposedly imposed on individuals, here women, inside the Muslim community. Nevertheless, there would be no controversy about Muslim headscarves if they did not fall within the liberal order, or in other words if it was impossible to make plausible claims to support the legality of this practice, whether in public schools or elsewhere; needless to say, such claims were made by one of France's highest judicial authorities in 1989. Broadly speaking, this also holds true for other contentious Muslim practices. Now, the case of the Muhammad cartoons differs significantly from this pattern, as the demands made by most Muslim associations are for restrictions on freedom of expression. Placing Muslims and Islam in a negative position in relation to freedom therefore facilitated rationalizations of this conflict as an Islamic threat to the liberal order.

These ideas were on the mind of the editors of the Danish journal *Jyllands-Posten* in 2005. They were convinced that "Denmark had succumbed to fear-induced political correctness" and a mix of censorship and self-censorship when it came to Islam, so they commissioned "drawings" of Muhammad both as a provocation and a kind of experiment to test the willingness of Danish illustrators to depict the prophet (Klausen 2009: 13ff.).

The basic claim about Islam and certain Muslims posing a threat to freedom of expression first put forward by the Danes was picked up by multiple other actors. In France, this assertion about the menace to freedom of expression was central to those who defended the (re)publication of these cartoons, notably the editor-in-chief of *Charlie Hebdo*, Philippe Val (2008). From the standpoint of Val and others, Muslim criticism of the cartoons was in fact part of a much more comprehensive attack, by "Islamism" or totalitarian forms of Islam, on freedom of expression. This thesis was set out—within a global frame of reference—in the so-called Manifesto of the Twelve, published by *Charlie Hebdo* on March 1, 2006 and signed by prominent intellectuals and journalists from France and abroad. In this manifesto, the cartoon controversy is seen as just one small element in a broader confrontation between "totalitarianism"—i.e., "Islamism" conceived as the successor to fascism and communism—and free democracies. The global protests against the cartoons are presented as evidence for the need to work for "the promotion of liberty, equal opportunity and secularism for all." This "struggle of ideas," it is argued, is not a conflict between civilizations, but rather opposes democrats anywhere against theocrats anywhere. This was soon followed by another manifesto signed by journalists from *Charlie Hebdo*, "Against a new obscurantism," in which references to France mingle with references to Islam around the globe (Cassen et al. 2006).

The two petitions center their description of France and the West around the Islamic threat to the liberal order. The picture of the threat posed by forms of Islam to the West is almost inverted in another document signed by Muslim organizations, including the Union. In this national petition against Islamophobia, addressed to President Chirac, which was launched after the publication of the cartoons (Pétition 2006), the climate at the time is described as one of growing "Islamophobia," where "citizens of Muslim confession" are "stigmatized" and "their image and that of Islam are disfigured." Referring to this situation, the petition, which brought together all major federations and a number of larger mosques,[8] demanded that the "necessary legal provisions be enacted to prevent Islamophobia, insult, and the defamation of God and His prophets" (Pétition 2006).

The above texts indicate the outer edges of the space in which, since 2006, the cartoon controversies have been debated and diverse interpretations contested. As this shows, stereotypical and totalizing representations—of historical developments ("new obscurantism") and political Islam (a global "totalitarian" movement)—are central elements of this debate where Islam is regularly configured as an alterity of the West. Note that alterity constructions can to different degrees also rely upon arguments and knowledges raised in response to specific questions about free speech in Islam, such as about how Muslims perceive the existing laws on freedom of speech. The petition by Muslim associations quoted above (rejecting the defamation of God and his prophets) to some degree validates the idea that existing laws (which only prohibit the defamation of persons or groups on grounds of religion) are not sufficient. This question about Muslim views of legal provisions on free speech resonates with concerns, in the early 2000s, about attempts by Catholic groups to reinterpret existing laws, by means of a number of legal cases, as prohibiting the defamation of religions (Boulègue 2010).[9] In the Muslim case, the critique of existing laws on defamation can easily be portrayed as an expression of a particular civilizational identity proscribing blasphemy in contrast to the supposedly fully liberalized West (Asad 2009). The debate about the cartoons also poses questions about the normative status of images in Islam and representations of Muhammad in particular. Here, again, material exists to oppose a textualized and ahistorical Islam as the aniconic other to the West (Flood 2013a & 2013b; Naef 2004).[10] Finally, the mobilization of French Muslims raises the question of their place in global Islamic networks and debates and how this is relevant to the debates unfolding in France. While from this perspective Islam can be approached in terms of flows "as a global public space of normative reference and debate" (Bowen 2004), it can also be portrayed as a bounded space separated and different from the West.

In the court proceedings initiated in 2006, the cartoons feature in a different manner, in the sense that only a very small aspect mattered to the judges. Basically, they only took into account the context created by the publications, which resulted in Danish journalists being "threatened or sanctioned," in the words of the judgment.

Charlie Hebdo was sued by these Muslim organizations for reprinting the Danish cartoons and itself producing a number of drawings, one of which—the one on the journal's cover—provoked much debate.[11] In court, the litigants claimed that the drawings were part of "a well reflected plan of provocation aiming to hurt the Muslim community through its most profound beliefs, for reasons having to do with Islamophobia and purely commercial interests" (Leclerc 2015: 117). The court carefully scrutinized the claims about the hurtful nature of these images. However, the ultimate question examined was not whether there was injury, but whether there was an intention to hurt all Muslims gratuitously. When announcing its decision, roughly a year after the publication in March 2007, the court had taken into consideration that any cartoon must be analyzed as "a portrait which dispenses with good taste in order to fulfil a function of parody," and that the "literary genre of caricature" by being "intentionally provocative contributes in this way to freedom of expression and the communication of thoughts and opinions." Crucially, this acknowledgment of the particularity of the genre does not preclude injury. Indeed, the court ruled that one of the drawings, the one showing Muhammad with a turban-bomb, was "shocking, even hurtful ... to the sensibilities of Muslims," since it established a direct association between Muhammad and terrorism and thus "clearly implied" that "terrorist violence was inherent to the Muslim religion": "this drawing appears, taken for itself and in isolation, of a nature to offend all adherents of this faith ... because it assimilates them – without distinction or nuance – as believers in a teaching of terror" (Leclerc 2015: 115). However, the court reasoned that the drawing could not be evaluated in isolation and concluded that the texts and editorial accompanying it "seemed devoid of any deliberate desire to directly and gratuitously offend all Muslims" (Robert-Driard 2007).[12] Deciding in favor of *Charlie Hebdo*, the judgment argued that *Charlie Hebdo* did not publish these cartoons as a form of public information, but as "an act of resistance to intimidation and of solidarity with threatened or sanctioned journalists, by preaching 'provocation and irreverence' and by proposing to test the limits of freedom of expression."

What is *Charlie Hebdo* the Name of?

The strategy of the Muslim associations had been to emphasize the sensibilities of Muslims and the necessary limits to the freedom of expression. Although the French public recognized the notions of hurt and Muslim sensibility and took these into account, the case ultimately collapsed. The UOIF appealed the lower court's decision to no avail. Significantly, the decision to go to court had been contested within public Islam. Here, too, the debate reflected different rationalizations of the cartoons. Little was said about whether the cartoons were objectionable or hurtful to Muslims. Rather, the central question was: What is the status of these drawings in France? Are these cartoons a normal feature of public and in particular cultural life in France? Accordingly, different views were expressed about what constituted a reasonable reaction to the publication. The cartoon controversy provided a context in which Muslims inevitably had to engage in a concrete manner with the relation between Islam and France objectified as a cultural space. They had to define Islamic notions of appropriate public speech about religion and assess their potential difference from the features ascribed to French culture.

Tariq Ramadan was prominent among those who emphasized that the caricature enjoys a special status in French culture and that any decision should take this fact on board.[13] Ramadan sought to secure "respect" for Muslim sensibilities, but rejected the option of a lawsuit (2006). He argued that actions by European media, politicians, and intellectuals need to be viewed in a cultural context and in the light of historical developments:

> ... it was necessary for Muslims to bear in mind that, for the past three centuries, western societies – unlike Muslim-majority countries – have grown accustomed to critical, ironical – even derisive – treatment of religious symbols, among them the pope, Jesus Christ and even God. Even though Muslims do not share this attitude, it is imperative that they learn to keep an intellectual distance when faced with such provocations and do not let themselves be driven by zeal and fervour, which can only lead to undesirable ends (2006).

Ramadan goes beyond calling for a reconfiguration of the Muslim subject. Noting that freedom of expression is not unlimited and that Muslims do not seek "more censorship," he aims to reorient the debate away from legislation to "nurturing a sense of civic responsibility" enabling a different manner of exercising free speech. He asks whether it would not be "more prudent ... to take into account the diverse sensitivities that compose our pluralistic contemporary societies."

Coming down heavily on some Muslim reactions, which he describes at one point as being "as unproductive as ... insane," he sees the solution in "free, responsible and reasonable common citizenship" paired with a "self-critical approach" and the repudiation of "exclusive truths and narrow-minded, binary visions of the world" (2006). Importantly, Ramadan is careful not to reduce the conflict to a cultural issue. While he asserts the Islamic prohibition of representing any of the prophets ("a grave transgression") and frames the conflict at one point as "two universes of reference," he also emphasizes the contingency of the events and considers that the controversy came into being because it suited the political interests of various actors in Europe and the Middle East. Furthermore, like many other commentators, he alludes to supposedly commercial interests pushing *Charlie Hebdo* to publish the caricatures in order to increase sales. This line of reasoning is secondary, however, in the sense that the controversy is for him not just about a publicity stunt; it cannot be reduced to the financial exploitation of drawings.

Meanwhile, other voices in this milieu tried to radically alter the status of the drawings as satire and deprive them of any legitimacy. The solutions derived from this narrowly instrumentalist perspective were much more straightforward than those proposed by Ramadan. At the same time, a different picture of France is drawn. One example for this argumentation is provided by Ahmed Miktar, imam in Villeneuve-d'Ascq in the Lille region, in comments broadcast during the weekly radio show *La prophétie*, hosted by a local radio station. Miktar sees the cartoons basically as an instance of political "instrumentalization" targeting a people whose posture is reactive; he believes they were published to provoke disorder and violence and to prove the point that certain young people will never integrate into France.

In his comments, Miktar, unlike Ramadan, dismisses the genre of caricature.[14] He refuses to rationalize the cartoons in terms of the special status of fiction. Rejecting the criticism that Muslims are "too prickly," he argues that caricatures do not constitute a form of criticism, but are "lies, defamation. Criticism is done with real facts" (Miktar 2006). Miktar notes that there is a history of defaming Muhammad in the West and he concedes that art has been connected with "shock" and "conflict" in the West, but he basically sidelines cultural factors. Miktar reads the French context and societal views of the cartoons very differently from Tariq Ramadan. He considers that "the sensibilities of an important section of French society" have been "attacked"; according to one survey he quotes, 54 percent of respondents found them shocking. Explicit reference is made to Christians whose sensibilities had been repeatedly hurt by representations of Jesus and who went to court as a consequence. He thus supported the case brought against *Charlie Hebdo* (Miktar 2006).

There can be little doubt that most individuals in this milieu felt provoked or offended by the cartoons, but the feeling was by no means limited to this group. The prominent liberal Muslim intellectual Abdelwahab Meddeb, testifying in defense of *Charlie Hebdo* during the trial in 2007, was quoted by the judges when they concluded that the cartoon of Muhammad with a turban-bomb was, indeed, hurtful to Muslims.[15] One person who dissented was a blogger and writer from the Lille area, Mohamed Louizi.[16] A former member of the Union who left after disagreements in 2006, Louizi publishes a blog called "*Écrire sans censure*" ("Writing without Censorship").[17] Criticism of his erstwhile companions from the Muslim Brotherhood and inquiries into their activities are an important element of his writings.

Louizi aimed to disrupt the broad consensus on Muslim sensibilities. Reacting to the CFCM press release at the end of the first trial, Louizi poured scorn and contempt on the assertion by the plaintiffs that "the legitimate right of Muslims to feel hurt by the deliberate and racist violence of [these] publications" had been validated by the court. He felt that his "belief in [Muhammad's] prophecy and in his moral qualities and human values" simply could not be undermined by satirical drawings of this kind. While the dismissal of these drawings is not singular, Louizi's criticism is inseparable from his broader critique of the attempts by Muslim organizations in France to be recognized as the mouthpiece of all Muslims in France. Louizi perceives the creation of the CFCM as part of the establishment of a class of Muslim authorities who are supposed to lead ordinary believers. In his view, this is utterly illegitimate, as the role of scholars is restricted to that of issuing warnings (*nadhīr*). The constant claims made by Muslim organizations and notably the CFCM during the controversy that they were speaking in the name of Muslims in asserting this injury were yet another example of unacceptable tutelage. Declaring that he supported the CFCM's critique of the essentialization of Islam, Louizi added that the CFCM itself was practicing its own essentialist homogenization of Muslims. A second, central reason why Louizi rejects the protests against the cartoons is related to the "amalgamation of Islam and terrorism." Again, Louizi acknowledges the risk as "certainly real," but he importantly adds that "people must specify which 'Islam' they are referring to." From his point of view, the connection between terrorism and a certain interpretation of Islam—this interpretation of Islam is sometimes designated as "anti-Islam"—cannot simply be denied. He concludes that "it is not the Danish cartoons or those of *Charlie Hebdo* that cause the connection. It is produced by 'Muslims' themselves and those who pretend to represent them and defend them, right or wrong" (Louizi 2007a & 2007b).

The Republican March: An Imposture by Zombie Catholicism?

After the staff of *Charlie Hebdo*—who had been under police protection for several years—were murdered on January 7, 2015, more than 3 million people demonstrated in major French cities on January 10 and 11. There were other casualties, too, during this terrorist episode: a police officer was killed on January 8 and four customers were killed in a kosher supermarket on January 9, with several others wounded.[18] These other deaths, however, were of marginal significance to the mobilization which took place on January 10 and 11, when the protesters adopted the slogan *Je suis Charlie*, in white letters on black, echoing a hashtag created just hours after the attack. Although the scale of protest was unprecedented in modern French history, the debate about *Charlie Hebdo* and its drawings continued. This in itself is remarkable: in spite of massive efforts to rally the nation around *Charlie Hebdo*, the controversies about it continued. French Muslims were part of this debate, but the fault lines can by no means be reduced to a division between them and other French citizens. As we saw above, this was not a single-issue debate centered around the legality of these caricatures, nor was it simply about how to interpret specific caricatures. Rather, the debate about their meaning was entwined with a much broader discussion about the history and present state of France and of Muslims in France. At the same time, this debate was about thrashing out one aspect of normative Frenchness, namely attitudes toward the mockery of religions in public life.

This aspect became notably more important after the 2015 attack. To laugh when religions are mocked was declared specifically French early on by the political elite. During the court proceedings in 2007 after the first cartoon controversy, when a number of politicians—including the presidential candidates Sarkozy, Bayrou, and Hollande—testified, in person or in writing, in favor of "freedom of expression," Sarkozy had claimed that those who laugh at the drawings are keeping alive an "old French tradition." After 2015, the slogan *Je suis Charlie* soon came to be understood precisely as a call—in particular—to Muslims to accept the mockery of Islam and to identify with the work of *Charlie Hebdo*. While it is clearly plausible to see *Je suis Charlie* as a unifying statement in the sense that it expresses the simple idea that no one should die for any statement about any religion, in the context of France the message of *Je suis Charlie* was often seen as much more specific and tied to the magazine's views on Islam and other religions. This is, for instance, the position taken by Ahmed Jaballah from the Union in an op-ed which appeared in *Le Monde* a couple of days after the demonstrations (2015). Jaballah argued that he was Charlie as he wished to defend freedom of expression, but that he also disapproved of the "editorial line" of the journal—which he associated with a "provocation of Islam"—and in that sense he could not identify himself as Charlie. Jaballah also took care to point out that "numerous voices" had criticized *Charlie Hebdo* in the past.

In the aftermath of the attacks a wide range of voices in various fora emerged to denounce claims equating Frenchness with Charlie.[19] The constant assertions by the journal's staff that it criticized any religion restricting public liberties and fought any kind of racism were questioned by a significant number of commentators (Fourest 2015). Gauging the precise impact of these voices is not easy. However, they can and need to be situated in a societal context which, if we consider the poll data, had been far from unified ever since the attacks and in spite of the impressive demonstrations. According to one poll, 42 percent of French considered, a week after the demonstrations, that it would have been better not to publish the Danish cartoons (de Saint-Victor 2015). This "large minority of French," as de Saint-Victor calls it, manifests itself later in surveys. In 2016, 71 percent of French declared that they were Charlie, but in 2018 that number was down to 61 percent (Libération 2018).

After the attacks, the critique of *Charlie Hebdo* was fleshed out further. The most elaborate attempt to do so was the study by historian and anthropologist Emmanuel Todd, *Sociologie d'une crise religieuse: Qui est Charlie?* (Sociology of a Religious Crisis: Who is Charlie?), published in April 2015. Todd's widely discussed study triggered multiple responses, including one by Prime Minister Manuel Valls (2015), for its proposal of a radically different view of France and those French who mobilized under the banner *Je suis Charlie*.[20] Retracing the gradual process of the de-Christianization of France since the eighteenth century, Todd describes France as divided. His focus is on those regions in the periphery which were until the 1960s "Catholic bastions" and which converted over the following three decades to "unbelief" (2015: 30f.). According to Todd, the "division of space" between a Catholic periphery on the one hand and a de-Christianized center and Mediterranean coast on the other "remains active, subterranean and non-conscious" (2015: 42). "Zombie Catholicism" is his name for the life after death of "this residual form of a peripheral Catholic subculture" (2015: 55). Assuming that unbelief correlates with emptiness and anxiety, Todd argues that "unbelieving France needs a scapegoat in order to find her equilibrium and to replace her own now defunct Catholicism." It has found this scapegoat in Islam (2015: 66f.). From Todd's perspective, Charlie—the one who filled French streets and squares on January 10 and 11—is an "old acquaintance," who emerges from "the mutated forces which once supported the Catholic Church" and hail from regions with predominantly inegalitarian family structures; his home is not the revolutionary tradition (2015: 82, 89).

Todd acknowledges the many "positive elements" which are part of the "grandiose" national mobilization in the wake of the attacks (2015: 87). However, his central argument is that the analysis of events needs to focus on "sociological determinants" and unconscious mechanisms and much less on rationalizations provided by the actors (2015: 20f.). Against this backdrop, in a context of rising Islamophobia and anti-Semitism,[21] he sidelines Charlie's claims to defend freedom, wondering who he will resemble when he grows up and whether his basic values—namely authority and inequality—will then become more manifest (2015: 89). This outline of Todd's book is fragmentary but it suffices to show that here France, in whose name Charlie claims to speak, attacks Islam, which is characterized as the religion of an oppressed minority. The contrast can hardly be stronger with Charlie's advocates, who defended the demonstration as a call for dignity, tolerance, and *laïcité* and a rejection of jihadism (Valls 2015).

Mokhtar Awards: Making Manifest the Reality of Islam

Todd criticized the aftermath of the attacks for generating a confusion between the "*right*" and the "*duty*" to "blaspheme." The willingness to blaspheme, he maintained, had become an essential part of "being French" and was monitored in individuals in a manner reminiscent of "the Inquisition" (2015: 13; emphasis in the original). Attitudes in the French population toward *Charlie Hebdo*, largely focused on French Muslims, were coming under widespread scrutiny. Indeed, during the minute of silence observed in French schools after the attacks, a number of incidents were reported where pupils disrespected the silence, a fact that led to an ongoing public debate.[22]

Just as this claim to normative Frenchness was being expressed, a short video was published. It served as a call for contributions to a film festival—the Mokhtar Awards—whose annual theme was the title of the video: "Tell us about Prophet Muhammad" (Mokhtar Awards 2015). This short film—allegedly "inspired by a real fact"—depicts a scene in a classroom, on January 12, where pupils are asked to draw Muhammad "as if for the next cover of *Charlie Hebdo*." One pupil, heard as a voice off, writes a letter to Muhammad instead of producing the requested drawing. While viewers listen to the letter, they watch the teacher reading it after class has ended. Concise and fragmentary, the video nevertheless reframes the controversy about drawing Muhammad. The kernel of dissent is no longer about the permissibility of drawing Muhammad, but about the possibility and necessity of doing it. The student cannot depict Muhammad as he has never seen him, but by closing his eyes he sees images, images of people affected by Muhammad—"I saw a tear in the eyes of my mother while reading your story"—and other images of people he wants to draw. The teacher would not let him explain what he sees when Muhammad's name is evoked, but he does not bear her a grudge: "She probably never learned to love someone she does not see. But I love you without seeing you." The video concludes by expressing a hope: "If you only could come back amongst us for some hours, a few minutes, a few seconds, she could eventually understand . . ." (Mokhtar Awards 2015).

The cartoon controversy stimulated a host of counterinitiatives and publications aimed at acquainting people with the real Muhammad.[23] Often the guiding idea was to publicize the truth about Muhammad and Islam by, essentially, providing a factually correct account founded on Islamic sources.[24] The video "Tell us about Prophet Muhammad" is different. It emerged out of an initiative born in 2013, the short film festival known as the Mokhtar Awards. In fact, the Mokhtar Awards has become an all-year educational venture aimed at coaching young filmmakers in different French cities and putting young talents in touch with more established directors as part of a broader process to encourage Muslims to make films rather than merely watching them. Although this initiative was launched partly to correct the image of Islam current among the French public and partly to share with others, Muslims and non-Muslims alike, the joy which Islam procures, the usage of fiction sets it apart from many other projects.[25]

The festival features short movies—up to five minutes in French or English—from both fiction and documentary genres. All these films tell short stories about Muslims in France addressing a variety of topics. Here, I limit myself to highlighting two ways in which such films can intervene in constructions of reality and their contestation. On the one hand, not surprisingly, fiction is used to tell stories about who Muslims really are rather than how they are regularly perceived or depicted by non-Muslims. That is, fiction serves to counter representations which, ironically, usually pretend to the status of objective knowledge. On the other hand, these films are not simply attempts to correct distorted representations of social life in France. Rather, these films are also about a much more general theme, which is how Islam transforms individuals and allows them to act upon themselves, and more generally, what kind of changes encounters with Islam produce in social relations. In a sense, it is not so much the conflicts between different representations of the reality of Islam in/ and France which primarily matter here. Moving beyond the more narrowly apologetic concerns entailed by such conflicts, it shifts the focus to a broader question: How can individuals come to perceive reality?

Let me illustrate this by looking at the three prize-winning films in 2013. The film that emerged first in the public vote, "Le fil vert" ("The Green Thread") by

Sarah Sayd (2013), is about Hicham and his spiritual quest. More precisely, it is about Hicham discovering that it is his spiritual life which ultimately counts and brings fulfillment. The film starts with a short sequence showing Hicham as a young boy standing at his window at night, while a voice-over of Hicham as an adult recalls his father often telling him that "Islam was perfect" and advising him never to miss the morning prayer, for it is at this moment that God descends to the lowest sky in order to fulfill the wishes of believers. Hicham confesses that he had been somewhat dubious about this in younger days. The film then moves forward in time, depicting Hicham's life as an adult: "My life was just the daily grind.'" Islam was there, but a "feeling of emptiness" remained: "I fulfilled my obligations, prayer, *zakat* and fasting, but I felt that I was missing something." We then observe his attempts to change this state of affairs by following various kinds of advice: he studies, helps the "poor," defends "freedom and justice" (we see him with a Palestinian scarf coming home from a demonstration), he takes part in sport activities, helps a mother carry her shopping, marries ("marriage is half of religion" as a prophetic tradition proclaims), and helps his wife in the household "just like the Prophet". In spite of his efforts, he is unhappy, killing time with computer games until the day he wakes up and thinks about his death and how God will ask him "how he had spent his time." Panic grips Hicham who feels an urge to "find the mission that God had created me for, the goal of my existence." After reflection and prayer, reports Hicham years later, he grasped how Islam "is synonymous with gentleness, patience, trust and perseverance." In this sequence, he is shown as an entrepreneur engaged in fair trade with carpets. The film ends with images of Hicham performing the morning prayer just as his father had advised him to do: "The young kid I was has grown older and finally understood that to approach the Most High you have to bow low with humility. O *Allāh ʿazza wa-jalla* I need you so much, at every moment and forever. Only God knows."

This film, then, describes how Islam provides Hicham with the practical and cognitive means to change and thus fully realize himself. The film that took third prize, "Regarde plutôt la mer" ("Just Look at the Sea"), adopts a different approach to demonstrating the reality of Islam for Muslims, namely God's presence through his signs and messages: "for every moment of our lives, for every person, for every trial, God sends a Message, a Sign ... It is up to us to open our hearts, and to contemplate the marvels all about us." The film, by Sofiane Benabdallah, follows three individual men in Marseilles, all of them in some way experiencing unhappiness and difficulties in their life. All three pass through the same place at the port where women distribute small cards with a verse from the Qur'an. In the final sequences they read the cards, take in the beauty of the sea and setting sun, and contemplate qur'anic wisdom—about life and afterlife,[26] the aims of marriage,[27] and the inscrutability of God's decree[28] (Benabdallah 2013).

The winner of the second prize, the film "Sunna" by Hicham Ismaili, who also played the lead role, uses fictionalization to criticize prejudiced and mistaken views of Muslims by other French people (2013). The movie is about a young journalist, Carole, assigned to interview the author of a book entitled "My Fight against Islam." Her boss is explicit about the need to tap the public interest in anything negative about Islam. During her trip to see the author in the *banlieue*, Carole waits at the railway station eating biscuits from a bag which she believes she brought with her. The man sitting next to her, who is reading the Qur'an, also helps himself to her cookies, to her growing dismay. When he suggests sharing the last one with her, she gets up and gives vent to her anger. Sitting back down, she discovers her own biscuits and realizes that the man had shared his with her without her even asking. She tries to find him in the train and later on at a station. After a cut, we see Carole inside an apartment, opening the door to her station acquaintance who is now her husband. He has been shopping for the household and brings not only the same brand of cookies, but also the first copy of her published autobiography *Partage et vivre-ensemble* (Sharing and Living Together).

This narrative not only dissolves the fear of Islam by exposing it as based on prejudice consciously reproduced for mercantile ends. Significantly, it also suggests that Muslims strive to conduct themselves in the best possible manner, as exemplified in the practice of Muhammad. The love story unfolding between Carole and her future husband presupposes his love for the Prophet's "Sunna," which gives this film its title.[29] It is when Muslims seek to behave as well as possible that prejudice can be identified as prejudice and non-Muslims can be won over. To explain hostility toward Islam, this film relies on a single cause, which is the erroneous perception of Islam by non-Muslims. "Sunna" narrates how one non-Muslim woman comes to realize her mistake, and the title of Carole's autobiography, with its reference to "living together," takes on a new meaning. In its current usage, this notion assumes a problematic difference which must be overcome so that a common existence can be established or maintained. In the film, however, this problematic difference is simply dissolved by conversion to Islam.

Soumission as the Future of Multicultural France

The story of Carole and her husband is set in a context where the fear of Islam presents business opportunities for the media. This assessment of French society is shared by a significant number of observers. Numerous references in public discourse to the need to avoid speaking of Islam in general terms or amalgamating Islam with violence testify to an awareness that stereotyping, with all its social consequences, is a genuine phenomenon. However, there is no consensus on how to describe the social position of Muslims and Islam in society. In other words, there is no consensus at all that Muslims are subaltern. The French and international public were forcefully reminded of this fact the day the *Charlie Hebdo* massacre took place. That same day in 2015 saw publication of the widely anticipated novel *Soumission* by one of France's most successful, prominent, and controversial authors, Michel Houellebecq.

The plot of this bestselling novel presents a radical countervision to representations of Islam as a minority religion. The story is set in France in the year 2022 where, for two years, riots and clashes between nativist groups[30] and "Muslim immigrants" have been ongoing (Houellebecq 2015: 43). It begins shortly before presidential elections which will overturn the political system. The two candidates who make it to the runoff are Marine Le Pen from the extreme-right National Front and—to widespread surprise—the candidate of the Muslim Brotherhood, Mohammed Ben Abbes. Ben Abbes is a thoroughly moderate Muslim: "Unlike his sometime rival Tariq Ramadan ... Ben Abbes had kept his distance from the anti-capitalist left." Moreover, he had understood "that elections would no longer be about the economy, but about values, and that here, too, the right was about to win the 'war of ideas' without a fight." Whereas Ramadan presented Sharia "as forward-looking, even revolutionary," Ben Abbes emphasized its "reassuring traditional value – with a perfume of exoticism that made it all the more attractive" (2015: 125).[31] With socialists and conservatives voting to block the extreme-right candidate, Ben Abbes is elected by a narrow margin to the presidency of the Republic and will create a government of national unity with left- and right-wing forces. This is the context for the story of François, a university lecturer in Paris in his forties who is depressed, lonely, and alcoholic. François is a specialist in Joris-Karl Huysmans, a nineteenth-century writer who converted to Catholicism. The novel concludes with François deciding to convert to Islam.

The Islamization of France is a central element of the plot, as the fragmentary outline above shows. More particularly, the plot is predicated on a Muslim Brotherhood candidate being elected president of France in 2022. How can such a story be read as anything other than pure fiction? The basic plotline is "absurd," as Olivier Roy put it (Roy 2015). There can be no doubt that a "Muslim party" in France—and, moreover, a party winning more than 20 percent of the votes in the first round—is not a realistic option for a long time to come.[32] Indeed, minimal effort is made in the book to explain the emergence of this entity, which is supposed to occur after the presidential elections of 2017 (won by François Hollande, who garnered the vast majority of votes by citizens of Muslim faith). Houellebecq himself admits that the prospect of such a party is "not very realistic" and that its rise would take "several decades," even supposing that Muslims "succeed in getting along with each other" (Bourmeau 2015).

I want to suggest here that in spite of the novel's highly unlikely basic plot, incidentally lacking any element of fictionalization, the novel can be and is read in ways that help shape understandings of multicultural France. One reading of the novel considers it an intervention in debates about multicultural France today and processes of political and societal transformation which have been underway now for several decades and which provide multiple indicators for the kind of future which could become reality.[33] A second approach to the novel is, broadly speaking, historical. It reads *Soumission* as a narrative on the consequences or inherent problems of liberal modernity, that is, about the future of modernity. This is in line with how Houellebecq's earlier novels are often read (Morrey 2013). These approaches to the novel are not uncontested. Importantly, the differences between commentators partly relate to different understandings of the basic functioning of fiction, i.e., the relation between fiction and politics and the referentiality of the novel (performative or constative).

Soumission as Provocation

The question of the novel's plausibility is not central to all comments. Shifting focus to the novel's performative effects, it is possible to argue that Houellebecq seeks primarily to provoke readers and change attitudes.[34] Provocation can be easily detected on different levels—for example, in the ridicule underlying portrayals of politicians like President François Hollande or François Bayrou; it can also be detected in the claim implied in the novel's plot that French society would, on the whole, simply accept the new order.[35] More generally, one might see the basic plot as a insolent challenge to all those among the elite who naively believe that they are still in charge of things. The specter of imminent change passing unnoticed is expressed clearly after a reference to how intellectuals in the 1930s misread Hitler: "It may well be impossible for people who have lived and prospered under a given social system to imagine the point of view of those who feel it offers them nothing, and who can contemplate its destruction without any particular dismay" (Houellebecq 2015: 44). We might, like Pierre Assouline, refuse to condone this attitude: "What is more irresponsible than a fantasy that plays with fire about civil war in today's France?" Even if we leave aside the issue of how a novel might contribute to violent change,[36] we can still read this work as a gauntlet thrown down to the public, calling upon them to take sides in the ongoing restructuring of the political field, as Jean Birnbaum observes.[37]

What Does it Mean to be a Human Being Without Faith?

Other commentators object to political readings of the novel as these are seemingly oblivious to its literary form.[38] Indeed, there is some reason to be skeptical about identifying Houellebecq with statements by the main protagonist in this novel, or any other, as has regularly been the case. While Houellebecq, in interviews given after the publication of earlier novels, has sometimes reiterated statements by his protagonists,[39] this interpretive approach is basically inadequate, as it fails to reflect the internal complexity—both stylistic and philosophical—of the narrative voices in his novels.[40] In the particular case of *Soumission*, there are some good reasons for rejecting a simple reading of the novel as a programmatic statement on the situation of France. This point was made, for example, by Norwegian writer Karl Ove Knausgaard, who argued that the novel's "fundamental theme and issue" is "this lack of attachment, this indifference" on the part of the principal character, "much more so than the Islamization of France, which in the logic of the book is merely a consequence." Following Knausgaard, the novel's perhaps central question is "What does it mean to be a human being without faith?" Besides, until the very last sentence this lack of attachment never fully disappears, as the narrator does not actually convert in the final pages, but looks forward in time and describes his future conversion in the conjunctive mode.

Soumission and the Failure of Integration

To accept Knausgaard's claims that the novel's theme is the condition of immanence does not negate, however, that religion is recurrently discussed by characters in the novel with an eye to the social conditions and implications of religious faith. Importantly, some of these discussions primarily consist of monologues by experts, such as the lengthy analyses of French politics and the Muslim Brotherhood provided by an intelligence officer (Houellebecq 2015: 65–9, 116–22). As Raphaëlle Leyris has pointed out, while the novel is full of declarations of love to literature, the author often seems tempted by the essay genre.[41] This affinity with essay writing, against the background of Houellebecq's often noted affinities with realism, certainly facilitates a political reading of the novel. While the arguments exchanged by the novel's characters about religion in society and the situation in France do not simply add up to a party manifesto, they contribute to define parameters for what counts as legitimate in debates about multicultural France. In this case, they support the plausibility of claims that French politics are abysmally overwhelmed by the task of governing Muslims and that the presence of Muslims will alter France beyond recognition. Fleshing out the novel's title, they sow the most radical doubts about the integration of Islam as a normative project.

This fundamentally political dimension of the novel is widely noted by reviewers. Laurent Joffrin thus considers that "Houellebecq's fable" elevates "the ideas of the National Front or those of Éric Zemmour to the center of the intellectual elite"; "in a word, it keeps a place warm for Marine Le Pen in the Café de Flore," i.e., the archetypical site of Parisian intellectualism.[42] Importantly, this kind of analysis denies any significant distance between the novel and extreme-right thought, notably that associated with Éric Zemmour, Renaud Camus, and theories of the *Grand remplacement*. This directly frustrates Houellebecq's pretentions to neutrality beyond issues of literary concern (Leyris 2015; Bourmeau 2015). Like Joffrin, many reviews focused on what Houellebecq does or aims to do with this novel and where to situate Houellebecq on the political and ideological chessboard.[43] In many ways, this question is about the very (il)legitimacy of reading the novel. A central criterion for placing a tag on the author is the question "Islamophobic or not?"[44] There were some straightforward affirmative answers, like the one from the CFCM's expert on Islamophobia.[45] More attuned to the novel's complexity, Tareq Oubrou worried that the "seeming Islamophilia" of the novel might engender Islamophobia.[46]

For Sylvain Bourmeau—in an interview with Houellebecq and a review of the book (2015)—*Soumission* is quite simply "a novel-symptom" of the current context, which is primarily characterized by Islamophobia, understood as "cultural racism," a concept which Houellebecq fully rejects. Entitling his review "French literary suicide," Bourmeau argues that the novel should not be treated as fiction at all, as it merely repeats "fantasies" circulating in society. Houellebecq, it follows, has abandoned any artistic pretensions and committed "literary suicide." A very similar position is adopted by Tariq Ramadan, who does not address the comparison of civilizational ideologies in *Soumission* and reduces the book to an intervention—motivated, again, by pecuniary aims—in a debate heavily influenced by Islamophobia. His analysis, like Bourmeau's, attributes the narrative directly to the societal context and concludes that it does not merit analytical attention. He draws parallels to Éric Zemmour, again negating the difference in form between Houellebecq's novel and Zemmour's historical essay (Ramadan 2015).[47] Edwy Plenel, founder of the online news platform *mediapart* and author of a critique of Islamophobia (2014), formulates a fundamental criticism of the media response to the novel and warns his colleagues: "You turn a book which is an Islamophobic fiction into a political event."[48] For Plenel, the matter is clear. Politics and literature constitute qua epistemology two separate spheres. Journalists are charged with reporting "facts" about politics, whereas literary critics discuss fiction. In this perspective, the debate about Houellebecq's novel has no right to exist and Plenel's primary aim is to disrupt it.[49]

Changing Identities and Alliances in Multicultural France

In the course of public debates, significant reasons are identified for not seriously engaging with *Soumission*. This does not preclude readings that to different degrees aim to do just this. The theme of the reconfiguration of identities and structures of power in France's multicultural society frames one engagement with the novel. This kind of reading, whose validity Houellebecq has partly confirmed,[50] generates various reflections, often of fragmentary nature, on France. Despite the complex interweaving of satire, many aspects of the novel's—often very detailed—portrayal of France are recognizable. To quote Bernard Pivot, "everything is at the same time enormous and subtle, excessive and intelligent, unbelievable and logical."[51]

Among the transformation processes thematized in the novel, the reshaping of cultural and political identities, of alliances and antagonisms, is a major issue, as important to public debates as it is to the novel's plot. This transformation is partly enabled by the dysfunctionality of the current system, a system which is structured around the antithesis left/right, which places significant emphasis on antiracism, and which is largely oblivious to religion as an independent variable. This basic structure is a carryover and inadequate to the new context and this is one of the reasons why the future French president in the novel, Ben Abbes, is able to overhaul the system from the inside, as it were, in response to an increasing demand for religion. Thus the Muslim Brotherhood is able to "campaign … on family values, traditional morality and, by extension, patriarchy" without being called "reactionaries" or "even fascists" by the remnants of progressive forces—a fate that would have been reserved for conservatives or the National Front. The antiracist ideology of the left makes it impossible to fight Ben Abbes as he has a "multicultural background" (Houellebecq 2015: 126). After the elections, with the right in any case close to the Muslim Brotherhood, the left—divided between a "pro-immigrant wing" and "secularists"—ultimately accepts an alliance with the Brotherhood and the right (2015: 120), putting an end to "the politics of right versus left" (2015: 120) which had been a constituent factor in the Fifth Republic. Now the political struggle can center on "the real enemy" of Ben Abbes: secularism (2015: 127).

The web of interrelated issues picked up by the narrative in *Soumission* has been widely discussed since the 1980s. These debates reflect the changing meaning of political and cultural identities and the (re)alignment of parties and political alliances. Their fictionalization elicited diverse reflections. Olivier Roy, whose critique was mentioned earlier, sees the relationship between Islam, Christianity, and the nativist movement as "perhaps the most interesting" "theme" in the book: "Islam realizes the unthought of Christianity and the nativists."[52] In his review of this "satire," Bernard-Henri Lévy, coauthor of an epistolary exchange with Houellebecq,[53] dismisses the notion that fiction and reality relate in a uniform sense, emphasizing rather their multifaceted connections. Defending the novel's plausibility from this perspective, he points to the debilitated state of the major political parties and a willingness to rethink alliances.[54] Note that the novel's presentation of societal developments solicits critique which tends to reproduce the divisions in the broader debate about Islam. The novel's plot implies an "overwhelming return to Islam" among younger generations which is denied by Sylvain Bourmeau (Houellebecq 2015: 154). Rather, Muslims (as adherents of other religions) are affected by a trend toward secularization (Bourmeau 2015) and in this sense they are part of Houellebecq's secular modernity. Here, Bourmeau is proposing a variation on the typical argument that integration is quite simply not necessary, as Muslims are not different from other French and are not transforming France in any way.[55]

Religion and the Passing of Traditional Society

Soumission is also read as a narrative on the consequences of liberal modernity. One pivotal element of the novel is its vision of religion. In particular, a vision of Islam and its societal function is expounded by the converted nativist intellectual and university chancellor Robert Rediger, author of a thesis on René Guénon's reading of Nietzsche, and later by a university colleague of François, another former nativist called Godefroy Lempereur. For Rediger, Islam is the answer to the multidimensional crisis which has caught France and more generally Western Europe in its throes since at least the First World War. This crisis results, sociologically, from the inevitable failure of liberal individualism: it "triumphed as long as it undermined intermediate structures such as nations, corporations, castes, but when it attacked that ultimate social structure, the family, and thus the birth rate, it signed its own death warrant" (Houellebecq 2015: 139). The dysfunctional character of gender relations in the West is analyzed by the protagonist, François, in the very first chapter (2015: 12ff). Later, on behalf of the nativists, Lempereur explains the demographical advantage of cultural groups and societies where "couples... follow one of the three religions of the Book and maintain patriarchal values" (2015: 38).

The passing of "organic society" and the nefarious influence of various humanist philosophies—whether communism or forms of liberalism—have weakened Europe; it has turned away from what is essential (and what remains essential for humans outside Europe), namely metaphysics, even if the atheism of Westerners, in Rediger's view, is only superficial. While Rediger believes that "without Christianity, the European nations had become bodies without souls – zombies" (Houellebecq 2015: 130), Christianity, "based on the decadent, antisocial personality of Jesus" who "enjoyed the company of women ... *and it showed*" (2015: 140; emphasis in the original), is dismissed for the future. Islam, rational and reconciling man with the world as it is, offers the solution. Rediger presents this not just as a theoretical statement about (un)true philosophy, but as "the return of religion" (2015: 130).

The ramifications of this thinking are multiple, but the basic upshot is not difficult to name: the existence of religion—its content, form, and force—makes a difference to society.[56] This understanding of religion's social functions is the basis for a relatively distinct perspective on power in multicultural France and the recent presence of Islam. From this perspective, Islam constitutes—structurally—a real challenge to the political system and to the existing order, an order which is identified above all with secularism, seen not as the simple differentiation between state and religion, but as the overcoming of religion.

The historical perspective outlined in the novel is very broad. In a sense, it seeks to capture the totality of history. We may doubt, of course, that such a claim can be substantiated empirically. Hans Blumenberg has argued in the modern context that "to the extent that the philosophy of history continues to be fixated on the definition of an overall structure of its object, it is burdened by no longer realistically fulfillable obligations towards the persisting 'great questions'" (1983: 50). Leaving aside anthropological questions about why those "great questions" persist (and how questions relate to answers),[57] we shall confine ourselves to noting that some authors, such as the extraordinarily successful Houellebecq, continue to raise them, and consequently they can be used—or dismissed—to rationalize the situation of France.[58] Fragments of this broad historical perspective are outlined throughout the novel (and through Houellebecq's other novels). When taken up and examined by commentators, they feed into very different assessments of multicultural France and the cultural and power dynamics shaping its future. Emmanuel Carrère, in a review that is in some places rapturous, accepts the basic thesis of civilizational decline: "Many good spirits, again, consider this civilization to be threatened today, and I think this menace is real."[59] Himself the author of a well-received study on the origins of Christianity, *Le royaume* (The Kingdom, 2014), Carrère—while shying away from a judgment on the "slippery topic"—draws a comparison with antiquity. Between the first and fourth centuries, the Roman Empire faced a threat very similar to the one we are witnessing today, but the object in those days was Christianity. Carrère points out that at that time "the best spirits feared something like a 'great replacement'" and it actually occurred in an "unnatural *métissage* of Greco-Roman thought and alien Judeo-Christian superstition." "European civilization" is the result. Carrère imagines that a similar process can take place again and that "Islam will, over a shorter or longer term, constitute not the disaster, but the future of Europe, just as Judeo-Christianity was the future of Antiquity." Note that for Carrère the overarching theme of Houellebecq's œuvre is "the radical inversion of perspectives"—in religious terms we might call it "conversion" or in history "paradigm change"—and this, he claims, is why "we all" read Houellebecq "with amazement."[60] Nevertheless, he does not envisage the possibility of an Islamic future for Europe simply as a "radical inversion," but tempered by the hope that Islam will "adapt" to the "freedom of European thought." By adopting this broad historical perspective, Carrère deems the scenario outlined in *Soumission*, which he sees as an opportunity for France, plausible.

Conclusion

In debates about French Islam and secular politics, there are frequent calls to distinguish between facts on the one hand, and fictions, fantasies, or obsessions about Islam on the other. These calls are often legitimate responses to discourses which disregard any rules on evidence and reasoning and exempt themselves from argument. At the same time, they imply a certain risk of portraying the discursive space of secularism in a manner which obscures its fragmented structure, ambiguity, and potential for conflicts.

This chapter has attempted to account for part of this complexity by focusing on usages of fiction in rationalizations of secular politics. The works of fiction examined here set out as a minimum to contribute to representations of social reality; they thus play their part in the complexity of debates about secular politics, its objects and aims. While the works vary and present their own particular features, their common feature is that they refer to and reproduce recognizable elements of given understandings of reality and alter them by inserting them into different semantic contexts. They define specific conditions of social intelligibility by referring to a reality which is exterior and anterior to themselves (Dubois 2000: 43f.). Rather than conceiving of fiction in opposition to reality, we might draw on Dieter Henrich and Wolfgang Iser to say that a given understanding of reality is exceeded here through acts of fictionalization (1983). It is because fiction surpasses reality—and is not merely situated beyond reality in a different sphere—that it can both be criticized with reference to reality and constitute an inquiry into the understanding of reality, here notably the reality of multicultural French society, its changing identities and structures of power. The analysis has shown that fiction merits analytical attention not only because it is part, to different degrees, of rationalizations of secular politics. All the cases discussed here indicate that aesthetic rationalizations of politics are also a major domain of public dissonance. Here, too, Roy's insightful statement—"The debate with Islam is in fact a European search for a European soul" (2005a)—is significant; the massacres perpetrated in January 2015 have not simply obliterated these divisions in society about constitutive values.

Works of fiction have been approached here as directly relevant to the milieu of public Islam. This is one reason why *Charlie Hebdo* and Houellebecq occupy a central position in this chapter. From a comparative perspective, the impact of the Mokhtar Awards festival seems almost negligible. Given the imbalance in this chapter in favor of critical or hostile views of Islam, it is worth underlining that fictionalizations serve diverse and often opposing political ends. Suffice here to consider how the future of France and its presidential elections have been fictionalized by other (successful) authors, too. In 2011, well before *Soumission* appeared, Sabri Louatah started publishing *Les sauvages* (Savages), the four-volume story of Idder Chaouch, the first Socialist president of Algerian and

Kabyle descent who defeats Nicolas Sarkozy. The contrast between this story (to be turned into a TV series) and Houellebecq's account is significant: for a start, Chaouch, designated as a French Obama, is secular and married to a Jewish wife. Shortly after *Soumission*, sociologist Michel Wieviorka published a novel, *Le séisme* (The Earthquake, 2016), about the first six months of government under the next French president—in this case, Marine Le Pen. Some years before that, bestselling writer Corinne Maier coauthored with Frank Martin *Manuel de savoir-vivre en cas d'invasion islamique* (Handbook of Etiquette in the Event of an Islamic Invasion, 2008). While the *Manuel de savoir-vivre* shares with *Soumission* an interest in the instability and complexity of identities, the authors' political position is diametrically opposed to the views usually attributed to Houellebecq.[61] In a series of critical and mocking vignettes describing various dimensions of social life in future Islamic France, the authors seek to deconstruct the alterity of Islam. Systematically subverting hegemonic representations of France, the threat of Islamization is partly dissolved. As France is and remains the same in spite of some formidable moments of rupture, one example being the Vichy regime, the authors wonder: "Regimes perish, religions follow one upon the other, France remains. *Douce France*, is she not eternal?" (Maier & Martin 2008: 172).

The second argument explored here is that the works of fiction discussed operate in a social context whose delimitation and definition is always already contested—even without these controversial but by no means simply illegitimate representations of society. The scope of dissent is very significant when it comes to assessing the threat of political Islam globally and in France, or the hostility or hatred toward Islam or Muslims in France. This has led me to argue that the normative approach which often prevails when studying controversies about fictionalizations of Islam and Muslims should be reconfigured, giving greater consideration to how normative issues are entwined with controversies about defining fictionalized objects, their social contexts, and the requirements that a (present or future) social reality will impose on society and the state.

8

Islamophobia and the Critique of Integration

Introduction

In the course of the 2000s, the vocabulary available for describing French society and politics, in particular the politics of secularism, has changed. Notwithstanding many strong and persistent reservations, the term "Islamophobia" has become an integral part of the vocabulary used in public debates. As the *Commission nationale consultative des droits de l'homme* (National Consultative Commission on Human Rights, or CNCDH) states in its 2013 report: "One cannot deny that the word is today part of the political, media and institutional landscape" (13). This chapter examines the extent to which this term has altered the conditions of debate about Islam and Muslims in France. My interest here is not to reflect upon how best to conceptualize Islamophobia nor to contribute to the complex "on-going controversies over what it actually is that we are analysing when we study Islamophobia" (Opratko 2017: 86f.).[1] Rather, it is to grasp how the term is understood in France and what makes it both appealing and contentious to different parts of the French public. More particularly, the aim is to assess the potential for criticizing integration policies which this polyvalent term opens up.

In a first step, I will examine why this term has been increasingly found useful. While the term "Islamophobia" is often associated by its critics with restrictions of free speech, I will argue that Islamophobia functions primarily as a category of illegitimacy as opposed to illegality. Islamophobia designates phenomena (i.e., perceptions, discourses, and acts) which are considered illegitimate from an epistemic point of view and which are susceptible to engender harm notably to Muslims and, more generally, to negatively impact society. Needless to say, the identification of what exactly can be labeled Islamophobia is contested in France. Nevertheless, the term carries weight and its introduction into public debates, particularly those on the integration of Islam and Muslims, matters. In a second part, taking the case of the *Collectif contre l'islamophobie en France* (Collective against Islamophobia in France, or CCIF), I will scrutinize in more detail the arguments developed in the course of mobilizing against Islamophobia and assess their critical leverage in the debate on integration. More particularly, my interest here is to examine the reasons that are advanced to support the epistemic and moral disqualification of certain views or attitudes regarding Islam and Muslims. Ultimately, the question raised is whether the mobilization against Islamophobia gives rise to new arguments which have the potential to restructure the debate on integration and alter its disorderly nature.

I have chosen to focus on the CCIF because this group, notably its former spokesperson and director Marwan Muhammad,[2] has become, in the course of the 2010s, the public face of campaigns against Islamophobia and a major force in the broader debate about Islam.[3] The origins of the CCIF go back to 2003; its founders are described by its former president Samy Debah (2003–17), himself a teacher of history, as a group of teachers, sociologists, and engineers. The collective defines itself as "independent ... of any religious tradition" (CCIF 2012a).[4] The official definition of Islamophobia by the CCIF is clear-cut: "all acts of discrimination or violence against individuals or institutions based on actual or assumed belonging to Islam" (CCIF 2019a). This definition is closely related to a key aspect of the CCIF's work, namely to offer legal advice from professional staff to hundreds of victims of Islamophobia. Its website contains a wealth of information, including "first-aid packs" with legal advice for various situations. This legal counseling takes place alongside a second activity: monitoring Islamophobia. Since its inception, the CCIF has published annual reports which include statistics on "Islamophobic acts" (CCIF 2004, 2019a: 8f.).[5] In the often heated debates about the legitimacy of the notion "Islamophobia," and how to measure it, the data collected by the CCIF garners significant, partly critical, attention.[6] Finally, the annual reports (with regular contributions from various academics) and other publications by the CCIF or members provide an analysis of the causes and functioning of Islamophobia.

Rethinking the Separation Between "Belief" and "Believers"

Growing usage of the term "Islamophobia" has triggered an important discussion about its conceptualization. Questions of varying complexity have arisen: What precisely is the object of this "phobia"—Islam or Muslims or both? And how do they relate to each other? Should "Islamophobic" be replaced by "anti-Muslim," as this would distinguish the critique of Islam as religion from indiscriminate attacks on Muslims, the latter being subject to significant legal constraints contrary to the critique of religion? Does it make sense to speak of racism toward a religion and its members, given the individual or voluntary dimension of religious adherence? These and other questions are hotly debated by various experts.

While these questions are important, my focus here is slightly different. I aim to outline how the term is being used in the public sphere, what it names and what kind of difference it makes. The numerous critics of the term "Islamophobia" regularly portray it as a newly invented means to silence criticism of Islam. It is, as essayist Pascal Bruckner put it, an attempt to "intimidate" and to create a "crime of opinion," thus putting an end to intellectual debate (2017: 32–43).[7] From this perspective, the term "Islamophobia" is associated primarily with attempted legal restrictions and censorship (and more generally with the identification of judiciable acts).[8] This perspective is not unfounded, and the CCIF's motto "Islamophobia is not an opinion, but an offense" bears that out. However, by associating campaigns against Islamophobia primarily with legal restrictions and censorship, one partly misconstrues how the term functions and how it affects the debate about Islam. Here, I want to argue that Islamophobia does not only designate justiciable attitudes or perceptions of Islam which are considered to be illegal. It is also used in a routine manner to classify certain attitudes, perceptions, or acts as illegitimate. In this sense, Islamophobia creates new criteria, in addition to legal ones, for problematizing perceptions, attitudes, and speech acts about Islam and Muslims. At the same time, the term is used to describe a broader social context and this usage, in very different ways, raises questions as to the characteristic causes of the hostility toward Islam. From this perspective, Islamophobia is not so much a means of censorship which puts an end to critical debate, but rather contributes to reframing debates.

First, it is noteworthy that the campaigns against Islamophobia simply make use of existing legislation, whether it relates to discrimination or regulation of freedom of expression. As discussed in chapter six, the legal protection offered by the law of 1881 as amended in 1939 and 1972 covers "incitement to discrimination, hatred or violence" and "abuse" and "defamation" of groups or individuals on grounds of ethnicity, nationality, race, or religion.[9] Since 1939, social groups defined with reference to "race" or "religion" and targeted in defamatory or abusive speech are recognized by the law, even if their actual capacity to litigate remained extremely limited until 1972.[10] As we saw in the case of the caricatures of Muhammad with a turban-bomb, French law does recognize that any speech about a religion, or in this case, its prophet, can be hurtful to its adherents and thus subject to restrictions. Having said this, French legal provisions, like those of other Western liberal states, are founded on the distinction between "believers" and "beliefs," protection not being extended to the latter "as mere ideas" (Cumper 2017; see also Mahmood 2009). From the outset, of course, this limits what can be achieved, by recourse to legal action, in anti-Islamophobia campaigns aimed at public speech about Islam (as religion) as opposed to speech about Muslims.

I want to suggest that one central reason why the term "Islamophobia" is increasingly found useful is that it allows challenges to the idea that speech about Islam—as it supposedly concerns only ideas, and not people—should be totally unrestrained. In other words, it enables the distinctions between believers and belief—people and ideas—to be marked as problematic and arguments to be advanced for conceiving these boundaries in more complex ways. From this perspective, Islamophobia is used to designate a set of attitudes to and perceptions of Islam and persons identified as Muslims which are declared illegitimate, even if they are mostly not illegal. The claim to illegitimacy is based upon the fact that these attitudes and perceptions are negative *and* indiscriminate—and hence that they are unreasonable.[11] Needless to say, these attitudes and perceptions can lead to the targeting of Muslims or persons identified as such.

Islamophobia as a category of social illegitimacy underlies, for example, the statement, by the feminist philosopher Elisabeth Badinter: "One should not be afraid of being labelled an Islamophobe" (*Marianne* January 6, 2016). Basic elements of this notion of Islamophobia were defined and popularized in the 1990s by the influential Runnymede Report in the UK, which argued that criticism of Islam should be considered Islamophobic only when the internal diversity of Islam and its capacity to develop are negated (Runnymede 1997). This basic idea is of great significance to how many authors define Islamophobia in France. Thus, Islamophobia has been associated with the dual process of homogenization and racialization (Hajjat & Muhammad 2013: 96), with a failure to differentiate between the acts of "some individuals" and an "entire community" (Plenel 2014: 31), or with a "global, general and inconsiderate hostility towards a particular religion" (Boniface & Médine 2012: 63). Philosopher Pierre-André Taguieff, while critical of the term, likewise argued that it should be used to designate "the essentialization and demonization of all Muslims" (2017: 186). In this usage, Islamophobia is also closely associated with prejudice, ignorance, irrationality, and various emotional states of anxiety and fear. Taking issue with Islamophobic intellectuals and security experts, the political scientist Vincent Geisser commented: "What really galls them are the *imaginary Islam* and *fantasized Islam* placed in the service of an ideological combat where real Muslims are only extras and phantom shadows" (Geisser 2003: 115f.; emphasis in the original). In sum, Islamophobia functions as a category of social illegitimacy; it does not simply designate certain acts, attitudes, or perceptions as judiciable.

In another related usage, the term "Islamophobia" refers generally to a societal context characterized by various forms of hostility against Muslims and/or Islamic institutions. For the CNCDH, one reason for adopting the term after years of hesitation was, as the chair Christine Lazerges put it at the time, "to make available a term other than anti-Muslim acts in order to chart a disquieting context: the rejection of Islamic practices, which does not necessarily translate into a criminal act" (Mouillard & Sauvaget 2016). This definition can be used to garner survey data on "a quasi-phobia, that is, an intense fear of Islam and Muslims" to corroborate the description of societal contexts as Islamophobic, as the CNCDH does in its annual reports (2013: 20).

More importantly, the term "Islamophobia" constitutes a new factor which potentially allows the political configuration to be rearranged. The analytical framework for this study has conceptualized the politics of integration as a reversible power relation. Building on that, I want to argue that Islamophobia allows a shift in focus away from the supposedly problematic difference of Muslims toward their exclusion by various institutions and actors in state and society. Another way to describe the political effect of referencing Islamophobia is to say that it identifies actors, attitudes, views, and identities and problematizes them in relation to policies on Islam and Muslims and, more generally, the social position of French Muslims.

CCIF and Critique of Integration

The restating of mainstream debate about integration, as the anti-Islamophobia activists of the CCIF seek to do, may seem at first sight very critical, far-reaching, and unambiguous. Islamophobia is defined in the CCIF's motto categorically as "not an opinion, but an offence." Furthermore, Islamophobia tends to be equated with racism. The CCIF Manifesto asserts that Islamophobia "appears as the acceptable expression of disguised racism" (2019a). In his monograph *Nous (aussi) sommes la nation* (We, too, are the nation), Marwan Muhammad goes for full convergence and writes that Islamophobes "are simply racists" (2017: 99), placing the conceptual debate about the term in the field of racism (2017: 109). However, one of his articles, is titled "Islamophobia, this almost acceptable racism" (2013). The close association between Islamophobia and racism indicates a straightforward moral condemnation of Islamophobia and will be understood in this manner by readers. Robert Miles's statement that "throughout Europe, racism has become a category of abuse, a means of declaring one's political opponent an immoral and unworthy person" (1993: 83) applies here.[12] How should one read the fact that Islamophobia is, at least sometimes, not made fully convergent with racism? One could start by saying that this nonconvergence points to the complexity of the truth regimes within which Islamophobia functions.

Let me elaborate on this by taking the monograph *Nous (aussi) sommes la nation*, in which Muhammad outlines how to "deconstruct Islamophobic ideologies" (2017: 109–61) followed by a chapter about the "structural ambivalence" of the state with regard to Islamophobia (2017: 163–203). Muhammad, as I mentioned, frames his discussion of Islamophobia unambiguously as a specific kind of racism and discusses at length the question whether the notion "state racism" is applicable to the French republic.[13] At the same time, he touches on numerous issues routinely raised in the debate about the integration of Muslims. *Nous (aussi) sommes la nation* provides thus an opportunity to examine what critique of integration policies can be conducted within this approach to Islamophobia. Is this project of "deconstructing" Islamophobia taking down the edifice of integration with its underlying assumptions and the knowledges used here to govern? Is this critique able to delegitimize the debate on integration as we might expect, given that Islamophobia is conceptualized as a kind of racism? In brief, to the degree that the critique succeeds in demonstrating that the integration of Muslims is a nonissue, this is not so much the result of bringing in a notion of racism which functions as a discursive "game-changer." Rather, it results from strategic interventions in the reversible structure of the notion of integration. Importantly, Muhammad's critique is not situated outside of the space of disorderly secular politics: the identification of Muslims remains a centrally important topic as do the knowledges used to identify them. All this is done, as elsewhere, not in a manner which is always coherent from a logical point of view—which is not to say that it is inefficient.

Part of the critique articulated by Muhammad draws on arguments which have been circulating for some time and have figured in previous chapters. There is his critical examination of simplistic appropriations of Marxist theories on religion, appropriations which he sees as informed by particular experiences with Catholicism (2017: 111–14); his criticism of a pseudo-universalism associated with the French left, which mistakenly believes itself immune from racism because of its progressive identity (2017: 132–7); or the idea that the public problematization of Islam's difference results from displacing issues of (in)equality—social, economic, political—to the emotionalized rejection of specific groups (2017: 123). All three arguments displace the burden of integration. All identify factors outside the group of immigrant French and their descendants as causes for the perception of immigrants as problems. Muhammad invites "atheists" to abandon their prejudiced view of religion ("an internal revolution" is the condition for continuing the conversation with him) (2017: 114); the French left is invited to self-liberation, implying that it must read its own history critically if it wants to become (again) an "actor of change and liberating peoples" (2017: 137).

A second line of argument accomplishes a far-reaching dissolution of the problematic of integration. This is achieved by adopting a radical individualist perspective, positing abstract universal rationality as a yardstick of political legitimacy and by redefining the meaning of patriotism. From this perspective, Muhammad launches a full-frontal attack on the principle of assimilation illustrated here with the saying, "When in Rome, do as the Romans do" (2017: 143f.). In his view, this injunction is "nonsense" and causes harm to everyone involved. The saying is nonsense as it presupposes that the addressees of this injunction are not "Romans." As what matters for being "Roman" is simply nationality and residence in "Rome," this is not true for those to whom the injunction is addressed in France, i.e., immigrants and their descendants. Furthermore, there is no "homogeneous" "Roman" people which, in the author's view, seemingly invalidates the existence of "Romans" as a people altogether; "Romans" are fallible and should not be an automatic object of imitation; and "reason" is the only basis for judging what people say. "Critical distance" to what people say is a necessary element of "respect": "There is no higher form of attachment and sincere love for one's country, land and people than to express disagreement when they are exposed to danger or threatened with losing their capacity for discernment" (2017: 143f.).

The normative category "Roman" is thus rejected. It would seem easy to criticize the above argument for ignoring how this kind of normative category is in fact implemented in France[14] or how the historical legitimacy of practices, institutions, and their modes of change are reasoned beyond crude claims to an eternally self-same "Rome" which no one is allowed to change (2017: 143). However, this would surely miss the point that the individualist rights-based perspective outlined here, dismissing more complex notions of culture, society, or power and emphasizing that any regulation of social life requires direct democratic legitimation, can act as a powerful counterargument to assimilation. Second, such a critique would simply miss out on the fact that this argumentation partly functions as performative.

The line of argument concerning the hijab seems, at first sight, to be similar. Here, Muhammad adopts again a strongly individualist, liberal perspective to make the controversies appear, in a word, pointless. Referring to covered women, he emphasizes that "It seems to me that only *they* are qualified to choose freely the way in which *they* want to dress themselves and only *they* can define the meaning which they give (or not) to this choice" (2017: 118; emphasis in the original). The individualist perspective is also crucial for the claim that "The least one can say is that there are as many reasons to wear it as there are women wearing it." Through his total incomprehension of why some people would set out "to labor for the exclusion of Muslim women wearing the scarf," Muhammad negates the legitimacy of the entire debate, arguing that only the women wearing headscarf—if they want to—should talk about it (2017: 118).[15]

However, in contrast to the fundamental critique of "When in Rome . . .," this disavowal of integration rapidly turns out to be merely one aspect of the argument. Despite reaffirming his aim to advance "beyond sartorial polemics" (2018: 119), the author moves on to give responses to some of the usual questions around the hijab, thus reproducing the ground laid by previous debates. Why are Muslim women, if they are indeed forced to wear the headscarf, being "punished a second time by being excluded from education and work?" If these women have "a hidden political agenda," "how would unveiling them make it disappear?" And so on. Muhammad's responses compile often well-rehearsed arguments from a mixture of legal maxims, irony, and consequentialist ethics.

This argumentation is quite typical of how the author engages with the problematization of Islam: a good deal of what is presented here under the heading "deconstructing Islamophobic ideologies" turns out to be very similar to any other intervention in the debate on integration.[16] To put it differently, the scope of deconstruction is limited as is indicated by the fact that no systematic critique of the politics of asking "Who are Muslims?" and "What is normative Frenchness?" is conducted. Muhammad emphasizes his rejection of "generic categories" and, referring to the "generic category" of Muslims, he writes that it has a "dehumanizing" effect on Muslims. Restoring their "voice, way, and belief, which are personal, intimate, and singular" is to "reestablish their most essential dignity" (2017: 205).[17] However, French Muslims and other French are not dissolved by the author into a mass of individuals who would be—simply—free to define themselves.[18] To the contrary, in the concluding chapter "One Islam, Muslims," Muhammad proposes a "refined sociology of practices and modes of belonging" (2017: 216) among Muslims. This leads him to elaborate a "typology of trends and sensibilities" in French Islam which he uses to dispel misconceptions about certain groups, such as Salafis, while recognizing and decrying the insufficiency of these categories and their inability to do justice to "the complexity and fluidity of Islam in France as elsewhere" (2017: 219).[19]

These summary remarks suffice to indicate the considerable distance separating the categorical condemnation of Islamophobia succinctly expressed in the CCIF's motto "Islamophobia is not an opinion, but an offense" and the actual critique of French debates on Islam. In the course of this latter critique, Muhammad does, to some degree, seek to dismantle the legitimacy of debating the integration of Islam. At the same time, however, he is responding to central questions of this debate in a manner which accepts the necessary definition and classification of identities and which, fails to undo the discursive frames of integration politics.

It is from this perspective that Muhammd pursues the aim to demonstrate that "Muslims are normal" (2017: 97), an assertion which leads him to discuss, for example, the topic of Muslims and *communautarisme*. Muhammad rejects the designation of Muslims as communalist (*communautaristes*). He claims that "in their social interactions, whatever their level of [religious] observance, the conduct of Muslims debunks media depictions which describe them as withdrawn into themselves"; they "do not constitute an exception to the other national communities" (2017: 141). As I have argued before, this is the typical argument refuting the need for integration by claiming that Islam and Muslims are just not different. A brief look at the quantitative evidence presented by Marwan Muhammad (a financial mathematician by training) shows that Muhammad's argument is likely to dislodge a number of widespread assumptions about the self-segregation and difference of Muslims. However, the data presented—not suprisingly—is far from conclusive and argumentative gains are uncertain. For example, Muhammad presents data to assess the place of religion in the identity of French Muslims. The data supplied shows that 33 percent of self-identifying Muslims mention religion as a significant feature of their identity, as opposed to 45 percent of Jews and 7 percent of Catholics. While the second rank of Muslims and the relatively low absolute figure can be used to counter certain ideas about Muslim *communautarisme*, these figures can also be read in a different manner. In fact, the closeness to Jews can be read as a bad sign, as Jews are like Muslims scrutinized with regard to the "temptation of self-segregation" (Schnapper et al. 2009). Moreover, in both cases the comparatively high figures have a more general significance as they cohere with the exceptionally high number of believers who choose to describe their religiosity as "strong": 43 percent of self-identifying Jews and 49 percent of Muslims do so in contrast to less than 10 percent of Catholics (Simon & Tiberj 2013: 9f., 26). Finally, in the case of Muslims, this high figure, in turn, has to be partly explained with another important difference between Muslim and Catholic descendants of immigrants. Whereas Catholics are affected by secularization and manifest decreasing religiosity, gradually conforming to the general tendency in the population, Muslims are only weakly affected by this process of secularization (Simon & Tiberj 2013: 23f.).

Conclusion

Although activism against Islamophobia has largely focused on a limited number of religious practices, notably the headscarf,[20] the introduction of the term "Islamophobia," now regularly judged irreversible, is indicative and part of a broader movement that is reconfiguring integration politics.

Islamophobia names a perspective from which to study factors external to the French Muslim population which obstruct their inclusion as equal citizens into France. It is central to a narrative of France that counters many narratives of the secular-universalist Republic. It permits the definition of aims and criteria (of varying precision) for the necessary government of various groups of French with a hostile attitude toward and view of Islam and Muslims. Responding to certain critics of Islam, it allows a problematization of the notion of free speech and facilitates calls for freedom and responsibility to be more closely conjoined. Needless to say, there is significant resistance and criticism, but conditions of speech in debates on Islam and integration have changed to some degree.

It is important to recognize that referencing Islamophobia has allowed the articulation of a powerful critique of integration, triggering a systematic, monitoring of practices, arguments, and structures in French state and society defined as racist and designated as Islamophobic. At the same time, the analysis has made apparent the limits of this critique. In a certain sense, these limits find expression in the fact, earlier mentioned, that in some of its statements the CCIF does not fully converge Islamophobia and racism, such as in the Manifesto's claim that Islamophobia "appears as the acceptable expression of disguised racism" (CCIF 2019). This statement expresses both the clear will to establish Islamophobia as a form of racism, a category which continues to be seen by the broader public as one of unambiguous amorality, and the inability to do so fully. This is reflective of a broader discursive context, I want to suggest, where the moral disqualification of what is designated as Islamophobia is often difficult to realize as it cannot be separated from the simultaneous critique—complex and contestable—of various problematizations of Islam and Muslims. As in the previous chapters, the debate in this field is one where normative questions (about equality, subordination, and inclusion/exclusion) are closely entwined with the questions "Who are Muslims?" and "What is normative Frenchness?"

In the course of undoing problematizations of Islam and Muslims, the arguments examined here can sometimes be considered contradictory. At times, Marwan Muhammad seeks to demonstrate that the difference of Muslims is no cause for concern (or is simply not given), and at times a liberal, individualist discourse of human rights is adopted which seems to reject any legitimate interest by the state or public in citizens' private lives. In this sense, we can say that the mobilization against Islamophobia remains situated in the disorderly space of secular politics.

Conclusion

The claim that modernity, or secularism, does not constitute a coherent, well-ordered whole can be made to advance diverse arguments and different conclusions can be drawn from it. Talal Asad has pointed out that this claim in itself does not tell us much about the significance of modernity. One reason for this is simply that even if descriptions of modernity as fully integrated totality may be wrong, they may nevertheless be efficient as assumptions and "distinctive sensibilities, aesthetics, moralities" guiding people in their determination of how "modern life is required to take place" (Asad 2003: 14). Furthermore, it can be argued that "those who assume modernity as a *project* know" about the contradictions, contestations, and complexity characterizing "the West," another entity mistakenly reified, some would claim (Asad 2003: 13; emphasis in the original). From this perspective, the real question is not so much why modernity has been misdescribed as well-integrated totality, but "why it has become hegemonic *as a political goal*" and "what practical consequences follow from that hegemony" (Asad 2003: 13; emphasis in the original).

This general point is transposable to the case of secularism in France as it was studied here. To say that secularism does not fit orderly visions of politics is not to downgrade its significance nor to assert that complexity is necessarily an impediment to transformative action.[1] Furthermore, to claim that secularism is not fully coherent nor seamlessly integrated into the republican order does not amount to unmasking secularism, as these facts have not gone fully unnoticed by decision-makers (which is not to deny that they are sometimes rejected with great emphasis). One illustration of this is provided by an influential report on *laïcité* from 2003 where the author François Baroin, vice president of the *Assemblée Nationale*, states that "human rights and *laïcité* to some degree contradict each other" (Portier 2016). *Laïcité* is understood here by Baroin as implying that religion is a private affair, whereas human rights refers notably to the freedom to manifest religion, Baroin's central problem being the headscarf and its de facto authorization in public schools by the *Conseil d'État*. One year later, of course, the scope for conflict between this notion of *laïcité* and human rights had been significantly reduced by the law of March 15, 2004, which redefined the religion section of human rights as applicable in public schools.

Here, my interest in the complexity of secularism has been motivated by a more specific concern which has to do with the diverse ways of reasoning employed in and enabling secular politics. I suggested considering this plurality of rationalities as an effect of the double separation inherent in secularism. My contention was that the separation of state and religion needs to be thought together with what has been called the "definitive separation of words from things" (Singer & Weir 2008: 57). According to Foucault in *The Order of Things*, this "separation of words from things" happened in the late eighteenth century, when the conditions of possibility for knowledge moved from the field of "immediate visibility" to "a sort of behind-the-scenes world even deeper and more dense than representation itself" (2005: 259).[2] At that moment, "man" comes to occupy an "ambiguous position as an object of knowledge and as a subject that knows: enslaved sovereign, observed spectator" (2005: 340). Two aspects of this broad epistemological transformation are relevant here, both of which make for inherently contestable and instable knowledge. First, the emergence of new quasi-transcendental objects of (and conditions for) scientific inquiry, such as society, identity (and alterity), and memory. Second, the directly related inherent tendency to a form of immanent critique—the auto-demystification of human sciences—which in the context of this study takes shape notably in the critique of Orientalism and, more generally, postcolonial thought.

All through this investigation, I have indicated positive examples of disorderliness and analyzed why and how they matter to Muslims' engagement with secularism. Secular politics are not only disorderly in the sense that the identification of objects of government (notably Islam and Muslims) raises questions about how to define and delimit categories (e.g., worship, religion, culture) and categorical boundaries (e.g., between faith, identity, and religion; history and memory; morality and history; fiction and reality) or which criteria to use to distinguish past from present and determine how the past relates, on the one hand, to contemporary times and, on the other, to today's human subjectivities. These questions are not fully (or systematically) answered nor always explicitly asked. More importantly, there is regularly disagreement—in the face of diverse options—over what kind of knowledge can answer the questions which emerge in the course of governmental practices. These conflicts can be summarized in the following questions: Can Muslim identities be reduced to a result of social processes or do they have to be understood in their particularity as one religious tradition? If the latter, what is the particularity through which Muslim identity should be understood? How "much" do social factors matter in Muslim lives? If subjects are socially determined, does it limit their responsibility, and if so, how can determination and responsibility be distinguished? Is history, e.g., of colonialism, complex and discontinuous to a degree that the past can and must be neatly separated from the world of today? Or can it be subjected, partly or in its entirety, to moral or legal criticism by contemporaries according to their own standards? Can the reality or dimensions of it be made to appear through works of fiction? If so, how can their manifest and often drastic difference from conventional reality be explained? What kind of claims about essential properties of human collectives, like Muslims, and contextually meaningful objects, like the Islamic tradition, are reasonable and legitimate, and which ones not? Are there ways of perceiving or representing Islam and Muslims which are morally problematic even if legal, and what are their central features?

These and other acts of identification are accomplished with a greater or lesser degree of care and intelligence and can in this respect be very different from each other. Nevertheless, three general remarks can be made. First, they always imply that at some point arbitrary decisions are ultimately taken—or, more often, conventionalized decisions taken by others are accepted—about what is (and how it became what it is) and about how humans and things are to be classified. Second, these decisions regularly *need* to be taken, since the vocabulary which is available for reasoning in a particular case is partly insufficient, conflicted, or just not self-evident; at the same time, they are decisions which *can* be taken, i.e., they constitute repeated occasions when choices can be made. The regulation of Islamic worship and the government of Muslims are in multiple ways enmeshed with these more general acts of identification concerning various dimensions of France, Islam, and Muslims. In one sense, the conflicts about these questions constitute a basic form of power struggle between a broad variety of actors who seek to define, in terms favorable to them, the definition of integration, i.e., the inclusion of Islam, and the modalities of implementing this aim. As this study has made apparent, vastly different positions exist with regard to this question. I have shown, third and finally, that actors in the milieu of public Islam are part of this power struggle, actively using secular rationalities and contributing to reconfiguring the notion of integration and its implementation, whether this is through interventions in the field of social policies, notably in the *banlieue*, national memory and history writing, or Islamophobia.

The study of secular rationalities allows us to identify these sites and modalities of interweaving Islam and French contexts. If the question is how the practice and understanding of Islam change in relation to the French context, the concept of political rationality also allows France to be grasped as instable and multifaceted—and Muslims as part of it. Specifically, studying the usage of political rationalizations allows us to understand how Muslim discourses change in correlation with how transformations in and of France are reasoned and fought over. The controversies about French history, the *banlieue*, various works of fiction, and Islamophobia constitute significant cases for this correlative process. Here, the variety and breadth of Muslim positions rivals those defended more generally in French debates. The limits inherent in the question whether Muslims adapt to France become clearly apparent; the question "to which France" gains in salience.

This brings me back to the beginning, where I took up the suggestion to study it through its multiple heterogeneous rationalizations. This study indicates that there is a crucial analytical distinction to be made between secularism on the one hand and sovereignty as bounded and unconditioned power on the other. Rationalizations of power as sovereign in this sense do play a central role in secular politics and the government of Muslims: imaginations of the sovereign French state, legitimated through its past exercise of glorious-lawful power, and of the French population as a sovereign nation, i.e., a cohesive group of people with certain distinct characteristics which constitute normative points of reference for the integration of Muslims. Moreover, a largely unfettered decision-making power is wielded by the state in various fields and independent of any powers of emergency, e.g., in the selection of Muslim interlocutors, in the process of granting citizenship to Muslims (Hajjat 2010 & 2012), or in the granting of work permits to imams and in the surveillance of mosques and expulsion of imams (Jouanneau 2013; Human Rights Watch 2007). However, the exercise of this power has to be placed in a broader context, which structurally inhibits sovereign power from being exercised in the name of France. Sovereign power is inhibited by the necessary, and always to some degree impossible, representation of the "immanent but largely invisible" sovereign people (Singer & Weir 2006: 455)—invisible in spite of or precisely because of the increase in means and acts of representation (Rosanvallon 1988). The people as "the inevitable and ultimate horizon of all political interpellation" (Singer & Weir 2006: 455) is durably divided among itself and its representatives.

Joan Scott has argued that "the seeming resolution of the impossibility of representation" theorized here is the difference of sex (2018: 103). Which is to say that the "indeterminacy of democracy" resulting from its foundational "abstractions (the individual, rights, nations, representation)" is "resolved by grounding them in a seemingly concrete referent: the visible, sexed bodies of women and men" (2018: 120). Needless to say, this reference is instable and requires repeated efforts to secure the definitions and boundaries, even more so in the age of "sexual democratization" where "the order of things is presented explicitly as a social, not a natural, order, steeped in history and thus subject to change, fundamentally political and thus an object of critique" (Fassin 2011: 148). In this context, as Eric Fassin underlines, the very "status of norms" changes (2006: 125f.). Here, I have emphasized that definitions of France as the indispensable reference in discourses calling for the "integration" of Muslims, if these definitions are undertaken and transcend invocations of polysemic values, are essentially contested if only because there is a multiplicity of truth regimes and rationalizations. Sayad has argued that emigration and immigration "are a cross-check or a borderline situation which force us to reflect on the notion of the nation, obliging the latter to reveal its truth" (1984: 189). This fits the current situation of France. It is a situation in which the double question of how to define the nation (and its criteria of membership) and how to impose the latter as binding recurrently incites the French to engage in sovereign imaginations of power; however, these are, more often than not, impossible to perform.

Notes

Introduction

1. The secular was seen "as the natural and universal substratum that emerges once the superstructural religious addition is lifted" (Casanova 2011: 56).
2. "Where are the pure enclaves of secularism ... to be found?" asks Graham Ward and points out that such claims about secularism "to an extent" depend upon the "homogenising of myriad social, economic and cultural projects" (Ward 2005: 118).
3. See Peter 2008.
4. See notably Caeiro 2003, 2004, 2005b, 2006a, 2006b, 2011a, 2011b; Bowen 2009; Shavit 2016; March 2007, 2008, 2011; Baylocq Sassoubre 2008; Rohe 2003, 2004; Olsson 2016; Albrecht 2018; Larsen 2018.
5. It has been argued that integration policies are committed to a "totalist logic" (Parekh 2005: 187) aiming at interrelated processes of change in all social spheres. Such claims fail to address the crucial fact that deliberations on integration invariably draw on diverse political rationalities, thus fragmenting this policy field and the "totalist" aims which may be associated with integration policies.
6. The constitutive act of integration politics, i.e., the act of denying full membership in the nation to the group of non-European immigrants irrespective of their citizenship, can be seen as an act of sovereign power. However, this act in itself already indexes its own inherent limitations. This discourse not only asserts categorically that one kind of immigration constitutes a problem, but also indicates the ultimate aim, namely integration, and asserts, again and again, that the inclusion of immigrants into the nation is in principle possible.
7. Cf. Rose 1999: 187–91.
8. In contexts prior to 2017, I will refer to this organization as *Union des organisations islamiques de France*.
9. In her study on the Muslim Brotherhood in Europe, Brigitte Maréchal indicates that their "influence ... seems totally disproportionate to their numerical weakness" (2008: 77; see also Kepel 1994: 293ff.). In 2017, *Musulmans de France* was reported to claim 1,600 members (La Croix 2017). For an identical statement about the United Kingdom, see Bowen (2014: 101f.). In the course of the 2010s, the increasing appeal of Salafi groups and the large audiences reached by a new generation of preachers via social media is changing this configuration.

10 As regards educational institutions, other federations have undertaken efforts, too. In 1995, the *Mosquée de Paris* (Mosque of Paris), directing a network of mosques linked to Algeria, founded an institute for higher education, the Institut al-Ghazali; however, it only started to function properly (after an intermittent closure) in the late 2000s (Stegmann 2017). The Moroccan *Union des Mosquées de France* (Union of Mosques of France) relies upon training facilities in Morocco. On the major, but unsuccessful attempt to create a Theology Faculty in Strasbourg (2011–14) by the French branch of the Turkish Presidency of Religious Affairs, see Bruce (2018: 237–41).
11 See Peter forthcoming for a survey of Muslim organizations and community structures in France.
12 See Sellam 2006; Godard & Taussig 2007; Godard 2015; Leschi 2018; see also chapter three.
13 See notably Césari 1998; Khosrokhavar 1997; Marongiu 2002.
14 See notably Marongiu 2002 and de Lavergne 2003/4.
15 See notably Caeiro 2011 and Larsen 2018.
16 For two small studies, see Peter 2006d, 2010.
17 Didier Leschi, former head of the *Bureau central des cultes* in the Interior Ministry, mocks those who claim that *Musulmans de France* and Tariq Ramadan are part of an International of Muslim Brothers. His main argument is that many divergencies and differences can be observed between the organizations that supposedly form part of this international structure (Leschi 2017: 79f.).
Compare this with how Lorenzo Vidino justifies his reference to *The New Muslim Brotherhood in the West*: "Understanding that those operating in the West are not subsidiary branches of any Middle East-based organization and that affiliation to the movement is not based on formal membership, it is fair to call them Muslim Brotherhood legacy groups or New Western Brothers. Though the primacy of the legacy of Hassan al-Banna is undisputed, the New Western Brothers are now inspired by a heterogeneous ensemble of works and ideas of many thinkers and activists" (2010: 53). In the conclusion, Vidino adds: "Today it is not unreasonable to speak of some of these organizations as 'post-Brotherhood,' even though the real meaning of this expression is still to be defined" (2010: 224). For accounts from former members of *Musulmans de France* discussing their relation to the Muslim Brothers, see Abdelkrim 2015 and Louizi 2016.
18 This is not to deny that the relations between *Musulmans de France* and Tariq Ramadan on the one hand and the Muslim Brothers in the Middle East (and related individuals, institutions, or states) on the other regularly lead to controversies; for a more recent example, see Chesnot & Malbrunot 2019.

Notes to pp. 15–17   211

1 Beyond an Orderly Vision of Politics

1 The book was researched and written by a team of five young journalists supervised by the two official authors. The journalists are Ivanne Trippenbach, Célia Mebroukine, Romain Gaspar, Hugo Wintrebert, and Charles Delouche.
2 Unless otherwise indicated, translations are my own.
3 I use religious freedom as shorthand for a series of expressions, especially *"liberté de religion"* or *"liberté religieuse"* (Conseil d'État 2004: 276), *"libre exercice des cultes"* (Law of 1905; 2012-297 QPC February 21, 2013), *"liberté d'expression et de manifestation de croyances religieuses"* (Conseil d'État, November 27, 1989).
4 General limitations to proselytism have been enacted in two areas. Proselytism of any kind is prohibited for civil servants (Fortier 2008). Proselytist conduct by pupils wearing headscarves in public schools was a factor, since 1989, which limited the right to wearing the headscarf and justified the exclusion of pupils (Conseil d'État, November 27, 1989). Initially, the headscarf was not considered "a sign which is in itself characterized by ostentation or claims-making whose usage would constitute in any case an act of pressurizing or proselytism" (Conseil d'État, November 27, 1996). The law of 15 March 2004 prohibiting headscarves in public schools changed this categorization. Henceforth, as Fortier writes, the hijab of students constitutes in general an act of "silent or passive proselytism" (Fortier 2008; cf. Tawil 2016: 174 and Portier 2016: 278f.).
5 Article 1 of the current constitution states: "France is an indivisible, *laïque*, democratic and social Republic. It ensures equality of all citizens before the law with no distinction made on the basis of origin, race or religion. It respects all beliefs." The preamble to the constitution of the Fourth Republic (1946) includes a reference to "secular education": "The establishment of free, *laïque*, public education on all levels, shall be a duty of the State."
6 This point will be further discussed in chapters three and eight. Many studies have examined this issue. See notably Adrian 2016; Amir-Moazami 2007; Bowen 2007; Fernando 2014; de Galembert 2009, 2014; Joppke 2009; Jouili 2015; Lorcerie 2005; Nordmann 2004; Scott 2007; Winter 2009.
7 France Inter, Le grand entretien 2018.
8 See notably Koussens 2015.
9 See Conseil d'État 2004: 272. The definition of religious freedom as one aspect of *laïcité* was not made explicit by the *Conseil d'État* in a general manner until 2004; it had been established in the context of schools in November 1989 in response to the first hijab crisis (cf. Portier 2016: 278). On the definition of *laïcité* by the *Conseil d'État* and *Conseil constitutionnel* (Constitutional Council) (which did not provide a complete definition until 2013), see notably Tawil 2016, Philip-Gay 2016, and Guillaumont 2005.
10 France Inter, Le grand entretien 2018.

11 This is not to say that Zemmour's thought can be reduced to his interventions into the debate about Islam and immigration. Marc Lilla emphasizes the complexity of his writings: "Zemmour's views are simply too eclectic to be labeled and dismissed *tout court*. And they can be surprising" (Lilla 2015: 78). Writing in the early 2000s, Daniel Lindenberg, author of an influential essay on "the new reactionaries," praises his "impressive historical and political culture" (2016 [2002]: 95). Cf. Corcuff 2014 and Noiriel 2019.

12 The authors state that "one may rejoice at or deplore" this process of Islamization, which incidentally triggers "both negative and positive developments" (2018: 11, 14). For statements contradicting this neutrality, see, e.g., France Inter Le grand entretien 2018, and below.

13 The reference to *laïcité* is made by Fabrice Lhomme in the radio show (France Inter Le grand entretien 2018). On the term *communautarisme*, see Dufoix 2016, 2018. Note that this term, widely criticized as stigmatizing, is used less or with more caution by the government; "separatism" is seemingly introduced as substitute (Couvelaire 2020; Lemarié 2020).

14 81 percent of respondents consider that *laïcité* is under threat as opposed to 58 percent in 2005. One element perceived as threat is the wearing of ostensible religious signs in public (43 percent). The law of March 15, 2004 enacted to prohibit these signs is approved by 85 percent as opposed to 55 percent in October 2003 (IFOP 2015).

15 The expression "fake news" is part of the French title (Touche pas à mon poste 2018).

16 For an outline of how data—including data on religion—for the study *Trajectoires et Origines* (Trajectories and Origins) was collected in 2008/9, see Algava and Lhommeau 2016. See also Héran 2016: 13f. and Fassin 2012.

17 This figure is extrapolated from self-declarations by individuals in the age group 18–60 in a representative survey conducted in 2008/9 (Simon & Tiberj 2013).

18 Bergeaud-Blackler 2017 dates the take-off of this economic sector to the mid-1990s.

19 See Tadros 1998, on whom I draw here, for Foucault's usage of the concept "juridical" and its distinction from law.

20 From a legal perspective, this claim about the "retreat" of the state would need to be specified further. It may suggest a degree of systematicity which is not warranted here. According to Curtit and Fornerod, French law of religions is a network of superimposed norms from various legal branches "which do not emanate from a general supra-legislative principle" and "the guarantee of fundamental rights and in particular freedom of religion seems disconnected from the provisions regulating faith-based organizations and activities." Moreover, "the juridical norms draw the outlines of a law on faith-based organizations rather than a law of religious practices" (2016: 113f.). Hennette-Vauchez likewise emphasizes that the recent and ongoing "redefinition or reorientation of the principle" of *laïcité* imply a shift from

questions about the organization of public authorities to the "individual activation of the guarantee of free exercise of worship" (2016: 13f.).

21 See chapter eight for a detailed discussion of other usages of the term "Islamophobia."

22 I draw here on Bleich's work, who defines Islamophobia as "*indiscriminate negative attitudes or emotions directed at Islam or Muslims.*" Bleich adds: "These are the ontologically significant aspects of Islamophobia because they are the ones that we assume influence societal interactions that we care about" (2011: 1585; emphasis in the original).

23 In his review of definitions of Islamophobia, Bleich points out that "[a]s much as they may lack precision or coherence, what unites all of the above definitions, proto-definitions, and underlying assumptions is a sense that Islamophobia is a social evil" (2011: 1583). One may object here that it is possible to bracket off the question of Islamophobia's illegitimacy and only focus on whether a given perception of Islam and/or Muslims or attitude is undifferentiated—i.e., monolithic, essentialist, etc. —or not (2011:1586). However, the labeling of a perception as undifferentiated will be mostly understood as implying a critique as illegitimate.

24 Stolz adds: "Definitions that try to circumvent the 'pathological element' in stereotypes, prejudice or Islamophobia are generally not very convincing" (2005: 549).

25 See Rose & Miller 1992.

26 Given that rationalities are not conceived here as systems, the search for and identification of contradictory features in the politics of secularism is only of limited analytical importance. Cf. Jon Elster: "The term contradiction is basically a logical one and should not be extended in a way that is totally divorced from its primary meaning. If by contradiction we mean only opposition, conflict or struggle, then we should say opposition, conflict or struggle" (1978: 3). In a discussion of European liberalism's multiple and simultaneous notions of law and freedom, Foucault points out that "heterogeneity is never a principle of exclusion; it never prevents coexistence, conjunction, or connection. And it is precisely in this case, in this kind of analysis, that we emphasize, and must emphasize a non-dialectical logic if want to avoid being simplistic" (2008: 42).

27 As John Milbank puts it in more general terms, it is the social which "supplies the categorical universals under which are to be comprehended all empirical contents. Traditional and particular religions are thought to encode in a non-perspicuous fashion this priority of the social (...)" (1990: 103).

28 This difficulty and the conceptual problems related to using the terms Islam and Muslim have been noted by various authors. See, for example, Diop & Kastoryano 1991: 107 and de Galembert 2004.

29 The term is, of course, not used as normative concept; it simply denotes a power constellation.
30 In 1992, an amendment to Article 2 of the Constitution adds "The language of the Republic is French."
31 The "national" framing of this study is far from exceptional, although the more recent interest in secularism certainly has had the effect of diminishing the attention paid to the post-migration dimension, as Modood has pointed out (2012).
32 See Weil 2004.
33 For a discussion of the term "integration" and integration policies, see chapter three.
34 In the words of the Council of State, the Republic "does not recognize any form of worship," as stipulated in section 1 of the law of 1905, but in order to guarantee the free exercise of religions it needs to be able to "identify them" (Conseil d'État 2004: 284).
35 No conclusive statement can be made here given the lack of studies systematically examining the impact of the judiciary's basic framework on judicial and administrative decisions relating to Islam. Examining this impact is complicated by the fact that cases exist where the framework is misinterpreted due to prevalent concepts of religion in the cultural space of France. E.g., Auvergnon reports a case where the question whether *ministres du culte* (religious officials) can conclude an employment contract is wrongly answered from a Catholic perspective, as it were. Equating the function of *ministre du culte* with Catholic clergy, the administration in this case denied the imam his rights. Whereas the option of an employment contract is excluded for Catholic priests (notably because an essential element of a contract, the subordination to a superior, is lacking in accordance with doctrine), imam and mosque association are free to give their relation the form of an employment contract (Auvergnon 2019: 112; Hafiz & Devers 2005: 130f.; see also Forey 2007; Jouanneau 2013: 97f.). Back in 1829, freedom of religion and the system of state-recognized forms of worship—Jewish, Catholic, and Protestant—were already understood by some as being applicable to Muslims. That year the Protestant pastor Vincent wrote that if "Muhammadans" (*mahométans*) were to "travel and settle in our ports," they would be entitled to the rights established in the Charter of 1814 (Despland 1999: 260), notably in Article 5: "Everyone may manifest his religion (*religion*) with equal liberty, and obtain for his worship (*culte*) the same protection" (the Jewish religion being excluded by this Charter from public subsidies). Then as now, the basic recognition of Islam as one religion and form of worship to which the general regime of rights and obligations is applicable, is not contested.
36 Jean-Marie Woehrling considers that the poverty of jurisprudential thought in this field may be explained by the fact that a definition of religion is after all of "in practice of little use" (2003: 29).

37 Indeed, the law requires "religious officials" (*ministres du culte*) to take out specific insurance, but does not define the group of persons to which it applies (Woehrling 2003: 34).
38 See Rolland 2005, Philip-Gay 2016: 225f.
39 See also Messner 1999: 337f.
40 Alain Boyer points out that the case law tends to be conservative and to disadvantage new religions, as two criteria regularly used in French jurisdiction are "seniority" and "universality" (2005: 40). From a similar perspective, the *Conseil d'État* considers that the "main difficulties" in the identification of worship appear "in the case of movements which pretend to be religious or spiritual but which cannot be related to a 'known' religion" (Conseil d'État 2004: 383). Conflicts about the identification of religions are played out on a much larger scale with regard to "sects," another term not defined in law (Woehrling 1999). Since the 1980s, a series of parliamentary commissions have been investigating "sectarian deviances." In 1995, a list based on information gathered by the home intelligence agency in France was published by parliament, characterizing 173 groups as "sects" (Chantin 2007). The usage of this controversial list (without any legal force) was abandoned in 2005, although the surveillance of "sects" by a state agency created in 2002 still continues.
41 Conseil d'État , 27 June 2008 (no. 286798).
42 This attempt failed when the *Conseil constitutionnel* obliged the government to include in the proposed law a clause making the prohibition of "burqas" inapplicable in spaces of worship (Joppke & Torpey 2013: 40–6; Weil 2010).
43 This decision is taken in a context where the classification of the headscarf as Islamic practice is contested. See *Le Monde* for the response of Ahmed Jaballah, president of the *Union des organisations islamiques de France*, to Prime Minister Rocard. Jaballah argues, against Rocard, that the hijab is a Qur'anic prescription (23 and 25 November 1989). Note, however, that in the course of implementing the law of March 15, 2004 prohibiting ostensible religious signs in public schools headcovers worn by Muslim students in overseas territories such as Mayotte and Réunion were declared to be cultural. Other "religious signs" were equally classified "cultural."
44 For a recent overview of legislation in this matter, see Fornerod 2018.
45 See below.
46 Note that the European Council for Fatwa and Reserch describes the headcover both as act of modesty and sign: "Allah (swt) decreed this modesty upon the Muslim woman so that she is easily distinguished from the non-Muslim and from the non-obedient" (ECFR 2002: 18).
47 The above discussion of the belief-centered notion of religion leads up to the question of whether or not this notion is being transformed in relation to the new presence of Muslims. Based upon research among students in French high schools, Séverine Mathieu argues that an "islamization of the representation of religion" is

observable among students and teachers, i.e., that the "religious" is "primarily" "associated with Islam and its practices" (2009: 85–9).

48 See Fernando 2014 and Jouili 2019 for different perspectives on the usage of "culture" in French debates.

49 See chapters two and three.

50 Note that administrative practices have contributed to this blurring (Boyer 1993: 88; Commission Debré 2003: I, 64). Note also that the same phenomenon exists for Catholic associations (Hafiz & Devers 2005: 96). The blurring of boundaries has a long history. The association owning the first mosque constructed in metropolitan France, the Mosque of Paris, had two distinct legal identities (Islamic and French secular, respectively founded in 1917 in Algiers and 1921 in Paris); its legal form in France was that of a nonprofit association which allowed it to receive public subsidies (Boyer 1992: 23–7).

51 The registration of a worship association at the *préfecture* is not compulsory, nor does it suffice to obtain any of the privileges that are reserved for cultic associations (Hafiz & Devers 2005: 101; Conseil d'État 2004: 283f.).

52 For example, Islam and other religions are also classified, by the *Conseil constitutionnel*, as one element constituting the "pluralism of currents of sociocultural thought" in France which warrants representation on public television in weekly shows devoted to each religion (Forey 2001).

53 Mohamed Merah killed two French soldiers in Toulouse on March 15, 2012. He had killed another soldier on March 11 in Montauban and went on to kill four persons, including three children, in a Jewish school in Toulouse on March 19. He died in a shoot-out with French police on March 22, 2012.

54 See Todd 2006: 230ff. on how "Muslim" became a racialized ethnicity when the French left Algeria in 1962. Muslim was "no longer an adjective for 'French', or even for 'civil status', but an 'origin' [*origine*]" (231).

55 See Pratten (2012) on two senses of essence (concrete-explanatory and defining) and the different effects of essentialism.

56 "It is on the basis of these forms, which prowl around the outer boundaries of our experience, that the value of things, the organic structure of living beings, the grammatical structure and historical affinities of languages, attain our representations and urge us on to the perhaps infinite task of knowing" (2005: 265).

57 Foucault also notes that "it is always possible to make human sciences of human sciences – the psychology of psychology, the sociology of sociology, etc." (2005: 387).

58 On constructions of Islam as France's other, see Lorcerie 2005/6.

59 See Gingrich 2004 and also Grossberg 1996 for a discussion of the different articulations of this approach.

60 See chapter six.

61 Said 1995.

62 See notably 2008a, 2008b. Daniel Reig similarly argues that the transformation and decline of Arabic Orientalist studies (*orientalisme arabisant*) in France, due to decolonization, immigration, and cultural revolution, begins in the mid-twentieth century (Reig 1988: 167f., 178).
63 "Specialists and the public at large became aware of the time-lag, not only between orientalist science and the material under study, but also – and this was to be determining – between the conceptions, the methods and the instruments of work in the human and social sciences and those of orientalism" (Said 1995: 105). Said himself refers to the "Crisis of Orientalism," starting in the 1920s, but as to its outcome, no clear picture emerges from his account. The more recent history of scholarship covered by him contains breaks and processes of internal differentiation (1995: 290, 291, 300, 320f.) —as one would expect in a context of "crisis"—but there are also very important lines of continuity (e.g., 1995: 6, 287, 290, 322). Some of the changes are qualified as limited or superficial; notably, the usage of social sciences is repeatedly presented as merely a matter of using new jargon (1995: 109, 296, 300, 321). The relative unclarity of Said's account may be due to the fact, reported by Roger Owen, that he was "in such a hurry to finish [the book] that he raced through Chapter 3, 'Orientalism now,' without … thinking through his argument as far as the relationship between Orientalism and the centers of modern Middle Eastern studies was concerned" (2012).
64 I leave aside here Achcar's analysis of the studies by Kepel, Roy, and Burgat. My concern is with studies on French Islam, which is only of secondary importance to Achcar, who concentrates on their early work on the Islamic world.
65 Peter 2006d.
66 Wael Hallaq argues that the Saidian critique of Orientalism has created a discursive context in which scholars studying Islam are incited to depict the latter in ways which conform to the central features of liberal modernity: "To the critics who espouse this position, Islam can be neither good nor bad, and the only way to escape the charge of Orientalism, it would seem, is to construct a vision of Islam and Islamic history consistent with, though perhaps not a replica of, modernity, and most especially its liberalism. This much, it will be my argument, was Said's legacy, although he advanced his case with some subtlety. Thus any scholar who depicts Islam negatively or positively is an Orientalist, the former emerging as a bigot, the latter as an exoticizer" (2018: 10).
67 "Indeed, my real argument is that Orientalism is—and does not simply represent—a considerable dimension of modern political-intellectual culture, and as such has less to do with the Orient than it does with 'our' world" (Said 1995: 12).
68 Nor are these works of fiction understood as realizing a kind of supreme reason which transcends the cognitive structure of rationalities and disables them, as could be argued for certain forms of art (Seel 1997: 46).

69 This is taken from a comment by Trilling on *Don Quixote*: "It can be said that all prose fiction is a variation on the theme of *Don Quixote*. Cervantes sets for the novel the problem of appearance and reality: the shifting and conflict of social classes becomes the field of the problem of knowledge, of how we know and of how reliable our knowledge is, which at that very moment of history is vexing the philosophers and scientists" (209). Cf. the comment by Hans Robert Jauß on this novel: "Never before had the reality of this-world in its contingency and polyvalence been so exposed and describable" (1983: 430).
70 "What is common to art and science is vastly more important than what is different" (Nisbet 1976: 10).
71 Furthermore, he connects "themes" to "styles."

2 The Social Republic

1 Historian Jean Baubérot, renowned authority on the history of *laïcité*, was the only member to abstain. For his account of the Commission's work, see Baubérot 2006.
2 Cf. John Bowen's analysis: "It is a particularly intriguing feature of the headscarf debates that although 'defending *laïcité*' was cited as the major justification of the law on religious signs, the arguments carried out in the media linked the scarves to more concrete social concerns. I highlight three such concerns: the growth in 'communalism' at the expense of social mixing, the increasing influence of international 'Islamism' in France, and the denigration of women in the poor suburbs" (2007: 4f.).
3 "The history of republican doctrine confirms in fact the intuition of common opinion: *laïcité* remains the most original trait of French political history, but also its most burning and debated sign of contradiction" (Nicolet 1994: 484).
4 Rosanvallon discusses the role of social thought in the chapter "Sociology against Jacobinism" (1994: 265–75).
5 Cf. Hazareesingh, who states that "[r]epublicanism was not a rigid ideological construct" (1994: 69); see also Berstein & Rudelle 1992 and Audier 2015.
6 As I will show all through the book, these rationalizations of Islam, while they differ sometimes greatly in regard to authors and complexity, do share many elements and are interconnected.
7 For Émile Durkheim's critique of Rousseau's theory of social contract, see Donzelot 1994: 76–81, Rosanvallon 2004: 271ff., and Fournier 2007: 149–55, 707–11.
8 For further discussion, see Schulze 2013.
9 See chapter one.

10 Analyzing developments in the eighteenth century, Foucault writes: "Society as a specific field of naturalness peculiar to man, and which will be called civil society, emerges as the vis-à-vis of the state. What is civil society if not, precisely, something that cannot be thought of as simply the product and result of the state? But neither is it something like man's natural existence. Civil society is what governmental thought, the new form of governmentality born in the eighteenth century, reveals as the necessary correlate of the state. With what must the state concern itself? For what must the state be responsible? What must it know? What must the state, if not control, at least regulate, or what kind of thing is it whose natural regulations it must respect?" (2009: 449).

11 This implied a new notion of rights, i.e., social rights, entailing shifts in the understanding of responsibility (now partly detached from individual actors) and the broad circulation of imperatives (solidarity and cohesion) which partly substituted or recombined with the notion of justice in regulating the conduct of individuals in society.

12 For historical accounts of Islam in France, see notably Arkoun 2007, Sellam 2006, and Telhine 2013.

13 Early in the 1970s, the number of prayer rooms was estimated at only 100. In the following two decades, the Islamic landscape in France changed completely. The estimated number of prayer rooms and mosques in metropolitan France rose to 500 in 1985, 1,279 in 1992, and 1,600–1,800 in 2002/3. In 2012, 2,449 prayer spaces and mosques were identified by the French Ministry of Home Affairs, including 318 in nonmetropolitan territories. The number of purpose-built mosques increased significantly in the 2000s (more than forty-five mosques built in 2000–13); about 200 were undergoing construction or fitting (Zwilling 2015).

14 See Sbaï 2018 and Burke 2014.

15 Their work is also indissociable from their Catholic faith, which led them to set up in France, on their own account, projects aiming to turn away Maghrebi migrants from nationalist propaganda and, ultimately, to win them over to Catholicism (Sbaï 2018: 108–19).

16 As pointed out already, the subsequent period also witnesses a fundamental shift in the academic world that especially affected Islamic studies (*islamologie*). See chapter one.

17 On the early history of the INED, see Rosenthal 2003.

18 See also Amiraux & Simon 2006.

19 See Kepel 1991. Hamès 1989 claims that Islam again became an object for "non-anecdotal" studies in the mid-1980s, the last study on Muslims in France–a PhD thesis submitted to the University of Algiers–having been published in 1950.

20 See, e.g., Achcar 2008: 136; Fernando 2014: 27; cf. Geisser 2012: 359; Geisser 2016; Dakhli 2016; and see below.
21 He limits his analysis of it by saying: "This phenomenon is too recent to narrate its history, measure its scope, analyze its causes or predict its evolution" (1991: 376).
22 See chapter three. Similar arguments have been properly elaborated in other studies (see, e.g., Khosrokhavar 1997).
23 Note that Kepel himself has often been criticized for a lack of differentiation and for contributing to unreasonable fears of Islam. These accusations date back to the study discussed here. In a review, Olivier Carré draws attention to the "sometimes regrettable" usage of terminology, the term "Islamism," for example, denoting both violent activism and "the simple activities of Muslims as one would talk about *Action catholique*" (1988: 405). Constantin Hamès, also in a review, deplores the discrepancy between the "image" of "an important process of Islamization ongoing in France," painted by Kepel, and the data presented, which does not reveal to what "proportion and degree the immigrant and French population are touched by this phenomenon" (1989: 146). In 2016, a similar question was raised about jihadi Islam by Vincent Geisser, who criticizes Kepel's "ambivalence" with regard to the "idea that jihadism had become the new mobilizing utopia in the '*banlieues* of Islam'" (2016).
24 Together with the volume *Les musulmans dans la société française* (Muslims in French Society) coedited by Kepel and Leveau (1988).
25 The picture he draws is one of a "complex demand" (for Islam) in France and "even more complex offer" which "has a thousand origins, French and foreign ones" (1991: 61).
26 See also Burgat 2016.

3 Rationalizing Integration

1 See the list in *Islam de France* 2000: 38.
2 *Le Monde*, November 11, 1999.
3 On the creation of the CFCM, see Laurence 2005; Boyer 2005; Geisser & Zemouri 2007; Godard & Taussig 2007; Zeghal 2008; Godard 2015.
4 See Ministère de l'Intérieur 2000a.
5 Ternisien 2000; Amiraux 2003; Zeghal 2008.
6 In 2008, more than two thirds of Muslims were French citizens or were to become citizens or have this option upon reaching adulthood (Tribalat 2013a: 117).
7 In another statement by the Interior Minister, the rationale of the document was described as allowing Islam to "join in a formal and irrevocable manner and in all clarity" "the other religions which have been established longer in France" (*Islam de France* 2000: 34).

8 Amiraux 2003.
9 See, e.g., Ramadan 2003b; Hajjat & Makri 2004; Makri 2005; Blanchard et al. 2005; Geisser & Zemmouri 2007a; see also chapter six.
10 From a historical perspective, government attempts to create a unified structure for Islamic institutions are often compared to the precedent of creating a Jewish consistory and integrating Judaism into the regime of recognized worships under the reign of Napoleon. See Cohen 2001, who identifies some limits to this comparison, Grand Sanhédrin 2007 and more generally Jansen 2013.
11 Tareq Oubrou contests this claim and alleges that the controversy was merely about the formulation which ultimately led to the Ministry retracting this passage (Babès & Oubrou 2002: 60f.). For Babès's original critique of the amendment (coauthored with Michel Renard) see Babès & Renard 2000.
12 See chapter one.
13 Note that disagreements on this issue continue in later discussions. The "recommendation" addressed to mosque associations using the legal regime of nonprofit association, to "also" constitute themselves as worship association does not find unanimous support among members of the working group on Muslim places of worship (Ministère de l'Intérieur 2000b).
14 Adrien Favell refers to "the ineffectiveness of formal political and legal institutions in governing social life" (Favell 2001: 45).
15 Emile Chabal (2015: 103f.) emphasizes that there is "no need to modify France's model of integration" from the perspective of republican thinkers. At the same time, he notes that "the reality of identity politics, socio-economic exclusion and the battles over the French empire have all posed a formidable challenge to neo-republican definitions of *intégration*."
16 This is not to say that this contrast is necessarily acknowledged by all political actors and in an identical manner. As we will see below, one way to deal with this discrepancy consists in only partly acknowledging it or simultaneously acknowledging and negating it, which leads to adopting positions which are not fully coherent.
17 See Peter 2013.
18 The positions of the HCI differed considerably from that of the *Observatoire*. For example, the HCI's recommendation to prohibit headscarves in university classrooms, made in its last report, met with disapproval by the universities, and the vast majority of politicians did not support it. The *Observatoire* took the position, after its own inquiry, that the facts were very different from those reported by the HCI (Bianco 2014).
19 During the debates about the reform of the Nationality Code, the focus was placed squarely on immigration from North Africa. Feldblum notes that the Commission on Nationality "had neglected to invite a representative of the Portuguese

community" in spite of the fact that the "Portuguese population was the second largest foreign group in France (21 percent of the foreign population), barely less numerous than the Algerians (22 percent)" (1999: 19).
20 Feldblum 1999: 76.
21 Beaugé & Hajjat 2014: 57f.
22 Cf. Lochak 2011: 14.
23 On these policies see notably Prévert 2014. While the principle of nondiscrimination is enshrined in the preamble to the constitution of the Fourth Republic (1946), Aline Prévert notes that it took more than half a century before "the fight against discriminations as a category of public action ... became meaningful and took shape" (Prévert 2014: 364). Anti-discrimination policies are placed on the agenda when the Socialist Party comes to power through legislative elections in 1997. According to Didier Fassin the HCI report on discrimination (HCI 1998), submitted to the prime minister, "can be considered a symbolic turning-point" in discussions about immigration (Fassin 2002: 405).
24 See Bertossi 2010, Goodman 2014, and Hajjat 2012. This procedure, mandatory since 2006, is also applied to applicants for residence permits. Goodman considers that the contract is "part of a mild, but unambiguous strategy of contained restriction" (2014: 197, cf. 195). Françoise Lorcerie argues that "via the '*contrat d'accueil et d'intégration*' (CAI) henceforth imposed on newcomers, integration has become a condition of entry and residence in France" (2014a: 52). Gourdeau argues that signatories to the CAI see it as a necessary administrative procedure (2018).
25 Gaspard refers here to Dominique Schnapper's study with the subtitle "Sociology of the Nation in 1990" (1991).
26 Vincent Geisser emphasizes the need "not to succumb to the myth of a *deus ex machina* as if the doctrine of integration were totally coherent or even totalizing" (2005: 147).
27 See Lorcerie 1994: 250f.
28 Indeed, one of the HCI's members, demographer Michèle Tribalat, says so much when she claims that the notion of assimilation—"implying the resorption of migratory specificities and reduction of specificities relating to social, cultural and religious practices"—is "ultimately close to that developed by the *Haut Conseil à l'intégration* under a different name" (Tribalat 1995: 13; cf. Tribalat 2013b).
29 This is also applicable to the terms "racialization" and "racializing." While these terms are often criticized for lack of clarity (Murji & Solomos 2005), they do involve, like culturalism, the construction of social groups as human lineages (Meer & Modood 2019).
30 The rest of the chapter will give examples for this claim. Cécile Laborde argues that "the understanding of integration defended by national republicans relies on a sociological and psychological theory of the development of patriotic loyalty and

'affection' (the socio-psychological explanation of 'the will to be French') and of cultural resemblance (the social process of 'assimilation' studied by sociologists)" (2008b: 190).

31 The term "culturalism," if it implies "essentializing culture by fixing it as immutable tradition and turning it into an universal explanation" (Fassin 2011: 785), is regularly used in a more loose manner in French debates. For example, the work of Gilles Kepel is designated "culturalist" by François Burgat who at the same time criticizes Kepel for giving too much weight to "social variables" (2016: 266, 277). (Note that Kepel in turn criticizes other authors—the philosopher Pierre Manent [2015]—for failure to take into account the "social construction" of French Islam [Kepel 2015: 367].) In a similar vein, Vincent Geisser remarks that "socioeconomic readings" of terrorism are "often combined with culturalist interpretations" (2015: 9).

32 On the changes, starting in the mid-1970s, in systems for classifying the population, see also Le Bras 1998.

33 "Being a foreigner is a matter of will: one can stop being a foreigner, supposing that one makes an effort to satisfy the criteria of naturalization. Being an immigrant is a matter of destiny. No effort from your side will change your conditions if you stay in France" (Le Bras 2014: 106).

34 For a critique by a demographer of these attempts to subdivide the France's population with reference to the "origins" of citizens, see Le Bras 1998.

35 See Keyhani 2014 on precursors of this policy.

36 The *Haut Conseil* also points out that some Islamic associations defend a "social and political Islam rather than a religious and moral" one, and that this becomes a "source of potential conflict with French society once it causes them to reject secular values" (1995: 41).

37 In 2000, the HCI considers that it is impossible to identify an exlusive set of criteria allowing to estimate the number of Muslims on the basis of figures about religious practices. In this report, the HCI distinguishes between "persons 'of Muslim culture' and persons who practise their worship more or less regularly," i.e., persons "of Muslim faith"; this results in a figure of less than 1 million (2005: 27). In the second report, when evaluating the number of Muslims (3 million), the HCI notes that it is impossible to make a distinction between "traditional practitioners, rigorous practitioners and 'sociological' Muslims" (1992: 40) without defining these terms further. In a later report, the HCI advances a new figure (4 million), stating that these individuals "do not necessarily define themselves as Muslim, but they are perceived as such without their practice being clearly measured" (1995: 31). For more recent discussions of the counting of Muslims in France, see notably Simon & Tiberj 2013, Tournier 2013 and Tribalat 2013a.

38 "The majority of young Maghrebi with roots in immigration continue to have **a more cultural than religious relation with Islam** by perpetuating traditions which

mark membership of a group. The festivities are occasions for socializing and identitarian and communitarian reunions rather than for asceticism" (1995: 34; emphasis in the original). See also HCI 1995: 17f.

39 On this issue, see notably Hafiz & Devers 2005, Césari 2005, Fonds de soutien pour l'intégration et la lutte contre les discriminations 2006, Duthu 2008, Maussen 2009, Zwilling 2015, Sénat 2015, and Fornerod 2016.

40 When set in relation to state neutrality, equality is considered to restrict the duty of neutrality: "The absolute neutrality of the state could in fact thwart individual beliefs. The public authorities cannot leave a category of persons unable to live in conformity with their conscience" (2000: 60).

41 The HCI itself considers that in spite of "the flexibility of the law" (2000: 39) "no really satisfactory response" is possible (2000: 39).

42 See also Leveau & Mohsen-Finan 2001: 11 and, more generally Guélamine 2014 and Verba & Guélamine 2014.

43 After 2002, the *Haut Conseil de l'intégration* will move away from this position.

44 Nine out of twenty members of the Stasi Commission had been, were (in 2003–4), or were to become members of the HCI (Beaugé & Hajjat 2014: 48).

45 On the Stasi commission, see Bowen 2007, Akan 2009, and Koussens 2011.

46 The public order argument had been rejected in strong terms by Interior Minister Sarkozy when presenting the available statistics on girls wearing headscarves in state schools in 2003; see Commission Debré (2003: II, 642).

47 In line with this reasoning, the HCI, after 2002, makes a series of proposals aiming to reinforce "the rights of women of immigrant background" (*issues de l'immigration*) (see, e.g., 2004).

48 However, the recommendation to enact a law is only one of many proposals set out by the Commission. In many other respects the Commission simply continues established ways of thinking which rely upon social rationality. This can be illustrated by the following explanation of communalism (*communautarisme*): "Discontent is the breeding ground on which communalist extremism develops: *laïcité* has no chance and no legitimacy unless equality of opportunity is guaranteed in every corner of the territory, unless the diverse histories which found our national community and multiple identities are respected" (Commission Stasi 2003: 4.1.2.). Likewise, the Commission champions "respect for diversity" (Commission Stasi 2003: 4.1.2.3.). Neglect of this aim is, according to the Commission, one of the causes of failed integration in the past two decades. On the "outcome of the Stasi report," see Fornerod 2017.

49 The UOIF was not invited to join by Sarkozy but by Interior Minister Chevènement (see above).

50 See chapter three.

51 The report was submitted to the prime minister on November 26, 2005.

52 "It is correct to say that what defines a French person is neither race nor religion. This is a positive abstraction. But in the lived world, a black French person lives differently from a white French person, and the latter can consider him-/herself more French than the former. While education policy, notably national education, can help to correct such disparities, this cannot be enough. The role of the media is just as important in this field. Identity is also shaped in the imaginary, and we have seen how publicity and the media have historically produced a derogatory image of people from the ex-colonies. The matter needs to be corrected, via a broadening and an enrichment of our cultural horizon" (HCI 2006: 78). On the measurement of diversity, see Ghosn 2010 and the report of the media regulator (Conseil Supérieur de l'Audiovisuel 2018).
53 Note that when Kriegel held the chair the aim to restrict public religion was manifest in the proposal for a *Charte de la laïcité dans les service publics* ("Charter of *laïcité* in public services") (HCI 2007); see below.
54 The *Conseil d'État* rejected the creation by the ministry of a third category of persons in addition to the users and employees of public services. However, the conduct of parents can be restricted in order to maintain the functioning of the service; the legal battles around the exclusion of Muslim mothers continue (Collectif contre l'Islamophobie 2013; Hennette-Vauchez 2017a; Fornerod 2017).
55 Hennette-Vauchez & Valentin 2014: 32f.
56 See Ministère du Travail 2017: 7ff. and Hennette-Vauchez 2017b. On the limited judicial importance of the judgment in the case of the day-care facility *Baby Loup*, which sacked an employee who came back from maternity leave with a headscarf, see Hennette-Vauchez 2017a: 311; see also Hennette-Vauchez & Valentin 2014: 52.
57 See Philip-Gay 2016: 194f.; Koussens 2011: 71f.; Portier 2016: 265f.; Fornerod 2017: 84; HCI 2010. On the issue of the supposed spread of religious practices and demands by users of public services, notably in hospitals, see Azouvi 2013 and Bertossi & Bowen 2015.
58 See, e.g., HCI 2007: 24 for a similar argument about the way in which the principle of *laïcité* needs to be not only understood, but acknowledged.
59 The study focusing on two communes in Seine-Saint-Denis, Clichy-sous-Bois and Montfermeil was conducted by a team of researchers led by Gilles Kepel (Kepel 2012).
60 See the description of Tuot's mission in Tuot 2013: 79.
61 In the first case, the report written by Thierry Tuot was met with "a mitigated even openly hostile reception, on the right as on the left, including among those who commissioned it" (Geisser 2013: 4; cf. Tuot 2014: 201f.). In the second case—five reports prepared by working groups tasked by Prime Minister Ayrault with reflecting upon the "refounding of integration policy"—criticism in the media and from opposition parties led to the reports being retracted (Dhume 2014).
62 See Lorcerie 2014a: 50.

63 "Has France ever depended upon whether a piece of cloth – *boubou*, Breton headgear, tagelmust or beret – was worn in this way or another? It doesn't take much to pacify our shared mental horizon" (Tuot 2013: 65; see also 2013: 21). Nevertheless, a dose of cultural adaptation is welcome: "It would be good if architects could conceive a French mosque ... that does not ape the accomplishments of previous centuries spent in other climates ..." (Tuot 2013: 65).
64 On these reports, see notably the contributions in Lorcerie 2014b.
65 Tuot discusses the place of immigration in "national memory." The necessary reconfiguration of the latter is imagined as an act of inclusion of hitherto invisible groups (Tuot 2013: 35).
66 See chapter six.

4 Islam and Society: Entwinement and Differentiation

1 These comments are made in a study by Dounia Bouzar on "Muslim preachers" as "social workers" (2001). On Bouzar, anthropologist, former educator, and consultant in matters of religion, see also below.
2 Bouzar 2001: 42.
3 Bouzar 2001: 45. Lasfar notes the municipality's surprise and inability to understand that the "mosque [was] the sole interlocutor of youth" (Bouzar 2001: 42).
4 Bouzar 2001: 45.
5 Bouzar 2001: 38f., 45.
6 See Chatriot & Lemercier 2002 and Behrent 2008.
7 See Scott 2018.
8 See Wieviorka 2006; Silverstein 2008. For Tariq Ramadan's controversial intervention in this debate, see 2003a; see also Ramadan 2001b.
9 See the analysis in *Commission nationale consultative des Droits de l'homme* 2017: 64f.
10 See Kokoreff et al. 2006; Lagrange & Oberti 2006; Lapeyronnie 2006; Harsin 2015; Murphy 2011; Leonard 2016. Note that in an inquiry into what it called an "urban insurrection" the police intelligence agency (*Direction centrale des renseignements généraux*) rejected these associations categorically. See *Le Monde*, December 7, 2005; *Le Parisien*, December 7, 2005.
11 See also Guibet-Lafaye & Brochard 2016 and de Galembert 2016.
12 See below.
13 See notably the studies by Andrew March 2006, 2007, and 2009.
14 See Introduction.
15 John Bowen described that seminal distinction between *Islam en France* and *Islam de France* as "a hackneyed rhetorical device for signaling one's allegiance both to the French Republic and to Islam" (2004: 44).

16 See Caeiro 2011a.
17 See Frégosi 1998; Peter 2006a, 2006b.
18 See also Najjar 2005: 207f.
19 As the subsequent discussion shows (Ramadan 1994: 94–7 and 119–22), Ramadan's central concern is not legal changes. Elsewhere, Ramadan specifies that the issue of modifying legislation applies to "very few" laws (1999: 178). Rather, he criticizes here the widespread idea in France that the subject of "integration" is the abstract individual, an approach which strongly tends to problematize any reference to "community," a term which has become, as Ramadan notes, "the symbol of all dangers" (1994: 94).
20 Sadri Khiari considers that Ramadan "thinks more in terms of 'social support' (*accompagnement social*) for the excluded, and in particular for populations with an immigrant background, than in terms of struggle" (2004).
21 It would be a mistake to simply identify the work of this fatwa council with "adaptation" to Europe conceived as a given context different from Muslim lands. In fact, the analysis of the Council's fatwas shows that "neither is the reference to the context unambiguous nor does it permeate all of the ECFR's written production." Importantly, in the Council's fatwas, "parallels seem to be established between Muslim and non-Muslim countries more often than the two are distinguished" (Caeiro 2011a: 228). One may think that the implementation of "*wasaṭī* ideology and methodology" could lead to the "gradual creation of a unique system of religious law for Muslim minorities"; however, "[t]o date, this has not happened" (Shavit 2012: 457; see also Shavit 2016). Note also that, according to Lena Larsen, Ahmed Jaballah believes that references to a minority will decrease in proportion to the "establish[ment]" of Muslims in France (2018: 115).
22 One could add that Ramadan's usage of civilizational frames offers another point of convergence with integration discourse. In his second monograph published in 1995, his broader vision of the present context was that the Islamic revival had led to a "civilisational face to face" unprecedented in history: "For the first time in two centuries, and in a more 'confrontational' manner, that even the Chinese or Japanese horizon could not pose, the Islamic world contests the universality of Western values either by relativising or questioning them" (2001a: 202). Ramadan distinguishes the challenge posed by the Islamic world from that of "traditional cultures such as the Indians of North America and the Aborigines of Australia," as "[t]hese ethnicities do not endanger the supremacy of rationalist and modernist points of reference" (2001a: 202). Since his third major publication *To be a European Muslim*, Ramadan has started to elaborate a terminology which contests binary models (1999). This does not necessarily exclude a description of "the West" as a distinct space different from Muslim countries: "On the whole, the situation was quite bad and remains so: to be a Muslim man or woman in the West while trying to respect one's values and

principles is not easy. To maintain a spiritual life, carry out the ritual obligations (prayer, *zakat*, and fasting), and keep to an ethical way of life is a daily test" (2004a: 217).

23 This is the concluding passage of an op-ed for *Le Monde* which was not included in the newspaper (1998: 211–17).

24 Ramadan makes the same point in 2016b.

25 Note that Ramadan's implicit notion of culture here is homogeneous. There are French, Arab North-African, Turkish, and Indo-Pakistani cultures, but no mention is made of a hybrid culture (1998: 37). More programmatically, the relation between religion, culture, and civilization is defined in the following manner:

> "Islam is not a culture. Whether we like it or not, the essence of Islam is religious. (…) Around the body of principles that define the fundamentals of allegiance to Islam, the area of social affairs is a field that is open to the cultures, customs, discoveries, and creativity of humankind as long as they do not violate a prohibition that is specific and explicit and recognized as such. The 'way of faithfulness' integrates all the knowledge, arts, and skills for people's well-being that humankind has been able to produce. (…) This principle of integration (…) has made it possible for Muslims to live in very varied cultural environments and to feel at home. (…) Islam stands as a civilization as a result of this singular ability to express its universal and fundamental principles across the spread of history and geography while integrating the diversity and taking on the customs, tastes, and styles that belong to the various cultural contexts" (2003: 214).

26 Thus Ramadan writes in 1999 that "[f]rom the Muslims' point of view, this means they should acquire the confidence that they are *at home* and that they must become more involved within European societies which are henceforth their own" (1999: 229; emphasis in the original).

27 For similar positions in more recent work, see the new introduction to a reedition of *Western Muslims and the Future of Islam* (Ramadan 2016a: 15–21). Note also that the essay discussed above, "Integration – a conceptual trap?" (2008c), is reprinted in Ramadan 2014.

28 Oubrou took care to emphasize that he did not break with *Musulmans de France*: "I am a person who likes relations and reconciliation and not ruptures, even more with an institution which has partly made me who I am now. It is not because you leave the home where you have grown up to live as an adult that you necessarily break with your family." One of the "main reasons" for leaving *Musulmans de France* was that Oubrou does not want to "be perceived as an organic intellectual theologian (*théologien intellectuel organique*), as my ideas cannot be contained within a system, even less in an associative structure." See Ben Rhouma 2018.

29 Oubrou 2004: 207.
30 See Oubrou 2013.
31 Oubrou acknowledges the positive work done by the ECFR, but also claims that it is "culturally alien to Western civilization. It is too Arab in all respects" (2009: 181). He also deplores the absence of theological considerations in their methodology, a field where he sees himself engaged (2007).
32 In a recent publication, he states with regard to Ramadan: "We are radically different, we do not have the same ambition and do not live in the same world. I find that his discourse contributed to creating confusion between different registers [of discourse] and that he mobilized a whole Muslim youth behind him in an intellectual and social fight which is about claim-making (*revendicatif*), divisive and leads to nowhere" (Colombani & Oubrou 2016: 65, cf. 88f.).
33 Oubrou 1998: 27; emphasis in the original.
34 Oubrou 2012: 47.
35 Note that Oubrou also emphasizes the significance of change occurring in society. With regard to "Western society," he writes that its "principal characteristics are complexity and rapid evolution." France is described as "once again searching for identity, for a new basis of citizenship and a new cultural foundation" (1998: 28).
36 Oubrou 2004: 225.
37 Oubrou 2009: 43.
38 Oubrou 2009: 39f.
39 Cf. Colombani & Oubrou 2017: 76ff. In some of his statements, Oubrou almost entirely disconnects the wearing of the hijab from modesty norms and "the problem of sexual appeal" (2009: 81–4).
40 With regard to covered women, he has claimed that "many of them are very unstable" and that their practice is "sometimes" motivated "unconsciously" by a will to "stand up" to society and not always part of a "very sincere spiritual approach." Oubrou acknowledges that "many young girls and boys construct their spirituality on this kind of detail," i.e., hijab or gandoura. However, Oubrou considers that "wearing the headscarf is not part of faith and does not augment it. Sometimes it causes real problems for faith …" (2009: 86).
41 Needless to say that in the case of the hijab, Oubrou is not in any way redefining Islamic norms so as to diminish the potential for conflict in France. Rather, he argues that the covering of the hair by women can be seen, in light of scripture and scholarly tradition, as not being obligatory, and thus dispensable (2009: 84; see also p. 38 for his view on the "heritage of classical Muslim theology" as shield against "religious anarchy").
42 During the presidential primary elections of *Les Républicains*, Juppé's supposedly close relations to Oubrou were used against the former in campaigns alleging Juppé was compromising with Islamists (*Le Figaro*, November 24, 2016). See Dazey 2019

for a study of the Bordeaux branch of *Musulmans de France* in its local political context and see Malogne Fer on religion in local politics (2019).
43 Oubrou has been called out for statements on the conflict between Israel and Palestine which were seen as unsupportive of Palestinian causes (see, e.g., Oubrou 2014b; *oumma.com* 2014). While I cannot discuss this point here, any discussion needs to take into consideration Oubrou's general stance toward Israel which is highly critical. Israel, he claims, has created the "unity of the Jewish people of Israel" in "common opposition against an absolute foreign enemy, the Arab and Muslim neighbor." For this reason, "peace is not a solution for Israel": "It would not receive any more foreign subsidies nor support and would be left on its own with the administration of one of the most complex societies of this world" (2014a: 271f.). Israel's basic flaw, in Oubrou's view, has to do with its "ethnico-religious ambiguity": "To reduce an entire nation, a religion to the politics of a State whose doctrine, since its birth until today, has been to maintain ethnico-religious ambiguity – this is the trap which needs to be avoided." Oubrou advocates universal access to citizenship in Israel (2014a: 311).
44 Note that the need not to "provoke" "identitarian Christianity" is presented by Oubrou as a reason why Muslims should practice discretion (2019: 22).
45 Elsewhere Oubrou relates this problematic visibility to the "failure of integration"; see France 24 2019.
46 For Ramadan's account of the campaign, see Ramadan 2011b. The topic of "stoning" had been a major theme in the TV debate between Nicolas Sarkozy and Tariq Ramadan in 2003; Ramadan's call for a moratorium was considered "shocking" by Sarkozy.
47 See also Bowen 2009:169–73.
48 Cédric Baylocq Sassoubre suggests classifying Oubrou as practicing a "measured conservatism" (*conservatisme mesuré*) (2008: 304).
49 As the electoral system of the CFCM and the regional councils is structured around prayer spaces, the CFCM's creation sparked the foundation of associations of secular Muslims (*musulmans laïques*) and debates about whether and how to grant them a public voice. On the CFCM and preceding government attempts to establish an official interlocutor, see notably von Krosigk 2000; Terrel 2004; Frégosi 2005b; Laurence 2005; Laurence & Vaisse 2006; Sellam 2006; Godard & Taussig 2007; Telhine 2013.
50 See chapter three.
51 Fundamentalism should be understood here as designating a form of religiosity characterized by the fact that its practitioners believe "fundamentally," as Sarkozy elaborates shortly afterwards. *Intégrisme*, in contrast, is characterized by its illiberal attitude toward others. The latter is fought against, not the former (Sarkozy 2004: 87).
52 "I chose to believe them [the UOIF]. Was there another solution?" (2004: 83).

53 Sarkozy 2004: 83, 90f.
54 Sarkozy 2004: 85; see also 78.
55 *Le Monde*, December 24, 1994.
56 Geisser & Zemouri 2007: 116.
57 See notably Makri 1998 & 2008. On the *Union des Jeunes Musulmans*, see Marongiu (2002).
58 Akan 2009; Geisser & Zemouri 2007; Baubérot 2008.
59 "Everywhere in France, and more so in the *banlieues*, where all despairs condense, it is much preferable that the young can hope spiritually instead of having as their only 'religion', violence, drugs, or money" (Sarkozy 2004: 18).
60 Sarkozy 2004: 21f.
61 In the context of debates about the reform of the CFCM, the Union suspended its participation in its activities between 2011 and 2016 and boycotted the elections in 2013.
62 In 2003, just after the creation of the CFCM, Sarkozy was welcomed as a "friend" by the Union's leadership at their Annual Meeting in Le Bourget. In 2012, during the presidential election campaign and after the killings perpetrated by Merah, Sarkozy publicly announced that any speaker at the Annual Meeting opposing "republican values" would be evicted from French territory. A number of invited scholars had been denied a visa.
63 Sarkozy 2007; Lindner 2017; De Cock et al. 2008; Noiriel 2007a.
64 *oumma.com* 2005.
65 *oumma.com* 2005.
66 Note the convergences between Ramadan and Oubrou. Oubrou cites the prohibition of the headscarf in 2004 as a case of Islamization: By enacting it French politicians in effect sidestepped the "real problems"—i.e., social problems—relating to the Muslim presence in France (2012: 97).
67 Elsewhere, Ramadan has marked a certain distance from sociological analyses of Muslim religiosities, notably the tendency to explain the turn to Islam as typical for the socially excluded. "Material and socially visible causalities" cannot fully grasp the "act of faith, the birth of an intimate commitment" (1994: 87; cf. Geisser & Chaambi 2007: 132).
68 The Union's "final declaration" at the Annual Meeting which followed the attacks of 2015 is very similar to this statement, although its rejection of an "Islamizing" framework reducing complex phenomena to purely religious factors is more explicit: "This phenomenon of radicalization goes beyond the reading of Islam; other parameters – social, economic, psychological, or related to family or international politics – intervene. However, Muslim leaders assume their responsibility for the production and diffusion of a religious discourse [that is] balanced" (UOIF 2016).
69 See Sedgwick 2015 on different usages of this term.

70 While the state of emergency was ended in 2017, some of its provisions were then integrated into law. See Halpérin et al. 2017.
71 For a review of "radicalization" studies, see Dalgaard-Nielsen 2010.
72 Khosrokhavar continues: "Modern societies of which Durkheim spoke in terms of a broken social bond, combined with economic exclusion within a mass culture which is egalitarian by essence, create new harm which our societies master only very imperfectly" (2014: 184).
73 Compare this with Ramadan's critique of the social order in an opinion piece published after the death of Mohamed Merah. Ramadan finds that Merah is "guilty and to be condemned beyond the shadow of a doubt" and adds that "even though he himself was the victim of a social order that had already doomed him, and millions of others like him, to a marginal existence, and to the non-recognition of his status as a citizen equal in rights and opportunities" (2012c). Cf. Oubrou who, commenting on the cases of Merah and Mehdi Nemmouch who had attacked the Jewish Museum in Brussels, refers to the "massive process of identification with the Palestinian people" by "a vulnerable Muslim population." The underlying lack of "social and moral education" is linked to the abandonment of these territories by the Republic (2014b).
74 See Daumas 2016 for an account of these exchanges.
75 Burgat's agreement with Roy is only partial. In Burgat's view, Roy depoliticizes jihadism by explaining it as "a psychosocial state of tension of individuals who are relatively ungrounded in their historical and social environment" (2016: 279, 281). Burgat disapproves of this depoliticizing move.
76 Furthermore, while Roy emphasizes commonalities between forms of radical contestation (i.e. "leftist and radical Islamist"), such as their generational nature and their Third-Worldism, he also acknowledges distinctive features of al-Qaʿida and Daesh, namely the "fascination for death, what I have called nihilism," "the hatred of existing societies," and the singular prospects offered by Daesh for "transfiguring loser into superhero" and playing a role in a kind of "grand narrative of the return to the golden age of Islam" (2016: 122f., 126).
77 Mahajan 2012. Roy says as much when writing: "I say simply that *this fundamentalism does not suffice to produce violence*" (2016: 16; emphasis in the original).
78 Only two elements of the debate about Roy's work can be mentioned here. An important piece of evidence for Roy's central thesis that radicalization precedes any kind of attachment to Islam (the so-called Islamization of radicality) is his claim that jihadists are uprooted individuals "who almost never have a religious education" and "reject the authority of parents as much as their Islam" (2016: 60, 46f.). This claim has been nuanced with reference to the social and religious profile of jihadists, a significant number of whom are arguably less uprooted and ignorant than is sometimes claimed (Thomson 2016). As importantly, Roy's emphasis on the

individualized nature of radicalization processes is problematized with reference to the social geography of French jihadism, i.e., the fact that the vast majority of individuals come from a small number of localities (Micheron 2020; Rougier 2020; cf. Roy 2016: 44f.).

79 In this context, the problematic of defining the individual's moral responsibilities while taking into account social forces is very similar. See, e.g., Mucchielli 2006: 51ff. This set of questions has been widely debated in French media in 2010 following the publication of *Le déni des cultures* (The Denial of Cultures) by Hugues Lagrange (2010). Lagrange attempts to establish a causal link between misconduct by young descendants of sub-Saharan immigrants on the one hand and family structure and socialization on the other. For a critical discussion, see Fassin 2011 and Blanchard 2017; Lagrange responds to Fassin in Lagrange 2011.

80 Lahire 2016: 11f.

81 Needless to say, as Lahire points out, understanding the logics "which have contributed to making the crimes, incivilities, delinquency, and attacks possible" means "giving oneself the chance with time to avoid new dramas" (2016: 46).

82 See, for example, Bronner & Géhin 2017.

83 See Schnapper 2017: 115. Schnapper refers here to the exceptional case of historian Olivier Pétré-Grenouilleau, who had declared that the slave trade obeyed primarily a commercial logic and was not a genocide. He criticized the *loi Taubira* (Law 2001-434, May 21, 2001) for designating the slave trade, as the Shoah, a "crime against humanity." The case is particular, as a group of associations from Guyane, Réunion, and the Antilles sued Pétré-Grenouilleau in court for "denying a crime against humanity," but later withdrew the case (Bertrand 2006a: 167–200). Pétré-Grenouilleau's global history of slavery had also triggered a number of critiques aiming at the prominent place he accorded to the "oriental" slave trade (see N'Diaye 2005).

84 Official figures vary somewhat due to different classifications; more than 10,000 individuals were classified as "radicalized" in 2017/18. See *Libération*, March 25, 2018.

85 This is not to say that the entire phenomenon is reduced to "sectarian deviance" by the experts of the interior ministry (see Ministère de l'Intérieur 2015: 33). See Sèze 2019: 165f; cf. 34f. on how MIVILUDES (see also chapter one) became involved in this policy field.

86 The Union's leadership emphasized its intention to continue its preventive work through education as the "best antidote to immunize coming generations against Muslim radicalism," as President Amar Lasfar put it. See *Le Figaro*, January 11, 2015.

87 "... identifying one or several signs does not necessarily imply radicalization." See Ben Rhouma 2015. This campaign is hosted on stop-djihadisme.gouv.fr.

88 See Sèze 2019: 163–71. On related policies, see for example Vincent & Couvelaire 2019.

89 See Peter 2006b, 2006c.
90 Practical conflicts entailed by this ambivalence are thematized in different ways by the authors. See, for example, Ramadan's reasoning regarding the still insufficient but rapidly developing status of associational structures and the need not to move too quickly in the dialogue with the French state: "It would be a pity if by going too fast today, we would break a dynamic which is part of the necessarily long process of settling of a minority religion" (2000).
91 See Ramadan's assessment of the state of associations, characterized by "division and fragmentation" (2014: 175–9) and compare this to his reflections from 2000. On the critical internal debate about the CFCM, see notably Geisser et al. 2017.
92 This is particularly true for the issue of "Salafi jihadism." While a critical view of "literalist" Salafism is widespread in the milieu of public Islam, these groups were long considered marginal in the West (see, e.g., Ramadan 2004a and Oubrou 2012:20f.). While Mohamed Merah's much debated trajectory was often associated with Salafi milieus, Ramadan discards this perspective, as does the Union's leadership, declaring that "terrorism and murderous insanity do not have any religion" (UOIF 2012). Ramadan discusses aims and types of jihad and offers a brief critique of the "'Islamic state' or Da'esh" in Ramadan 2014.

5   Teaching Freedom

1 Meziani 2009b.
2 Meziani 2010, 2011.
3 Meziani 2015.
4 Meziani 2017.
5 Meziane (*sic*) 2008.
6 Meziani 2009a.
7 Meziani criticizes the excessive focus on Palestine in the Muslim community (Meziani 2015: 18).
8 Meziani 2009a: 71.
9 See chapter three.
10 Meziani 2012.
11 Meziani 2012.
12 Meziani 2010. The work is described as a novel of "initiation" (or coming-of-age) on the cover of his subsequent book, *Le Chemin de la liberté* (The Way of Liberty).
13 Meziani 2010: 16.
14 Meziani 2009a: 32.
15 Meziani 2009a: 30.
16 Meziani 2009a: 39f.

17 Meziani 2010: 71f.
18 Meziani 2010: 81.
19 Meziani 2009a: 49.
20 Meziani 2009a: 50.
21 Meziani 2009a: 87f.
22 Meziane 2008: 10.
23 Meziani claimed, as reported above, that this debate belonged to the past.
24 On this notion, see Wagemakers 2008 and Shavit 2016.
25 Ramousi 2012: 9, 29.
26 Ramousi 2012: 18.
27 Ramousi 2012: 51.
28 Ramousi 2012: 11.
29 Ramousi defends the idea that the successful identification of Muslims with French citizenship demands a certain level of education. Citing a *Le Monde* poll in 2008 about—French and/or Muslim—identity, Ramousi argues that "the samples show that the majority of those who describe themselves as first of all Muslim and then French have no qualifications or only primary education qualifications" (2012: 43). The majority of respondents had described themselves as French and Muslim. Ramousi considers that "citizenship" and "Muslimness" are terms referring to different categories and do not compete, like a lemon which is "oval and yellow at the same time, not more oval than yellow" (2012: 43).
30 Ramousi 2012: 51.
31 Ramousi 2012: 66.
32 Ramousi 2012: 61f.
33 Ramousi 2012: 65. In this context, he points out that the caliphate was historically seen as a means to achieve justice and not as an "end in itself."
34 Ramousi 2012: 9.
35 Ramousi 2012: 10.
36 Ramousi 2012: 43.
37 Ramousi 2012: 46.
38 Ramousi 2012: 49.
39 Ramousi 2012: 45.
40 Ramousi 2012: 106.
41 Ramousi 2012: 38.
42 Ramousi 2012: 136.
43 Ramousi 2012: 149.
44 Ramousi 2012: 150f.
45 Ramousi 2012: 151.
46 Ramousi 2012: 159.
47 Ramousi 2012: 158–60.

48 Ramousi 2012: 162.
49 Ramousi 2012: 162ff.
50 Ramousi 2012: 163.
51 See http://farid-abdelkrim.fr/mqvb.
52 Abdelkrim 2002a.
53 Abdelkrim 2002b.
54 Abdelkrim 2005.
55 This book was followed shortly afterwards by *"L'islam sera français ou ne sera pas"* ("Islam will be French or it will not be") (Abdelkrim 2015b).
56 Abdelkrim 2015a, 2016b.
57 In the book, Abdelkrim formulates differently and refers to his "hope" that some readers "perhaps" will recognize themselves in this writing (2002a: 21).
58 His book is prefaced by Ahmed El Mcherfi, a former member of the Union's youth organization and then a deputy mayor in Reims. In the preface, Mcherfi claims that through this book "thousands of young French Muslims" speak to the reader (Abdelkrim 2002a: 8).
59 Abdelkrim 2002a: 132.
60 Abdelkrim 2002a: 113.
61 Abdelkrim 2002a: 139.
62 Abdelkrim 2002a: 92.
63 Abdelkrim 2002: 98f.
64 Abdelkrim 2002a: 105. Hasan al-Banna was an important reference for Abdelkrim whose "way of seeing the world, to practice Islam and to make myself useful" and "modest spiritual and mystical aspirations" are due to al-Banna (2002: 19).
65 Abdelkrim 2002a: 129.
66 Abdelkrim 2002a: 128.
67 Abdelkrim 2002a: 132.
68 Abdelkrim 2002a: 110.
69 Abdelkrim 2002a: 111.
70 Abdelkrim 2002a: 112.
71 In the conclusion, Abdelkrim ascribes the injustices committed in France—a "beautiful and good country"—to "a handful" of people only (2002a: 145).
72 See notably Abdelkrim 2015a, 2015b.
73 Abdelkrim 2015a: 243.
74 Abdelkrim 2015a: 141, 147, 176f., 179f., 230; emphasis in the original).
75 Abdelkrim 2015a: 68.
76 Abdelkrim 2015b: 23, 35–41.
77 Abdelkrim 2015a: 57. On this point, see chapter eight.
78 Abdelkrim 2015a: 40.

79 Abdelkrim 2015a: 242.
80 The fact that some of these critics even "draw a parallel" between the situation of Muslims in present France with that of Jews during the Second World War incites Abdelkrim to contradict (2015a: 40).
81 Abdelkrim 2015a: 58f., 69, 239, 242.
82 Abdelkrim 2015a: 47.
83 Abdelkrim 2015a: 17.
84 Abdelkrim 2015a: 19.
85 Abdelkrim 2015a: 19. Furthermore, the somber description of these difficult years is partly revised as these were also the years, until his conversion to Islam, when he joined as singer a local band covering songs by Elvis and Taj Mahal (2015a: 38f., 50f., 224).
86 Abdelkrim 2015a: 40.

6 "The History of Some is not the History of Others"

1 See *Le Monde*, November 29, 2005. Defense minister Michèle Alliot-Marie traveled to the Czech Republic to attend an event.
2 This comes in reaction to the emancipation which had been decreed previously in Saint-Domingue in 1793 after a successful revolt.
3 On the history of the revolution and the French war efforts in Saint-Domingue, see Dubois 2004.
4 Note that the *loi Taubira* adopted in 2001 had branded certain forms of slave trade and slavery a "crime against humanity." Article 1 of the law reads: "The French Republic recognizes both the transatlantic and Indian Ocean Negro (*négrière*) slave trade, on the one hand, and slavery itself, on the other, that were practiced from the 15th century, in the Americas, the Caribbean, the Indian Ocean, and Europe against African, Amerindian, Malagasy and Indian populations, as constituting crimes against humanity."
5 For a survey with a focus on parts of the Islamic world, see Luizard 2019.
6 On the movement—since 2010, *Parti des indigènes de la République*—see Robine 2006, 2011. It is difficult to evaluate the outreach capacity of this movement, but there can be no doubt that it has significantly influenced the public debate since 2005 (see Bertrand 2006b). Reflecting on the state of affairs in 2012, Houria Bouteldja, one of its founders, acknowledges its limited audience "in the housing projects" (*dans les quartiers*), but claims that there is "no immigrant organization with the same influence, audience, outreach, and impact as ours" (Bouteldja & Khiari 2012: 272).

7 Bouteldja & Khiari 2012: 19–22. The usage of the term "*indigène*" by the movement has been discussed in more detail since its inception; see Bouteldja & Khiari 2012: 39–78 and Saïd Bouamama cited in Robine 2011: 152.
8 *Le Monde*, December 5, 2005.
9 On Nora, see Dosse 2011. For Ribbe's response, see Ribbe 2005b.
10 This op-ed does not capture Nora's thinking on changes in French politics of commemoration and the shifting relation between collective memories and historiography; see notably Nora 2008, 2011.
11 The *Lieux de mémoire* are limited to mainland France and colonial France is hardly paid any attention. For an entry into the debate about this project, see Valensi 1995, Judt 1998, Tai 2001, and Anderson 2004; Nora responds to Anderson in Nora 2005b.
12 Quoting historian Marc Bloch on the conditions for understanding French history, Nora claimed:

> "'There are two categories of French people who will never understand the history of France: those who refuse to tremble at the memory of the Coronation in Reims and those who are unmoved by the story of the *Fête de la Fédération*.' He [Bloch] could have added: those who do not feel something rise in their heart with the sun at Austerlitz" (2011: 494).

13 Emile Chabal points out: "For if, as many have argued, the French Academy has been slow to absorb the lessons of Anglo-American post-colonial theory, this does not mean that a French post-colonial critique has not emerged in the past three decades" (2015: 186); see also Smouts 2007 and Saada 2014.
14 Such attempts in France go back to the 1760s, according to Foucault 2003: 136f.
15 See also Safran 2003.
16 I cannot deal here with how the shape and intensity of these memory controversies relate to the current "regime of historicity" which, as François Hartog argues, emerges after the crisis of the modern regime in the late twentieth century and is "presentist," i.e., an alignment of past, present, and future where the latter has almost disappeared from the horizon (Hartog 2016).
17 Sébastien Ledoux notes that the term "duty to remember," widely used in politics in the 1990s, has been replaced by "duty of history" (*devoir d'histoire*) and "memory work" (*travail de mémoire*); see Ledoux 2013a: 241, 250. The parliamentary commission on "memory-related questions" uses the term "memory work" to shift the focus of attention from commemorating past events to future actions; memories of particular events are used as reminder of the general duty to continue the struggle for more liberty, equality and fraternity (Assemblée Nationale 2008: 84–90).
18 See Rousso 1990.

19 A directive (n° 93-150, February 3, 1993) had previously established a day of commemoration for the victims of persecution committed "under the *de facto* authority of the so-called 'government of the French state' (1940–1944)."
20 Note that the law, in contrast to some demands, does not contain any apology for France, nor does the law accuse her, as Taubira pointed out later (Michel 2010: 131f.)
21 See De Cock 2018: 178–92, Ledoux 2013a, and Coquery-Vidrovitch 2009: 66ff.
22 This law had already been voted through parliament in 1998, but was then blocked by the senate. In 2006 a new law was passed, modeled upon the *loi Gayssot*, which made denial of the "Armenian genocide" a punishable offence (the *loi Masse*, October 12, 2006). This law was declared unconstitutional by the Constitutional Council on February 28, 2012 (see Garibian 2013).
23 On this law, see notably Bertrand 2006a and Liauzu & Manceron 2006. An amendment to this law included "recognition" by France of the massacres committed after the conclusion of the Evian Accords, and of her responsibility for the fate of Algerian loyalist troops (*harkis*) who were simply abandoned and all those who were repatriated. Supported by Socialists, Communists, and Centrists, the amendment failed; see Michel 2010:160f.
24 On this report, see Michel 2011.
25 On the "normativity" of memory laws, see notably Garibian 2013 and Michel 2010: 186ff.
26 See Bachir 2014 and De Cock et al. 2008. In 2010, Sarkozy had declared an intention to abandon, after strong critique, the term "national identity" as a source of "misunderstandings"; during the presidential election campaign of 2012, it was rehabilitated (*Le Monde*, March 5, 2012).
27 The basic vocabulary of contemporary national politics—*nation*, *patrie*—is recent (Beaune 1985; Fehrenbach 1986; Nora 2007). However, the writing of history of the nation France goes back to the late medieval period. Starting in the twelfth century, "France" "becomes the normal framework of historical reflection" and remains so until the end of the nineteenth century (Beaune 1985: 13f.).
28 See chapter one.
29 Cf. Klein: "The prosaic emancipation is tremendous, for an author can move freely from memories as individual psychic events to memories as a shared group consciousness to memories as a collection of material artifacts and employ the same psychoanalytic vocabularies throughout" (2000: 135).
30 The subtitle is *French society through the prism of colonial heritage*. The volume is coedited by historian Pascal Blanchard. On Blanchard and the *Association pour la connaissance de l'histoire de l'Afrique contemporaine*, see De Cock 2018: 212–19 and Chabal 2015: 199–202.
31 For an account of French historiography on colonialism, see Coquery-Vidrovitch 2009.

32 See Legris 2010 and De Cock 2018 on the complex and rapidly changing institutional setup in which history programs are written in France.
33 For further discussion, see Zancarini 2001, Golder 2005, and references cited therein as well as Nichols 2013.
34 Florence Hulak 2018 argues that these lectures propose on one level an ultimately unsuccessful "new genealogy of the social sciences presented as negating" the relations of domination, struggle, and submission, constitutive of the scientific object of society. On this question, see also Salmon 2016.
35 For another example, see the comic-book story *Le Caïd de Naphte* by Farid Abdelkrim, which introduces children to Arabic words in French (Abdelkrim & Mahouin 2008).
36 The monograph is based on his PhD thesis (2003).
37 The fact that one volume of the prestigious series *Trente journées qui ont fait la France* (Thirty days which made France) is dedicated to the battle may indicate its significance (Roy & Deviosse 1966).
38 See Arkoun 2007 and Terrisse 2014.
39 For a review discussing the place of colonialism in this global history of France, see Huard 2018.
40 For a critical discussion of this "minimalist" perspective on the battle as "one event among others," see Micheau & Sénac 2007: 10f.
41 See the YouTube show "Let's deconstruct prejudices" with rapper Médine and Mouslim (Mouslim & Médine 2014). On Médine, see Jouili 2013.
42 Apart from this, the handout implicitly accepts the view that the incursion of troops from al-Andalus into the north of what is now France cannot be considered an invasion, but rather constitutes a raid. The significance of the battle of 732 is argued by presenting raids as reconnaissance operations for a future invasion, averted by this battle (Les Identitaires 2017).
43 On Iquioussen, see Bouzar 2001 and Peter 2006d.
44 See Lasfar 2017 for another example for this usage of history.
45 References to the sacrifices made by Muslims soldiers in the World Wars are frequent; see, e.g., Musulmans de France 2018 and below. In 2014, President Hollande inaugurated the "Memorial to the Muslim Soldier" in the Mosque of Paris. The memorial is designed to allow visitors to identify relatives who had fought in the army (Boubakeur & Thréard 2014; *Le Monde*, February 18, 2014).
46 Iquioussen discusses Arab racism in al-Andalus (2015b).
47 Mouslim 2007 makes a similar point with regard to the conquest of the Iberian peninsula.
48 Examples given by Iquioussen include the sources of La Fontaine's *Fables* (i.e., *Kalila wa-Dimna*) and the importance of Islamic imagery in Dante's *Divine Comedy*.
49 Ramadan points out that he has been calling for this "for years" (Ramadan 2000:202).

50 A strong identification with the nation is desirable, according to Ramadan, but its realization may be problematic and is directly prevented if Muslims are treated as foreigners: "The passport does not create the feeling of belonging, just as legal membership in a state does not create affective identification with the nation" (Morin & Ramadan 2014: 28; see also 236). Ramadan has drawn attention to the dangerous emergence of a new status of citizens, which he calls "foreign citizens" (quotation marks included). He describes a group as "citizens when it comes to their papers, but foreigners in their self-identification or their perception by others" (Morin & Ramadan 2014: 28). Against this background, some of Ramadan's criticism sounds hollow. When he writes of the immigration debate that "the difference between immigrants and 'new citizens' and ethnic French [*citoyens de souche*] is down to the fact that the latter are simply immigrants who arrived much earlier" (2009: 218), the usage of "simply" suggests that the "feeling of belonging" is generated automatically over time, which is what he had doubted.

51 Cultural conditions of integration find particularly strong emphasis in an audiocassette entitled "Urban violence: how can we act?" (Ramadan 2001). Ramadan discusses the causes of urban violence—a notion which is not defined in the talk—and how Muslim activists can help to counter it. Criticizing those who see violence as a merely structural question, he argues that any causal analysis of urban violence must also take into account the factors that make a human feel "in equilibrium." Islamic associations thus need to pay more attention to "the interior, the heart." The aim here is to enable the Muslim subject "to modify the way in which one looks at oneself." It is this kind of "deep" analysis he advocates, and it is here that memory comes into play. Ramadan demands a "discourse to revalue" the history of North African countries, an enterprise which he distinguishes sharply from the way "Oriental music" or certain foods are rated in France. At the same time, deeply concerned with the negative "image of parents" among youths, he draws attention to the need to recognize the contribution of immigrants to France and to its wealth, "because the immigrants who came to work in this country after the Second World War, they made this country," not least as soldiers serving in the armed forces (Ramadan 2001). See also Ramadan 2012b.

52 Its inaugural meeting was attended by Nicolas Dupoint-Aignan, souverainist presidential candidate, Michel Lelong, formerly in charge of relations with Islam at the Catholic Church and dialogue activist, Robert Ménard, journalist and far-right politician, Tareq Oubrou, and others. Former Interior Minister Jean-Pierre Chevènement, whose policies have been criticized by the association, had been invited, too (Ben Rhouma 2012).

53 Bechikh also was editor-in-chief of the short-lived magazine *Actualis: Islam et Société* published by the Union in 2004.

54 On Soral and the "new red-brown" (*noveaux rouges-bruns*), see Lebourg 2015, Amselle 2014, and Birnbaum 2015. See Fourquet 2015 on Muslim and Jewish votes for the National Front.

55 Soral 2004.
56 Such claims in favor of acculturation also impact structures of leadership. Bechikh considers that more space should be given to Francophone Muslims in the Union (Bechikh 2012).
57 On the significance of the cooperation between the two rulers for the relations between the Ottoman Empire and Western powers see Poumarède 2004: 624 and *passim*.
58 Baghezza argues that any vote in France necessarily implies making certain concessions. He gives priority to the preservation of family, morality, and patriotism. Sharply critical of the historical preference of Muslims for the Socialist Party, he considers these values are best served by the National Front (Baghezza 2012).
59 Which is an incomplete reading, as the above shows.
60 In a sense, historians today are perhaps moving beyond the empirical critique of supposedly pure origins and identities and are questioning the basic notion of identity which triggers such claims. Introducing the *Histoire mondiale de la France*, Patrick Boucheron seemingly gestures towards a different notion of identity when wondering why a country's "openness toward the world" has come to be associated with diminishing its "greatness." The very idea that a country's history can be conceived as a "struggle without end to maintain its sovereignty safe from foreign influences" triggers only incomprehension (Boucheron 2017: 11).

7 Islam and Fiction beyond Freedom of Speech

1 Following general usage, I refer to them as cartoons, even though not all of them are cartoons and their classification is contentious. See Seurrat 2008 and Klausen 2009.
2 See Klausen 2009.
3 The law of July 1, 1972 amends article 24 of the law of 1881 and makes "incitement to discrimination, hatred or violence toward a person or group of persons because of their origin, belonging or non-belonging in an ethnic group, a nation, race, or specific religion" a punishable offence.
4 On the history of the regulation of public speech in France, see Boulègue 2010, de Saint-Victor 2016 and Soula 2018.
5 See below.
6 See Boulègue 2010 for an account of court cases from 1984 until 2009.
7 *Charlie Hebdo* had addressed accusations of racism in an op-ed "No, Charlie Hebdo is not racist!" in *Le Monde* (Charlie Hebdo 2013a).
8 The petition to President Chirac was signed by the UOIF, the Mosque of Paris, FNMF (*Fédération Nationale des Musulmans de France*), CCMTF (*Comité de Coordination des Musulmans Turcs de France*), *Foi et Pratique*, the Great Mosque of

Saint-Denis la Réunion, the Mosque of Lyon, the Mosque Al-Islah in Marseille, the *Islamic Center in Évry*, and the Mosque in Mantes-la-Jolie.

9 See Langer 2014: 160–98 on attempts, before and after the cartoons, to mobilize against the defamation of religions on the international level since the 1990s.

10 Cf. Avon 2020.

11 It showed Muhammad saying "It is hard to be loved by idiots" (*C'est dur d'être aimé par des cons*) and was subtitled "Muhammad overwhelmed by fundamentalists" (*Mahomet débordé par des intégristes*). The Muslim organizations united behind this legal action—which initially included the Muslim World League—claimed that three drawings in fact constituted "public abuse of a group of people because of their religious adherence," an offence under the law of 1881 mentioned above. Apart from the cover of the magazine, the three drawings denounced by the Muslim organizations included the depiction of Muhammad with a turban-bomb and a drawing showing Muhammad greeting suicide bombers with "Stop, we have run out of virgins".

12 The cover of *Charlie Hebdo* was designed in a way that made it impossible or very difficult to separate the text—indicating that Muhammad was not addressing all Muslims, but only "fundamentalists"—from the drawing, as chief editor Val testified during the trial.

13 Note that Ramadan had defended a basically identical position in the case brought in 2002 against the writer Michel Houellebecq (see below) by several Muslim associations, including the Mosque of Paris. Houellebecq had been accused of incitement to discrimination, hatred, or violence, and offense on the basis of an interview in which he had notably stated his "hatred" of Islam and declared it to be the "dumbest" (*con*) religion. The court dismissed the case, ruling that Houellebecq had been targeting Islam and not Muslims, nor had he incited to hatred, discrimination, or violence. Note, too, that in 1993 Ramadan had warned strongly against the staging of Voltaire's play "Mahomet the Prophet or Fanaticism" in Geneva: "you cannot prevent this [Voltaire's] description [of Muhammad] violently hitting the heart and conscience of Muslims who are now part of Europe, for whom Muhammad is the way and horizon of their identity and sacrality" (quoted in Hamel 2007: 181). At the time, Ramadan had argued that this should not be seen as an act of censorship, but rather of "delicacy" (*délicatesse*).

14 Hasan Iquioussen, speaking a week later on the same radio show, makes a similar argument. The genre of caricature is not addressed. He deplores the absence of source-based criticism and urges following the prophet's model and keeping calm (Iquioussen 2006).

15 Meddeb's position on the cartoon is relatively complex. In Meddeb's account, free speech and the right to profane the sacred figure as historical European achievements. At the same time, Meddeb considers there is an old dispute between Europe and Islam;

the historically rooted negative stereotypical image of Muhammad which continues to be present subconsciously and shapes the Danish cartoons is one part of it. In the current multicultural context, there is need for deconstruction and more generally to enter into dialogue with the aim of "reconciliation" (2008: 63–7). Meddeb is disturbed by reactions to the cartoons. They indicate the "sensitivity of Muslim subjects in a position of weakness." The reaction of self-confident Muslims to these drawings, whose weakness and ugliness he bemoans, would have been "indifference or contempt" (2008: 125). This is not to say that the drawings are meaningless; rather, Meddeb considers that they respond to the real problem of violence in Islam, a problem not particular to Islam and equally present in the Bible (2008: 125–9). This posture cannot be separated from Meddeb's project to reconstruct a transcultural history of Islam, a history rejected by "common sense" and the scholars (2003: 16).

16 mlouizi.unblog.fr.
17 On Louizi, see Peter 2008b.
18 See Kepel & Jardin 2015.
19 See Badouard 2016.
20 Tiberj and Mayer offer an important critique of major elements in Todd's study. Using data from the annual poll conducted for the *Commission nationale consultative des droits de l'homme* (National Consultative Commission on Human Rights), the authors claim that the "motivation of demonstrators" "did not have anything to do with Islamophobia or intolerance towards any minority. It was the opposite." In other words, the approval rating for statements designating Islam as a threat or as denying Frenchness to descendants of immigrants was significantly lower among demonstrators and those who approved of the marches (Tiberj & Mayer 2015).
21 Todd considers that "the problem no. 1 of French society" is "the diffusion of antisemitism in the banlieues"; however, this phenomenon is addressed only in the most summary and general manner in his essay (2015: 106, 217–20). He also considers that the "primal sin" of Charlie was his silence after the "massacre" in a Jewish school in Toulouse in 2012 and other similar events (2015: 106). He claims that "*the definition of Islam as the central problem in French society has to led to an increase in physical risk not for the majority of French, but for Jews*" (emphasis in the original). While hardly addressing the causal connection, he argues that it deserves study given the importance of nonconscious factors and "the identification of Zombie Catholicism at the core of the Charlie phenomenon" (2015: 107).
22 This has been examined as part of a broader research project; see Galland & Muxel 2018 and reviews by Baubérot 2018 and Lamine 2018.
23 See, for example, Tariq Ramadan's biography of Muhammad (2007); on this see Haourigiui's study on it (2011).
24 In 2013 *Charlie Hebdo* published a two-volume account of Muhammad's life, written and drawn by Charb and Zineb El Rhazoui. The comic claims to present

Muhammad's life "as it is described in Islamic sources themselves" and refers to *sīra* literature (2013b: 4). Charb states: "No humor whatsoever is added. If the form appears to some blasphemous, the content is perfectly halal ... for you to judge" (back cover) (2013b).

25 Speech by the founder of the Mokhtar Awards, Gibran Hasnaoui, at the award ceremony in 2013.
26 "And do not gaze longingly at what We have given some of them to enjoy, the finery of this present life: We test them through this, but the provision of your Lord is better and more lasting" (Qur'an 20: 131).
27 "Another of His signs is that He created spouses from among yourselves for you to live with in tranquility: He ordained love and kindness between you" (Qur'an 30: 21).
28 "You may dislike something although it is good for you, or like something although it is bad for you: God knows and you do not" (Qur'an 2: 216).
29 As was pointed out by the director during his speech at the ceremony.
30 The nativists include a group called "Indigenous Europeans" who "started out as a direct response to the *Indigènes de la République*" (Houellebecq 2015: 55).
31 This assessment is made in the novel by a member of the French intelligence service.
32 Ajala 2013, Brouard & Tiberj 2005, Peace 2015, and Tiberj & Simon 2016.
33 This presentist reading is greatly facilitated—or encouraged—by frequent references in the narrative to present-day institutions and individuals, notably politicians and journalists.
34 De Cabarrus 2014; Lancon 2015.
35 Béglé 2014.
36 Houellebecq rejects any responsibility for supposed effects of his books, arguing that novels are too complex to produce any effects. Moreover, the topic of Islam had already been on the social agenda: "It would be impossible to talk about it more than [the media] already do, so my book won't have any effect" (Bourmeau 2015).
37 Birnbaum 2015.
38 See the critique of this position by Joffrin 2015. While Joffrin rigorously asserts the political character of the book, he acknowledges that the irony makes it impossible to read the author's intentions: "[O]ne does not know whether he approves or condemns what he describes."
39 Meizoz 2013.
40 This point is argued by Boris Viard in a study on Houellebecq. He notes that Houellebecq relies heavily on antiphrasis and should really be seen as a moralist. However, "a certain collaboration" with his often vile and cynical protagonists and "a little complicity with what he condemns" can be observed. See Viard 2013: 29f.
41 Leirys 2015.
42 Joffrin 2015.

43 Sometimes to the point that this is all that is talked about; see, e.g., Kantcheff 2015.
44 Roy 2015: 438. Note that Roy considers that it does not make sense to read Houellebecq from the perspective of Islamophobia (Bruckner & Roy 2017).
45 *saphirnews.com* 2015.
46 Oubrou 2015.
47 See Ramadan 2015. Ramadan notes that he appreciates "certain provocateurs," "but today there is a real lack of finesse … and basic intelligence" (2015).
48 See also Plenel 2015.
49 C à vous 2015.
50 Bourmeau 2015.
51 Pivot 2015.
52 Roy 2015.
53 Houellebecq & Lévy 2011.
54 See also Delorme 2014.
55 A similar argument can be made about the discussion of the religiosity of French fighting in Syria (Bourmeau 2015).
56 Houellebecq himself has always been explicit on this point. Bruno Viard writes that for Houellebecq, "far from being opium, religion is the infrastructure of any society. *Modern society* is thus not a society, but the painful assemblage of particles! This is the fundamental cause of Houellebecq's antiliberalism" (2013: 69; emphasis in the original). See Betty 2016 and Ungureanu 2017 on religion in Houellebecq's œuvre.
57 See Brient 2002: 27–38.
58 Houellebecq's fame is arguably founded on contributing a new question of public concern specific to the present context. It is the question how to think about love after recognizing that "desire" cannot be turned into "a generalized cultural project," nor can sexuality, which "remains resistant to the logic of marketing distribution (i.e. democratization)," be integrated "into the regime of liberty" (Abecassis 2000: 802, 810).
59 This and all following quotes are from Carrère 2015.
60 "What we feared the most is what, once we have passed to the other side, seems the most desirable – to the point that one will be astonished to not have desired it earlier. This radical inversion of perspectives, this is what in religious terms is called conversion, and in historical terms paradigm change. This is what Houellebecq talks about, he never talks about anything else, he is practically the only one to talk about it, at least in this way, as if he had access to the history books of the future – supposing there still are history books, and a future –, and this is why we all read him, dumbfounded."
61 See *On n'est pas couché* 2008.

8 Islamophobia and the Critique of Integration

1. See Meer & Modood 2009, 2019, Sayyid 2010, 2014, Bleich 2011, Klug 2012, Tyrer 2013, and Asal 2014.
2. Muhammad left the post of director of the CCIF in 2017. In 2018, he initiated a national consultation of French Muslims; see https://lesmusulmans.fr/ and Doucouré & Trinh Nguyen 2018.
3. In 2012, the CCIF managed to fully enter the national debate by launching its campaign *Nous (aussi) sommes la nation* (We [too] are the nation) presenting the case for a republican mobilization against Islamophobia (Collectif contre l'islamophobie en France 2012a). In 2016, it made a widely noted intervention into the burkini ban controversy, successfully challenging these bans together with the *Ligue des droits de l'homme* (Human Rights League) at the *Conseil d'État*. In the same year, a debate between Marwan Muhammad and Jean-François Copé, leader of the principal conservative party, took place (Sciences Po TV 2016). In 2019, the CCIF co-organized the first major demonstration against Islamophobia in Paris, attended by numerous politicians from the left (excluding the Socialist Party).
4. In the media, the CCIF is regularly associated with a number of Muslim groups deemed suspicious, including most prominently the Muslim Brotherhood and Tariq Ramadan (who supports its work and was one of the first to use the term "Islamophobia" in France). See, e.g., Mouillard & Sauvaget 2016; Chambraud 2016; Pina 2016. See also Marwan Muhammad 2017: 45f., where the author briefly presents his understanding of Tariq Ramadan's vision of Islam.
5. The figures for the last years are: 262 (2011), 469 (2012), 691 (2013), 764 (2014), 905 (2015), 580 (2016), 446 (2017), 676 (2018), and 789 (2019). The figures from the CFCM diverge greatly (e.g., 2019: 100), mainly because they only take into account complaints registered with public authorities (on methods of calculation, see also Zekri 2019).
6. See, for example, Kersimon & Moreau 2014, Moreau 2016, Gresh 2015, and CCIF 2015.
7. Similar arguments are made in Zineb 2016, Fourest 2015, and in the posthumously published essay by Charb 2015. See also Manent 2015: 112–15.
8. In 2010, the CFCM concluded an agreement with the Interior Ministry and created the *Observatoire national contre l'islamophobie* (National Monitoring Centre against Islamophobia) to count what are listed as "anti-Muslim acts" by the ministry. See, e.g., https://www.gouvernement.fr/bilan-2018-des-actes-racistes-antisemites-antimusulmans-et-antichretiens.
9. This point is sometimes missed by critics of the notion "Islamophobia" arguing that "anti-racist" legislation is being misused. See, e.g., Zineb 2016: 16. The *décret-loi Marchandeau* (1939) mentions both "religion" and "race" as grounds of "incite(ment) to hatred," defamation, and abuse.

10 See Soula 2018 on the conditions for implementing these provisions, which were primarily conceived in 1939 in the context of virulent anti-Semitism and preparations for war, as a means for the government to safeguard national cohesion by prosecuting those who "incite to hatred" (*excitent à la haine*), as the *décret-loi* put it. "It is not the community being attacked which is primarily protected, but the nation, union, unity, the society" (Soula 2018: 244). Since 1972 antiracist associations have been entitled to litigate as civil party.

11 I am drawing here on the discussion by Erik Bleich 2011; see also chapter one.

12 Making a similar point for France, Rokhaya Diallo points out that the accusation of racism constitutes a problem for the reputation and that the debate about racist statements is conducted on the level of the morality of the accused and not on the level of ideas (2011: 46f.).

13 Muhammad considers that the logic of racism is "utilitarian." Racism is defined as a means to "change the *game* of power" (2017: 123; emphasis in the original), i.e., a means to disable claims to equality from newcomers. This "utilitarian" dimension of racism is conceived as foundational and "creating the conditions of possibility" for a second level of racism, which is emotional (2017: 122f.).

14 Most obviously, through verifying the "assimilation" of candidates to naturalization. See Hajjat 2012.

15 Elsewhere, Muhammad argues that the question "Why is the headscarf worn?" is the wrong one: "In reality we should not intrude into their personal life," arguing that this is what respect of *laïcité* implies (CCIF 2012b).

16 Which, as I said, does not simply reproduce integration politics, but may to different degrees imply its reconfiguration.

17 Muhammad asserts his belief in the ultimately unrestricted possibility for individuals to choose their own identity: "Human beings in their magnificent and infinite complexity are able to construct ways of being themselves and to define themselves which liberate them from all these categorizations" (2017: 103), i.e., nationality and religion.

18 Another example of this can be found in the 2012 nationwide media campaign *Nous (aussi) sommes la nation*, which established that the CCIF can redefine media agendas. In the second campaign image, entitled "A French Family – 2012", we see a couple sitting on a sofa with their two young blond children. According to the Collective, the image is intended to refute several common stereotypes about Muslims: one which equates Muslims with foreigners—"this series shows also that a Muslim is not necessarily Maghrebi"—and a second one associating Muslims with strict behavior, violence, and the submission of women (CCIF 2012c). In the video presentation of this element of the campaign, Marwan Muhammad stresses that the image is not in any sense 'normative': "This visual is not supposed to fix a norm of what is or what should be the French nation, the French population, or French

identity" (CCIF 2012d). Rather, as his subsequent statements make clear, the visual is intended to show that Muslims fulfill the normative criteria for Frenchness.
19 Muhammad claims that "sociologically speaking, there is no 'Muslim community' as such" (2017: 140), meaning that a "generic, uniform and unified category" is being incorrectly imposed upon a diverse group of Muslims (2017: 140).
20 The controversies about the headscarf in public schools (and, importantly, beyond) occupy a central place in the work of the CCIF. At its creation in 2003, according to Marwan Muhammad's account, the CCIF "responded to an elementary need," namely to help women who were discriminated against in public services outside school because of their sartorial choices. Importantly, this "constitutes the majority of cases that we have to deal with today" (2017: 70f.). The CCIF identifies major continuities in the phenomenon at issue: "Islamophobia remains primarily a gendered racism" (i.e. 70 percent of documented acts target women), and public services, with more than 55 percent are the "main discriminating agent" (CCIF 2019b: 1). Marwan Muhammad considers that the date of the CCIF's creation— during debates about the ban of headscarves in 2003—is not insignificant, as this ban set in motion a broader political and societal dynamic which, as he states in conclusion, had made the CCIF "necessary" (2017: 71, 75).

Conclusion

1 In a discussion of European liberalism's multiple and simultaneous notions of law and freedom, Foucault points out that "heterogeneity is never a principle of exclusion; it never prevents coexistence, conjunction, or connection. And it is precisely in this case, in this kind of analysis, that we emphasize, and must emphasize a non-dialectical logic if we want to avoid being simplistic" (2008: 42).
2 Cf. Foucault: "No composition, no decomposition, no analysis into identities and differences can now justify the connection of representations one to another; order, the table in which it is spatialized, the adjacencies it defines, the successions it authorizes as so many possible routes between the points on its surface – none of these is any longer in a position to link representations or the elements of a particular representation together. The condition of these links resides henceforth outside representation, beyond its immediate visibility, in a sort of behind-the-scenes world even deeper and more dense than representation itself" (2005: 259).

Works Cited

Abdelkrim, Farid. 2002a. *Na'al bou la France?!* La Courneuve: Éditions Gedis.
Abdelkrim, Farid. 2002b. *Les jeunes, l'islam et le sexe. Des réalités cachées.* La Courneuve: Éditions Gedis.
Abdelkrim, Farid. 2005. *La France des islams. Ils sont fous ces musulmans?!* La Courneuve: Bayane Éditions.
Abdelkrim, Farid and Romain Mahouin. 2008. *Le Caïd de Naphte.* La Courneuve: Bayane Éditions.
Abdelkrim, Farid. 2015a. *Pourquoi j'ai cessé d'être islamiste. Itinéraire au cœur de l'islam en France.* Paris: Les points sur les i.
Abdelkrim, Farid. 2015b. *L'islam sera français ou ne sera pas.* Paris: Les points sur les i.
Abdelkrim, Farid. 2016. "J'ai une responsabilité dans la radicalisation de l'islam en France." *Le Monde.* 4 September.
Abecassis, Jack I. 2000. "The Eclipse of Desire: L'Affaire Houellebecq." *MLN*, 115.4: 801–26.
Achcar, Gilbert. 2008. "L'orientalisme à rebours. De certaines tendances de l'orientalisme français après 1979." *Mouvements*, 54: 127–44.
Adrian, Melanie. 2016. *Religious Freedom at Risk: The EU, French School, and Why the Veil was Banned.* Cham: Springer.
Ajala, Imène. 2013. "Muslims and Foreign Policy in France: A Case-study of UOIF and the Palestinian Issue." *French Politics*, 11.3: 259–71.
Ajbli, Fatiha. 2016. "Les Françaises 'voilées' dans l'espace public: entre quête de visibilité et stratégies d'invisibilisation." *Nouvelles Questions Féministes*: 35.1: 102–17.
Akan, Murat. 2009. "Laïcité and multiculturalism: the Stasi Report in context." *British Journal of Sociology*, 60.2: 237–56.
Albrecht, Sarah. 2018. *Dār al-Islām Revisited. Territoriality in Contemporary Islamic Legal Discourse on Muslims in the West.* Leiden: Brill.
Algava, Élisabeth and Lhommeau, Bertrand. 2016. "Échantillonage, collecte et pondérations de l'enquête Trajectoires et origines." In *Trajectoires et origines. Enquête sur la diversité des populations en France* edited by Chris Beauchemin, Christelle Hamel, and Patrick Simon, 585–606. Paris: INED.
Alouane, Rim-Sarah. 2014. "Bas Les Masques! Unveiling Muslim Women on Behalf of the Protection of Public Order: Reflections on the Legal Controversies Around a Novel Definition of 'Public Order' Used to Ban Full-Face Covering in France." In *The Experiences of Face Veil Wearers in Europe and the Law* edited by Eva Brems, 194–205. Cambridge: Cambridge University Press.

Amghar, Samir. 2006. "Les trois âges du discours des Frères musulmans en Europe." In *Islamismes d'Occident. État des lieux et perspectives* edited by Samir Amghar, 49–62. Paris: Éditions Lignes de repères.

Amghar, Samir. 2008. "Europe puts Islamists to the Test: The Muslim Brotherhood (France, Belgium and Switzerland)." *Mediterranean Politics*, 13.1: 63–77.

Amir-Moazami, Schirin. 2007. *Politisierte Religion. Der Kopftuchstreit in Deutschland und Frankreich*. Bielefeld: transcript.

Amiraux, Valérie. 2003. "CFCM – A French Touch?" *ISIM Newsletter*, 12: 24f.

Amiraux, Valérie. 2004. "Expertises, savoir et politique. La constitution de l'islam comme problème public en France et en Allemagne." In *Les sciences sociales à l'épreuve de l'action. Le savant, le politique et l'Europe* edited by Bénédicte Zimmermann, 209–45. Paris: Éditions de la Maison des Sciences de l'Homme.

Amiraux, Valérie and Patrick Simon. 2006. "There are no Minorities Here: Cultures of Scholarship and Public Debate on Immigrants and Integration in France." *International Journal of Comparative Sociology*, 47: 191–215.

Amiraux, Valérie. 2007. "The Headscarf Question: What is Really the Issue?" In *European Islam. Challenges for Public Policy and Society* edited by Samir Amghar, Amel Boubekeur, and Michael Emerson, 124–43. Brussels: Centre for European Policy Studies.

Amselle, Jean-Loup. 2014. *Les nouveaux rouges-bruns*. Fécamp: Lignes.

Anderson, Benedict. 1983. *Imagined Communities. Reflections on the Origin and Spread of Nationalism*. London: Verso.

Anderson, Perry. 2004. "Union sucrée." *London Review of Books*. 23 September. 26,18. https://www.lrb.co.uk/the-paper/v26/n18/perry-anderson/union-sucree

Arkoun, Mohammed, ed. 2007. *Histoire de l'islam et des musulmans en France du Moyen Âge à nos jours*. With a preface by Jacques Le Goff. Paris: Albin Michel.

Arslan, Leyla and Éric Marlière. 2014. "Les jeunes, l'islam et les travailleurs sociaux: concurrence ou complementarité? Etude comparée de deux quartiers populaires de la banlieue nord de Paris." In *Interventions sociales et faits religieux. Les paradoxes des logiques identitaires* edited by Daniel Verba and Faïza Guélamine, 63–76. Paris: Presses de l'EHESP.

Asad, Talal. 1993. *Genealogies of Religion: Discipline and Reasons of Power in Christianity and Islam*. Baltimore: Johns Hopkins University Press.

Asad, Talal. 2003. *Formations of the Secular: Christianity, Islam, Modernity*. Stanford: Stanford University Press.

Asad, Talal. 2006. "Trying to Understand French Secularism." In *Political Theologies: Public Religions in a Post-Secular World* edited by Hent de Vries and Lawrence E. Sullivan, 494–526. New York: Fordham University Press.

Asal, Houda. 2014. "Islamophobie: la fabrique d'un nouveau concept. État des lieux de la recherche." *Sociologie*, 5.1: 13–29.

Assemblée nationale. 2008. *Rapport d'information fait en application de l'article 145 du règlement au nom de la Mission d'information sur les questions mémorielles.* Président-Rapporteur M. Bernard Accoyer. 18 November. http://www.assemblee-nationale.fr/13/pdf/rap-info/i1262.pdf

Assouline, Pierre. 2015. "Michel Houellebecq, subversif et irreponsable comme jamais." *larepubliquedeslivres.com.* 5 January. http://larepubliquedeslivres.com/michel-houellebecq-subversif-et-irresponsable-comme-jamais/

Audier, Serge. 2015. *Les théories de la république.* New edition. Paris: La Découverte.

Auvergnon, Philippe. 2019. "Ministres du culte et exclusion du contrat de travail: à propos d'un changement de paradigme." *Revue du droit des religions.* 8. http://journals.openÉdition.org/rdr/432

Avon, Dominique. 2015. "Islam und Muslime im europäischen Kontext. Reden eines medienwirksamen Menschen (1993-2013): Tariq Ramadan." In *Muslimische Identitäten in Europa. Dispositive im gesellschaftlichen Wandel* edited by Sabine Schmitz und Tuba Işik, 267-97. Bielefeld: transcript.

Avon, Dominique. 2020. "Juristes musulmans contemporains, images et caricatures." *Revue de l'histoire des religions,* 237.1: 83-109.

Ayari, Michael Bechir. 2007/8: "Rester le même tout en devenant un autre. Les 'islamistes' tunisiens exilés en France." *Maghreb Machrek,* 194: 55-69.

Azouvi, Alain. 2013. "Religions et *laïcité* à l'hôpital public : enjeux et propositions." *Gestions hospitalières,* 523: 92-5.

Babès, Leila. 1997. *L'islam positif. La religion des jeunes musulmans de France.* Paris: Éditions de l'Atelier/Éditions ouvrières.

Babès, Leila and Michel Renard. 2000. "Quelle liberté de conscience?." *Libération.* 26 June. https://www.liberation.fr/tribune/2000/06/26/quelle-liberte-de-conscience_328669

Babès, Leila and Tareq Oubrou. 2002. *Loi d'Allah, loi des hommes. Liberté, égalité et femmes en Islam.* Paris: Albin Michel.

Bachir, Myriam. 2014. "La démocratie participative au service de l'identité nationale. Retour sur l'instauration gouvernementale d'un débat public (2009-2010)." In *L'identité nationale: instruments et usages* edited by Céline Husson-Rochcongar and Laurence Jourdain, 127-50. Amiens: Éditions du CURAPP.

Badinter, Elisabeth, Hervé Le Bras, et al. 2009. *Le retour de la race. Contre les "statistiques ethniques."* Paris: Éditions de l'Aube.

Badouard, Romain. 2016. "'Je ne suis pas Charlie.' Pluralité des prises de parole sur le web et les réseaux sociaux." *Le Défi Charlie. Les médias à l'épreuve des attentats.* <hal-01251253> https://hal.archives-ouvertes.fr/hal-01251253/document

Bahri, Fouad. 2009. "Les surprenantes déclarations de Tareq Oubrou." *oumma.com.* 2 November. https://oumma.com/les-surprenantes-declarations-de-tareq-oubrou/

Balibar, Etienne. 2005. "Difference, Otherness, Exclusion." *Parallax,* 11.1: 19-34.

Balke, Friedrich. 2007. "Tumulto. Regime des Bildes in Hobbes' *Leviathan*." In *Bildregime des Rechts* edited by Jean-Baptiste Joly, Cornelia Vismann, and Thomas Weitin, 62–82. Akademie Schloss Solitude: merz&solitude.

Bancel, Nicolas, Pascal Blanchard, and Françoise Vergès, eds. 2003. *La République coloniale*. Paris: Hachette.

Bancel, Nicolas, Florence Bernault, Pascal Blanchard, Ahmed Boubeker, Achille Mbembe, and Françoise Vergès, eds. 2010. *Ruptures postcoloniales*. Paris: La Découverte.

Basset, Karine-Larissa. 2013. "Le site de '732 La Bataille'. Ethnographie d'un récit historique, entre legs colonial et reconfiguration nationale." *Genèses*, 92.3: 76–101.

Bassiouni, Moustapha Chérif. 2008. "La naissance du collège-lycée Al-Kindi à Décines: une réussite conflictuelle." *L'Année du Maghreb*, 4: 401–21.

Baubérot, Jean. 1996. "L'affaire des foulards et la laïcité à la française." *L'homme et la société*, 120: 9–16.

Baubérot, Jean. 2001. "La laïcité comme pacte laïque." In *La laïcité une valeur d'aujourd hui?* edited by Jean Baudouin and Philippe Portier, 39–50. Rennes: Presses universitaires de Rennes.

Baubérot, Jean. 2006. "Le dernier des Curiace. Un sociologue dans la Commission Stasi." In *The New Religious Question/La nouvelle question religieuse. Régulation ou ingérence de l'État? State Regulation or State Interference?* edited by Pauline Côté and Jeremy Gunn, 247–73. Brussels: Presses Interuniversitaires Européennes.

Baubérot, Jean. 2008. *La laïcité expliquée à M. Sarkozy. . .et à ceux qui écrivent ses discours*. Paris: Albin Michel.

Baubérot, Jean. 2015. *Les sept laïcités françaises: Le modèle français de laïcité n'existe pas*. Paris: Éditions Maison des Sciences de l'Homme.

Baubérot, Jean. 2018. "L'ouvrage 'La tentation radicale' d'O. Galland et d'A. Muxel: une enquête défectueuse." *Mediapart*. 10 April. https://blogs.mediapart.fr/jean-bauberot/blog/100418/l-ouvrage-la-tentation-radicale-d-o-galland-et-d-muxel-une-enquete-defectueuse

Baudouin, Jean and Philippe Portier, eds. 2001. *La laïcité une valeur d'aujourd hui?* Rennes: Presses universitaires de Rennes.

Baumann, Gerd and André Gingrich, eds. 2004. *Grammars of Identity/Alterity. A Structural Approach*. New York: Berghahn.

Bauman, Zygmunt. 2005. "Durkheim's Society Revisited." In *The Cambridge Companion to Durkheim* edited by J.C. Alexander and P. Smith, 360–82. Cambridge: Cambridge University Press.

Bayart, Jean-François. 2005. *The Illusion of Cultural Identity*. Chicago: The University of Chicago Press.

Baylocq Sassoubre, Cédric. 2008. "Questions de pratiquants et réponses d'imam en contexte français. Économie de la fatwa dans les 'consultations juridiques' de Tareq Oubrou." *Revue des mondes musulmans et de la Méditerranée*, 124: 281–308.

Beauchemin, Cris, Christelle Hamel, and Patrick Simon, eds. 2015. *Trajectoires et origines. Enquête sur la diversité des populations en France*. Paris: INED.

Beaugé, Julien. 2015. "Stigmatisation et rédemption. Le port du voile comme 'épreuve.'" *Politix*, 111.3: 153–74.

Beaune, Collette. 1985. *Naissance de la nation France*. Paris: Gallimard.

Bechikh, Camel. 2012. "Beaucoup de jeunes imams sont les vrais promoteurs d'un islam français." *Le Monde*. 6 April. https://www.lemonde.fr/idees/article/2012/04/06/beaucoup-de-jeunes-imams-sont-les-vrais-promoteurs-d-un-islam-francais_1681810_3232.html

Beckford, James A. 1999. "The Politics of Defining Religion in Secular Society. From a Taken-for-Granted Institution to a Contested Resource." In *The Pragmatics of Defining Religion* edited by Platvoet and Arie Molendijk, 23–40. Leiden: Brill.

Béglé, Jérôme. 2014. "Houellebecq va faire une peur bleue à la France!" *Le Point*. 31 December.

Benabdallah, Sofiane. 2013. *Regarde plutôt la mer*. Video. https://www.youtube.com/watch?v=MYFZj5V3Ijs.

Ben Rhouma, Hanan. 2012. "Fils de France lève le tabou sur le patriotisme des musulmans français." *saphirnews.com*. 13 March. https://www.saphirnews.com/Fils-de-France-leve-le-tabou-sur-le-patriotisme-des-musulmans-francais_a14097.html

Ben Rhouma, Hanan. 2015. "#Stop Djihadisme: une infographie sur les 'signes de radicalisation' fait polémique." *saphirnews.com*. 29 January. https://www.saphirnews.com/StopDjihadisme-une-infographie-sur-les-signes-de-radicalisation-fait-polemique_a20352.html

Ben Rhouma, Hanan. 2018. "Départ de Tareq Oubrou de MF: 'Je ne suis pas un théologien organique.'" *saphirnews.com*. 14 May. https://www.saphirnews.com/Depart-de-Tareq-Oubrou-de-MF-Je-ne-suis-pas-un-theologien-organique_a25180.html

Behrent, Michael. 2008. "The Mystical Body of Society: Religion and Association in Nineteenth-Century French Political Thought." *Journal of the History of Ideas*, 69.2: 219–43.

Bergeaud-Blackler, Florence. 2017. *Le marché halal ou l'invention d'une tradition*. Paris: Éditions du Seuil.

Berstein, Serge and Odile Rudelle, eds. 1992. *Le modèle républicain*. Paris: Presses universitaires de France.

Bertossi, Christophe and Catherine Wihtol de Wenden. 2007. *Les couleurs du drapeau. L'armée française face aux discriminations*. Paris: Éditions Robert Laffont.

Bertossi, Christophe. 2010. *Country Report: France*. Florence: EUDO Citizesnhip Observatory/Robert Schuman Centre for Advanced Studies. https://cadmus.eui.eu/bitstream/handle/1814/19613/France.pdf?sequence=1&isAllowed=y

Bertossi, Christophe. 2012. "French Republicanism and the Problem of Normative Density." *Comparative European Politics*, 10: 248–65.

Bertossi, Christophe and John Bowen. 2015. "Practical schemas, conjunctures, and social locations: laïcité in French schools and hospitals." In *European States and their*

Muslim Citizens: The Impact of Institutions on Perceptions and Boundaries edited by John Bowen, Christophe Bertossi, Jan Willem Duyvendak, and Mona Lena Krook, 104–31. Cambridge: Cambridge University Press.

Bertrand, Romain. 2006a. *Mémoires d'empire. La controverse autour du "fait colonial"*. Bellecombe-en-Bauges: Éditions du croquant.

Bertrand, Romain. 2006b. "La mise en cause(s) du 'fait colonial'. Retour sur une controverse publique." *Politique africaine*, 102.2: 28–49.

Betty, Louis. 2016. *Without God: Michel Houellebecq and Materialist Horror*. University Park: Penn State University Press.

Billig, Michael. 1995. *Banal Nationalism*. London: Sage.

Birnbaum, Jean. 2015. "Houellebecq et le spectre du califat." *Le Monde*. 9 January.

Birnbaum, Jean. 2016. *Un silence religieux. La gauche face au djihadisme*. Paris: Éditions du Seuil.

Birnbaum, Pierre. 2015. "Jour de colère." *Revue d'histoire moderne & contemporaine*, 62–63: 245–59.

Bishri, al-'Arabi al-. 2004. "Muntalaqat li-fiqh al-aqalliyyat." *Al-Majalla al-'ilmiyya li-majlis al-urubbi li-l-ifta' wa-l-buhuth*. 227–44.

Bitèye, El Hadji Babou. 2013. *Vivre le pluralisme*. La Courneuve: Bayane Éditions.

Blanc, William and Christophe Naudin. 2015. *Charles Martel et la bataille de Poitiers de l'histoire au mythe identitaire*. Clermont-Ferrand: Éditions Libertalia.

Blanchard, Pascal, Nicolas Bancel, Sandrine Lemaire, and Olivier Barlet, eds. 2005. *La fracture coloniale. La société française au prisme de l'héritage colonial*. Paris: La Découverte.

Blanchard, Pascal. 2017. "Inequality between humans: From 'Race wars' to 'Cultural hierarchy'." In *The Colonial Legacy in France. Fracture, Rupture, and Apartheid* edited by Nicolas Bancel, Pascal Blanchard, and Dominic Thomas, 220–30. Bloomington: Indiana University Press.

Bleich, Erik. 2011. "What Is Islamophobia and How Much Is There? Theorizing and Measuring an Emerging Comparative Concept." *American Behavioral Scientist*, 55.12: 1581–600.

Bloc identitaire. 2012. "Les identitaires et la mosquée de Poitiers . . . dans les coulisses de l'opération." 23 December. http://www.bloc-identitaire.com/actualite/2765/minute-identitaires-coulisses-operation-mosquee-poitiers

Blumenberg, Hans. 1983. *The Legitimacy of the Modern Age*. Translated by Robert M. Wallace. Cambridge, MA: MIT Press.

Borghée, Maryam. 2012. *Voile intégral en France. Sociologie d'un paradoxe*. Paris: Michalon.

Bouamama, Saïd. 2004. *L'affaire du foulard islamique. La production d'un racisme respectable*. Roubaix: Le Geai Bleu.

Bouamama, Saïd. 2010. *Les discriminations racistes. Une arme de division massive*. Paris: L'Harmattan.

Boubakeur, Dalil and Yves Thréard. 2014. "Mémorial du Soldat musulman: Dalil Boubakeur répond à Yves Thréard." *Le Figaro*. 17 February. https://www.lefigaro.fr/

politique/2014/02/17/01002-20140217ARTFIG00144-memorial-du-soldat-musulman-dalil-boubakeur-repondez-moi.php

Boucheron, Patrick, ed. 2017. *Histoire mondiale de la France*. Paris: Éditions du Seuil.

Boulègue, Jean. 2010. *Le blasphème en procès 1984–2009*. Paris: Nova.

Bourget, Carine. 2019. *Islamic Schools in France: Minority Integration and Separatism in Western Society*. Cham: Palgrave Macmillan.

Bourmeau, Sylvain. 2015. "Scare Tactics: Michel Houellebecq Defends His Controversial New Book." January 2. https://www.theparisreview.org/blog/2015/01/02/scare-tactics-michel-houellebecq-on-his-new-book/

Boussinesq, Jean. 1994. *La laïcité française. Memento juridique*. Paris: Éditions du Seuil.

Bouteldja, Houria and Sadri Khiari. 2012. *Nous sommes les indigènes de la république*. Coordination and interviews by Félix Boggio-Éwanjé-Épée and Stella Magliani-Belkacem. Paris: Éditions Amsterdam.

Bouzar, Dounia. 2001. *L'islam des banlieues. Les prédicateurs musulmans: nouveaux travailleurs sociaux?* Paris: Syros/La Découverte.

Bouzar, Dounia. 2004. *Monsieur Islam n'existe pas : Pour une désislamisation des débats*. Paris: Hachette.

Bouzar, Dounia. 2005. *Ça suffit!* Paris: Éditions Denoël.

Bowen, John R. 2004. "Does French Islam Have Borders? Dilemmas of Domestication in a Global Religious Field." *American Anthropologist*, 106.1: 43–55.

Bowen, John R. 2007. *Why the French don't like Headscarves. Islam, the State, and Public Space*. Princeton: Princeton University Press.

Bowen, John R. 2009. *Can Islam be French? Pluralism and Pragmatism in a Secularist State*. Princeton: Princeton University Press.

Bowen, John R. 2012. "Working Schemas and Normative Models in French Governance of Islam." *Comparative European Politics*, 10.3: 354–68.

Boyer, Alain. 1992. *L'Institut Musulman de la Mosquée de Paris*. Paris: Centre des hautes études sur l'Afrique et l'Asie modernes.

Boyer, Alain. 1993. *Le droit des religions en France*. Paris: Presses universitaires de France.

Boyer, Alain. 2005. "La représentation du culte musulman en France." *French Politics, Culture & Society*, 23.1: 8–22.

Boyer, Alain. 2005. "Comment l'État laïque connaît-il les religions?" *Archives de sciences sociales des religions*, 37–49.

Bowen, Innes. 2014. *Medina in Birmingham, Najaf in Brent. Inside British Islam*. London: Hurst.

Bréchon, Pierre and Jean-François Tchernia, eds. 2009. *La France à travers ses valeurs*. Paris: Armand Colin.

Brèze, Lhaj Thami. 2006. "L'UOIF, Réalisations et orientations." 7 May. http://www.uoif-online.com/modules.php?op=modload&name=News&file=article&sid=453

Brisson, Thomas. 2008a. "Les intellectuels arabes et l'orientalisme parisien (1955–1980): comment penser la transformation des savoirs en sciences humaines?" *Revue française de sociologie*, 49.2: 269–99.
Brisson, Thomas. 2008b. *Les intellectuels arabes en France*. Paris: La Dispute.
Bronner, Gérald and Étienne Géhin. 2017. *Le danger sociologique*. Paris: Presses universitaires de France.
Brouard, Sylvain and Vincent Tiberj. 2005. *Français comme les autres? Enquête sur les citoyens d'origine maghrébine, africaine et turque*. Paris: Fondation Nationale des Sciences Politiques.
Brown, Wendy. 2001. *Politics out of History*. Princeton: Princeton University Press.
Brown, Wendy. 2006. "Power after Foucault." In *Oxford Handbook of Political Theory* edited by John S. Dryzek, Bonnie Honig, and Anne Phillips, 65–85. Oxford: Oxford University Press.
Brubaker, Rogers. 1992. *Citizenship and Nationhood in France and Germany*. Cambridge, MA: Harvard University Press.
Brubaker, Rogers and Frederick Cooper. 2000. "Beyond 'Identity.'" *Theory and Society*, 29.1: 1–47.
Bruce, Benjamin. 2018. *Governing Islam Abroad: Turkish and Moroccan Muslims in Western Europe*. London: Palgrave Macmillan.
Bruckner, Pascal. 2010. *The Tyranny of Guilt. An Essay on Western Masochism*. Princeton: Princeton University Press.
Bruckner, Pascal. 2017. *Un racisme imaginaire. Islamophobie et culpabilité*. Paris: Bernard Grasset.
Burgat, François. 2003. *Face to Face with Political Islam*. London: I.B. Tauris.
Burgat, François. 2016. *Comprendre l'Islam politique*. Paris: La Découverte.
Burke, Edmund. 2014. *The Ethnographic State. France and the Invention of Moroccan Islam*. Berkeley: University of California Press.
C à vous. 2015. "Houellebecq et islamophobie: clash entre Cohen et Plenel – C à vous – 06/01/2015." https://www.youtube.com/watch?v=zZT-4bleAkU
Caeiro, Alexandre. 2003. "Adjusting Islamic Law to Migration." *ISIM Newsletter*, 12: 26–7.
Caeiro, Alexandre. 2004. "The Social Construction of Šarīʿa. Bank Interest, Home Purchase, and Islamic Norms in the West." *Die Welt des Islams*, 44.3: 351–75.
Caeiro, Alexandre. 2005a. "Religious Authorities or Political Actors? The Muslim Leaders of the French Representative Body of Islam." In *European Muslims and the Secular State* edited by Jocelyn Cesari and Séan McLoughlin, 71–84. Ashgate: Aldershot.
Caeiro, Alexandre. 2005b. "An Imam in France. Tareq Oubrou." *ISIM Review*, 15: 48–9.
Caeiro, Alexandre. 2006a. "The Shifting Moral Universes of the Islamic Tradition of Iftā': A Diachronic Study of Four Adab al-Fatwā Manuals." *Muslim World*, 96.4: 661–85.
Caeiro, Alexandre. 2006b. "The Mufti and the Home Minister. Gearing Muslim Technologies towards Social Governance in France." Paper presented at 40th MESA Meeting, Boston, 18–21 November.

Caeiro, Alexandre. 2011a. *Fatwas for European Muslim: The Minority Fiqh Project and the Integration of Islam in Europe*. PhD Dissertation, Utrecht University.

Caeiro, Alexandre. 2011b. "Islamic Authority, Transnational 'Ulama, and European Fatwas. A Case-Study of the ECFR." In *Producing Islamic Knowledge: Transmission and Disseminaton in Western Europe* edited by Martin van Bruinessen and Stefano Allievi, 121–41. London: Routledge.

Calhoun, Craig. 1993. "Nationalism and Ethnicity." *Annual Review of Sociology*, 19: 211–39.

Calhoun, Craig. 2006. *Nations Matter: Culture, History and the Cosmopolitan Dream*. London: Routledge.

Camus, Jean-Yves. 2006. "The Commemoration of Slavery in France and the Emergence of a Black Political Consciousness." *European Legacy*, 11.6: 647–55.

Camus, Renaud. 2012. *Le grand remplacement suivi de Discours d'Orange*. N. pl.: Renaud Camus.

Candiard, Adrien. 2016. *Comprendre l'Islam – ou plutôt: pourquoi on n'y comprend rien*. Paris: Flammarion.

Carpentier, Jean. 2004. "L'histoire récente de l'enseignement du fait religieux en France." *Revue d'histoire critique*, 83: 2–11.

Carrère, Emmanuel. 2015. "Emmanuel Carrère sur Houellebecq: Un roman d'une extraordinaire consistance romanesque." *Le Monde*. 6 January. https://abonnes.lemonde.fr/livres/article/2015/01/06/emmanuel-carrere-la-resistance-n-interesse-pas-houellebecq_4550129_3260.html?

Casanova, José. 1994. *Public Religions in the Modern World*. Chicago: The University of Chicago Press.

Casanova, José. 2011. "The Secular, Secularizations, Secularisms." In *Rethinking Secularism* edited by Craig Calhoun, Mark Juergensmeyer, and Jonathan VanAntwerpen, 54–74. Oxford: Oxford University Press.

Cassen, Pierre, Caroline Fourest, and Corinne Lepage. 2006. "Contre un nouvel obscurantisme." *Liberation*. 28 April. https://www.liberation.fr/tribune/2006/04/28/contre-un-nouvel-obscurantisme_37612

Carré, Oliver. 1988. "Les banlieues de l'Islam." *Arabica*, 35.3: 404–6.

Césari, Jocelyne. 1994. *Être musulman en France: associations, militants et mosquées*. Paris: Karthala.

Césari, Jocelyne. 1998. *Musulmans et républicains: les jeunes, l'islam et la France*. Brussels: Éditions Complexe.

Césari, Jocelyne. 2005. "Mosques in French Cities. Towards the End of a Conflict?" *Journal of Ethnic and Migration Studies*, 31.6: 1025–43.

Chabal, Emile. 2015. *A Divided Republic. Nation, State and Citizenship in Contemporary France*. Cambridge: Cambridge University Press.

Chakrabarty, Dipesh. 2000. *Provincializing Europe. Postcolonial Thought and Historical Difference*. Princeton: Princeton University Press.

Chambraud, Cécile. 2016. "Marwan Muhammad, porte-voix combatif des musulmans." *Le Monde*. 31 October. https://www.lemonde.fr/societe/article/2016/10/31/marwan-muhammad-porte-voix-combatif-des-musulmans_5022868_3224.html

Champion, Françoise and Cohen, Martine, eds. 1999. *Sectes et démocratie*. Paris: Éditions du Seuil.

Chantin, Jean-Pierre. 2007. "Les sectes en France. Quel questionnement sur la laïcité?" In *Pratiques de la laïcité au XXᵉ siècle* edited by Patrick Weil, 553–69. Paris: Presses universitaires de France.

Charb. 2015. *Lettre aux escrocs de l'islamophobie qui font le jeu des racistes*. Paris: Librio.

Charlie Hebdo. 2013a. "Non, 'Charlie Hebdo' n'est pas raciste!" *Le Monde*. 20 November.

Charlie Hebdo. 2013b. *La vie de Mahomet. 1ère partie. Les débuts d'un prophète*. Hors-serie. N. pl.

Chatriot, Alain and Claire Lemercier. 2002. "Les corps intermédiaires." In *Dictionnaire critique de la République* edited by Vincent Duclert and Christophe Prochasson, 691–8. Paris: Flammarion.

Chauveau, Stéphanie. 2014. "Au-delà du cas Soral. Corruption de l'esprit public et postérité d'une nouvelle synthèse réactionnaire." *Agone*, 54.2: 95–122.

Chesnot, Christian and Georges Malbrunot. 2019. *Qatar papers. Comment l'émirat finance l'islam de France et d'Europe*. Paris: Michel Lafon.

Citron, Suzanne. 1987. *Le mythe national. L'histoire de France en question*. Paris: Les Éditions ouvrières.

Cohen, Martine. 2001. "L'intégration de l'islam et des musulmans en France: modèles du passé et pratiques actuelles." In *La laïcité, une valeur d'aujourd'hui?* edited by Jean Beaudouin and Philippe Portier, 315–30. Rennes: Presses universitaires de Rennes.

Collectif contre l'islamophobie en France. 2004. *Rapport d'étape du CCIF sur l'Islamophobie en France 2003–2004*. www.islamophobie.net/wp-content/uploads/.../ccif_rapport_2004.pdf

Collectif contre l'islamophobie en France. 2012a. "Campagne #NSLN: Présentation du CCIF par Samy Debah." 30 October. https://www.youtube.com/watch?v=lefgeyLKTb4

Collectif contre l'islamophobie en France. 2012b. "Marwan Muhammad vs Mohamed Sifaoui." 12 November. https://www.youtube.com/watch?v=YfrE84VYvw0

Collectif contre l'islamophobie en France. 2012c. "Présentation de la campagne du CCIF 'Nous Sommes La Nation' par Marwan Muhammad." 10 January. https://www.youtube.com/watch?v=PkVZiEBPvdU

Collectif contre l'islamophobie en France. 2012d. "Campagne CCIF, #NSLN Visuel 2: Une famille française." https://www.youtube.com/watch?v=vsgvUfMQ9m0

Collectif contre l'islamophobie en France. 2015. "Islamophobie: Mise au point sur une contre enquête." 7 July. https://www.islamophobie.net/2015/07/07/qui-veut-faire-taire-le-ccif/

Collectif contre l'islamophobie en France. 2019a. "Notre manifeste." https://www.islamophobie.net/manifesto/

Collectif contre l'islamophobie en France. 2019b. *Rapport sur l'islamophobie pendant l'annee 2018*. https://www.islamophobie.net/wp-content/uploads/2018/04/ccif-rapport-2018.pdf

Colombani, Marie-Françoise and Tareq Oubrou. 2017. *La féministe et l'imam*. Paris: Éditions Stock.

Commission Debré. 2003. *Rapport fait au nom de la mission d'information sur la question du port des signes religieux à l'école*. Paris: La Documentation française.

Commission Machelon. 2006. *Les Relations des cultes avec les pouvoirs publics*. Paris: La Documentation française.

Commission Nationale Consultative des Droits de l'Homme. 2013. *Rapport annuel*. https://www.cncdh.fr/fr/publications/rapport-racisme-antisemitisme-et-xenophobie-2013-banalisation-de-la-parole-raciste-et

Commission Nationale Consultative des Droits de l'Homme. 2017. *Rapport annuel*. https://www.cncdh.fr/sites/default/files/cncdh_rapport_2017_bat_basse_definition.pdf

Commission Stasi. 2003. *Commission de réflexion sur l'application du principe de laïcité dans la République: rapport au Président de la République*. Paris: La Documentation française. http://lesrapports.ladocumentationfrancaise.fr/BRP/034000725/0000.pdf

Conseil d'État. 2004. *Rapport public 2004. Jurisprudence et avis de 2003. Un siècle de laïcité (Études et documents n. 55)*. Paris: La documentation française.

Coquery-Vidrovitch, Cathérine. 2009. *Enjeux politiques de l'histoire coloniale*. Marseille: Agone.

Corcuff, Philippe. 2014. *Les années 30 reviennent et la gauche est dans le brouillard*. Paris: Éditions Textuel.

Corcuff, Philippe. 2015. "Prégnance de l'essentialisme dans les discours publics autour de l'islam dans la France postcoloniale." *Confluences Méditerranée*, 95.4: 119–30.

Courtois, Stéphane and Gilles Kepel. 1988. "Musulmans et prolétaires." In *Les musulmans dans la société française* edited by Rémy Leveau and Gilles Kepel, 27–38. Paris: Presses de la Fondation Nationale des Sciences Politiques.

Couvelaire, Louise. 2020. "Sur l'islam et la République, les dangers de l'amalgame." *Le Monde*. 17 February. https://www.lemonde.fr/societe/article/2020/02/17/communautarisme-separatisme-secession-les-dangers-de-l-amalgame_6029833_3224.html

Culture et dépendances. 2005. "Tariq Ramadan Vs Manuel Valls La Colonisation, La France est elle coupable, doit elle s'excuser." *France 3*. 14 December. https://www.youtube.com/watch?v=P2nBO_2DvhY

Cumper, Peter. 2017. "Blasphemy, Freedom of Expression and the Protection of Religious Sensibilities in Twenty-First Century Europe." In *Blasphemy and Freedom of Expression. Comparative, Theoretical and Historical Reflections after the Charlie Hebdo Massacre* edited by Jeroen Temperman and Andras Koltay, 137–66. Cambridge: Cambridge University Press.

Curtit, Françoise and Anne Fornerod. 2016. "Manifestations de la *soft law* en droit français des religions." *Studies in Religion*, 45.2: 111–26.

Dakhli, Leyla. 2016. "L'islamologie est un sport de combat." *Revue du Crieur*. https://hal.archives-ouvertes.fr/hal-01325340/document

Dalgaard-Nielsen. 2010. "Violent Radicalization in Europe: What We Know and What We Do Not Know." *Studies in Conflict & Terrorism*, 33.9: 797–814.

Daumas, Cécile. 2016. "Olivier Roy et Gilles Kepel, querelle française sur le jihadisme." *Libération*. 14 April. https://www.liberation.fr/debats/2016/04/14/olivier-roy-et-gilles-kepel-querelle-francaise-sur-le-jihadisme_1446226

Davet, Gérard and Fabrice Lhomme. 2016. *Un président ne devrait pas dire ça...Les secrets du quinquennat*. Paris: Stock.

Davet, Gérard and Fabrice Lhomme. 2018. *Inch'Allah: l'islamisation à visage découvert*. Paris: Fayard.

Davidson, Naomi. 2012. *Only Muslim. Embodying Islam in Twentieth-Century France*. Ithaca: Cornell University Press.

Dazey, Margot. 2019. "Les conditions de production locale d'un islam respectable." *Genèses*, 117.4: 74–93.

De Cabarrus, Thierry. 2014. "Dans 'Soumission', Houellebecq met l'islam au pouvoir: de la provoc' à la Zemmour?." *leplus.nouvelobs.com*. 18 December. http://leplus.nouvelobs.com/contribution/1293518-dans-soumission-houellebecq-met-l-islam-au-pouvoir-de-la-provoc-a-la-zemmour.html

De Cock, Laurence, Fanny Madeline, Nicolas Offenstadt, and Sophie Wahnich, eds. 2008. *Comment Nicolas Sarkozy écrit l'histoire de France*. Marseille: Agone.

De Cock, Laurence. 2018. *Dans la classe de l'homme blanc. L'enseignement du fait colonial en France des années 1980 à nos jours*. Lyon: Presses universitaires de Lyon.

Défenseur des droits. 2013. *L'égale accès des enfants à la cantine de l'ecole primaire*. 28 March. https://www.ladocumentationfrancaise.fr/rapports-publics/134000207/index.shtml

de Galembert, Claire. 2001. "La régulation étatique du religieux à l'épreuve de la globalisation." In *La globalisation du religieux* edited by Jean-Pierre Bastian, Françoise Champion, and Kathy Rousselet, 223–34. Paris: L'Harmattan.

de Galembert, Claire. 2004. "Islam et intégration." In *Les modèles d'intégration en question: Enjeux et perspectives* edited by Michel Pélissier and Arthur Paecht, 103–10. Paris: Presses universitaires de France.

de Galembert, Claire. 2006. "L'islam des acteurs publics territoriaux: entre incertitude et ressource d'autorité politique." *Cahiers de la Sécurité Intérieure*. 33–53.

de Galembert, Claire. 2009. "Cause du voile et lutte pour la parole musulmane légitime." *Sociétés contemporaines*, 74.2: 19–47.

de Galembert, Claire. 2014. "Forcer le droit à parler contre la burqa. Une *judicial politics* à la française?" *Revue française de science politique*, 64.4: 647–68.

de Galembert, Claire. 2016. "Le 'radical', une nouvelle figure de dangerosité carcérale aux contours flous." *Critique internationale*, 72.3: 53–71.

de Lavergne, Nicolas. 2003/4. "L'Islam, moteur de la citoyenneté. Le cas de 'jeunes musulmans de France.'" *Sociétés*, 82: 29–41.

de Saint Victor, Jacques. 2015. "Du blasphème dans la République." *Le Débat*, 185.3: 11–20.

de Saint Victor, Jacques. 2016. *Blasphème. Brève histoire d'un 'crime imaginaire.'* Paris: Gallimard.

Delorme, Marie-Laure. 2014. "Alain Finkielkraut:'Le parti de Houellebecq, c'est le neutre.'" *Le Journal du Dimanche*. https://www.lejdd.fr/Culture/Livres/Alain-Finkielkraut-Le-parti-de-Houellebecq-c-est-le-neutre-708942

Descombes, Vincent. 2016. "The Order of Things: An Archaeology of What?" *History & Theory*, 55.4: 66–81.

Despland, Michel. 1999. *L'émergence des sciences de la religion. La monarchie de Juillet: un moment fondateur*. Paris: L'Harmattan.

Dewitte, Philippe. 1991. "La dette du sang." *Hommes & Migrations*, 1148: 8–11.

Dhume, Fabrice and Khalid Hamdani. 2013. *Vers une politique française de l'égalité. Rapport du groupe de travail "Mobilités sociales" dans le cadre de la "Refondation de la politique d'intégration"*. November. https://www.vie-publique.fr/sites/default/files/rapport/pdf/134000758.pdf

Dhume, Fabrice. 2014. "L'intimidation. Retour sur la campagne de presse qui a mené à l'enterrement des rapports." *Migrations Société*, 155.5: 129–52.

Diallo, Rokhaya. 2011. *Racisme: mode d'emploi*. n.pl.: Soulajah Éditions.

Diop, A. Moustapha. 1989. "Immigration et religion. Les musulmans négro-africains En France." *Migrations Société*, 1.4: 45–57.

Diop, A. Moustapha and Riva Kastoryano. 1991. "Le mouvement associatif islamique en Île-de-France." *Revue européenne des migrations internationales*, 7.3: 91–117.

Djavann, Chahdortt. 2003. *Bas les voiles!* Paris: Gallimard.

Donnet, Claire. 2013. *Des mobilisations autour de la reconnaissance de l'islam en France: étude de la puissance d'agir de sujets musulmans intégralistes*. PhD thesis. Université de Strasbourg.

Donzelot, Jacques. 1993. "The promotion of the social." In *Foucault's New Domains*, edited by Mike Gane and Terry Johnson, 106–38. London: Routledge.

Donzelot, Jacques. 1994 [1984]. *L'invention du social. Essai sur le déclin des passions politiques*. Paris: Éditions du Seuil.

Dosse, François. 2011. *Pierre Nora. Homo historicus*. Paris: Perrin.

Doucouré, Samba and Trinh Nguyen, Huê. 2018. "Consultation initiée par Marwan Muhammad: des chiffres ... et des luttes." *saphirnews.com*. 2 October. https://www.saphirnews.com/Consultation-initiee-par-Marwan-Muhammad-des-chiffres-et-des-luttes_a25638.html

Doytcheva, Milena. 2010. "Usages français de la notion de diversité: permanence et actualité d'un débat." *Sociologie*, 1.4: 423–38.

Dubois, Jacques. 2000. *Les romanciers du réel. De Balzac à Simenon*. Paris: Éditions du Seuil.

Dubois, Laurent. 2004. *Avengers of the New World. The Story of the Haitian Revolution*. Cambridge, MA: Belknap Press.

Dufoix, Stéphane. 2006. "Historiens et mnémographes." *Controverses*, 2: 15–38.

Dufoix, Stéphane. 2016. "Nommer l'autre: L'émergence du terme communautarisme dans le débat français." *Socio*. 7. http://journals.openÉdition.org/socio/2524.

Dufoix, Stéphane. 2018. "Communautarisme: une formule diabolique." In *Communautarisme?* edited by Marwan Mohammed and Julien Talpin, 13–25. Paris: Presses universitaires de France.

Duthu, Françoise. 2008. *Le maire et la mosquée. Islam et laïcité en Île-de-France*. Paris: L'Harmattan.

Dutrieux, Damien. 2014. "Laïcité et sépultures: aspects juridiques." https://www.resonance-funeraire.com/index.php/reglementation/1340-laicite-et-sepultures-aspects-juridiques-1re-partie

Elster, Jon. 1978. *Logic and Society. Contradiction and Possible Worlds*. London: John Wiley & Sons.

Escafré-Dubet, Angéline and Lionel Kesztenbaum. 2011. "Mesurer l'intégration des immigrés. Genèse et histoire des enquêtes Girard-Stoetzel, 1945–1953." *Genèses*, 84.2: 93–112.

Estier, Samuel. 2015. *À propos du "style" de Houellebecq. Retour sur une controverse (1998–2010)*. Second edition. Lausanne: Archipel Essais.

Étienne, Bruno. 1989. *La France et l'islam*. Paris: Hachette.

European Council for Fatwa and Research. 2002. *First Collection of Fatwas*. Dublin.

Fassin, Didier. 2002. "L'invention française de la discrimination." *Revue française de science politique*, 52.4: 403–23.

Fassin, Didier. 2011. "Qu'il ne suffit pas d'être politiquement incorrect pour être scientifiquement fondé." *Revue française de sociologie*, 52.4: 777–86.

Fassin, Didier and Éric Fassin. 2006. "Introduction." In *De la question sociale à la question raciale? Représenter la société française* edited by Didier Fassin and Éric Fassin, 5–16. Paris: La Découverte.

Fassin, Eric. 2006. "La démocratie sexuelle et le conflit des civilisations." *Multitudes*, 26.3: 123–31.

Fassin, Eric. 2011. "A Double-edged Sword: Sexual Democracy, Gender Norms, and Racialized Rhetoric." In *The Question of Gender: Joan W. Scott's Critical Feminism* edited by Judith Butler and Elizabeth Weed, 143–58. Bloomington: Indiana University Press.

Fassin, Eric. 2012. "Statistiques raciales ou racistes? Histoire et actualité d'une controverse française." In *Les nouvelles frontières de la société française* edited by Didier Fassin, 427–51. Paris: La Découverte.

Favell, Adrian. 2001. *Philosophies of Integration. Immigration and the Idea of Citizenship in France and Britain*. Second edition. Basingstoke: Macmillan.

Fauvelle, François-Xavier. 2017. "L'Afrique frappe à la porte du pays des Francs." In *Histoire mondiale de la France* edited by Patrick Boucheron, 124–9. Paris: Éditions du Seuil.

Febvre, Lucien and François Crouzet. 2012 [1950]. *Nous sommes des sang-mêlés: Manuel d'histoire de la civilisation française*. Paris: Éditions Albin Michel.

Federation of Islamic Organizations in Europe. 2000. "Muslims of Europe Charter." http://www.methaq.eu/

Fehrenbach, Elisabeth. 1986. "Nation." In *Handbuch politisch-sozialer Grundbegriffe in Frankreich, 1680–1820* edited by Rolf Reichhardt, Eberhard Schmitt, and Hans-Jürgen Lüsebrink, VII:75–107. Munich: R. Oldenbourg.

Feldblum, Miriam. 1999. *Reconstructing Citizenship. The Politics of Nationality Reform and Immigration in Contemporary France*. Albany: State University of New York Press.

Fernando, Mayanthi L. 2014. *The Republic Unsettled. Muslim French and the Contradictions of Secularism*. Durham, NC: Duke University Press.

Figaro Live. 2018. "Le livre 'scoop' de Davet & Lhomme arrive-t-il trop tard?." 21 October. https://www.youtube.com/watch?v=JRRFM5ZG4vs

Fils de France. 2012a. "Notre Charte." http://www.filsdefrance.fr/notre-charte/

Fils de France. 2012b. "Fils de France invité de la 29ème Rencontre annuelle des Musulmans de France." http://www.youtube.com/watch?v=XRuUJs5FPic

Fils de France. 2014a. "Conférence Fils de France – Français, Musulman et Patriote – par Camel Bechikh." https://www.youtube.com/watch?v=vaKGjPENJ9M

Fils de France. 2014b. "Camel Bechikh à propos de *Fils de France*, Tareq Oubrou et l'UOIF." http://www.filsdefrance.fr/breves/camel-bechikh-fils-de-france-tareq-oubrou-luoif/#more-2284

Fils de France. 2014c. "Camel Bechikh: La France est ontologiquement catholique et européeenne." http://www.youtube.com/watch?v=LszXzMsksfk

Fils de France. 2016. "Fils de France donne la parole à Farid Abdelkrim, ex-'Frère Musulman'." 9 May. https://www.youtube.com/watch?v=LQY4-3PvRV0

Flood, Finbarr Barry. 2013a. "Lost Histories of a Licit Figural Art." *International Journal of Middle East Studies*, 45: 566–9.

Flood, Finbarr Barry. 2013b. "Inciting Modernity? Images, Alterities and the Contexts of 'Cartoon Wars.'" In *Images That Move* edited by Patricia Spyer and Mary Margaret Steedly, 41–72. Santa Fe: School for Advanced Research Press.

Foblets, Marie-Claire. 2016. "Gender, Islam and Family Law in Europe: The broken promises of human rights." In *Beiträge zum Islamischen Recht XI* edited by Irene Schneider and Thoralf Hanstein, 125–49. Frankfurt: Peter Lang.

Fonds de soutien pour l'intégration et la lutte contre les discriminations. 2006. *L'exercice du culte musulman en France: lieux de prière et d'inhumation*. Paris: Documentation française.

Forey, Elsa. 2001. "Du 'cultuel' au 'culturel', vers une remise en cause du principe de séparation de 1905?" In *La laïcité, une valeur d'aujourd'hui? Contestations et renégociation du modèle français* edited by Jean Baudouin and Philippe Portier, 285–96.

Forey, Elsa. 2007. *État et institutions religieuses. Contribution à l'étude des relations entre ordres juridiques*. Strassburg: Presses universitaires de Strasbourg.

Fornerod, Anne. 2006. "Affectation cultuelle et affectation culturelle." In *Le patrimoine culturel religieux. Enjeux juridiques et pratiques cultuelles* edited by Brigitte Basdevant-Gaudemet, Marie Cornu, and Jérôme Fromageau, 237–47. Paris: L'Harmattan.

Fornerod, Anne. 2016. *Annotated Legal Documents on Islam in Europe: France*. Leiden: Brill.

Fornerod, Anne. 2017. "The outcome of the Stasi report in France: Much ado about nothing?" In *Public Commissions on Cultural and Religious Diversity: Analysis, Reception, and Challenges* edited by Solange Lefebvre and Patrick Brodeur, 80–97. London: Routledge.

Fornerod, Anne. 2018. "Wearing a veil in the French context of laïcité." In *The Routledge International Handbook of Veils and Veiling Practices* edited by Anna-Mari Almila and David Inglis, 53–62. London: Routledge.

Fortier, Vincente. 2000. *Justice, religions et croyances*. Paris: CNRS Éditions.

Fortier, Vincente. 2008. "Le prosélytisme au regard du droit: une liberté sous contrôle." *Cahiers d'études du religieux. Recherches interdisciplinaires*. Published online 4 July. http://journals.openÉdition.org/cerri/144

Foucault, Michel. 1981. "The Order of Discourse." In *Untying the Text: A Post-Structuralist Reader* edited by Robert C. Young, 51–78. London: Routledge & Kegan Paul.

Foucault, Michel. 1988. "The Ethics of Care for the Self as a Practice of Freedom." In *The Final Foucault* edited by James W. Bernauer and David M. Rasmussen, 1–20. Cambridge, MA: MIT Press.

Foucault, Michel. 1990. *The Use of Pleasure. Vol. 2 of History of Sexuality*. Translated by Robert Hurley. New York: Vintage Books.

Foucault, Michel. 1994. "Nietzsche, Freud, Marx." In *Essential Works of Foucault. Vol. 2. Aesthetics, Methods and Epistemology* edited by James Faubion, 269–78. London: Penguin.

Foucault, Michel. 2000. *Power. Essential Works of Foucault 1954–1984* edited by James Faubion. New York: New Press.

Foucault, Michel. 2003. *'Society Must Be Defended': Lectures at the Collège de France, 1975–1976*. New York: Picador.

Foucault, Michel. 2005 [1966]. *The Order of Things. An Archaeology of the Human Sciences*. London: Routledge.

Foucault, Michel. 2008. *The Birth of Biopolitics. Lectures at the Collège de France, 1978–79*. London: Palgrave Macmillan.

Foucault, Michel. 2009. *Security, Territory, Population. Lectures at the Collège de France 1977–1978*. New York: Palgrave Macmillan.

Fournier, Lydie. 2008. *Le fait musulman à Montpellier: Entre réalités sociologiques et enjeux politiques*. Paris: Dalloz-Sirey.

Fournier, Marcel. 2007. *Émile Durkheim (1858–1917)*. Paris: Fayard.

Fourquet, Jérôme. 2015. "Le vote National Front dans les électorats musulman et juif." In *Les faux-semblants du National Front* edited by Sylvain Crépon, Alexandre Dézé, and Nonna Mayer, 375–94. Paris: Presses de Sciences Po.

France. 1789. "Déclaration des Droits de l'Homme et du Citoyen de 1789." 26 August.
France 24. 2019. "Tareq Oubrou: 'L'islam de France est inaudible et inintelligible'." 11 June. https://www.youtube.com/watch?v=FlPLwnkZkKw
France Inter Le grand entretien. 2018a. "Le grand entretien avec Gérard Davet et Fabrice Lhomme." 15 October. https://www.youtube.com/watch?v=q5BiS0jgJaA
France Inter L'Instant M. 2018b. "Inch'Allah: l'enquête sur l'islamisation qui divise les générations." 18 October. https://www.youtube.com/watch?v=1bYypGrAkKA
Frégosi, Franck. 1998. "Les filières nationales de formation des imams en France." In *La formation des cadres religieux musulmans en France. Approches socio-juridiques* edited by Franck Frégosi, 101–39. Paris: L'Harmattan.
Frégosi, Franck. 2005. "Les musulmans laïques, une mouvance plurielle et paradoxale." *Maghreb Machrek*, 183: 33–43.
Garibian, Sévane. 2013. "La mémoire est-elle soluble dans le droit ? Des incertitudes nées de la décision n°2012-647 DC du Conseil constitutionnel français." *Droit et cultures*, 66: 25–56.
Gaspard, Françoise and Farhad Khosrokhavar. 1995. *Le foulard et la république*. Paris: La Découverte.
Gaspard, Françoise et al. 2003. "Petition: Oui au foulard à l'école laïque." *Libération*. 20 May. https://www.liberation.fr/tribune/2003/05/20/oui-au-foulard-a-l-ecole-laique_434258
Geisser, Vincent. 2003. *La nouvelle islamophobie*. Paris: La Découverte.
Geisser, Vincent. 2005. "L'intégration républicaine: Réflexions sur une problématique post-coloniale." In *Culture post-coloniale en France. Traces et mémoires coloniales en France* edited by P. Blanchard, N. Bancel with the collaboration of S. Lemaire, 145–64. Paris: Éditions Autrement.
Geisser, Vincent and Aziz Zemouri. 2007. *Marianne & Allah. Les politiques françaises face à la "question musulmane"*. Paris: La Découverte.
Geisser, Vincent and Abdelaziz Chaambi. 2007. "La fabrication médiatique de 'l'Islamiste des banlieues d'ici et d'ailleurs'." *Migrations Société*, 111–12.3: 123–34.
Geisser, Vincent. 2012. "La 'question musulmane' en France au prisme des sciences sociales: Le savant, l'expert et le politique." *Cahiers d'études africaines*, 206–7: 351–66.
Geisser, Vincent. 2013. "L'indésirable rapport. Pourquoi les analyses de Thierry Tuot dérangent-elles autant?" *Migrations Société*, 146.2: 3–14.
Geisser, Vincent. 2015. "Limites et dangers des réponses culturalistes et misérabilistes au terrorisme." *Migrations Société*, 157.1: 3–14.
Geisser, Vincent, Omero Marongiu-Perria, and Kahina Smaïl, eds. 2017. *Musulmans de France. La grande épreuve*. Ivry-sur-Seine: Éditions de l'Atelier/Éditions Ouvrières.
Gérin, André. 2009. *Proposition de résolution tendant à la création d'une commission d'enquête sur la pratique du port de la burqa ou du niqab sur le territoire national*. Paris: Assemblée nationale. 9 June. http://www.andregerin.com/admin/img/eve/00001.1832.prop_resolution_burqa.pdf
Ghosn, Catherine. 2010. "Représentation de la diversité à la télévision française: à partir de quelles normes?" *Sciences de la société*, 81: 27–43.

Gingrich, André. 2004. "Conceptualising Identites." In *Grammars of Identity/Alterity. A Structural Approach* edited by Gerd Baumann and André Gingrich, 3–17. New York: Berghahn.

Glavany, Jean, ed. 2011. *Le guide pratique de la laïcité. Une clarification par le concret.* Paris: Fondation Jean Jaurès.

Godard, Bernard and Sylvie Taussig. 2007. *Les musulmans en France. Courants, institutions, communautés: un état des lieux.* Paris: Robert Laffont.

Godard, Bernard. 2015. *La question musulmane en France. Un état des lieux sans concessions.* Paris: Fayard.

Golder, Ben. 2005. "Review." *Foucault Studies*, 3: 121–6.

Göle, Nilüfer. 2002. "Islam in Public: New Visibilities and New Imaginaries." *Public Culture*, 14.1: 173–90.

Göle, Nilüfer. 2010. "The Civilizational, Spatial, and Sexual Powers of the Secular." In *Varieties of Secularism in A Secular Age* edited by Michael Warner, Jonathan VanAntwerpen, and Craig Calhoun, 243–64. Cambridge, MA: Harvard University Press.

Göle, Nilüfer. 2015. *Islam and Secularity: The Future of Europe's Public Sphere.* Durham, NC: Duke University Press.

Goodman, Sarah Wallace. 2014. *Immigration and Membership Politics in Western Europe.* Cambridge: Cambridge University Press.

Gouguenheim, Sylvain. 2008. *Aristote au mont Saint-Michel. Les racines grecques de l'Europe chrétienne.* Paris: Éditions du Seuil.

Gourdeau, Camille. 2018. "'Le CAI, c'est bien pour les autres'. L'injonction à l'intégration du point de vue des signataires du contrat d'accueil et d'intégration (CAI)." *Politiques de communication*, 2.11: 73–101.

Grand Sanhédrin. 2008. *Les décisions doctrinales du Grand Sanhédrin réuni sous les auspices de Napoléon le Grand.* Lagrasse: Éditions Verdier.

Gresh, Alain and Tariq, Ramadan. 2000. *L'Islam en questions. Débat animé et présenté par Françoise Germaine-Robin.* Arles: Actes Sud.

Gresh, Alain. 2004. *L'islam, la république et le monde.* Paris: Fayard.

Gresh, Alain. 2015. "Islamophobie: Vous avez dit contre-enquête?" *blog.mondediplo.net*. 6 January. https://blog.mondediplo.net/2015-01-06-Islamophobie-vous-avez-dit-contre-enquete

Grossberg, Lawrence. 1996. "Identity and Cultural Studies: Is That All There Is?" In *Questions of Cultural Identity* edited by Stuart Hall and Paul Gay, 88–107. London: Sage.

Gruson, Luc. 2011. "Un musée peut-il changer les représentations sur l'immigration?" *Hommes & migrations*, 1293: 12–21.

Guélamine, Faïza. 2014. "L'inscription du fait religieux dans le champ de l'intervention sociale. Enjeux, paradoxes et modalites de traitement." In *Interventions sociales et faits religieux. Les paradoxes des logiques identitaires* edited by Faïza Guélamine and Daniel Verba, 129–44. Paris: Presses de l'EHESP.

Guibet-Lafaye, Caroline and Pierre Brochard. 2016. "La radicalisation vue par la presse – Fluctuation d'une représentation." *Bulletin of Sociological Methodology/ Bulletin de Méthodologie Sociologique*, 131.1: 25–48.

Guibet-Lafaye, Caroline and Ami-Jacques Rapin. 2017. "La 'radicalisation'. Individualisation et dépolitisation d'une notion." *Politiques de communication*, 8.1: 127–54.

Guillaumont, Olivier. 2005. "Le Conseil d'État et le principe constitutionnel de laïcité, à propos de l'arrêt du 16 mars 2005, Ministre de l'outre-mer c/gouvernement de la Polynésie française." *Revue française de droit constitutionnel*, 63.3: 631–8.

Gutting, Gary. 1990. *Michel Foucault's Archaeology of Scientific Reason*. Cambridge: Cambridge University Press.

Habermas, Jürgen. 1980. "Kritische und konservative Aufgaben der Soziologie." *Theorie und Praxis. Sozialphilosophische Studien*, 290–306. Frankfurt am Main: Suhrkamp.

Hacking, Ian. 1994. "Memoro-politics, trauma and the soul." *History of the Human Sciences*, 7.2: 29–52.

Hacking, Ian. 1999. *The Social Construction of What?* Cambridge, MA: Harvard University Press.

Hafiz, Chems-eddine and Devers, Gilles. 2005. *Droit et religion musulmane*. Paris: Éditions Dalloz.

Hajjat, Abdellali and Yamin Makri. 2004. "'Madame douce France' n'existe pas non plus!" oumma.com. 29 November. https://oumma.com/madame-douce-france-nexiste-pas-non-plus/

Hajjat, Abdellali. 2010. "'Bons' et 'mauvais' musulmans. L'État français face aux candidats 'islamistes' à la nationalité." *Cultures & Conflits*, 79–80: 139–59.

Hajjat, Abdellali. 2012. *Les frontières de 'l'identité nationale'. L'injonction à l'assimilation en France métropolitaine et coloniale*. Paris: La Découverte.

Hajjat, Abdellali and Marwan Mohammed. 2013. *Islamophobie. Comment les élites françaises fabriquent le "problème musulman."* Paris: La Découverte.

Hallaq, Wael. 2018. *Restating Orientalism. A Critique of Modern Knowledge*. New York: Columbia University Press.

Halpérin, Jean-Louis, Stéphanie Hennette-Vauchez, and Eric Millard, eds. 2017. *L'état d'urgence: de l'exception à la banalisation*. Paris: Presses universitaires de Paris Nanterre.

Hamel, Ian. 2007. *La vérité sur Tariq Ramadan. Sa famille, ses réseaux, sa stratégie*. Lausanne/Paris: Favre.

Hamès, Constant. 1989. "La construction de l'islam en France: du côté de la presse." *Archives de sciences sociales des religions*, 68.1: 79–92.

Haourigui, Khaddija. 2011. "L'humanisme exemplaire du prophète dans la lecture de Tariq Ramadan." In *Discours musulmans contemporains. Diversité et cadrages* edited by Felice Dassetto, 45–56. Paris: L'Harmattan.

Harsin, Jayson. 2015. "Cultural Racist Frames in TF1's French Banlieue Riots Coverage." *French Politics, Culture & Society*, 33.3: 47–73.

Hartog, François. 2016. *Regimes of Historicity: Presentism and Experiences of Time*. New York: Columbia University Press.

Haut Conseil à l'intégration. 1991. *Pour un modèle français d'intégration. Premier rapport annuel*. Paris: La Documentation française.
Haut Conseil à l'intégration. 1992. *Conditions juridiques et culturelles de l'intégration*. Paris: La Documentation française.
Haut Conseil à l'intégration. 1995. *Liens culturels et intégration*. Paris: La Documentation française.
Haut Conseil à l'intégration. 1997. *Affaiblissement du lien social, enfermement dans les particularismes et intégration dans la cité*. Paris: La Documentation française.
Haut Conseil à l'intégration. 2000. *L'Islam dans la République*. Paris: La Documentation française.
Haut Conseil à l'intégration. 2004. *Le Contrat et l'intégration*. Paris: La Documentation française.
Haut Conseil à l'intégration. 2006. *Le bilan de la politique d'intégration 2002–2005*. Paris: La Documentation française.
Haut Conseil à l'intégration. 2007. *Charte de la laïcité dans les services public et autres avis*. Paris: La Documentation française.
Haut Conseil à l'intégration. 2011. "Expression religieuse et laicité dans l'entreprise." Avis. 1 September. http://archives.hci.gouv.fr/IMG/pdf/HCI-Avis-laicite-entreprise-pdf-2.pdf
Haut Conseil à l'intégration. 2012. *Investir dans les associations pour réussir l'intégration – Charte des droits et devoirs du citoyen français – De la neutralité religieuse dans l'entreprise: rapport d'activité de la Mission Laïcité*. Paris: La Documentation française.
Hébrard, Gabrielle. 2014. "L'éclairage du Conseil d'État sur les obscurités de l'exigence de neutralité religieuse." *La Revue des droits de l'homme*. 17 January. http://revdh.revues.org/504
Heilbron, Johan. 1995. *The Rise of Social Theory*. Cambridge: Polity Press.
Hennette-Vauchez, Stéphanie and Vincent Valentin. 2014. *L'affaire Baby Loup ou la Nouvelle Laïcité*. Issy-les-Moulineaux: LGDJ.
Hennette-Vauchez, Stéphanie. 2016. "Séparation, garantie, neutralité…les multiples grammaires de la laïcité." *Les Nouveaux Cahiers du Conseil constitutionnel*, 53.4: 9–19.
Hennette-Vauchez, Stéphanie. 2017a. "Is French laïcité Still Liberal? The Republican Project under Pressure (2004–15)." *Human Rights Law Review*, 17.2: 285–312.
Hennette-Vauchez, Stéphanie. 2017b. "Equality and the Market: the unhappy fate of religious discrimination in Europe: ECJ 14 March 2017, Case C-188/15, Asma Bougnaoui & ADDH v Micropole SA; ECJ 14 March 2017, Case C-157/15, Samira Achbita & Centrum voor gelijkheid van kansen en voor racismebestrijding v G4S Secure Solutions NV." *European Constitutional Law Review*, 13.4: 744–58.
Henrich, Dieter and Wolfgang Iser. 1983. "Entfaltung der Problemlage." In *Funktionen des Fiktiven* edited by Dieter Henrich and Wolfgang Iser, 9–14. Munich: Wilhelm Fink.

Héran, François. 2016. "Préface." In *Trajectoires et origines. Enquête sur la diversité des populations en France* edited by Chris Beauchemin, Christelle Hamel, and Patrick Simon, 7–16. Paris: INED.

Hervieu-Léger, Danièle. 2000. "Le miroir de l'islam en France." *Vingtième Siècle*, 66: 79–89.

Hirschkind, Charles. 2011. "Is there a Secular Body?" *Cultural Anthropology*, 26.4: 633–47.

Houellebecq, Michel and Bernard-Henri Lévy. 2011. *Ennemis publics*. Paris: J'ai Lu.

Houellebecq, Michel. 2015. *Submission*. Translated from the French by Lori Stein. London: William Heinemann.

House, Jim. 2001. "Antiracist memories: the case of 17 October 1961 in historical perspective." *Modern and Contemporary France*, 9.3: 355–68.

Huard, Raymond. 2018. "Patrick Boucheron (dir.), *Histoire mondiale de la France*." *Revue d'histoire du XIXe siecle*, 57: 202–4.

Hulak, Florence. 2018. "La guerre et la société. Le problème du 'savoir historico-politique' chez Foucault." *Philosophie*, 138.3: 61–75.

Human Rights Watch. 2007. "In the Name of Prevention." 19,3. June. https://www.hrw.org/sites/default/files/reports/france0607_0.pdf

IFOP. 2015. "Sondage. Les Français et la laïcité." *Ifop.com*. 9 December. https://www.ifop.com/publication/les-francais-et-la-laicite-3/

Institut Montaigne. 2013. "Faire vivre la promesse laïque." https://www.institutmontaigne.org/ressources/pdfs/publications/note_-_faire_vivre_la_promesse_laique.pdf

Iquioussen, Hassan. 1990. "Comment un musulman vit l'intégration." 21–3 December. Video. Amiens: Euro-Médias.

Iquioussen, Hassan. 2006. "La Zakat Almaal et Les caricatures du Prophète." 17 February. *Pastel FM*. http://acmr1.free.fr/index.php?page=telechargements.

Iquioussen, Hassan. 2013. "L'Andalousie musulmane (1ère partie) - Hassan Iquioussen." *Hassan Iquioussen*. 29 May. https://www.youtube.com/watch?v=gzBEtHQUTC0

Iquioussen, Hassan. 2014. "L'Islam de France: de 1945 à 2114 (sic)." *Hassan Iquioussen*. 27 May. https://www.youtube.com/watch?v=40UgpVR-ccI

Iquioussen, Hassan. 2015a. "L'importance de l'Histoire en Islam." *Havre de Savoir*. 3 July. https://www.youtube.com/watch?v=D_46xSt6bgE

Iquioussen, Hassan. 2015b. "Histoire de l'Andalousie Musulmane par Hassan Iquioussen – Partie 1." *Havre de Savoir*. 23 January. https://www.youtube.com/watch?v=gYKOeRQ4sfQ

Iquioussen, Hassan. 2015c. "Histoire de l'Andalousie Musulmane par Hassan Iquioussen – Partie 2." *Havre de Savoir*. 22 February. https://www.youtube.com/watch?v=71kfRVSrgVc

Iquioussen, Hassan. 2015d. "Reponse aux orientalistes sur les 'Conquêtes Musulmanes'." *Havre de Savoir*. 29 June. https://www.youtube.com/watch?v=WOx1IiNd78w

Iser, Wolfgang. 1975. "The Reality of Fiction: A Functionalist Approach to Literature." *New Literary History*, 7.1: 7–38.

Islam de France. 2000. "Dossier al-istichâratou." No. 7:33–78.
Ismaili, Hicham. 2013. *Sunna*. Video. https://www.youtube.com/watch?v=6ex9fS1Gg1A
Jaballah, Ahmed. 2000. "Dans quelle mesure la pratique de l'Islam s'adapte-t-elle au contexte ?" Video cassette. Paris.
Jaballah, Ahmed. 2003. "Le Conseil européen de la fatwa. Adapter la pratique musulmane au contexte occidentale." In *L'avenir de l'islam en France et en Europe: Les Entretiens d'Auxerre* edited by Michel Wieviorka, 137–41. Paris: Balland.
Jaballah, Ahmed. 2008. "Al-Wasatiyya bayna muqtadayat al-muwatana fi-urubba wa-l-hifaz ʿala l-huwiyya al-islamiyya." *Al-Majalla al-ʿilmiyya li-l-majlis al-urubbi li-l-iftaʾ wa-l-buhuth*, 12/13: 257–72.
Jaballah, Ahmed. 2015. "Je suis et je ne suis pas Charlie." *saphirnews.com*. https://www.saphirnews.com/Ahmed-Jaballah-Je-suis-et-je-ne-suis-pas-Charlie_a20336.html Originally published in *Le Monde*, January 15, 2015.
Jaballah, Ahmed. 2016. "Colloque de l'UOIF – Ahmed Jaballah – Les bases de la pensée et du discours du juste milieu." https://www.youtube.com/watch?v=PcmTQ2VbkgQ
Jansen, Yolande. 2006. "Laïcité or the Politics of Republican Secularism." In *Political Theologies: Public Religions in a Post-secular World* edited by Hent de Vries and Lawrence E. Sullivan, 475–93. New York: Fordham University Press.
Jansen, Yolande. 2013. *Secularism, Assimilation and the Crisis of Multiculturalism. French Modernist Legacies*. Amsterdam: Amsterdam University Press.
Jauß, Hans Robert. 1983. "Zur historischen Genese der Scheidung von Fiktion und Realität." In *Funktionen des Fiktiven*, edited by Dieter Henrich and Wolfgang Iser, 423-31. Munich: Wilhelm Fink.
Joffrin, Laurent. 2015. "'Soumission', Le Pen au Flore." *Libération*. 2 January. https://next.liberation.fr/livres/2015/01/02/le-pen-au-flore_1173182
Jonker, Gerdien and Valérie Amiraux, eds. 2006. *Politics of Visibility. Young Muslims in European Public Spaces*. Bielefeld: transcript.
Joppke, Christian. 2009. *Veil: Mirror of Identity*. London: Polity Press.
Joppke, Christian and John Torpey. 2013. *Legal Integration of Islam. A Transatlantic Comparison*. Cambridge, MA: Harvard University Press.
Jouanneau, Solenne. 2013. *Les imams en France. Une autorité religieuse sous contrôle*. Marseille: Agone.
Jouili, Jeanette. 2013. "Rapping the Republic. Utopia, Critique, and Muslim Role Models in Secular France." *French Politics, Culture & Society*, 31.2: 58–80.
Jouili, Jeanette. 2015. *Pious Practice and Secular Constraints: Women in the Islamic Revival in Europe*. Stanford: Stanford University Press.
Judt, Tony. 1998. "A la Recherche du Temps Perdu." *The New York Review of Books*, 45.19: 51–8.
Kantcheff, Christophe. 2015. "'Soumission' de Michel Houellebecq: La conversion pour les nuls." *Politis*. https://www.politis.fr/auteurs/christophe-kantcheff-6/

Karsenti, Bruno. 2006. *Politique de l'esprit. Auguste Comte et la naissanace de la science sociale*. Paris: Hermann.

Kastoryano, Riva. 2002. *Negotiating Identities: States and Immigrants in France and Germany*. Princeton: Princeton University Press.

Kepel, Gilles. 1985. "La leçon de Cheikh Faycal. Les enjeux d'un discours islamiste dans l'immigration musulmane en France." *Esprit*. 186–96.

Kepel, Gilles. 1991 [1987]. *Les banlieues de l'Islam. Naissance d'une religion en France*. Paris: Éditions du Seuil.

Kepel, Gilles. 1994. *À l'ouest d'Allah*. Paris: Éditions du Seuil.

Kepel, Gilles. 2012. *Banlieue de la République: Société, politique et religion à Clichy-sous-Bois et Montfermeil*. In collaboration with Leyla Arslan and Sarah Zouheir and the participation of Mohamed-Ali Adraoui, Dilek Yankaya, and Antoine Jardin. Paris: Gallimard.

Kepel, Gilles with Antoine Jardin. 2015. *Terreur sur l'Hexagone. Genèse du djihad français*. Paris: Gallimard.

Kepel, Gilles and Bernard Rougier. 2016. "'Radicalisations' et 'islamophobie': le roi est nu." *Libération*. 14 March. https://www.liberation.fr/debats/2016/03/14/radicalisations-et-islamophobie-le-roi-est-nu_1439535

Kersimon, Isabelle and Jean-Christophe Moreau. 2014. *Islamophobie, la contre-enquête*. Paris: Plein Jour.

Keyhani, Narguesse. 2014. "De la régulation des 'opinions' sur l'immigration à la mise l'agenda d'un problème de 'l'identité nationale.'" In *L'identité nationale: instruments et usages* edited by Céline Husson-Rochcongar and Laurence Jourdain, 43–62. Amiens: Éditions du CURAPP.

Khiari, Sadri. 2004. "Tariq Ramadan, mythologie de la Umma et résistance culturelle." *Critique communiste*. 172. Published March 28, 2005 at http://www.preavis.org/breche-numerique/article151.html#nh7

Khosrokhavar, Farhad. 1997. *L'islam des jeunes*. Paris: Flammarion.

Khosrokhavar, Farhad. 2014. *Radicalisation*. Paris: Éditions de la Maison des Sciences de l'Homme.

Khosrokhavar, Farhad. 2018. *Le nouveau jihad en Occident*. Paris: Robert Laffont.

Kimmel-Alcover, Anne. 2014. "Restauration scolaire et laïcité: quand la religion de l'élève s'invite à la table de la cantine." *Revue de droit sanitaire et social*. 146–57.

Klausen, Jytte. 2009. *The Cartoons that Shook the World*. New Haven: Yale University Press.

Klein, Kerwin Lee. 2000. "On the Emergence of Memory in Historical Discourse." *Representations*. 127–50.

Klug, Brian. 2012. "Islamophobia: A Concept Comes of Age." *Ethnicities*, 12.5: 665–81.

Knausgaard, Karl Ove. 2015. "Michel Houellebecq's 'Submission.'" *The New York Times*. 2 November.

Kokoreff, Michel, Patricia Osganian and Patrick Simon, eds. 2006. "Emeutes, et après?" *Mouvements*, 44.2.

Koselleck, Reinhart. 1991. "Wie sozial ist der Geist der Wissenschaften?" In *Geisteswissenschaften heute. Eine Denkschrift*, by Wolfgang Frühwald, Hans Robert Jauß, Reinhart Koselleck, Jürgen Mittelstraß, and Burkhart Steinwachs, 112–141. Frankfurt am Main: Suhrkamp.

Koselleck, Reinhart. 2004. *Futures Past. On the Semantics of Historical Time*. New York: Columbia University Press.

Koussens, David. 2011. "Expertise publique sous influence?" *Archives de sciences sociales des religions*, 155: 61–79.

Koussens, David. 2015. *L'épreuve de la neutralité. La laïcité française entre droits et discours*. Brussel: Bruylant.

Krosigk, Constanze von. 2000. *Der Islam in Frankreich. Laizistische Religionspolitik von 1974 bis 1999*. Hamburg: Dr. Kovač.

Kuru, Ahmet T. 2009. *Secularism and State Policies toward Religion. The United States, France, and Turkey*. Cambridge: Cambridge University Press.

Laborde, Cécile. 2008a. "Toleration and laïcité." In *The Culture of Toleration in Diverse Societies. Reasonable Tolerance* edited by Catriona McKinnon and Dario Castiglione, 161–78. Manchester: Manchester University Press.

Laborde, Cécile. 2008b. *Critical Republicanism. The Hijab Controversy and Political Philosophy*. Oxford: Oxford University Press.

Laborde, Cécile. 2010. *Français, encore un effort pour être républicains!* Paris: Éditions du Seuil.

Laborde, Cécile. 2015. "Religion in the Law: The Disaggregation Approach." *Law and Philosophy*, 34.6: 581–600.

La Croix. 2017. "Qu'est-ce que l'UOIF?" Anne-Bénédicte Hoffner. 4 May. https://www.la-croix.com/print/article/1200844613

Lægaard, Sune. 2014. "The Case of the Danish Cartoons Controversy: The Paradox of Civility." In *Islam and Public Controversy in Europe* edited by Nilüfer Göle, 123–36. Aldershot: Ashgate.

Lagrange, Hugues and Marco Oberti, eds. 2006. *Émeutes urbaines et protestations. Une singularité française*. Paris: Presses de la Fondation Nationale des Sciences Politiques.

Lagrange, Hugues. 2010. *Le déni des cultures*. Paris: Éditions du Seuil.

Lagrange, Hugues. 2011. "Réponse à Didier Fassin." *Revue française de sociologie*, 52.4: 787–96.

Lahire, Bernard. 2016. *Pour la sociologie. Et pour en finir avec une prétendue "culture de l'excuse."* Paris: La Découverte.

Lalieu, Olivier. 2001. "L'invention du 'devoir de mémoire.'" *Vingtième Siècle*, 69.1: 83–94.

Lamarre, Chantal and Murielle Maffessoli. 2013. *Refondation de la politique d'intégration. Groupe de travail "Connaissance – reconnaissance."* 15 November. https://www.vie-publique.fr/rapport/33621-refonder-la-politique-dintegration-groupe-de-travail-connaissance-r

Lamine, Anne-Sophie. 2015. "Média minoritaire, diversité intra-religieuse et espace public. Analyse du site *Saphirnews.com*." *Sociologie*, 6.2: 139–56.

Lamine, Anne-Sophie. 2018. "L'islam des jeunes, un révélateur de nos impensés sur le religieux?." *Archives de sciences sociales des religions*, 184.4: 289–91.

Lançon, Philippe. 2015. "Houellebecq et le Coran ascendant." *Libération*. 2 January. https://www.liberation.fr/Houellebecq-soumission-islam,100480

Langer, Lorenz. 2014. *Religious Offence and Human Rights*. Cambridge: Cambridge University Press.

Lantheaume, Françoise. 2011. "La prise en compte de la diversité: émergence d'un nouveau cadre normatif? Essai de généalogie et identification de quelques conséquences." *Les Dossiers de sciences de l'éducation*, 26: 117–32.

Lapeyronnie, Didier. 2006. "Révolte primitive dans les banlieues françaises." *Déviance et Société*, 30.4: 431–48.

Larsen, Lena. 2018. *How Muftis Think. Islamic Legal Thought and Muslim Women in Western Europe*. Leiden: Brill.

Lasfar, Amar. 2017. "GML AMAR LASFAR un peu d'histoire." Sermon of 21 July held at Al-Imane Mosque. https://www.youtube.com/watch?v=EyKgyyXMxSE

Laurens, Henry. 2004. *Orientales II. La IIIe République et l'Islam*. Paris: CNRS Éditions.

Laurence, Jonathan. 2005. "From the Élysée Salon to the Table of the Republic. State-Islam Relations and the Integration of Muslims in France." *French Politics, Culture & Society*, 23.1: 37–64.

Laurence, Jonathan. 2012. *The Emancipation of Europe's Muslims. The State's Role in Minority Integration*. Princeton: Princeton University Press.

Laurence, Jonathan and Justin Vaisse. 2006. *Integrating Islam. Political and Religious Challenges in Contemporary France*. Washington, DC: Brookings Institution Press.

Lean, Nathan C. 2019. "The debate over the utility and precision of the term 'Islamophobia.'" In *The Routledge International Handbook of Islamophobia* edited by Irene Zempi and Imran Awan, 18–31. London: Routledge.

Le Bras, Hervé. 1998. *Le démon des origines. Démographie et extrême droite*. La Tour d'Aigues: Éditions de l'Aube.

Lebourg, Nicolas. 2015. "Le National Front et la galaxie des extrêmes droites radicales." In *Les faux-semblants du National Front* edited by Sylvain Crépon, Alexandre Dézé, and Nonna Mayer, 121–40. Paris: Presses de Sciences Po.

Leclerc, Henri. 2015. "Caricatures, blasphème et défi." *Légicom*, 55.2: 114–19.

Ledoux, Sébastien. 2013a. "'Devoir de mémoire': The post-colonial path of a post-national memory in France." *National Identities*, 5.3: 239–56.

Ledoux, Sébastien. 2013b. "Les historiens face aux nouveaux usages du mot *mémoire*." *Mots. Les langages du politique*, 103: 137–43.

Lefebvre, Solange and Patrice Brodeur, eds. 2017. *Public Commissions on Cultural and Religious Diversity: Analysis, Reception and Challenges*. London: Taylor & Francis.

Le Figaro 2017. "Laurent Bouvet: Il faut distinguer la question de la laïcité et celle de l'insécurité culturelle." *Le Figaro*. 3 November. http://www.lefigaro.fr/vox/societe/2017/11/03/31003-20171103ARTFIG00330-laurent-bouvet-il-faut-distinguer-la-question-de-la-laicite-et-celle-de-l-insecurite-culturelle.php

Lefranc, Sandrine. 2008. "Repentance." In *Comment Nicolas Sarkozy écrit l'histoire de France* edited by Laurence De Cock, Fanny Madeline, Nicolas Offenstadt, and Sophie Wahnich, 156–60. Marseille: Agone.

Le Goff, Jacques. 2007. "Préface." In *Histoire de l'islam et des musulmans en France du Moyen Âge à nos jours* edited by Mohammed Arkoun and Jacques Le Goff, xii–xvii. Paris: Albin Michel.

Legris, Patricia. 2010. *L'écriture des programmes d'histoire en France (1944–2010). Sociologie historique d'un instrument d'une politique éducative.* PhD thesis. Université de Paris-I Panthéon-Sorbonne.

Lejbovicz, Max, ed. 2008. *L'islam médiéval en terres chrétiennes: science et idéologie.* Villeneuve d'Ascq: Presses universitaires du Septentrion.

Lemarié, Alexandre. 2020. "Contre le 'séparatisme islamiste', Macron veut se positionner entre répression et intégration." *Le Monde.* 20 February. https://www.lemonde.fr/politique/article/2020/02/19/a-mulhouse-macron-veut-combattre-le-separatisme-islamiste-sans-froisser-les-musulmans_6030026_823448.html

Le Monde. 2013. "La France n'a pas de problème avec sa laïcité." 25 June. https://www.lemonde.fr/societe/article/2013/06/25/la-france-n-a-pas-de-probleme-avec-sa-laicite_3436086_3224.html?xtmc=jean_louis_bianco&xtcr=80

Le Monde. 2018. "Eric Zemmour condamné en appel pour des propos islamophobes." 3 May. https://www.lemonde.fr/police-justice/article/2018/05/03/eric-zemmour-condamne-en-appel-pour-des-propos-islamophobes_5293921_1653578.html

Léonard, Marie des Neiges. 2016. "The Effects of Political Rhetoric on the Rise of Legitimized Racism in France: The Case of the 2005 French Riots." *Critical Sociology*, 42.7: 1087–107.

Lepenies, Wolf. 2002. *Die drei Kulturen: Soziologie zwischen Literatur und Wissenschaft.* Munich: Fischer Verlag.

Les Identitaires. 2017. "Argumentaire XIV. 'La bataille de Poitiers n'a pas eu lieu.'" 27 December. https://www.les-identitaires.com/identite-europeenne/publications/argumentaires/

Leschi, Didier. 2017. *Misère(s) de l'islam de France.* Paris: Éditions du Cerf.

Leschi, Didier. 2018. "L'organisation du culte musulman: un regard de praticien administratif." *Revue du droit des religions*, 6: 27–42.

Leveau, Rémy and Gilles Kepel, eds. 1988. *Les musulmans dans la société française.* Paris: Presses de la Fondation Nationale des Sciences Politiques.

Leveau, Rémy and Khadija Mohsen-Finan. 2001. "France-Allemagne: nouvelles perspectives, identités et sociétés." In *L'islam en France et en Allemagne. Identités et citoyennetés* edited by Rémy Leveau and Khadija Mohsen-Finan, 9–15. Paris: La documentation française.

Leveau, Rémy and Catherine Wihtol de Wenden. 2001. *La Beurgeoisie. Les trois âges de la vie associative issue de l'immigration.* Paris: CNRS Éditions.

Levey, Geoffrey Brahm and Tariq Modood. 2009. "The Muhammad Cartoons and Multicultural Democracies." *Ethnicities*, 9: 427–47.

Lévy, Bernard-Henri. 2015. "Houellebecq, écrivain." *La règle du jeu*. 6 January. https://laregledujeu.org/2015/01/06/18624/houellebecq-ecrivain/

Lévi-Strauss, Claude and Jean-Marie Benoist. 1979. "Conclusions." In *L'identité* edited by Claude-Lévi Strauss, 317–32. Paris: Bernard Grasset.

Leyris, Raphaëlle. 2015. "Michel Houellebecq, ambigu et pervers." *Le Monde*. 6 January. https://abonnes.lemonde.fr/culture/article/2015/01/06/michel-houellebecq-ambigu-et-pervers_4550125_3246.html

Liauzu, Claude and Gilles Manceron, eds. 2006. *La colonisation, la loi et l'histoire*. Paris: Éditions Sylepse.

Lilla, Mark. 2015. "Slouching toward Mecca." *The New York Review of Books*. 2 April. 41–3.

Lindenberg, Daniel. 2016 [2002]. *Le rappel à l'ordre. Enquête sur les nouveaux réactionnaires*. Avec une postface inédite de l'auteur. Paris: Éditions du Seuil.

Lindner, Kolja. 2017. *Die Hegemoniekämpfe in Frankreich. Laizismus, politische Repräsentation und Sarkozysmus*. Hamburg: Argument.

Liogier, Raphaël. 2006. *Une laïcité légitime. La France et ses religions d'État*. Paris: Éditions Médicis-Entrelacs.

Lochak, Danièle. 2010. *Le droit et les paradoxes de l'universalité*. Paris: Presses universitaires de France.

Lochak, Danièle. 2011. "Le Haut Conseil à la (dés)intégration." *Plein droit*, 91.4: 12–15.

Lorcerie, Françoise. 1991. "L'islam au programme." *Annuaire de l'Afrique du Nord*, 27: 161–92.

Lorcerie, Françoise. 1994. "Les sciences sociales au service de l'identité nationale. Le débat sur l'intégration en France au début des années 90." In *Cartes d'identité. Comment dit-on nous en politique?* edited by D.-C. Martin, 245–81. Paris: Presses de la Fondation nationale des sciences politiques.

Lorcerie, Françoise, ed. 2005. *La politisation du voile en France, en Europe et dans le monde arabe*. Paris: L'Harmattan.

Lorcerie, Françoise. 2005–6. "L'islam comme contre-identification française: trois moments." *L'Année du Maghreb*, 2: 509–36.

Lorcerie, Françoise. 2014a. "Intégration: la 'refondation' enlisée." *Migrations Société*, 155: 47–66.

Lorcerie, Françoise, ed. 2014b. "Dossier. Intégration. La 'refondation' enlisée." *Migrations Société*, 155: 47–232.

Louatah, Sabri. 2014. *Les sauvages*. Volumes 1 & 2. Paris: J'ai lu.

Louizi Mohamed. 2007a. "De la caricature censurée (1)." 23 March. http://mlouizi.unblog.fr/2007/03/23/de-la-caricature-censuree-1/

Louizi, Mohamed. 2007b. "De la caricature censurée (2)." 25 March. http://mlouizi.unblog.fr/2007/03/25/de-la-caricature-censuree-2/

Louizi, Mohamed. 2016. *Pourquoi j'ai quitté les frères musulmans. Retour éclairé vers un islam apolitique*. Paris: Michalon.

Luizard, Pierre-Jean. 2019. *La République et l'islam. Aux racines du malentendu*. Paris: Éditions Tallandier.

Maffesoli, Michel. 2015. "Michel Maffesoli: Houellebecq a raison, les Lumières sont éteintes." *Le Figaro*. 7 January. https://www.lefigaro.fr/vox/culture/2015/01/07/31006-20150107ARTFIG00149-michel-maffesoli-pour-houellebecq-les-lumieres-sont-eteintes.php

Mahajan, Gurpreet. 2012. *Explanation and Understanding in the Human Sciences*. Third edition. Oxford: Oxford University Press.

Mahmood, Saba. 2005. *Politics of Piety. The Islamic Revival and the Feminist Subject*. Princeton: Princeton University Press.

Mahmood, Saba. 2009. "Religious Reason and Secular Affect: An Incommensurable Divide?" *Critical Inquiry*, 35.4: 836–62.

Makri, Yamine. (sic) 1998. "Sur l'évolution des jeunes musulmans et de leurs pratiques." *Islam de France*, 2: 82–6.

Makri, Yamin. 2003. "Islam de France: le retour à une gestion coloniale?" *oumma.com*. 16 December. https://oumma.com/islam-de-france-le-retour-a-une-gestion-coloniale/

Makri, Yamin. 2005. "Les 'nouveaux notables' de la République." *oumma.com*. 25 April. https://oumma.com/les-nouveaux-notables-de-la-republique/

Makri, Yamin. 2008. "Aux origines du mouvement des jeunes musulmans: L'Union des Jeunes Musulmans." In *Histoire politique des immigrations (post)coloniales. France, 1920-2008* edited by Ahmed Boubeker and Abdellali Hajjat, 217–24. Paris: Éditions Amsterdam.

Makri, Yamin. 2012. "'Pour qui voter?' ou 'Pourquoi voter?'". *oumma.com*. 20 March. https://oumma.com/pour-qui-voter-ou-pourquoi-voter/#_ftn1.

Malogne Fer, Gwendoline. 2019. "La laïcité en pratique. L'exemple de la diversité religieuse sur les listes municipales à Bordeaux." *Archives de sciences sociales des religions*, 185: 147–67.

Manent, Pierre. 2015. *Situation de la France*. Paris: Desclée de Brouwer.

March, Andrew F. 2006. "Liberal Citizenship and the Search for an Overlapping Consensus: The Case of Muslim Minorities." *Philosophy & Public Affairs*, 34.4: 373–421.

March, Andrew F. 2007. "Reading Tariq Ramadan: Political Liberalism, Islam, and 'Overlapping Consensus.'" *Ethics & International Affairs*, 21.4: 399–413.

March, Andrew. 2009. *Islam and Liberal Citizenship. The Search for an Overlapping Consensus*. New York: Oxford University Press.

March, Andrew F. 2011. "Law as a Vanishing Mediator in the Theological Ethics of Tariq Ramadan." *European Journal of Political Theory*, 10.2: 177–201.

Maréchal, Brigitte. 2008. *Muslim Brothers in Europe. Roots and Discourse*. Leiden: Brill.

Marongiu, Oméro. 2002. *L'islam au pluriel. Etude de rapport au religieux chez les jeunes musulmans*. PhD thesis. University Lille I.

Martiniello, Marco and Patrick Simon. 2005. "Les enjeux de la catégorisation. Rapports de domination et luttes autour de la représentation dans les sociétés post-migratoires." *Revue Européenne des Migrations Internationales*, 21: 7–18.

Marzouki, Nadia. 2004. "Théorie et engagement chez Edward Said." *Mouvements*, 33-4: 162-7.

Mas, Ruth. 2006a. *Margins of Tawhid. Liberalism and Plurality in the Discourse of Contemporary Islam*. PhD thesis. University of Toronto.

Mas, Ruth. 2006b. "Compelling the Muslim Subject: Memory as Post-Colonial Violence and the Public Performativity of 'Secular and Cultural Islam.'" *Muslim World*, 96.4: 585-616.

Mathieu, Séverine. 2009. "Les adolescents et la religion." In *Les jeunes, l'école et la religion* edited by Céline Béraud and Jean-Paul Willaime, 85-102. Paris: Bayard.

Maussen, Marcel. 2009. *Constructing Mosques. The Governance of Islam in France and the Netherlands*. Amsterdam: Amsterdam School for Social Science Research.

Mayeur, Jean-Marie. 1997. *La question laïque (XIXe-XIXe siècle)*. Paris: Fayard.

Mayeur, Jean-Marie. 2005 [1966]. *La Séparation de l'Église et de l'État*. Paris: Éditions de l'Atelier.

Mechaï, Hassina and Sihem Zine. 2018. *L'état d'urgence (permanent)*. Courbevoie: MeltingBook.

Meddeb, Abdelwahab. 2006. *Contre-prêches. Chroniques (mars 2003-janvier 2006)*. Paris: Éditions du Seuil.

Meer, Nasar and Tariq Modood. 2009. "Refutations of Racism in the 'Muslim Question.'" *Patterns of Prejudice*, 43.3-4: 335-54.

Meer, Nasar and Tariq Modood. 2019. "Islamophobia as the racialisation of Muslims." In *The Routledge International Handbook of Islamophobia* edited by Irene Zempi and Imran Awan, 18-31. London: Routledge.

Meizoz, Jérôme. 2003. "*Le roman et l'inacceptable*: polémiques autour de Plateforme de Michel Houellebecq." *Études de Lettres*, 4: 125-48.

Messner, Francis. 1999. "La législation cultuelle des pays de l'Union européenne face aux groupes sectaires." In *Sectes et démocratie* edited by Françoise Champion and Martine Cohen, 331-58. Paris: Éditions du Seuil.

Messner, Francis. 2001. "Les relations entre les communes et les groupements religieux: perspective juridique." In *Le religieux dans la commune* edited by Franck Frégosi and Jean-Paul Willaime, 29-46. Geneva: Labor et Fides.

Messner, Francis, Pierre-Henri Prélot, and Jean-Marie Woehrling, eds., with the collaboration of Isabelle Riassetto. 2003. *Traité de droit français des religions*. Paris: Litec.

Messner, Francis. 2010. "Les pouvoirs publics et la formation des cadres religieux en France." In *Formation des cadres religieux. Une affaire d'État?* edited by Francis Messner and Anne-Laure Zwilling, 13-24. Geneva: Labor et Fides.

Meziane (sic), Sofiane. 2008. *L'islam entre cœur & intélligence. Un pas vers la réforme par un retour à l'essentiel*. Paris: Maison d'Ennour.

Meziani, Sofiane. 2009a. *Réforme ta vie*. Lourches: Éditions Iquioussen.

Meziani, Sofiane. 2009b. *La sîra du Prophète expliqué aux jeunes. Pour une réforme de la jeunesse musulmane*. Paris: Maison d'Ennour.

Meziani, Sofiane. 2009c. "Biographie." *sofianmeziani.net*. http://www.sofianemeziani.net/qwy329xpx2322775/biog.php?page=Infos

Meziani, Sofiane. 2010. *L'ambition du vainqueur. Un intinéraire au service de la réforme*. N.pl.: Éditions Beaurepaire.

Meziani, Sofiane. 2011. *Le chemin de la liberté*. With a preface by Hani Ramadan. N.pl.: Éditions Beaurepaire.

Meziani, Sofiane. 2012. "L'opportunité de l'Islam dans les quartiers populaires." https://oumma.com/lopportunite-de-lislam-dans-les-quartiers-populaires/

Meziani, Sofiane. 2015. *Le défi du sens. Pour une nouvelle poetique de l'Homme*. Paris: Albouraq.

Meziani, Sofiane. 2017. *Petit manifeste contre la démocratie: Pour une redéfinition de l'homme et de la société*. Paris: Les points sur les i.

Micheau, Françoise and Sénac, Philippe. 2007. "La bataille de Poitiers, de la réalité au mythe." In *Histoire de l'islam et des musulmans en France du Moyen Age à nos jours* edited by Mohammed Arkoun, 7–15. Paris: Albin Michel.

Michel, Johann. 2010. *Gouverner les mémoires: Les politiques mémorielles en France*. Paris: Presses universitaires de France.

Michel, Johann. 2011. "Regards croisés sur les rapports Kaspi et Accoyer. Le retour du régime mémoriel d'unité nationale." In *La Mémoire et le crime* edited by Michel Danti-Juan, 199–216. Paris: Éditions CUJAS.

Micheron, Hugo. 2020. *Le jihadisme français. Quartiers, Syrie, prisons*. Paris: Gallimard.

Miktar, Ahmed. 2006. "Les caricatures du Prophète." *Pastel FM*, 10 February. http://www.mosquee-acmr.fr/article/les-caricatures-du-prophete-ahmed-miktar_181.

Milbank, John. 2006 [1991]. *Theology and Social Theory*. London: Blackwell.

Miles, Robert. 1993. *Racism After 'Race Relations.'* London: Routledge.

Ministère de l'Intérieur. 2000a. "Principes et fondements juridiques régissant les rapports entre les pouvoirs publics et le culte musulman en France." 28 January. https://fondationdelislamdefrance.fr/wp-content/uploads/2017/05/Principes-et-fondements-juridiques-r%C3%A9gissant-des-rapports-entre-les-pouvoirs-publics-et-le-Culte-musulman-en-France.pdf

Ministère de l'Intérieur. 2000b. *Al-Istichara*. No. 2. May. N.pl.: Service logistique de l'administration centrale.

Ministère de l'Intérieur. 2015. "Prévention de la radicalisation. Kit de formation." Secretariat général du Comité interministériel de prévention de la délinquance. https://philosophie.ac-versailles.fr/IMG/pdf/kit_de_formation_prevention_radicalisation.pdf

Ministère du Travail. 2017. *Guide pratique du fait religieux dans les entreprises privées. (Version employeurs)*. Revised in February 2018. https://travail-emploi.gouv.fr/IMG/pdf/guide_employeursmajfevrier2018valide.pdf

Mission d'information sur le port de signes religieux à l'école. 2003. *La laïcité à l'école: un principe républicain à réaffirmer. Rapport N° 1275 tome 1*. Paris: Assemblée nationale.

Mission d'information sur la pratique du port du voile intégral sur le territoire national. 2010. *Rapport d'information N° 2262*. Paris: Assemblée nationale.

Mission de réflexion sur la formation des imams et des cadres religieux musulmans. 2017. Rachid Benzine, Catherine Mayeur-Jaouen, Mathilde Philip-Gay. https://www.letudiant.fr/static/uploads/mediatheque/EDU_EDU/6/3/1455063-rapport-sur-la-formation-des-imams-4-original.pdf

Modood, Tariq, 1998. "Anti-Essentialism, Multiculturalism and the 'Recognition' of Religious Minorities." *Journal of Political Philosophy*, 6.4: 378–99.

Modood, Tariq. 2010. "Moderate Secularism, Religion as Identity and Respect for Religion." *Political Quarterly*, 81.1: 4–14.

Mokhtar Awards 2015. "Dessinez le Prophète / Draw the Prophet [*Lancement du concours Mokhtar 2015*]." https://www.youtube.com/watch?v=uUcxQRkZg_c

Moreau, Jean-Christophe. 2016. "Le Collectif contre l'islamophobie en France, un mal nécessaire?" *slate.fr*. 30 September. http://www.slate.fr/story/123875/ccif-fachosphere

Morin, Edgar and Tariq Ramadan. 2014. *Au péril des idées. Les grandes questions de notre temps*. Paris: Presses du Châtelet.

Morrey, Douglas. 2013. *Michel Houellebecq. Humanity and its Aftermath*. Liverpool: Liverpool University Press.

Mouillard, Sylvain and Bernadette Sauvaget. 2016. "Au Collectif contre l'islamophobie, de la suite dans les données." *Libération*. 3 April. https://www.liberation.fr/france/2016/04/03/au-collectif-contre-l-islamophobie-de-la-suite-dans-les-donnees_1443712

Mouslim, Charafeddine. 2007. "Aux origines de la présence musulmane en France (1/2)." *Saül Productions*. https://www.dailymotion.com/video/x26ffu

Mouslim, Charafeddine. 2014a. *La bataille de Poitiers. L'histoire d'un mythe*. La Courneuve: Bayane Éditions.

Mouslim, Charafeddine and Médine. 2014b. "La Bataille de Poitiers – Déconstruisons les Préjugés #2." 24 December. https://www.youtube.com/watch?v=0iYpd7KehWU

Mucchielli, Laurent. 2006. "Immigration et délinquance: fantasmes et réalités." In *La république mise à nu par son immigration* edited by Nacira Guénif-Souilamas, 39–61. Paris: La fabrique.

Muhammad, Marwan. 2013. "L'islamophobie, ce racisme presque acceptable." 16 December. https://www.islamophobie.net/2013/12/16/lislamophobie-ce-racisme-presque-acceptable/

Muhammad, Marwan. 2017. *Nous (aussi) sommes la nation. Pourquoi il faut lutter contre l'islamophobie*. Paris: La Découverte.

Murji, Karim and John Solomos. 2005. "Introduction: racialization in theory and practice." In *Racialization: Studies in Theory and Practice* edited by Karim Murji and John Solomos, 1–27. Oxford: Oxford University Press.

Musulmans de France. 2018. "Centenaire de l'armistice du 11 Novembre 2018." *musulmansdefrance.fr*. 15 November. http://www.musulmansdefrance.fr/centenaire-de-larmistice-du-11-novembre-1918/

Muxel, Anne and Olivier Galland. 2018. *La tentation radicale. Enquête auprès des lycéens.* Paris: Presses universitaires de France.
Naudin, Christophe, William Blanc, and Aurore Chéryl. 2013. "Loràent Deutsch et le mythe de l'invasion musulmane." *Huffpost*. 30 September. https://www.huffingtonpost.fr/christophe-naudin/lorant-deutsch-hexagone_b_4015871.html
Naef, Silvia. 2004. *Y a-t-il une 'question de l'image' en Islam?* Paris: Téraèdre.
N'Diaye, Pap. 2005. "Les traites négrières: Essai d'histoire globale." *Critique internationale*, 3.28: 201–5.
Nef, Annliese. 2017. *L'Islam a-t-il une histoire?* Lormont: Le Bord de l'eau.
Neirynck, Jacques and Tariq Ramadan. 1999. *Peut-on vivre avec l'islam ? Le choc de la religion musulmane et des sociétés laïques et chrétiennes.* Lausanne: Favre.
Nichols, Robert. 2013. "Of First and Last Men. Contract and Colonial Historicality in Foucault." In *The Ends of History. Questioning the Stakes of Historical Reason* edited by Amy Swiffen and Joshua Nichols, 64–83. London: Routledge.
Nicolet, Claude. 1994 [1982]. *L'idée républicaine en France. Essai d'histoire critique (1789-1924).* Paris: Gallimard.
Noiriel, Gérard. 1988. *Le creuset français. Histoire de l'immigration XIXe-XXe siècles.* Paris: Éditions du Seuil.
Noiriel, Gérard and Nicolas Offenstadt. 2006. "Histoire et politique. Autour d'un débat et de certains usages." *Nouvelles FondationS*, 2.2: 65–75.
Noiriel, Gérard. 2007a. *À quoi sert 'l'identité nationale.'* Marseille: Agone.
Noiriel, Gérard. 2007b. *Immigration, antisémitisme et racisme en France (XIXe-XXe siècle). Discours publics, humiliations privées.* Paris: Fayard.
Noiriel, Gérard. 2019. *Le venin dans la plume. Édouard Drumont, Éric Zemmour et la part sombre de la République.* Paris: La Découverte.
Nora, Pierre. 1996. "General Introduction: Between Memory and History." In *Realms of Memory* (3 volumes) edited by Pierre Nora, I:1–20. New York: Columbia University Press.
Nora, Pierre. 2005a. "Plaidoyer pour les indigènes d'Austerlitz." *Le Monde*. 13 December. https://www.lemonde.fr/idees/article/2005/12/12/plaidoyer-pour-les-indigenes-d-austerlitz-par-pierre-nora_720278_3232.html
Nora, Pierre. 2005b. "La pensée réchauffée." In *La pensée tiède. Un regard critique sur la culture française* edited by Perry Anderson, 99–137. Paris: Éditions du Seuil.
Nora, Pierre. 2007. "Nation." In *Dictionnaire critique de la révolution française* edited by François Furet and Mona Ozouf, 339–58. Paris: Flammarion.
Nora, Pierre. 2008. "Malaise dans l'identité historique." In *Liberté pour l'histoire* edited by Pierre Nora and Françoise Chandernagor, 11–24. Paris: CNRS.
Nora, Pierre. 2011. *Présent, nation, mémoire.* Paris: Gallimard.
Nordmann, Charlotte, ed. 2004. *Le foulard islamique en questions.* Paris: Éditions Amsterdam.
Offenstadt, Nicolas. 2014. *L'Histoire. Un combat au présent. Conversation avec Régis Meyran.* Paris: Éditions Textuel.

Onfray, Michel (with Asma Kouar). 2016. *Penser l'islam*. Paris: Bernard Grasset.

On n'est pas couché. 2008. "Manuel de savoir-vivre en cas d'invasion islamique" – On n'est pas couché 6 septembre 2008 #ONPC." *France 2*. Published October 23, 2014. https://www.youtube.com/watch?v=Z_G26F2mwhM

On n'est pas couché. 2013. "On n'est pas couché – Loràmt Deutsch 12/10/13 #ONPC." *France 2*. Published October 15, 2013. https://www.youtube.com/watch?v=HAUuVXPfICY

Opratko, Benjamin. 2017. "Islamophobia: The bigger picture." *Historical Materialism*, 25.1: 63–89.

Oubrou, Tareq. 1998. "Introduction théorique à la charî'a de minorité." *Islam de France*, 2: 27–41.

Oubrou, Tareq. 2004. "La sharî'a de minorité: réflexions pour une intégration légale de l'islam." In *Lectures contemporaines du droit islamique. Europe et monde arabe* edited by Franck Frégosi, 205–30. Strasbourg: Presses universitaires de Strasbourg.

Oubrou, Tareq. 2006. "Quelle est la part du religieux, et quelle est la part du psycho-sociologique dans le comportement d'un musulman?" In *Quelle éducation face au radicalisme religieux?* edited by Dounia Bouzar, 124–37. Paris: Dunod.

Oubrou, Tareq. 2009. *Profession imâm. Entretiens avec Michaël Privot and Cédric Baylocq*. Paris: Albin Michel.

Oubrou, Tareq. 2012. *Un imam en colère. Intégration, laïcité, violence. Entretien avec Samuel Lieven*. Montrouge: Bayard.

Oubrou, Tareq. "Cette affaire va laisser des séquelles." *Libération*. 23 March. http://www.liberation.fr/societe/01012397757-cette-affaire-va-laisser-des-sequelles

Oubrou, Tareq. 2013. "Le foulard est devenu un object obsessionnel." *saphirnews.com*. 28 October. https://www.saphirnews.com/Tareq-Oubrou-Le-foulard-est-devenu-un-objet-obsessionnel_a17803.html

Oubrou, Tareq. 2014a. "Perspectives musulmanes." In *La Vocation de la Terre sainte. Un juif, un chrétien, un musulman s'interrogent* edited by David Meyer, Michel Remaud, and Tareq Oubrou, 205–311. Namur: Éditions Lessius.

Oubrou, Tareq. 2014b. "Amis juifs et musulmans, restons français avant tout." *Huffingtonpost.fr*. 13 July. https://www.huffingtonpost.fr/tareq-oubrou/importation-conflit-en-france_b_5580766.html

Oubrou, Tareq. 2015. "Pour l'imam de Bordeaux, 'Soumission' de Houellebecq relève d'un 'scénario invraisemblable.'" *20minutes.fr*. https://www.20minutes.fr/culture/1511191-20150106-imam-bordeaux-soumission-houellebecq-releve-scenario-invraisemblable

Oubrou, Tareq. 2016. *Ce que vous ne savez par sur l'islam. Répondre aux préjugés des musulmans et des non-musulmans*. Paris: Fayard.

Oubrou, Tareq. 2019. *Appel à la réconciliation! Foi musulmane et valeurs de la République française*. Paris: Plon.

oumma.com. 2013. "Tareq Oubrou nommé Chevalier de la Légion d'Honneur." 3 January. https://oumma.com/tareq-oubrou-nomme-chevalier-de-la-legion-dhonneur/

oumma.com. 2014. "Gaza: Tareq Oubrou met sur un pied d'égalité l'Occupant oppressuer et l'Occupé opprimé." 15 July. https://oumma.com/gaza-tareq-oubrou-met-sur-un-pied-degalite-loccupant-oppresseur-et-loccupe-opprime/#_ftn3

Owen, Roger. 2012. "Edward Said and the Two Critiques of Orientalism." April 20, 2012 (originally published in April 2009). https://www.mei.edu/publications/edward-said-and-two-critiques-orientalism

Papi, Stéphane. 2012. "Islam, laïcité et commensalité dans les cantines scolaires publiques." *Hommes & Migrations.* 1296. http://hommesmigrations.revues.org/1522

Parekh, Bhiku. 2005. "Europe, Liberalism and the 'Muslim Question.'" In *Multiculturalism, Muslims and Citizenship* edited by Tariq Modood, Anna Triandafyllidou, and Ricardo Zapata-Barrero, 179–203. London: Routledge.

Peace, Timothy. 2015. *European Social Movements and Muslim Activism: Another World but with Whom?* London: Palgrave Macmillan.

Peter, Frank. 2006a. "Leading the Community of the Middle Way: A Study of The Muslim Field in France." *Muslim World*, 96.4: 707–36.

Peter, Frank. 2006b. "Islamism, Islamic Reformism and the Public Stigmatization of Muslims: A Study of Muslim Discourses in France." *Oriente Moderno.* n.s. 25.3: 443–60.

Peter, Frank. 2006c. "Islamic Sermons, Religious Authority and the Individualization of Islam in France." In *Religiosität in der säkularisierten Welt. Theoretische und empirische Beiträge zur Säkularisierungsdebatte in der Religionssoziologie* edited by Manuel Franzmann, Christel Gärtner, and Nicole Köck, 303–20. Wiesbaden: V.S. Verlag.

Peter, Frank. 2006d. "Individualization and Religious Authority in Western European Islam." *Islam and Christian-Muslim Relations*, 17.1: 105–18.

Peter, Frank. 2008a. "Political Rationalities, Counter-Terrorism and Policies on Islam in the United Kingdom and France." In *The Social Life of Anti-Terrorism Laws. The War on Terror and the Classifications of the 'Dangerous Other'* edited by Julia Eckert, 79–108. Bielefeld: transcript.

Peter, Frank. 2008b. "Impossible religious freedom? Mullahs, liberal Muslims, and the institutionalization of Islam in France." Workshop "Understanding Immanent Critique. Cultural Politics and Islamic Activism", ISIM Leiden.

Peter, Frank. 2010. "Les fruits de la foi et l'universalité de l'islam: une étude de cas sur l'activisme musulman en France." *Sociologie et sociétés*, 42.1: 95–114.

Peter, Frank. 2013. "The Ambiguity of Law and Muslim Debates about the Contextualisation of Islam in France." In *Debating Islam. Negotiating Religion, Europe, and the Self*, edited by Samuel Behloul, Susanne Leuenberger, and Andreas Tunger-Zanetti, 163–80. Bielefeld: transcript.

Peter, Frank. Forthcoming. "France." *Encyclopaedia of Islam* 3. Leiden: Brill.

Pethes, Nicolas. 2010. *Kulturwissenschaftliche Gedächtnistheorien zur Einführung.* Hamburg: Junius.

Pétition. 2006. "Pétition nationale contre l'islamophobie." *Yabiladi.com.* 25 February. http://www.yabiladi.com/forum/petition-nationale-contre-l-islamophobie-1-985632.html

Pétré-Grenouilleau, Olivier. 2004. *Les traites négrières. Essai d'histoire globale*. Paris: Gallimard.

Pettit, Philip. 2008. *Made with Words. Hobbes on Language, Mind, and Politics*. Princeton: Princeton University Press.

Philip-Gay, Mathilde. 2016. *Droit de la laïcité*. Paris: Ellipses.

Pina, Céline. 2016. "Marwan Muhammad, porte-parole des musulmans, pardon ... des islamistes." *Le Figaro*. 2 November. https://www.lefigaro.fr/vox/societe/2016/11/02/31003-20161102ARTFIG00182-celine-pina-marwan-muhammad-porte-parole-des-musulmans-pardon-des-islamistes.php

Pivot, Bernard. 2015. "Michel Houellebecq, extension du domaine de l'islam." *Le Journal du Dimanche*. 4 January. https://www.lejdd.fr/Chroniques/Bernard-Pivot/La-chronique-de-Bernard-Pivot-sur-le-livre-Soumission-de-Michel-Houellebecq-710244

Plenel, Edwy. 2014. *Pour les musulmans*. Paris: La Découverte.

Plenel, Edwy. 2015. "L'idéologie meurtrière promue par Zemmour." *Mediapart*. 4 January. https://www.mediapart.fr/tools/print/485783

Portier, Philippe. 2016. *L'État et les religions en France. Une sociologie historique de la laïcité*. Rennes: Presses universitaires de Rennes.

Poumarède, Gérard. 2004. *Pour en finir avec la Croisade. Mythes et réalités de la lutte contre les Turcs aux XVIe et XVIIe siècles*. Paris: Presses universitaires de France.

Pratten, Stephen. 2012. "Essentialism and the social." *The Sociological Review*, 60.2: 242–66.

Prélot, Pierre-Henri. 2018. "Les tentatives d'organisation du culte musulman en France au prisme du principe de laïcité." *Revue du droit des religions*, 6: 13–26.

Prévert, Aline. 2014. *La lutte contre les discriminations. Genèse et usages d'une politique publique*. Paris: L'Harmattaan.

Ramadan, Tariq. 1994. *Les musulmans dans la laïcité. Responsabilités et droits des musulmans dans les sociétés occidentales*. Lyon: Éditions Tawhid.

Ramadan, Tariq. 1998 [1994]. *Les musulmans dans la laïcité. Responsabilités et droits des musulmans dans les sociétés occidentales*. Lyon: Éditions Tawhid.

Ramadan, Tariq. 1999. *To be a European Muslim. A Study of Islamic Sources in the European Context*. Markfield: The Islamic Foundation.

Ramadan, Tariq. 2000. "Islam de France: essayons." *Le Monde*. 21 April. https://www.lemonde.fr/archives/article/2000/04/21/islam-de-france-essayons_3682712_1819218.html

Ramadan, Tariq. 2001a [1995]. *Islam, the West and the Challenges of Modernity*. Markfield: The Islamic Foundation.

Ramadan, Tariq. 2001b. "Existe-t-il un antisémitisme islamique?." *oumma.com*. 23 December. https://oumma.com/existe-t-il-un-antisemitisme-islamique/

Ramadan, Tariq. 2002. "Conseil européen des fatwas et de la recherche." *Recueil de fatwas. Avis juridiques concernant les musulmans d'Europe (Série n° 1)*. Lyon: Éditions Tawhid.

Ramadan, Tariq. 2003a. "Critique des (nouveaux) intellectuels communautaires." https://oumma.com/critique-des-nouveaux-intellectuels-communautaires/
Ramadan, Tariq. 2003b. "Pas de loi contre le foulard." *Libération*. 7 May.
Ramadan, Tariq. 2004a. *Western Muslims and the Future of Islam*. Oxford: Oxford University Press.
Ramadan, Tariq. 2004b. "Antisémitisme et communautarisme: des abcès à crever." *Le Monde*. 12 January. https://www.lemonde.fr/societe/article/2004/01/12/antisemitisme-et-communautarisme-des-abces-a-crever-par-tariq-ramadan_348896_3224.html
Ramadan, Tariq. 2005a. "La Fracture sociale: la France et l'Angleterre en miroir." *oumma.com*. 8 November. https://oumma.com/la-fracture-sociale-la-france-et-langleterre-en-miroir/
Ramadan, Tariq. 2005b. "Islam allows us to integrate into Britain's shared national culture." *The Guardian* 21 January. https://www.theguardian.com/uk/2005/jan/21/islamandbritain.comment14
Ramadan, Tariq. 2006. "Cartoon conflicts." *The Guardian*. 6 February. https://www.theguardian.com/media/2006/feb/06/homeaffairs.comment
Ramadan, Tariq. 2007. *The Messenger: The Meanings of the Life of Muhammad*. London: Allen Lane.
Ramadan, Tariq. 2008a. *Islam: La réforme radicale. Éthique et libération*. Paris: Presses du Châtelet.
Ramadan, Tariq. 2008b. *Face à nos peurs. Le choix de la confiance*. Lyon: Éditions Tawhid.
Ramadan, Tariq. 2008c. *Un chemin, une vision*. Lyon: Éditions Tawhid.
Ramadan, Tariq. 2010a. *What I Believe*. Oxford: Oxford University Press.
Ramadan, Tariq. 2010b. *The Quest for Meaning. Developing a Philosophy of Pluralism*. London: Allen Lane.
Ramadan, Tariq. 2011 *L'Islam et le réveil arabe*. Paris: Presses du Châtelet.
Ramadan, Tariq. 2011b. "A call for a moratorium on corporal punishment—the debate in review." In *New Directions in Islamic Thought: Exploring Reform and Muslim Tradition* edited by Kari Vogt, Lena Larsen, and Christian Moe, 163–74. London: I.B. Tauris.
Ramadan, Tariq. 2012a. *The Quest for Meaning. Developing a Philosophy of Pluralism*. London: Penguin.
Ramadan, Tariq. 2012b. "Islamophobie en France: actions et perspectives (Tariq Ramadan)." 30 November. https://www.youtube.com/watch?v=Tm5VDN_7PjE
Ramadan, Tariq. 2012c. "Les enseignements de Toulouse." *tariqramadan.com*. 22 March. https://tariqramadan.com/les-enseignements-de-toulouse/
Ramadan, Tariq. 2014. *De l'islam et des musulmans. Réflexions sur l'Homme, la réforme, la guerre et l'Occident*. Paris: Presses du Châtelet.
Ramadan, Tariq. 2015. Tariq Ramadan: "Houellebecq est au roman ce que Zemmour est à l'essai." *Lepoint.fr*. 6 January. https://www.lepoint.fr/societe/tariq-ramadan-houellebecq-est-au-roman-ce-que-zemmour-est-a-l-essai-06-01-2015-1894441_23.php

Ramadan, Tariq. 2016a. *Être occidental et musulman aujourd'hui*. Paris: Archipoche.
Ramadan, Tariq. 2016b. "14e RAMS 2016 – Tariq Ramadan 'Le vivre ensemble.'" https://www.youtube.com/watch?v=j09x7-aihdw
Reig, Daniel. 1988. *Homo orientaliste*. Paris: Maisonneuve & Larose.
Renaut, Alain. 2005. *Qu'est-ce qu'un peuple libre? Libéralisme ou républicanisme*. Paris: Bernard Grasset.
Ribbe, Claude. 2005a. *Le crime de Napoléon*. Paris: Éditions Privé.
Ribbe, Claude. 2005b. "A l'Esclave inconnu." *Le Monde*. 23 December. https://www.lemonde.fr/idees/article/2005/12/23/a-l-esclave-inconnu-par-claude-ribbe_724146_3232.html
Robert-Diard, Pascale. 2007. "Attendu que Charlie Hebdo est un journal satirique . . . ." *Le Monde*. 22 March. https://www.lemonde.fr/justice/article/2007/03/22/attendu-que-charlie-hebdo-est-un-journal-satirique_5976521_1653604.html
Robine, Jérémy. 2006. "Les 'indigènes de la République': nation et question postcoloniale." *Hérodote*, 120: 118–48.
Robine, Jérémy. 2011. *Les ghettos de la nation. Ségrégation, délinquance, identités, islam*. Paris: Vendémiaire.
Rochefort, Florence. 2002. "Foulard, genre et laïcité en 1989." *Vingtième siècle*, 75: 145–56.
Rodinson, Maxime. 1974. "The Western Image and Western Studies of Islam." In *The Legacy of Islam. Second Edition*, edited by Joseph Schacht with C. E. Bosworth, 9–62. Oxford: Oxford University Press.
Rohe, Mathias. 2004. "Application of Sharīʻa Rules in Europe – Scope and Limits." *Die Welt des Islams*, 44.3: 323–50.
Rolland, Patrice. 2005. "Qu'est-ce qu'un culte aux yeux de la République?" *Archives de sciences sociales des religions*, 50.129: 51–63.
Rosanvallon, Pierre. 1999. *Le peuple introuvable. Histoire de la représentation démocratique en France*. Paris: Gallimard.
Rose, Nikolas. 1998. *Inventing Our Selves: Psychology, Power, and Personhood*. Cambridge: Cambridge University Press.
Rose, Nikolas. 1999. *Powers of Freedom. Reframing Political Thought*. Cambridge: Cambridge University Press.
Rose, Nikolas and Peter Miller. 1992. "Political Power beyond the State: Problematics of Government". *The British Journal of Sociology*. 43.2: 173-205.
Rosenberg, Clifford. 2006. *Policing Paris: The Origins of Modern Immigration Control between the Wars*. Ithaca: Cornell University Press.
Rosenthal, Paul-André. 2003. *L'intelligence démographique. Sciences et politiques des populations en France (1930–1960)*. Paris: Éditions Odile Jacob.
Rougier, Bernard, ed. 2020. *Les territoires conquis de l'islamisme*. Paris: Presses universitaires de France.
Rousso, Henry. 1990. *Le syndrome de Vichy. De 1944 à nos jours*. Second edition. Paris: Éditions du Seuil.
Roy, Jean-Henri and Jean Deviosse. 1966. *La bataille de Poitiers*. Paris: Gallimard.

Roy, Olivier. 1992. *L'échec de l'islam politique*. Paris: Éditions du Seuil.
Roy, Olivier. 2004. *Globalised Islam. The Search for a New Ummah*. London: Hurst.
Roy, Olivier. 2005a. "A Clash of Cultures or a Debate on European Values." *ISIM Newsletter* 15:6f.
Roy, Olivier. 2005b. "La peur d'une communauté qui n'existe pas." *Le Monde*. 9 January. https://www.lemonde.fr/idees/article/2015/01/09/la-peur-d-une-communaute-qui-n-existe-pas_4552804_3232.html
Roy, Olivier. 2007. *Secularism Confronts Islam*. New York: Columbia University Press.
Roy, Olivier. 2011. "Du rôle consensuel des experts: La norme religieuse dans l'espace public." *Archives de sciences sociales des religions*, 155: 11–19.
Roy, Olivier. 2015. "L'Islam, dernier réfuge du chrétien décati." *Critique*, 816: 438–42.
Roy, Olivier. 2016. *Le djihad et la mort*. Paris: Éditions du Seuil.
Saada, Emmanuelle. 2014. "More than a Turn? The 'Colonial' in French Studies." *French Politics, Culture & Society*, 32.2: 34–9.
Sabot, Philippe. 2014. *Lire Les mots et les choses de Michel Foucault*. Paris: Presses universitaires de France.
Safran, William. 2003. "Pluralism and Multiculturalism in France: Post-Jacobin Transformations." *Political Science Quarterly*, 118.3: 437–65.
Said, Edward. 1995 [1978]. *Orientalism. Western Conceptions of the Orient*. London: Penguin.
Salmon, Gildas. 2016. "Foucault et la généalogie de la sociologie." *Archives de Philosophie*, 79.1: 79–102.
Saphirnews. 2015. "Le CFCM déplore 'la publicité médiatique' pour Houellebecq." *saphirnews.com*. 7 January. https://www.saphirnews.com/Le-CFCM-deplore-la-publicite-mediatique-pour-Houellebecq_a20200.html
Sarkozy, Nicolas. 2004. *La République, les religions, l'espérance. Entretiens avec Thibaud Collin et Philippe Verdin*. Paris: Éditions du Cerf.
Sarkozy, Nicolas. 2007. "Le discours d'investiture de Nicolas Sarkozy." *Le Monde*. 15 January. https://www.lemonde.fr/societe/article/2007/01/15/le-discours-d-investiture-de-nicolas-sarkozy_855369_3224.html
Sayad, Abdelmalek. 1984. "État, nation et l'immigration. L'ordre national à l'épreuve de l'intégration." *Peuples méditerranéens*, 27–8: 187–205.
Sayad, Abdelmalek. 1999. *La double absence. Des illusions de l'émigré aux souffrances de l'immigré*. With a preface by Pierre Bourdieu. Paris: Éditions du Seuil.
Sayd, Sarah. 2013. *Le fil vert*. Video. https://www.youtube.com/watch?v=gl4Jj6plLd8
Sayyid, Salman. 2010. "Thinking through Islamophobia." In *Thinking through Islamophobia. Global Perspectives* edited by Salman Sayyid and AbdoolKarim Vakil, 1–4. London: Hurst.
Sayyid, Salman. 2014. "A Measure of Islamophobia." *Islamophobia Studies Journal*, 2.1: 10–25.
Sbaï, Jalila. 2018. *La politique musulmane de la France. Un projet chrétien pour l'islam? 1911–1954*. Paris: CNRS Éditions.

Salzbrunn, Monika. 2019. *L'islam (in)visible en ville. Appartenances et engagements dans l'espace urbain*. Geneva: Labor & Fides.

Schnapper, Dominique. 1988. "La Commission de la Nationalité, une instance singulière (Entretien avec Jacqueline Costa-Lascoux)." *Revue européenne des migrations internationales*, 4: 9–28.

Schnapper, Dominique. 1991. *La France de l'intégration. Sociologie de la nation en 1990*. Paris: Gallimard.

Schnapper, Dominique. 2003. *La communauté des citoyens. Sur l'idée moderne de nation*. Second edition. Paris: Gallimard.

Schnapper, Dominique, Chantal Bordes-Benayoun, and Freddy Raphaël. 2009. *La condition juive en France. La tentation de l'entre-soi*. Paris: Presses universitaires de France.

Schnapper, Dominique. 2017. "De la difficulté à comprendre la société." *Le Débat*, 197.5: 114–18.

Schulze, Reinhard. 2013. "On relating religion to society and society to religion." In *Debating Islam. Negotiating Religion, Europe, and the Self* edited by Samuel Behloul, Susanne Leuenberger, and Andreas Tunger-Zanetti, 333–56. Bielefeld: transcript.

Sciences Po TV. 2016. "Le Grand Oral: Jean-Francois Copé face à Marwan Muhammad." 3 October. https://www.youtube.com/watch?v=OAUM14K8SP0

Scott, Joan W. 2007. *The Politics of the Veil*. Princeton: Princeton University Press.

Scott, Joan W. 2018. *Sex and Secularism*. Princeton: Princeton University Press.

Sedgwick, Mark. 2015. "Jihadism, Narrow and Wide: The Dangers of Loose Use of an Important Term." *Perspectives on Terrorism*, 9.2: 34–41.

Sellam, Sadek. 2006. *La France et ses musulmans: Un siècle de politique musulmane (1895–2005)*. Paris: Fayard.

Sénat. 2015. *Rapport d'information fait au nom de la délégation aux collectivités territoriales et à la décentralisation sur le financement des lieux de culte*. N° 345. Paris: La documentation française.

Sénat. 2016. *Rapport d'information fait au nom de la mission d'information sur l'organisation, la place et le financement de l'islam en France et de ses lieux de culte*. N° 757. Paris: La documentation française.

Seurrat, Aude. 2008. "La mise au jour des médiations à travers l'affaire des caricatures." *Communication & Langages*, 155: 27–38.

Sévillia, Jean. 2003. *Historiquement correct. Pour en finir avec le passé unique*. Paris: Perrin.

Sèze, Romain. 2014. "Condamnations des crimes perpétrés par l'État Islamique par les leaders musulmans de France. De l'unanimisme aux débats." *Observatoire Pharos*. October. https://www.observatoirepharos.com/wp-content/uploads/2014/10/S%C3%88ZE-Romain_Mobilisations-et-d%C3%A9bats-EI_Phar.pdf

Sèze, Romain. 2019. *Prévénir la violence djihadiste. Les paradoxes d'un modèle sécuritaire*. Paris: Éditions du Seuil.

Shakman Hurd, Elizabeth. 2007. *The Politics of Secularism in International Relations*. Princeton: Princeton University Press.

Shavit, Uriya. 2012. "The Wasaṭī and Salafī Approaches to the Religious Law of Muslim Minorities." *Islamic Law and Society*, 19: 416–57.
Shavit, Uriya. 2016. *Shari'a and Muslim Minorities. The wasati and salafi approaches to fiqh al-aqalliyyat al-Muslima*. Oxford: Oxford University Press.
Silverstein, Paul. 2008. "The Context of Antisemitism and Islamophobia in France." *Patterns of Prejudice*, 42.1: 1–26.
Simon, Patrick. 2006. "L'arbre du racisme et la fôret des discriminations." In *La république mise à nu par son immigration* edited by Nacira Guénif-Souilamas, 160–77. Paris: La fabrique.
Simon, Patrick and Vincent Tiberj. 2013. *Sécularisation ou regain religieux: la religiosité des immigrés et de leurs descendants (Documents de travail n° 196)*. Paris: Institut national d'études démographiques.
Simon, Patrick. 2014. "Commentary. The Republican Model: Myth of the Governance of Immigration and Integration." In *Controlling Immigration. A Global Perspective* edited by James F. Hollifield, Philip L. Martin, and Pia M. Orrenius, 194–8. Third edition. Stanford: Stanford University Press.
Simon, Patrick, Cris Beauchemin, and Christelle Hamel. 2015a. "Introduction." In *Trajectoires et origines. Enquête sur la diversité des populations en France* edited by Chris Beauchemin, Christelle Hamel, and Patrick Simon, 21–30. Paris: INED.
Simon, Patrick, Cris Beauchemin, and Christelle Hamel. 2015b. "Conclusion générale." In *Trajectoires et origines. Enquête sur la diversité des populations en France* edited by Chris Beauchemin, Christelle Hamel, and Patrick Simon, 607–16. Paris: INED.
Singer, Brian C. and Lorna Weir. 2006. "Politics and Sovereign Power: Considerations on Foucault." *European Journal of Social Theory*, 9.4: 443–65.
Singer, Brian C. and Lorna Weir. 2008. "Sovereignty, Governance and the Political: The Problematic of Foucault." *Thesis Eleven*, 94: 49–71.
Smouts, Marie-Claude. 2007. *La situation postcoloniale. Les postcolonial studies dans le débat français*. Paris: Presses de la Fondation Nationale des Sciences Politiques.
Soral, Alain. 2004. "La culture musulmane produit des hommes élevés dans des valeurs." *oumma.com*. 29 January. https://oumma.com/alain-soral-la-culture-musulmane-produit-des-hommes-eleves-dans-des-valeurs/
Soral, Alain. 2011. *Comprende l'empire. Demain la gouvernance globale ou la révolte des Nations?* Paris: Éditions Blanche.
Soula, Mathieu. 2018. "L'espace de la 'haine', les tensions de la 'race'. La diffamation et l'injure raciale du décret-loi du 21 avril 1939 à la loi du 1er juillet 1972." *Droits*, 68.2: 237–59.
Soullier, Lucie. 2019. "A Paris, la 'convention de la droite' de Marion Maréchal rejoue les classiques de l'extrême droite." *Le Monde*. 28 September. https://www.lemonde.fr/politique/article/2019/09/28/l-immigration-et-l-islam-au-c-ur-de-la-convention-de-la-droite_6013471_823448.html
Stegmann, Ricarda. 2017. *Verflochtene Identitäten: Die Große Moschee von Paris zwischen Algerien und Frankreich*. Göttingen: Vandenhoeck & Ruprecht.

Stolz, Daniel. 2005. "Explaining Islamophobia. A Test of Four Theories Based on the Case of a Swiss City." *Schweizerische Zeitschrift für Soziologie*, 31.3: 547–66.

Stora, Benjamin. 1999. *Le transfert d'une mémoire. De l'Algérie française' au racisme anti-arabe*. Paris: La Découverte.

Stora, Benjamin and Thierry Lecère. 2007. *La guerre des mémoires. La France face à son passé colonial*. Paris: Éditions de l'Aube.

Sullivan, Winnifred Fallers, Elizabeth Shakman Hurd, Saba Mahmood, and Peter G. Danchin. 2015. "Introduction." In *Politics of Religious Freedom* edited by Winnifred Fallers Sullivan, Elizabeth Shakman Hurd, Saba Mahmood, and Peter G. Danchin, 1–9. Chicago: The University of Chicago Press.

Taguieff, Pierre-André. 2017. *L'islamisme et nous. Penser l'ennemi imprévu*. Paris: CNRS Éditions.

Tai, Hue-Tam Ho. 2001. "Remembered Realms: Pierre Nora and French National Memory." *The American Historical Review*, 106.3: 906–22.

Tawil, Emmanuel. 2016. *Justice et religion. La laïcité à l'épreuve des faits*. Paris: Presses universitaires de Farnce.

Telhine, Mohammed. 2013. *L'islam et les musulmans en France. Une histoire de mosquées*. Paris: L'Harmattan.

Ternisien, Xavier. 2000. "La consultation Chevènement en débat au rassemblement musulman du Bourget." *Le Monde*. 3 May.

Ternisien, Xavier. 2005. *Les Frères musulmans*. Paris: Fayard.

Terrel, Hervé. 2004. "L'État et la création du Conseil français du culte musulman (CFCM)." *Cités*. Hors-série. 67–92.

Terrisse, Marc. 2014. "La présence arabo-musulmane en Languedoc et en Provence à l'époque médiévale." *Hommes & migrations*, 1306: 126–8.

Tévanian, Pierre. 2005. *Le voile médiatique. Un faux débat: 'l'affaire du foulard islamique'*. Paris: Raisons d'agir.

Thomas, Dominic. 2013. *Africa and France: Postcolonial Cultures, Migration, and Racism*. Bloomington: Indiana University Press.

Thomson, David. 2014. *Les Français jihadistes*. Paris: Édition des Arènes.

Thomson, David. 2016. *Les revenants. Ils étaient partis faire le jihad, ils sont de retour en France*. Paris: Éditions du Seuil.

Thuot, Thierry. 2013. *Rapport au Premier ministre sur la refondation des politiques d'intégration*. 1 February. https://www.vie-publique.fr/rapport/32981-pour-une-societe-inclusive-refondation-des-politiques-integration

Tiberj, Vincent and Nonna Mayer. 2015. "Le simplisme d'Emmanuel Todd démonté par la sociologie des 'Je suis Charlie.'" *Le Monde*. 20 May.

Tiberj, Vincent and Patrick Simon. 2016. "La fabrique du citoyen: origines et rapport au politique en France." In *Trajectoires et origines. Enquête sur la diversité des populations en France* edited by Chris Beauchemin, Christelle Hamel, and Patrick Simon, 501–29. Paris: INED. 2016.

Todd, Emmanuel. 2015. *Sociologie d'une crise religieuse. Qui est Charlie?* Paris: Éditions du Seuil.

Todorov, Tzvetan. 2004. *Les abus de la mémoire.* Paris: Arléa.

Touche pas à mon poste. 2018. "L'islamisation de la Seine-Saint-Denis: un fait ou une fake news?" *C8.* 4 November. https://www.youtube.com/watch?v=3-h0KPpxc9A

Touraine, Alain. 2005. "Les Français piégés par leur moi national." *Le Monde.* 7 November. https://www.lemonde.fr/idees/article/2005/11/07/les-francais-pieges-par-leur-moi-national-par-alain-touraine_707333_3232.html?xtmc=&xtcr=13

Tournier, Vincent. 2013. "Les musulmans en France: religiosité, politisation et capital social. Enseignements de l'enquête 'Trajectoires et origines.'" *Politique et sociétés*, 32.2: 89–120.

Tribalat, Michèle. 1995. *Faire France. Une grande enquête sur les immigrés et leurs enfants.* Paris: La Découverte.

Tribalat, Michèle. 2013a. *Assimilation. La fin du modèle français.* Paris: Éditions du Toucan.

Tribalat, Michèle. 2013b. "Intégration: les 5 rapports qui poussent la France sur la voie du multiculturalisme choisi sans le dire trop haut." *Atlantico.fr.* 11 December. https://www.atlantico.fr/decryptage/920510/integration--les-5-rapports-qui-poussent-la-france-sur-la-voie-du-multiculturalisme-choisi-sans-le-dire-trop-haut-michele-tribalat

Trilling, Lionel. 2008. *The Liberal Imagination. Essays on Literature and Society.* New York: New York Review Books.

Truong, Fabien. 2017. *Loyautés radicales. L'islam et les "mauvais garçons" de la Nation.* Paris: La Découverte.

Tuot, Thierry. 2014. "Pour une société inclusive. Entretien avec Thierry Tuot, réalisé par Françoise Lorcerie." *Migrations Société*, 155.4: 207–19.

Tyrer, David. 2013. *The Politics of Islamophobia. Race, Power and Fantasy.* London: Pluto Press.

Ungureanu, Camil. 2017. "Michel Houellebecq's shifting representation of Islam: From the death of God to counter-Enlightenment." *Philosophy and Social Criticism*, 43.4–5: 514–28.

UOIF. 2006. *Qu'est-ce que l'UOIF?* Paris: Éditions de l'Archipel.

UOIF. 2012. "Communiqué – Tueries de Toulouse et de Montauban." *havredesavoir.fr.* 21 March. https://www.havredesavoir.fr/communique-tueries-de-toulouse-et-montauban/

UOIF. 2016. "Déclaration finale – 33ème RAMF." *musulmansdefrance.com.* 17 May. http://www.musulmansdefrance.fr/declaration-finale-33eme-rencontre-annuelle-musulmans-de-france/

Ural, Nur Yasemin. 2014. "A Genealogy of Muslims Dying in France: Strasbourg Cemetery as a Contested Space." *Sociology of Islam*, 2.1–2: 1–20.

Ural, Nur Yasemin. 2016. *Mourir en Diaspora. Les pratiques funéraires des "minorités" musulmanes originaires de Turquie en Allemagne et en France.* PhD Thesis. Paris: EHESS.

Val, Philippe: *Reviens Voltaire, ils sont devenus fous.* Paris: Grasset. 2008.

Valensi, Lucette. 1995. "Histoire nationale, histoire monumentale. Les Lieux de mémoire (note critique)." *Annales*, 50.6: 1271–7.

Valls, Manuel. 2015. "Non, la France du 11 janvier n'est pas une imposture." *Le Monde*. 7 May.

Verba, Daniel and Guélamine Faïza, eds. 2014. *Interventions sociales et faits religieux. Les paradoxes des logiques identitaires*. Paris: Presses de l'EHESP.

Viard, Bruno. 2013. *Les tiroirs de Michel Houellebecq*. Paris: Presses universitaires de France.

Vidino, Lorenzo. 2010. *The New Muslim Brotherhood in the West*. New York: Columbia University Press.

Vincent, Elise and Louise Couvelaire. 2019. "Une circulaire de Castaner demande aux préfets de faire du 'combat contre l'islamisme' une priorité." *Le Monde*. 2 December https://www.lemonde.fr/politique/article/2019/12/02/christophe-castaner-mon-adversaire-c-est-l-islamisme_6021334_823448.html

Von Stuckrad, Kocku. 2013. "Secular Religion: A Discourse–historical Approach to Religion in Contemporary Western Europe." *Journal of Contemporary Religion*, 28.1: 1–14.

Wagemakers, Joas. 2008. "Framing the 'Threat to Islam'. Al-Wala' wa al-Bara' in Salafi Discourse." *Arab Studies Quarterly*, 30.4: 1–22.

Wahnich, Sophie. 2017. "L'immigration produit du patrimoine négatif. Le rôle du musée." *Communications*, 100: 119–35.

Ward, Graham. 2005. *Cultural Transformation and Religious Practice*. Cambridge: Cambridge University Press.

Watt, Ian. 1957. *The Rise of the Novel. Studies in Defoe, Richardson, and Fielding*. Berkeley: University of California Press.

Weibel, Nadine. 2000. *Par-delà le voile. Femmes d'islam en Europe*. Bruxelles: Éditions Complexe.

Weil, Patrick. 2004. *La France et ses étrangers. L'aventure d'une politique de l'immigration de 1938 à nos jours*. Revised edition. Paris: Gallimard.

Weil, Patrick. 2010. "La loi sur la burqa risque l'invalidation par l'Europe." *Le Monde*. 23 November.

Weitzmann, Marc. 2015. "Toxicité de Houellebecq." *Le Monde des livres*. 6 January. https://abonnes.lemonde.fr/livres/article/2015/01/06/marc-weitzmann-toxicite-de-houellebecq_4550131_3260.html?

Wesselhoeft, Kirsten M. Yoder. 2011. "Gendered Secularity: The Feminine Individual in the 2010 Gerin Report." *Journal of Muslim Minority Affairs*, 31.3: 399–410.

Wieviorka, Michel. 2006. *La tentation antisémite. Haine des Juifs dans la France d'aujourd'hui*. Paris: Hachette.

Wieviorka, Michel. 2016. *Le séisme*. Paris: Robert Laffont.

Willaime, Jean-Paul. 2005. "1905 et la pratique d'une laïcité de la reconnaissance sociale des religions." *Archives de sciences sociales des religions*, 129: 67–81.

Winter, Bronwyn. 2009. *Hijab and the Republic: Uncovering the French Headscarf Debate*. Albany: Syracuse University Press.

Winter, Jay. 2007. "The Generation of Memory. Reflections on the 'Memory Boom' in Contemporary Historical Studies." *Archives & Social Studies: A Journal of Interdisciplinary Research*, 1: 363–97.

Woehrling, Jean-Marie. 2003. "Définition juridique de la religion." In *Traité de droit français des religions* edited by Francis Messner, Pierre-Henri Prélot and Jean-Marie Woehrling with the collaboration of Isabelle Riassetto, 23–39. Paris: Litec.

Zancarini, Jean-Claude, ed. 2001. *Lectures de Michel Foucault. Volume 1. A propos de 'Il faut défendre la société'*. Lyon: ENS Éditions. https://books.openÉdition.org/ensÉditions/1772

Zeghal, Malika. 2008. "La constitution du Conseil Français du Culte Musulman: reconnaissance politique d'un Islam français?" *Archives de sciences sociales des religions*, 129: 97–113.

Zekri, Abdallah. 2019. "Baisse des actes anti-musulmans en France." *oumma.com*. 13 February. https://oumma.com/baisse-des-actes-anti-musulmans-en-france/

Zemmour, Eric. 2014. *Le suicide français*. Paris: Albin Michel.

Zemouri, Aziz. 2005. *Faut-il faire Tariq Ramadan? Suivi d'un entretien avec Tariq Ramadan*. Paris: Éditions de l'Archipel.

Zenati, Moncef. 2008. *La fraternité humaine*. Paris: Maison d'Ennour.

Zerouala, Faïza and Nasisra El Moaddem. 2018. "'Inch'Allah:' deux journalistes forment des étudiants en déformant le 93." *Mediapart*. 25 October. https://www.mediapart.fr/journal/france/251018/inch-allah-deux-journalistes-forment-des-etudiants-en-deformant-le-93?onglet=full

Zineb. 2016. *Détruire le fascisme islamique*. Paris: Éditions Ring.

Zitouni, Soufiane. 2015. "Pourquoi j'ai démissionné du lycée Averroès." *Libération*. February 5, 2015. https://www.liberation.fr/societe/2015/02/05/pourquoi-j-ai-demissionne-du-lycee-averroes_1196424

Zwilling, Anne-Laure. 2014. "L'enseignement de l'islam dans les universités en France: une histoire mouvementée." In *Droit et religion. Études en l'honneur de Francis Messner* edited by Marc Aoun and Jeanne-Marie Tufferie-Andrieu, 239–59. Strasbourg: Presses universitaires de Strasbourg.

Zwilling, Anne-Laure. 2015. "A century of mosques in France: building religious pluralism." *International Review of Sociology*, 25.2: 1–8.

Index

ʿAbd al-Rahman al-Ghafiqi, 151
Abdelkrim, Farid, 129–35, 159, 240 n.35
   autobiographical account of, 134f.
   on confusing culture and religion, 134
   on contingency of subject formation, 135
   and critique of Islamism, 130, 133f., 159
   on ethics of citizenship, 130ff.
   on France as Islamophobic country, 133f., 236 n.71, 237 n.80
   social rationalization and self-making, 130–5
academic research on immigration
   development of, 57f.
   externalization of immigrants, 58
academic research on Islam
   and auto-demystification in debate on Islam, 63
   and its critique of essentialism and stereotyping, 41f.
   and decline and transformation of Orientalist studies, 40ff., 217 n.63, 217 n.64
   disregard of Islam's textual tradition in, 42
   and Islam as constitutive Other, 40
   la politique musulmane and its decline, 56ff.
   see also integration, *Les banlieues de l'islam*
aesthetic rationalizations of Islam and/in France, 12, 26f.
   change of identities and structures of power in, 44, 166, 176, 180f., 184, 186ff.
   distinction between fiction and reality in, 12, 44f., 167, 176f., 180–4, 187f.
   and freedom of expression, 12, 166f.
   rivalry and mutual determination of literature and social sciences, 44
   usages of, 167, 177, 181, 188f.

   see also Charlie Hebdo; *Mokhtar Awards*; Muhammad cartoon controversy; *Soumission*; Todd, Emmanuel
Alaoui, Fouad, 34
Asad, Talal, 1f., 21, 33, 203
associations
   cultural (*association loi 1901*) and worship associations (*association cultuelle loi 1905*), 34, 69, 216 n.51, 221 n.13
   Muslim associations, 34f., 107, 168, 214 n.36, 216 n.52, 234 n.90f.
   see also integration; mosques

Babès, Leila, 221 n.11
Badinter, Élisabeth, 194
Baghezza, Abdelaali, 161ff.
   on distinguishing religion and culture, 161
   on forgotten Muslim master thinkers, 162
   on function and condition of reconciliation, 162
   on homogeneity and ethno-cultural fusion, 162
   on National Front, 242 n.58
   on religious freedom in France, 162
   on undoing otherness, 163
banlieue
   riots (2005), 41, 84, 94
al-Banna, Hasan, 125, 130, 132, 236 n.64
battle of Austerlitz, 137ff., 238 n.12
battle of Poitiers (732), 151–5
   contested revisions of history of, 151–4, 240 n.40
   in French imaginaries, 151
   as narrative of alterity, 152f.
Baubérot, Jean, 218 n.1
Bechikh, Camel, 159–62
   on distinguishing religion, culture and social, 160

on freedom of religion in France, 162
on French history, 160f.
on Muslim patriotism, 159f.
on Muslim victimhood and anti-racism, 160f.
see also *Fils de France*; counter-histories of Islam and/in France
Ben Mansour, Abdallah, 108
Benabdallah, Sofiane
"Regarde plutôt la mer," 178f.
Bencheikh, Soheib, 68
Bitèye, El Hadji Babou, 155f.
see also counter-histories of Islam and/in France
Blanchard, Pascal, 239 n.30
see also *La fracture coloniale*
Bloc identitaire see *Les Identitaires*
Bourmeau, Sylvain, 183ff., 246 n.55
Bouzar, Dounia, 116, 226 n.1
Bowen, John R., 94, 169, 218 n.2
Brèze, Lhaj Thami, 96, 112
Bruckner, Pascal, 193
Burgat, François, 63, 113, 232 n.75
burqa, 33, 87, 215 n.43

Camus, Renaud
Le grand remplacement, 147, 183
Candiard, Adrien, 116
Carrère, Emmanuel, 187
Catholicism 149f., 153, 196, 214 n.36
and churches as property of state, 34
and freedom of expression, 169
"Zombie Catholicism," 175
Centre de prévention contre les dérives sectaires liées à l'islam, 116
Césari, Jocelyne, 63
Charles Martel, 151, 153
Charlie Hebdo, 165f., 168, 170, 172–6, 180, 188, 243 n.12, 244 n.21, 244 n.24
attacks of January 7, 2015, 165, 173ff.
and marches for victims of attacks, 165, 173–6
and racism, 175, 242 n.7
see also Muhammad cartoon controversy; Todd, Emmanuel
Chevènement, Jean-Pierre, 67f., 91, 100, 220 n.7, 224 n.49, 241 n.52
Chirac, Jacques, 70, 142

citizenship
of Muslims, 206, 220 n.6
see also Abdelkrim, Farid; ethical self-making; integration; *Haut Conseil à l'intégration*; Meziani, Sofiane; public Islam; Ramousi, Mohamed
Collectif contre l'islamophobie en France, 12f., 191ff., 195, 199f., 247 n.3
definition of Islamophobia, 192
Comité de Bienfaisance et de Secours aux Palestiniens, 159
Commission nationale consultative des droits de l'homme, 191, 195
communautarisme see republicanism
Conseil français du culte musulman, 7, 67ff., 83f., 107f., 183, 230 n.49, 234 n.91, 247 n.4, 247 n.8
and Jewish consistory (1808), 227 n.10
Conseil représentatif des associations noires, 138
Copé, Jean-François, 247 n.3
counter-histories, 139f., 146ff., 163, 240 n.34
as challenge to historico-juridical discourse of sovereignty, 147
and history-writing in France, 164
"races" in, 146f.
vs. Roman historiography, 146
and "transcendental mobility" of human sciences, 146
see also counter-histories of Islam and/in France
counter-histories of Islam and/in France, 27, 147–64, 185ff., 206
and al-Andalus as point of indistinction between Islamic and French histories, 153ff.
and colonial continuum, 138, 143, 162f.
and deconstruction of republic, 149, 162f.
and Europe's difference, 148ff.
and French Algeria, 149, 162
and long history of Islam in France, 149–63, 240 n.45
and Muslims as memory collective, 12, 140
and nationalization of Islam, 163f.
and postcolonial thought, 11, 238 n.13

and relational identity of France, 155f.
  usages of, 12, 147f., 150f., 163
  see also Baghezza, Abdelaali; battle of
    Austerlitz; battle of Poitiers (732);
    Bechikh, Camel; Iquioussen,
    Hassan; Mouslim, Charafeddine;
    memory; Ramadan, Tariq;
    republicanism
culturalism
  as essentialism, 73
  as explanatory essentialism, 73
  loose usage of term, 223 n.31
  see also Haut Conseil à l'intégration

De Cock, Laurence, 141
Debah, Samy, 192
Debré Commission, 33f.
Declaration of the Rights of Man and of
  the Citizen, 67
Deutsch, Loránt, 153
discrimination 131, 141, 222 n.23
  measurement of, 75
  see also Haut Conseil à l'intégration;
    integration; Islamophobia

Égalité et réconciliation, 159
ethical self-making
  Foucault on, 119f.
  positive freedom, citizenship and,
    120
  and social rationalizations of Islam
    and/in France, 120, 122–35
  see also Abdelkrim, Farid; Iquioussen,
    Hassan; Meziani, Sofiane; Ramousi,
    Mohamed
Étienne, Bruno, 64
Étudiants Musulmans de France, 8, 121,
  155
European Council for Fatwa and Research,
  8, 96f., 99f., 227 n.21, 229 n.31

Fassin, Éric, 207
Federation of Islamic Organizations in
  Europe (renamed Council of
  European Muslims), 97
fiction, 43ff., 166f., 204
  and "themes," 44
  see also aesthetic rationalizations of
    Islam and/in France

Fils de France, 159ff.
  political identity of, 159, 241 n.52
Foucault, Michel, 4, 6, 11, 20ff., 25f., 30f.,
  54f., 96, 117, 139, 145, 163, 204,
  213 n.27
  see also counter-histories; ethical
    self-making; human sciences (in
    Les mots et les choses)
France
  and immanent contradiction of
    republic, 50f., 53
  immigration and contingency of
    national order, 30f., 206f.
  as nation-state, 29f., 72, 163, 214 n.32,
    239 n.27
  national identity of, 18, 141. 239 n.26
  postcoloniality of, 40f., 50, 62
  and problematic of representation, 206f.
  sovereignty of, 206f.
  see also Vichy regime
freedom of expression
  law of 1881 and, 165, 193, 242 n.3,
    243 n.11
  see also Muhammad cartoon
    controversy

Grand Mosque of Paris, 107

Haut Conseil à l'intégration, 10, 31, 70f.
  and anti-discrimination, 71f., 79, 84f.,
    222 n.23
  and changing Islam, 72f., 78
  and conditions of social
    rationalizations, 81–4
  and contractualism, 84
  and disregard for diversity of Islam, 76
  and effects of distinguishing between
    culture and religion, 76ff.
  and exclusionist policies and deficient
    commitment to laïcité, 86
  and headscarf, 78, 83, 85
  and identification of Islam and
    Muslims, 75ff., 223 n.37
  and integration, 72f., 78, 80, 84
  and legitimate state interventions into
    religion, 80f.
  and normative Frenchness, 78, 174
  and officialization of term immigrant,
    73ff.

and particularization of Islam, 88f.
and priority of political over social, 84f.
and relations between public authorities and local associations, 82, 93
and social rationalizations of Islam and/in France, 73–85
and state measures regarding exercise of worship, 79ff.
see also integration
Haute Autorité de lutte contre les discriminations et pour l'égalité, 79
Havre de Savoir, 148
headscarf
  banning of, 85, 197f., 221 n.18, 249 n.20
  conceptions and legal status of, 33, 215 n.44, 215 n.47
  controversy (1989), 8, 167f.
  controversy (2003), 47, 50f., 82f., 94, 161, 203f., 218 n.2, 231 n.66
  see also Haut Conseil à l'intégration; Islamophobia; Oubrou, Tareq
Hervieu-Léger, Danièle, 63
Histoire mondiale de la France (P. Boucheron, ed.), 152, 242 n.60
historical rationalizations of Islam and/in France *see* counter-histories of Islam and/in France
history teaching, 140f., 240 n.32
  and colonial history, 141
  Islam in, 141, 155, 162
  see also counter-histories of Islam and/in France; memory; republicanism
Hollande, François, 174, 181
Houellebecq, Michel, 232 n.13
  see Soumission
human sciences (in *Les mots et les choses*), 36–42, 216 n.58
  "constituent models" in, 4, 38, 140, 145
  and human as "observed spectator", 39
  and lack of positive object of study, 37f.
  "transcendental mobility" and auto-demystification of, 39ff., 204
  "transcendentals" of, 36f.
  and unthought of humans, 38
  see also academic research on Islam; counter-histories

Inch'allah: l'islamisation à visage découvert (G. Davet & F. Lhomme), 15–20
  and "Islamization" of France, 15–20
Indigènes de la République (renamed *Parti des Indigènes de la République*), 138, 237 n.6, 245 n.30
Institut Européen des Sciences Humaines, 7, 96f., 125, 148
Institut Montaigne, 86
Institut National d'Études Démographiques, 75
integration, 29ff.
  and ambivalence of rights, 70
  and anti-discrimination policies, 84f., 88, 222 n.23
  as assimilation, 222 n.28
  definitions of, 71, 87
  effective implementation of policies of, 69f., 89, 221 n.14
  and generating feeling of belonging, 88
  heterogeneity of rationalizations of, 89
  and imaginary of national sovereignty, 10, 30f., 69f., 88f., 206f.
  of Muslims, 18, 28, 45, 61f., 183
  and normative Frenchness, 6, 9, 18, 29f., 140, 143, 156, 201, 248 n.14
  reciprocity of, 87f.
  and reorientation of integration policies, 87f.
  as reversible relation of power, 5f., 10–13, 61f., 68–72, 75, 87, 117, 141, 183, 195, 200, 205, 209 n.6, 222 n.26
  and rewriting of French history, 88
  as self-willed commitment and change, 10f., 68, 222 n.30
  and unaccomplished nature of integration, 30, 68
  unnecessary as Muslims not different, 185
  see also Haut Conseil à l'intégration; Islamophobia; *Les banlieues de l'islam*; public Islam; Ramadan, Tariq; Ramousi, Mohamed; republicanism; Sarkozy, Nicolas; secularism; Tuot, Thierry
Iquioussen, Hassan, 154ff.
  on history, its universal laws and lessons, 154

on history, memory and French
    Muslim identity, 154f.
on Islam's contributions to Europe, 155,
    240 n.48
on jihad and freedom of religion in
    al-Andalus, 155
Islam
    and anti-Semitism, 94, 244 n.21
    as constitutive Other, 24, 40, 63, 151–4,
        164, 169, 216 n.59
    consular, 108f.
    differentiation and entwinement
        between France and, 5, 12, 119, 140,
        163, 206
    as exceptional object in knowledge
        production, 23
    in France as transnational, 169
    interpretive authority and
        individualization of, 63f.
    illiberalism of, 169
    and "Islamization" of social questions,
        110–15, 118
    and its legal tradition in Europe, 5, 8
    normative status of images in, 167
    racialization of, 35f., 109
    rationality of public debate about, 23, 25
    recognition as religion, 32
    secularization or revival of, 185, 200
    and social power of Muslims, 2, 4, 9ff.,
        18f., 29, 97, 99, 166, 185
    visibility of, 3f., 105f.
"Islamization" of France, 15–20, 180
Islamo-gauchistes, 17
Islamophobia, 17, 25, 35, 98, 159, 169, 176,
    179, 183f., 189, 213 n.25, 246 n.44,
    247 n.5
    as category of illegitimacy, 191, 193ff.
    conceptualizations of, 23f., 191,
        213 n.22, 213 n.23, 247 n.9
    and disorderly politics, 196, 200f.
    as framework for new governmental
        configuration, 13, 200
    and (limits of) critique of integration,
        12f., 196, 198ff.
    measurement of, 192, 247 n.5, 247 n.8,
        249 n.20
    as misperception and ignorance, 23f.
    and racism, 192f., 195f.
    usages of term, 193ff.

see also Abdelkrim, Farid; Islam; Islam
    and Muslim as proper names; racism
Ismaili, Hicham
    "Sunna", 179f.

Jaballah, Ahmed, 96–9, 174, 215 n.44
    on Muhammad cartoon controversy
        and *Charlie Hebdo*, 174
    and social rationalization of Islam and/
        in France, 98f.
    see also public Islam
Jama'at al-Tabligh, 60, 63, 76
Jeunes Musulmans de France, 8, 130, 154,
    161
jihadism, 112–15, 231 n.69
    see radicalization processes

Kepel, Gilles, 87, 123
    see also Les banlieues de l'islam
Khosrokhavar, Farhad, 63, 113
Klein, Kerwin Lee, 144f., 163
Kriegel, Blandine, 84

La fracture coloniale (P. Blanchard, N. Bancel,
    S. Lemaire & O. Barlet, eds.), 145
La Manif Pour Tous, 159
Lægaard, Sune, 166
Lagrange, Hugues
    Le déni des cultures, 233 n.79
Lahire, Bernard, 115
laïcité
    and autonomy, 16
    claim to universalism of, 9
    as condition for diversity, 17
    crisis of legitimacy of new, 85
    in constitution, 67
    diverse definitions of, 16ff., 47, 85, 89,
        211 n.9, 212 n.14
    and mandatory neutrality of
        citizens, 85f.
    as privatization of religion, 16, 19
    as tool of "cultural oppression," 86
Lasfar, Amar, 91ff., 96, 233 n.86, 240 n.44
Law of 1905, 34, 67, 214 n.35
Le Goff, Jacques, 152
Le Pen, Marine, 180, 183, 189
    on dissolution of UOIF, 159
Lelong, Michel, 241 n.52
Lepenies, Wolf, 44

Les banlieues de l'islam (G. Kepel), 10, 49, 58–62
   in context of French studies on Islam, 62ff.
   on integration of Muslims, 61ff.
   on Muslim identity, 63
   normalization-particularization of Islam in, 60
   rationalization of terrorist violence in, 61
   social functions of Islam in, 59ff.
   social power of Muslims in, 59–62
   transnational Islam in, 63
   transformation of national identity in, 61
   usages of social rationalization of Islam in, 59
   see also academic research on Islam; social rationalizations of Islam and/in France
Les Identitaires (formerly *Bloc identitaire*), 151, 153
   see also battle of Poitiers (732)
Les mots et les choses (M. Foucault), 36–9
   see also human sciences
L'invention du social (J. Donzelot), 48–53
   the crisis of contractualism and the antinomy between justice and freedom, 51ff., 218 n.7
   depoliticizing effects of, 55
   at the intersection of the civil and the political 55
   and the ontological priority of the social, 55
   see also society
Ligue des droits de l'homme, 68
Louatah, Sabri
   Les Sauvages, 188f.
Louizi, Mohamed, 173, 210 n.17

Maier, Corinne & Frank Martin
   Manuel de savoir-vivre en cas d'invasion islamique, 189
Makri, Yamin, 108f., 162f.
Marianne, 162
Meddeb, Abdelwahab, 172, 243 n.15
Médine, 240 n.41
memory, 4, 11f., 39, 140–5, 238 n.16
   of Algerian war, 142
   and commemorative practices, 137ff., 141–4, 153f.
   as "constituent model," 144f., 163, 239 n.29
   and debate about colonial history, 138, 141
   and *devoir de mémoire*, 141, 238 n.17
   of enslavement, 142, 233 n.83, 237 n.4, 239 n.20
   fragmentation of national, 141
   of Holocaust, 141f.
   legislation on, 141ff., 143, 233 n.83, 237 n.4, 239 n.20, 239 n.22, 239 n.25
   of Muslim soldiers, 154f., 240 n.45, 241 n.51
   and "positive role" of French colonization, 143, 239 n.23
   and *régime victimo-mémoriel de la Shoah*, 141f.
   See also battle of Austerlitz; battle of Poitiers (732); counter-histories of Islam and/in France; France; history teaching; historical rationality
Ménard, Robert, 241 n.52
Meziani, Sofiane, 120–5
   on ethics of citizenship in *banlieue*, 122f.
   on prayer, 124f.
   on self-mastery, 121–5
   on spirituality in modernity, 121
Michel, Johan, 141f.
Miktar, Ahmed, 172
Mission interministérielle de vigilance et de lutte contre les dérives sectaires, 116, 233 n.85
   see also religion
Mitterrand, François, 142
Modood, Tariq, 214 n.32
Mokhtar Awards, 176–9, 188
   "Tell us about Prophet Muhammad," 177
Morin, Edgar, 156f.
mosques, 59, 92f., 219 n.13
   construction of, 81, 151
   see also associations
Mouslim, Charafeddine, 151f.
   see also battle of Poitiers (732); counter-histories of Islam and/in France

Muhammad, Marwan, 192, 195–9
  Nous (aussi) sommes la nation, 195–9
  see also Islamophobia
Muhammad cartoon controversy
  as controversy and meta-controversy, 166f., 174
  in the courts, 169–72, 174
  distinguishing fiction and reality in, 167, 176, 244 n.24, 245 n.40
  diverse rationalizations of, 168f., 171ff., 174–7
  and freedom of expression, 168–72
  and divided public opinion, 174ff.
  and Manifesto of the Twelve, 168
  and normative Frenchness, 174ff.
  and performativity of cartoons, 169
  see also public Islam
Musulmans de France (formerly *Union des organisations islamiques de France*), 7ff., 96, 104, 209 n.9, 228 n.28

Napoleon (Bonaparte), 137–40
  see also battle of Austerlitz; Nora, Pierre; Ribbe, Claude; slavery
National Front (renamed National Rally), 70, 159, 162, 180, 183, 185, 241 n.54
nationality code, 70
  North African immigration in reform of, 221 n.19
Nisbet, Robert, 43
Noiriel, Gérard, 50, 57f., 71
Nora, Pierre, 138f., 146, 238 n.10
  Les Lieux de mémoire, 138, 238 n.11

Observatoire de la laïcité, 221 n.18
orderly vision of secularism, 2, 12, 15, 19ff., 165f.
  analytical insufficiency and critique of, 22f., 36, 39, 43, 45, 48, 203f.
  see also Islamophobia; public Islam; Ramadan, Tariq; Ramousi, Mohamed; secularism; secularism without religion
Orientalist studies in France *see* academic research on Islam
Oubrou, Tareq, 104–7, 117f., 133, 151, 160, 221 n.11, 234 n.92, 241 n.52
  on change and stability of context and necessary assimilation of Muslims, 104ff., 117f., 229 n.35
  and crisis and critique of context, 106f., 229 n.35
  distinguishing law, culture and religion, 104
  on hijab, 105f., 229 n.39ff., 230 n.44
  on integration, 104f., 117f., 230 n.45, 231 n.66, 232 n.73
  on Israel and Palestine, 105, 230 n.43
  and limits of assimilation of Muslims, 106f.
  and social rationalization of Islam and/ in France, 231 n.66, 232 n.73

Papon, Maurice, 142
Plenel, Edwy, 184
public Islam, 6–9
  and assessments of social power, 93–9
  and citizenship, 93, 95, 97, 135
  and conceptions of France, 95
  and contours of French Muslim identity, 97
  and diverse rationalizations of Muhammad cartoon controversy, 171ff.
  and distinction between Islam and society, 95
  and electoral politics, 161f.
  and ethical self-making, 11, 94f., 119
  fragmentation of discourse in milieu of, 135
  and integration, 92, 97, 99f., 205
  and Islam as tool for individual reform and social change, 93
  and "Islamization" of social questions, 95, 110–12, 118
  and *laïcité*, 95
  and orderly vision of secularism, 95ff.
  and political Islam, 8f., 210 n.17, 210 n.18
  and preserving Muslim identity, 97f.
  and renarrations of French history, 148–63
  and requirements of Muslim life in France, 93
  and social rationalizations, 10f.
  and social role of mosques, 92f.

racism, 50, 166, 196, 200, 242 n.7, 248 n.12
radicalization processes, 94f., 112–15, 130, 233 n.84

and counter-measures targeting
 Muslims, 116f.
and controversy about religious causes
 of violence, 112–15, 231 n.68,
 232 n.73, 232 n.76, 232 n.78,
 246 n.55
and distinction between Islam and
 Islamism, 115f.
and Salafi currents, 114, 116f.
and social rationalizations of, 112–15
Ramadan, Tariq, 6f., 99–104, 106, 180, 184,
 229 n.32, 234 n.92, 243 n.13, 247 n.4
 on contours of Muslim identity, 101f.
 on distinction between religion, culture
  and social, 102f., 110ff., 158, 160,
  228 n.25, 241 n.51
 on externality of Muslims to European
  history, 150
 on generating belonging and exclusion,
  102f., 228 n.26, 241 n.50
 on history as force of particularism, 149f.
 on inclusive history and memory, 156f.,
  159f., 241 n.51
 on indeterminacy of national identity,
  101
 on integration, 100, 102f., 156, 158,
  227 n.22, 228 n.27, 241 n.51
 and moratorium on corporal
  punishment, 106
 on Muhammad cartoon controversy,
  171f., 243 n.13
 and orderly vision of secularism, 101, 158
 on parameters of history and memory,
  157
 radicalization processes, 111, 232 n.73,
  234 n.92
 on secularism as liberation, 149
 on social participation and power, 99f.
 and social rationalizations of Islam
  and/in France, 100–4, 110ff.,
  231 n.67, 232 n.73
 on *Soumission*, 184, 246 n.47
 see also counter-histories of Islam and/
  in France; public Islam;
  radicalization processes
Ramousi, Mohamed, 125–9
 and civilizational role of Muslims, 125,
  127
 and critique of integration, 126

and *fiqh* debate on citizenship, 125f.
and ignorance as cause of deviance,
 126f.
imitation, social rationalization, and
 self-making, 125, 127ff.
and Islamophobia, 128
and orderly vision of secularism, 127f.,
 235 n.29
rationality
 aesthetic, 26ff.
 anticipatory, 94
 difference between system and, 26,
  213 n.27
 dimensions and functioning of
  political, 26
 diversity and cofunctioning of, 48, 53,
  204ff., 213 n.27
 historical, 11f., 26ff., 186f.
 juridical, 20f.
 political, 4, 26, 28, 48
 and scientific truth, 26
 secular, 24–8
 social, 10, 26ff., 53
rationalizations of Islam and/in France, 28,
 36, 48f., 206
 see also aesthetic rationalizations of
  Islam and/in France; counter-
  histories of Islam and/in France;
  Law of 1905; social rationalizations
  of Islam and/in France
religion
 and absence of separate legal regime
  for *cultes*, 32, 212 n.20
 as belief, 33f.
 changing meaning of, 215 n.48
 definitions of worship and, 32f.,
  214 n.36, 214 n.37, 215 n.51
 distinction between *culte* and culture,
  34
 as non-exclusive category, 34, 216 n.53
 and sects, 116, 215 n.41, 233 n.85
 secularism without, 3, 9, 28, 45
 state institutions identifying something
  as *culte* or, 32–5
 see also associations
religious freedom, 18, 34, 167f., 212 n.20,
 214 n.36
 deficient commitment to *laïcité* as
  effect of restrictions on, 86

effective force of, 22
governmentalities of, 2, 9, 16, 22, 45
legal restrictions of, 85f., 167f., 247 n.3.
and proselytism, 16, 34
and sectarian deviances, 116
Renaut, Alain, 47, 50
representation of Muslim worship, 63, 206, 247 n.2
see also Conseil français du culte musulman
republicanism, 4ff., 45, 48, 218 n.3
and diversité, 140f.
and communautarisme, 18, 47, 138, 199
and cultural difference, 48, 140
and equality as sameness, 50
illiberalism of, 48
and integration, 84, 221 n.15
and intermediary bodies, 92f.
and memory, 238 n.17
reduction of secular politics to, 51, 53
revival of, 48
and social thought, 49
and universalism, 9, 45, 47–51, 138, 196
see also Haut Conseil à l'intégration; Les banlieues de l'islam; L'invention du social; Tuot, Thierry
Ribbe, Claude, 137–40
Le crime de Napoléon, 137
Rougier, Bernard, 114
Roy, Olivier, 5, 42, 64, 113f., 181, 185, 188, 232 n.75ff., 246 n.44
Rushdie, Salman
The Satanic Verses, 165

Said, Edward
critique of Orientalism, 217 n.67
Orientalism, 40f.
social sciences in Orientalism, 217 n.64.
see also academic research on Islam
Saint-Domingue (Haiti), 137
Sarkozy, Nicolas, 107ff.
and Catholic national identity, 109
and ministry of immigration, integration, national identity and solidarity development, 143
on Muhammad cartoon controversy, 174
on normality of UOIF, 83f., 108
rationalizing state recognition of UOIF, 107f.

upgrading religious factor in policy-making in banlieue, 109.
see also racialization of Islam; UOIF
Sayad, Abdelmalek, 30f., 207
Sayd, Sarah
"Le fil vert," 177f.
Schnapper, Dominique, 84, 115, 233 n.83
Scott, Joan W., 24, 50f., 206
secularism
and governmentality, 21f., 45
and governing of Muslims, 22f., 28f.
and juridical conceptions of power, 20f., 27f., 51
and prognostic of the future, 4
and regimes of knowledge, 21, 24–8
and religious freedom, 2f., 15, 21f.
and secular-religious binary, 1ff.
see also orderly vision of secularism; secularism without religion
secularism without religion
and identification of Islam and Muslims, 3f., 9f., 15, 19f., 28f., 31–5, 39, 45, 49, 196, 198, 201, 204f., 213 n.29
Islam and Muslim as proper name, 35f.
and "the separation of words from things," 24ff., 28, 204
and sovereignty, 10, 20f., 27, 31, 206f.
see also human sciences (in Les mots et les choses); rationalizations of Islam and/in France
Seine-Saint-Denis, 15
Septimania, 151
slavery
abolition and reinstitution of 137
and memorial of Unknown Slave, 139
social rationalizations of Islam and/in France, 10f., 19, 27, 47ff., 53–6, 175f., 182f.
and assessment of changing conditions of integration, 11
and assessment of state policies, 56
and changing Islam, 10
critique of, 114ff.
and distinction between Islam and society, 11, 118
and functions of religion, 54
and individual responsibility, 115

and "Islamization" of social questions, 110–15, 118
and juridico-political rationality, 49–53
and the normalization-particularization of Islam, 10, 27
and particularization of Islam, 49
politically diverse effects of, 10
scrutinizing relation between freedom and determination through, 55f.
and social normality, 54f.
and terrorist violence, 61
truth claims of, 54
see also ethical self-making; *Haut Conseil à l'intégration*; Jaballah, Ahmed; Lasfar, Amar; *Les banlieues de l'islam*; Oubrou, Tareq; public Islam; radicalization processes; Ramadan, Tariq; Todd, Emmanuel
society, 4, 39, 49, 55, 96, 218f n.10
and difference between the social and the political, 49, 55f.
Soral, Alain, 159, 241 n.54
SOS Racisme, 161
Soumission (M. Houellebecq), 12, 167, 180–9, 245 n.36, 246 n.56, 246 n.58, 246 n.60
see also aesthetic rationalizations of Islam and/in France
Stasi Commission, 47, 83
state regulation of *cultes*, 28, 67f., 85
(neo)colonial, 68
see also Conseil français du culte musulman
statistical data, 212 n.16
on immigration, 74f.
on Muslims, 19, 199f., 212 n.17

Todd, Emmanuel
on anti-Semitism, 176, 244 n.21
social rationalization, 175f.
Sociologie d'une crise religieuse: Qui est Charlie?, 175f., 244 n.20

Touraine, Alain, 47f.
Tribalat, Michèle, 74f.
Truong, Fabien, 113
Tuot, Thierry
and abstract universalism, 87
and changing Islam, 226 n.63
and irrelevance of "the 'Muslim question,'" 87
and reorientation of integration policies, 87

Union des organisations islamiques de France (renamed *Musulmans de France*), 6, 34, 67, 69, 76, 83, 91, 93, 98, 101, 105, 107–10, 112, 121, 126, 130, 151, 160f., 165, 231 n.62, 241 n.53
and Muhammad cartoon controversy, 168–71
and Muslim Brotherhood, 7, 107, 159, 173, 201n17
and quest for state recognition, 108f.
and Salafi currents, 108, 126, 234 n.92
see also Le Pen, Marine; radicalization processes; Sarkozy, Nicolas

Valls, Manuel, 114f., 175f.
Vichy regime, 74, 142

Wieviorka, Michel
Le séisme, 189
worship (*culte*) *see* religion

Zemmour, Éric, 17, 183f.
Le suicide français, 147
Zenati, Moncef, 148f.
on Islamic foundations of political order, 149
on relations with non-Muslims, 148f.
see also counter-histories of Islam and/in France

www.ingramcontent.com/pod-product-compliance
Lightning Source LLC
Chambersburg PA
CBHW072123290426
44111CB00012B/1761